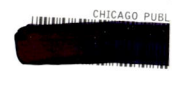

R00787 D1682669

```
LB           Assessment of
2838            teaching.
.A788
1990
```

$49.95

DATE			

SOCIAL SCIENCES AND HISTORY DIVISION

SOCIAL SCIENCES DIVISION
CHICAGO PUBLIC LIBRARY
400 SOUTH STATE STREET
CHICAGO, IL 60605

© THE BAKER & TAYLOR CO.

Assessment of Teaching:
Purposes, Practices, and
Implications for the Profession

Buros-Nebraska Symposium on Measurement & Testing

Series Editor

JANE CLOSE CONOLEY

Buros Institute of Mental Measurements
and
Department of Educational Psychology
University of Nebraska-Lincoln

Assessment of Teaching: Purposes, Practices, and Implications for the Profession

Edited by

JAMES V. MITCHELL, JR.
STEVEN L. WISE
BARBARA S. PLAKE
University of Nebraska-Lincoln

1990   LAWRENCE ERLBAUM ASSOCIATES, PUBLISHERS
       Hillsdale, New Jersey   Hove and London

Copyright © 1990 by Lawrence Erlbaum Associates, Inc.
All rights reserved. No part of this book may be reproduced in any form, by photostat, microfilm, retrieval system, or any other means, without the prior written permission of the publisher.

Lawrence Erlbaum Associates, Inc., Publishers
365 Broadway
Hillsdale, New Jersey 07642

Library of Congress Cataloging-in-Publication Data

Assessment of teaching : purposes, practices, and implications for the profession / edited by James V. Mitchell, Steven L. Wise, Barbara S. Plake.
    p. cm. -- (Buros-Nebraska symposium on measurement & testing)
  Includes bibliographical references.
  ISBN (invalid) 0-8058-0200-0
  1. Teachers--United States--Rating of--Congresses. 2. Teaching--Evaluation--Congresses. I. MItchell, James V., 1925- -Nebraska symposium on measurement & testing (Series)
LB2838.A788   1990
371.1'44--dc20

Printed in the United States of America
10 9 8 7 6 5 4 3 2 1

Contents

Preface *vii*

1. **Face Validity: Siren Song for Teacher-Testers** *1*
   W. James Popham

2. **Teacher Performance Assessments: A New Kind of Teacher Examination** *15*
   Edward H. Haertel

3. **Improving Teaching Through the Assessment Process** *37*
   Donald M. Medley

4. **Assessing the Quality of Teacher Assessment Tests** *77*
   William A. Mehrens

5. **Teacher Evaluation in the Organizational Context** *137*
   Linda Darling-Hammond

6. **Measuring Performance in Teacher Assessment** *183*
   Richard J. Stiggins

7. **Legal and Professional Issues in Teacher Certification Testing: A Psychometric Snark Hunt** *209*
   George F. Madaus

8. **Limitations of Using Student Achievement Data for Career Ladder Promotions and Merit Pay Decisions** *261*
   Ronald A. Berk

9. **Teaching Assessment: The Administrator's Perspective** *307*
   John R. Hoyle

10. **Appraisal: The Teacher's Perspective** *329*
    Peg Shafer

11. **The Assessment of Teacher Assessment: Concluding Thoughts and Some Lingering Questions** *347*
    James V. Mitchell, Jr.

    Author Index *377*

    Subject Index *385*

Preface

The Buros-Nebraska annual Symposia on Measurement and Testing are aimed at providing a forum for discussing important issues in the field of measurement and testing. The topic for the 1987 Symposium was "Assessment of Teaching: Purposes, Practices, and Implications for the Profession." This topic was selected because of the current interest in developing, designing, and implementing accountability programs for teaching that are present in many states and education programs. The complex nature of teaching, combined with the unique measurement issues for assessing outcomes in the teaching context, provided the basis for identifying the topic of teacher assessment for the 1987 symposium.

As is the tradition for the Institute, after each annual symposium a volume is prepared that contains written versions of the presentations from the symposium as well as additional chapters, invited by the editors, to complement the collection of chapters representing the symposium presentations. During the editorial process, each chapter for the current volume has external review by one or two professionals in the field in order to provide comments and suggestions for improvement of the chapter. We are very grateful to the dedicated efforts of the following persons who served as external reviewers for this volume: Peter Airasian, Jerrilyn Andrews, David Berliner, Carol Dwyer, Stephen Dunbar, Kim Hoogeveen, Ronald Joekel, Michael T. Kane, Steven Murray, Michael Rebell, Carol Robinson, Robert Stalcup, Charol Shakeshaft, Kenneth Strike, James Sweeney, Gary Sykes and Herbert Walberg. We also extend our gratitude to Jane Close Conoley, who as series editor provided the advice, oversight, and continuity necessary for an enterprise of this kind.

This volume provides a comprehensive look at the assessment of teaching, covering dimensions of assessment techniques, validity concerns, legal issues, application and implementation considerations, utility of assessment information, and views of the process of teacher assessment from the perspective of both an administrator and a teacher advocate. Therefore, this volume will focus on many related and vital facets of assessment of teaching.

The first chapter in the volume is authored by W. James Popham and is titled "Face Validity: Siren Song of Teacher-Testers." As the keynote speaker of the Buros-Nebraska Symposium on Measurement and Testing, Dr. Popham sets the stage for concern for validity in teacher assessment programs. The concerns raised by Dr. Popham are echoed by many authors in subsequent chapters in the volume.

Dr. Edward Haertel is the author of the second chapter, "Teacher Performance Assessments: A New Kind of Teacher Examination." As a member of the team involved in developing an instrument to credential teachers, Dr. Haertel is in a unique position to provide insights into the assessment methods for teaching. The methods identified give an overview for upcoming chapters in the volume on paper-and-pencil assessment instruments (Mehrens) and performance assessment techniques (Stiggins).

"Improving Teaching Through the Assessment Process" is the title of the next chapter authored by Dr. Donald Medley. Most practitioners agree that improvement of teaching should be the primary goal of teacher assessment programs. This chapter provides examples of teacher assessment programs that attempt to realize this critical goal for teacher assessment programs.

Dr. William Mehrens' chapter, "Assessing the Quality of Teacher Assessment Tests," provides an important continuation of the discussion on assessment methods identified by Dr. Haertel in Chapter 2. Focusing on paper-and-pencil assessment instruments, Dr. Mehrens addresses many critical psychometric issues related to the development and use of instruments for assessing teaching.

Highlighting the need for test validity, and focusing particularly on content validity, Dr. Mehrens provides an important contribution to teacher assessment evaluation.

The complex interrelationships among organizational/situational variables as they impact the teaching function are the focus of Dr. Linda Darling-Hammond's chapter, "Teacher Evaluation in the Organizational Context." The ecological validity of teacher assessment is portrayed as a critical requirement for such assessment. This chapter provides useful information for development and application of teacher assessment programs.

Dr. Richard Stiggins is the author of the next chapter, which focuses on another method of teacher assessment, "Measuring Performance in Teacher Assessment." Identifying this method as central to valid inferences about teacher performance, Dr. Stiggins lays out critical features to be considered in the development of a teacher assessment procedure. Coupled with Dr. Mehrens' chapter on paper-and-pencil techniques for teacher assessment, Dr. Stiggins' chapter provides important information for the application of performance assessment techniques to teacher assessment. Together, Dr. Mehrens' and Dr. Stiggins' chapters serve as useful applied examples of some of the assessment methods identified by Dr. Haertel in his chapter on teacher assessment methods.

"Legal and Professional Issues in Teacher Certification Testing: A Psychometric Snark Hunt" is the title of Dr. George Madaus' chapter. Dr. Madaus presents an interesting and important perspective on both legal and political implications for teacher assessment programs. Anyone seriously considering designing, implementing, or interpreting teacher assessment programs should carefully review Dr. Madaus' chapter.

Some teacher assessment program advocates suggest that useful information concerning teacher performance is shown through the performance of students on objective tests. Dr. Ronald Berk addresses this approach for merit pay decisions for teachers in Chapter 8 titled "Limitations of Using Achievement Data for Career Ladder Promotions and Merit Pay Decisions." Dr. Berk's chapter has important linkages to Dr. Darling-Hammond's chapter on organization variables influencing teacher performance and Dr. Madaus' chapter on legally defensible measures for assessing teacher performance.

The next two chapters in this volume are authored by practitioners directly impacted by teacher assessment programs. Chapter 9, "Teaching Assessment: The Administrator's Perspective" by Dr. John Hoyle addresses teacher assessment from an administrator's perspective. "Appraisal: The Teacher's Perspective" by Peg Shafer follows. Together, these chapters bring reality considerations to the broad goals and methods discussed in earlier chapters.

The final chapter is "The Assessment of Teacher Assessment: Concluding Thoughts and Some Lingering Questions" by Dr. James V. Mitchell, one of the coeditors of this volume in the Buros-Nebraska Symposium on Measurement and Testing series. The goal of his chapter is to provide synthesis of the earlier chapters, evaluating them on their approach to the topic, raising concerns as the topics are discussed, and then identifying a set of concerns that need to be addressed as the field of measurement moves more directly into the assessment of the teaching process.

The goal of this volume was to address the assessment of teaching from a variety of viewpoints relevant to measurement and testing. Through discussions of techniques, an evaluation of the utility of these techniques, an identification of contextual variables and concerns that impede direct linkages between teaching and student performance outcomes, and critical legal and political implications of teacher assessment, this volume provides the foundation for directed efforts toward improving the knowledge base for teacher assessment programs. It is clear that the cry for accountability in teacher performance is growing louder. This volume will hopefully serve as a tool for researchers, policy makers, and practitioners involved in developing, implementing, and evaluating the utility of teacher assessment programs.

Barbara S. Plake
Steven L. Wise

1

Face Validity: Siren Song for Teacher Testers

W. James Popham
UCLA and IOX Assessment Associates

The sirens of Greek mythology were a seductive set of women who, by singing melodies that apparently topped even those of Diana Ross and the Supremes, could lure mesmerized men to their doom. Greek mythology, it is clear, was solidly sexist, for the sirens used their supernatural singing talents to entice only unsuspecting males into trouble. Gender-equity considerations were conspicuously absent from the forays of Greek fablemakers. Sexism aside, however, it is certain that the sirens of yesteryear knew how to sing some truly enticing tunes.

FACE VALIDITY'S ALLURE

In today's current frenzy to develop teacher assessment devices that tap truly important dimensions of a teacher's skills, astute observers will recognize a melody subtly reminiscent of the ancient sirens' top 10 hits. The seductive refrain to which I refer is *face validity* or, as it can be more pedantically described, *verisimilitude*. With ever-increasing frequency, the architects of teacher tests are striving to create assessment instruments that simply reek of face validity, that is, assessment approaches consonant with the actual day-to-day requirements of teaching. Face validity is being touted by some as a genuinely indispensible element of new, more defensible teacher assessment devices. Paper-and-pencil tests, particularly those of the multiple-choice genre, are regarded by these new face-validity enthusiasts as assessment tools of a benighted past in which teacher tests yielded inferences of only debatable validity.

Many educators' experience with multiple-choice teacher tests has been based on the *National Teacher Examinations* (NTE) developed by the educational Testing Service (ETS). NTE tests have been available for some time. They deal not only with general knowledge and pedagogy, but also with an array of special subject fields such as chemistry and French. Originally constructed to assess the consequences of teacher preparation programs, NTE tests have recently been used in various states as part of licensure systems for prospective teachers. One suspects that when critics disparage multiple-choice teacher tests, they are generally thinking of the sorts of examinations that they imagine the NTE to represent.[1]

As indicated earlier, a dominant reason that today's teacher testers are scurrying from multiple-choice teacher tests is that examinees' responses to such tests do not resemble what goes on in teachers' classrooms. Instead, a new cadre of teacher testers is currently striving to create assessment approaches simply swimming in face validity, that is, assessment approaches unquestionably parallel to the activities in which classroom teachers must engage.

Webster's Dictionary defines an object possessing verisimilitude as one "having the appearance of truth." Therein, of course, is the attraction of face validity. It *looks* so appropriate. The appeal of verisimilitude in testing is compelling. But is that appeal warranted in the case of teacher testing?

---

[1]There are, to be sure, concerns abut NTE-type tests other than their lack of face validity. Some critics contend that such paper-and-pencil tests must be replaced or augmented with performance tests.

LICENSURE AND CERTIFICATION

Prior to looking more carefully at the pros and cons of face validity, we need to consider the various kinds of teacher tests to which face validity may be germane. Before doing so, however, it will be useful to engage in a bit of preliminary term tidying, for there is the potential for substantial confusion in the way that educators employ two key terms, namely, *licensure* and *certification.* Historically, many states have awarded teaching certificates to prospective teachers at the close of their teacher-education programs. Thus, the use of a test in conjunction with this process would typically lead us to describe such a test as a "teacher-certification" test.

Yet, in recent months the efforts of Lee Shulman and his Carnegie-supported associates (Shulman & Sykes, 1986) to devise what they refer to as "certification" tests has forced us to be more circumspect in using teacher-test descriptors.[2] Shulman employed the expression "certification test" to describe a test used with experienced, incumbent teachers. His use of the adjective *certification* coincides with the idea of a *certified* public accountant, this is, a professionally sanctioned, superior accountant. (Not all accountants, of course, are certified.) A certified teacher, to Shulman and his colleagues, is an incumbent teacher who has demonstrated clearly superior competence. Only a modest proportion of American teachers would, therefore, achieve such a state of certified excellence. Shulman would prefer to describe end-of-teacher-training tests as *licensure* tests.

Given the attention that Shulman's work is receiving these days, it seems that his licensure/certification distinction is apt to be used with increasing frequency in the field, hence, it is the distinction that will be employed in the remainder of this chapter. In other words, a *licensure* test will refer to tests given to prospective teachers at the end of their training programs. In contrast, a *certification* test will refer to tests given to incumbent teachers who aspire to be recognized for their advanced level of competence. (It should be noted, however, that in states where teachers have traditionally received certificates to teach, it may be difficult to persuade local educators to adopt the descriptor licensure test.)

---

[2]Shimberg (1981) drew this distinction between licensure and certification tests some years ago. See also Murray's (1986) essay dealing, in part, with this distinction.

DISTINCTIVE FUNCTIONS OF TEACHER TESTS

At the present, there are numerous varieties of teacher tests used in the U.S. To equate these diverse tests would be akin to considering a Lear jet and a San Francisco trolley as equivalent modes of transportation. We need to do some sorting out of the various species of teacher tests in order to decide which, if any, need to be face valid.

We can distinguish among teacher tests most conveniently by considering their functions. Let's look, therefore, at six relatively distinctive functions served by today's teacher tests.

Teacher-Education Screening Tests

One function of a teacher test is to screen applicants for admission to teacher-training programs. Technically, this use of the phrase "teacher test" is inaccurate. Clearly, if a test is being used to determine whether or not students are admitted to a teacher-education program, those students are not yet teachers. However, because the examinees have clearly set out in pursuit of teacherhood, it seems only a mild misnomer to consider such tests as members of the teacher-testing family. An example of such a teacher-education screening test would be the *Pre-Professional Skills Tests* (P-PST), tests of reading, writing, and mathematics distributed by ETS. Teacher-education screening tests characteristically focus on such subject matter. These sorts of screening tests are designed to determine whether an examinee is sufficiently literate to perform satisfactorily in a teacher-education program and, if successful in that program, thereafter as a classroom teacher.

Teacher-Licensure Tests

A second variety of teacher test is one used at the close of a teacher-education program to determine if examinees possess sufficient knowledge and/or skills to be granted a teaching license. As noted earlier, this is a function currently served by the NTE in many states. Generally, the focus of teacher licensure tests is on the examinee's mastery of a subject field or, perhaps, pedagogy. The content of teacher-licensure tests, as is the case with all varieties of teacher tests, is determined on a state-by-state basis. In California, for example, the *California Basic Education Skills Test* (CBEST) covers the same reading, writing, and mathematics content as the P-PST (the test from which the CBEST was originally derived). Thus, it would seem, teacher-licensure tests can cover the full gamut of content tapped by teacher tests, that is, subject matter, pedagogy, and basic skills.

In some instances it is useful to think of teacher-licensure tests as "initial" licensure tests because such tests may be *provisional* or *permanent* depending on the regulations of the particular state involved. In Connecticut, for example, the NTE are used at the close of an examinee's teacher training in order to grant an initial certificate to teach, a certificate that must be renewed by the state within 2 years. Other states grant more "permanent" licenses to teachers on the basis of an end-of-training licensure test.

Confirmatory Teacher-Licensure Tests

A third type of teacher tests is one employed to confer a permanent teaching license on those who have previously been only provisionally licensed to teach. In Connecticut, as previously indicated, a confirmatory licensure test will be administered to provisionally licensed teachers during their 1st or 2nd year of teaching.

Not all states issuing provisional teacher licenses rely on a formal teacher test to confer permanent licenses. In most states this function is accomplished chiefly by in-class observations and/or administrator' judgments regarding the neophyte teacher's competence. However, when a formal test is used as part of a process to confirm a teacher's provisional license, that test is clearly a distinctive species of teacher test.

In the main, confirmatory licensure tests deal with pedagogical content as opposed to subject matter content or the 3Rs. Typically, confirmatory licensure tests are used in concert with other indices of a teacher's skill, for example, classroom observations.

Career-Ladder Teacher Tests

A fourth function of teacher tests arises in connection with the educator career-ladder systems that have been established by an increasing number of our states. In Tennessee, for instance, in addition to relying on a host of other evaluative data, those who evaluate career-ladder candidates use teachers' scores on (a) a basic literacy test and (b) a test of pedagogical knowledge dealing with curriculum, instruction, and evaluation.

Teacher-Certification Tests

As indicated earlier, Shulman and his associates have set out to develop assessment prototypes suitable for use by a national teacher-certification board bent on bestowing special recognition on superior teachers. Shulman's approach rests on the assumption that many key teaching acts represent a teacher's pedagogically appropriate use of suitable subject matter (Shulman, 1986). Accordingly, the tests to be developed by Shulman and his colleagues seem destined to assess admixtures of both subject matter content and pedagogy. Shulman's group is eager to devise assessment schemes that are fundamentally different from conventional paper-and-pencil teacher tests. He hopes to rely far more heavily on the measurement of actual or simulated performance than is the case with most extant teacher tests.

Teacher-certification tests are at a particularly early stage of development. Preliminary assessment ploys devised by Shulman et al. will doubtlessly need to be revised, based on numerous tryouts, before they are perfected. New and better assessment tools are difficult to build. Nonetheless, a programmatic effort has been initiated to create certification tests for American teachers. The nation's educators will view with interest the endeavors of Shulman and his cohorts.

Teacher-Relicensure Tests

The final variant of teacher tests has been installed, thus far, in only three states, namely, Arkansas, Texas, and Georgia. Regulations in these three states oblige incumbent teachers to pass state-mandated tests as a condition for license renewal. Because incumbent teachers, as a consequence of results on such tests, could be excluded from teaching, these relicensure tests have received substantial media attention.

In Arkansas, the teacher-relicensure test deals with basic skills reading, writing, and mathematics. In Texas, the teacher-relicensure test measures examinees' mastery of rudimentary reading and writing skills. In Georgia, teachers are obliged to pass subject-matter oriented teacher-relicensure tests.

It is unclear whether additional states will require incumbent teachers to demonstrate mastery of basic skills as a condition for relicensure. In Arkansas and Texas, a predictably small percentage of teachers were denied license renewal as a consequence of the relicensure tests. That small percentage of teachers, however, interacted with many thousands of pupils each year. Arkansas and Texas policy makers conceived of the teacher-licensure test as a literacy test, that is, a test designed to identify teachers who were insufficiently literate to function as a classroom teacher. In Georgia, state policy makers were more concerned with teachers' mastery of subject matter.

A half-dozen varieties of teacher tests have now been described. Some of them deal with subject matter, some with pedagogy, and some with basic skills. For certain teacher-testing functions it is possible to develop tests that assess the *interaction* between certain pedagogical skills (e.g., task analysis) and particular subject content.

Although there are similarities among the six kinds of tests discussed, the functions served by each are meaningfully different. In Table 1.1 we see the six varieties of teacher tests alongside the types of content that has been used for such tests (● = already in place) or that could appropriately be used for such tests (○ = potential).

Let's turn now to the notion of face validity and the degree to which it is relevant to different types of teacher tests.

TABLE 1.1
Six Varieties of Teacher Tests
and Present/Potential Appropriate Content

Function	Basic Skills	Subject Matter	Pedagogy	Pedagogy Subject Interactions
Teacher education screening test	●	○	–	–
Teacher licensure test	●	●	●	○
Confirmatory teacher licensure test	–	–	○	○
Career-ladder teacher test	●	○	●	○
Teacher certification test	–	○	○	○
Teacher relicensure test	●	○	○	○

Note. ● = Already in place, ○ = Potential, – = Inappropriate

WHAT FACE VALIDITY ISN'T

Face validity is not regarded as a bona fide member of validity's blessed trinity. In the 1985 revision of the *Standards for Educational and Psychological Testing* (American Educational Research Association American Psychological Association, & National Council on Measurement in Education [AERA, APA, & NCME], 1985), as in the 1974 and earlier version of the *Standards*, we find no endorsement of face validity. The 1985 *Standards* accurately reflects an increasingly broad consensus in the measurement community that *validity* refers to the defensibility of an inference that is based on an examinee's test score. Thus, the 1985 *Standards* recommends that, to gauge the validity of score-based inferences, we assemble *content-related, criterion-related,* and *construct-related* evidence of validity. Face validity (or even face-related evidence) is not touted in the *Standards* as a fourth form of evidence pertinent to score-based inferences because it bears *no necessary relationship* to the validity of inferences we draw from an examinee's score. A test can yield valid score-based inferences even if it doesn't possess face validity. A test can yield invalid score-based inferences even if it does possess face validity.

Face validity constitutes the perceived legitimacy of a test for the use to which it is being put. Thus, if a teacher test is seen as appropriate for its particular function, it is said to possess face validity. Perceptions regarding the legitimacy of a test are held by a variety of individuals, not the least of whom are the examinees who are obliged to take the test. In a sense, therefore, face validity of teacher tests is a political rather than a psychometric consideration.

Today's teacher testers yearn for face-valid tests because they wish those tests to be perceived as appropriate by the numerous constituencies that might have a say regarding whether and how the tests are used. If state legislators enact laws calling for the creation of a teacher test, those legislators want a test that they and the public perceive to be a sensible approach to the testing of teachers. Such legislators, for example, would view with dismay a teacher test composed of ink-blot stimuli about which examinees were required to create fantasies. People simply don't see the relevance of such assessment approaches to the process of teaching.

As far as most of us are concerned, then, teacher tests ought to *look* like teacher tests. Teacher tests ought to look like teacher tests, however, only if other things are equal. And that, of course, is the nub of the problem. Those teacher testers who worship at the face-validity altar may fail to recognize that without other evidence of a score-based inference's validity, face validity creates a potentially false impression of a test's appropriateness. For such misguided teacher testers, face validity may not only be seen as necessary, it may be regarded as sufficient for the defensible testing of teachers. As will be demonstrated, that view is in error.

VALID INFERENCES AND FACE VALIDITY

Earlier it was indicated that face validity and the validity of a test's score-based inferences were not necessarily linked. Let's illustrate that point with a few examples drawn from existing teacher tests.

Consider an assessment approach drawn from a recently installed career-ladder teacher test in which applicants to a state's career-ladder program were obliged to assemble a portfolio of materials representative of certain aspects of their educational efforts. The portfolio was to include lesson plans, teacher-made tests, teacher-developed practice exercises, and so on. Because this portfolio assessment scheme dealt chiefly with teacher-generated materials of obvious relevance to instruction, it was generally regarded by outsiders as face valid. It was not widely known, however, that the state's teachers union had pressured career-ladder officials into making public the detailed scoring criteria that were to be used when the portfolios were being judged. As a consequence of the state's publicizing the portfolio-judging criteria, all career-ladder applicants, thereafter, assembled portfolios certain to earn the maximum possible points. Portfolios were created by assiduously attending to union-supplied guidelines and models. The result was, predictably, a flock of highest possible scores from which no valid inferences could be drawn regarding teachers' ability to generate such materials. A face-valid teacher assessment approach had been modified so that no sensible inferences could be drawn from examinee's performances.

This portfolio-judging debacle should not be used as evidence that teachers should not be informed of the criteria by which their performances will be judged. Teachers have a right to know the standards that will be applied to their test results. For instance, if teachers are asked to generate a brief written composition, it is perfectly sensible to let them know (in advance of the actual test) what criteria will be employed to judge the compositions. The difference between these two examination procedures is pivotal. In the case of the portfolio test, examinees can prepare their responses (with consultant help, if desired) in advance of providing those responses (the portfolios) to the examiners. In the case of the composition test, examinees must demonstrate in security monitored conditions that they can adhere to specified criteria by applying those criteria when generating an *original* response. If divulging of examination criteria for a teacher test distorts the defensibility of inferences we wish to draw from examinee's performances, then we ought not employ that teacher-testing strategy.

In another state we currently find a form of teacher performance test employed as part of a confirmatory teacher-licensure system. The state's beginning teachers are observed in their classrooms on several occasions to discern whether sound instructional practices are being employed. As far as the public is concerned, the assessment procedure is perceived to be legitimate. Teachers are being judged as they carry out classroom teaching responsibilities. Yet, because in all instances the observations are scheduled well in advance, that is, the teacher is aware of the specific date and time when observers will be present, we find nearly all teachers deliver polished lessons, many of which have been rehearsed at length with the aid of videotape recordings, consultants' reactions, and so on. The amount of performance variation is trivial. Almost everyone wins. Inferences about a teacher's actual classroom performance based on this face-valid approach are of little value.

The focus of validity, as indicated previously, must be on the defensibility of the score-based inferences that we attempt to draw from examinee's performances. Typically, in the case of teacher tests, we administer tests so that we can make inferences about how a teacher is apt to behave in an instructional setting. We use the examinee's score on the test as a proxy to represent aspects of future classroom performance. Even if a test focuses exclusively on a teacher's subject-matter knowledge, hence, we are more concerned with appropriateness of test's content, we still infer that the more knowledgeable teacher will dish out better content in the classroom. If, for a particular teacher test, we have reason to believe that the inferences we draw about teachers' classroom performances are not warranted, then the teacher test is of no utility irrespective of whether it possesses face validity.

Teacher tests can yield valid inferences even though they do not possess face validity. For example, biographical information often proves potent as a predictor of one's future success in many settings. Yet, even if biographical information yielded yummy predictions of a teacher candidate's future classroom performance, it would not possess face validity. Nonetheless, if an administrator is choosing among prospective teachers and has no other predictor available, the use of biographical information is apt to yield better decisions than a table of random numbers.

To repeat, the presence or absence of face validity bears little, if any, relationship to the defensibility of score-based inferences we make when we use tests to make decisions about examinees. Does this mean, then, that face validity is unimportant? The answer to that question is emphatically negative.

FACE VALIDITY'S IMPORT

As previously noted, face validity constitutes the perceived legitimacy of a test. Perceptions of legitimacy on the part of those concerned with a test's use are important. Take, for example, the teacher relicensure tests used in Arkansas and Texas. It was sufficiently traumatic for the teachers in those states to face the loss of their teaching licenses because of unsatisfactory results on a basic skills test, imagine how much more stress they would have experienced if the test itself appeared to be educationally irrelevant.

In Arkansas, for example, test items in the mathematics, reading, and writing sections of the Arkansas Educational Skills Assessment (AESA) were all couched in educationally relevant contexts. For instance, mathematics word problems dealt with the sorts of activities in which teachers typically engage such as calculating test-score averages or managing classroom materials budgets. One effect of this attention to the face validity of the AESA was at least a partial reduction in the strident, union-spurred resistance to the test. Had the AESA not been perceived as a legitimate measure of the basic skills needed by teachers, then the Arkansas Education Association would have been more effectively able to galvanize teacher resistance to the test.

Similarly, if the legislators of Arkansas who had mandated the teacher-licensure test perceived the AESA to be irrelevant to the requirements of teaching, then they would certainly have been less willing to support the AESA when it was under fire.

Over 40 years ago, Mosier (1947) argued that, when possible, tests which possessed face validity would be decisively superior to those which did not:

> In Civil Service situations, the candidate whose score is less than he expected is inclined to attribute his low score, not to his own defi-

ciencies but to the impractical nature of the test in relation to the job for which he is being examined. His dissatisfaction with the test results and his feeling of injustice may, of course, have real merit. We have not yet reached the era of public personnel examining where all tests are technically sound. Whether or not there is merit in his claim, the legislature, the courts, and public opinion, the court of last appeal, are more readily impressed by superficial appearances than by correlation coefficients. It becomes highly important, therefore, that a test to be used in such a situation not only be valid in the pragmatic sense of affording reasonably accurate predictions of job competence, but *have the appearance of validity* as well.

This appearance of validity as an added attribute is important in terms of the acceptance of the test, not only by the persons being examined, but also by those operating officials who are charged with the responsibility for taking action based upon the test results. If sound tests are given and accurately reported, but the supervisor, interviewer, or counselor has no confidence in them, the results will not be used effectively. (p. 200)

Clearly, face validity for teacher tests is always a plus. If teacher tests can yield valid inferences *and* also possess face validity, they are certainly apt to function more satisfactorily (for any of the six functions cited earlier) than tests that yield only valid inferences but possess no face validity. Hence, if other factors are equal, face validity is a quality earnestly to be sought for teacher tests. Yet, as we well know, how often do we find situations in which "other factors are equal"?

TRADE-OFFS IN TEACHER TESTING

If a teacher test can be created that simultaneously yields valid inferences and also possesses face validity, then it should be cherished. It should be cherished, that is, if the costs of achieving face validity are not prohibitively expensive. For example, future teacher tests might call for examinees to instruct specially assembled, randomly assigned pupils in one or more short lessons. These lessons could be videotaped so that, subsequently, the teacher's instructional prowess could be judged by a panel of experts. The costs associated with this sort of face-valid assessment approach, obviously, are far from trivial. If a state is not reasonably affluent, such assessment tactics would probably be out of the question on financial grounds alone.

It is possible that a less face-valid assessment approach, for

1. FACE VALIDITY

example, one involving the examinee's multiple-choice answers to verbal simulations of classroom situations, would be so highly correlated with the more elaborate test that it is quite clear the extra assessment dollars were being spent exclusively in quest of face validity. The key issue to be faced by decision makers in such situations is whether the boost in face validity is worth the boost in assessment costs.

There is another sort of trade-off that should be verboten to teacher testers, namely, the enhancement of face validity at the cost of validity regarding score-based inferences. To illustrate, suppose that examinees are presented with videotaped stimuli consisting of classroom vignettes in which teachers are functioning at differing levels of proficiency. In a multiple-choice version of the test, examinees select from a series of alternative interpretations the most appropriate analyses of the videotaped teachers. In an interview version of the test, an interviewer interacts with the examinee to record the examinee's appraisal of the videotaped sequence and also the examinee's rationale for that appraisal. This examinee–examiner interview is videotaped and, subsequently, the examinee's performance judged by a team of trained evaluators who view the examinee–examiner videotape.

In this comparison, the multiple-choice version appears to be a fairly conventional selected-response assessment approach whereas the interview version appears to be a far more face-valid scheme in which examinee and interviewer discuss at length the substance of classroom instruction. The interview version deals more directly with the "stuff" of teaching and, therefore, would typically get face-validity votes both from examinees as well as from those who subsequently viewed the interview videotapes. Indeed, in contrast to the multiple-choice version's prosaic selected-response strategy, the interactive interview version positively glistens.

Yet, suppose that intensive probing of both approaches reveals the dominant factor operative in determining the quality of an examinee's performance on the interview version is the examinee's skill in oral discourse. Examinees who can chatter comfortably with interviewers might secure better scores from judges irrespective of how much those examinees know about classroom instruction. For the interview version of the test, face validity has been purchased by reducing the validity of score-based inferences. That price is too great.

Yet, in today's highly publicized educational climate where teacher testers are eager to curry the favor of teachers unions, educational policy makers, and the public in general, this type of trade-off will, for some test developers, be too appealing to resist. Even worse, teacher tests may be created that are judged favorably on the basis of face validity alone. This would be truly deplorable.

REPRISE

In this analysis it has been argued that face validity may become an all too alluring magnet for teacher testers. Whereas face validity is an important consideration in a political context, it has precious little to do with the validity of the score-based inferences we draw from teacher tests. If face validity can be attained with tolerable increases in costs for teacher tests that otherwise yield valid inferences, face validity should be sought. Both examinees and others concerned with the teacher tests will be more positively disposed toward such face-valid tests. If, however, an increase in face validity causes a decrease in the validity of score-based inferences, then efforts to enhance face validity should be foregone. Teacher testers should not become so preoccupied with the appeal of face validity that they fail to scrutinize the validity of a test's score-based inferences.

In a politicized milieu, when we are eager to secure assessment approbation from many parties, face validity is an enormously attractive commodity. But face validity, as was true with siren-sung songs, is accompanied by both promise and peril. Teacher testers dare not allow face validity's promise to mask its perils.

REFERENCES

American Educational Research Association, American Psychological Association, & National Council on Measurement in Education. (1985). *Standards for educational and psychological testing.* Washington, DC: American Psychological Association.

Mosier, C. I. (1947). A critical examination of the concepts of face validity. *Educational and Psychological Measurement, 7,* 191–205.

Murray, S. L. (1986). *Considering policy options for testing teachers.* Northwest Regional Educational Laboratory. Portland, OR.

Shimberg, B. (1981). Testing for licensure and certification. *American Psychologist, 36,* 1138–1146.

Shulman, L. S. (1986). Those who understand: Knowledge growth in teaching. *Educational Researcher, 515*(2), 4–14.

Shulman, L. S., & Sykes, G. (1986). *A national board for teaching? In search of a bold standard.* Task Force on Teaching as a Profession, Carnegie Forum on Education and the Economy. New York: Carnegie Corporation of New York.

2

Teacher-Performance Assessments: A New Kind of Teacher Examination

Edward H. Haertel
Stanford University

During the last week of July 1987, 20 fourth- and fifth-grade teachers spent four days at a simulated assessment center in an elementary school. Each teacher completed 10 performance exercises on the teaching of equivalent fractions. The following week, 20 high school teachers of United States history spent four days completing a like number of exercises on the American revolution and the formation of the new government. These field tests were the culmination of over a year's work by the Teacher Assessment Project (TAP), sponsored by the Carnegie Corporation of New York, under the direction of Professor Lee S. Shulman at Stanford University.

The TAP prototype exercises represent a fundamentally new kind of teacher examination, based on structured observations of teachers' performance in situations designed to elicit the same kinds of knowledge and skills as they use in teaching, lesson planning, textbook selection, or related activities. Used in conjunction with more conventional examination formats and additional kinds of evidence (e.g., academic training or documentation of on-the-job performance), exercises based on some of these prototypes are expected to play an important role in the certification process being developed by the recently created National Board for Professional Teaching Standards. Some of the TAP prototypes directly simulate activities that are part of teaching or preparing to teach. Others, like discussing the performance of another teacher viewed on videotape, are more remote from the day-to-day work of teaching. All of the TAP exercises are designed to elicit forms of knowledge and analysis that may be critical for expert teaching.

For purposes of the TAP's research, prototypes were developed around two specific topics: the teaching of fractions, in particular the equivalence of fractions, at the upper elementary level, and the teaching of the American Revolution and the formation of the new government in a high school course on American history. Different exercises in each of these two content areas require from 45 minutes to 3 hours to complete and call on teachers to plan a lesson, critique a videotape of another teacher presenting a lesson, discuss the use of specific instructional materials, analyze and critique a textbook, or teach a lesson of their own choosing to a group of six students. Teacher examinees respond to particular student questions and comment on student homework problems (in mathematics) or brief essays (in history). Another exercise in elementary mathematics requires teachers to discuss the relationships among a set of possible topics from a unit on fractions, to select an appropriate sequence in which to teach those topics, and to explain their selection. They also demonstrate or describe methods of using specific household articles for teaching the equivalence of fractions, discuss the advantages and disadvantages of teaching students to use different methods for solving fraction problems, and describe their classroom routines for checking mathematics homework. High school history teachers engage in a group-planning exercise, in which three or four teachers work together to plan a unit on a specified topic. In another exercise, each teacher designs packets of instructional materials for a particular form of cooperative group-learning activity. The 1987 field tests of these exercises yielded a rich and extensive data base. In two weeks, they generated roughly 200 videotapes, 400 audiotapes, several thousand pages of observer notes, and hundreds of pages of notes and other writing by the 40 participating teachers themselves.

POLICY CONTEXT

Teachers in the United States take tests of various kinds, for various purposes. Their classroom performance as student teachers is observed and critiqued by supervising teachers and higher education faculty members. For state licensure, most complete objective paper-and-pencil tests like the National Teacher Examinations (NTE), or basic literacy and numeracy examinations like the California Basic Educational Skills Tests (CBEST). Increasing numbers of states are also turning to structured classroom observations, using instruments like the Florida Performance Measurement System (FPMS) or the Teacher Performance Assessment Instruments (TPAI) as requirements for obtaining a clear credential (Sandufer, 1986). Later, at the point of the school district's tenure decision and at intervals thereafter, teachers may be evaluated on the basis of brief, informal classroom observations by the principal (Bridges, 1986).

In an effort to improve teacher preparation, to help teachers through the first, difficult years in the classroom, and to encourage more beginning teachers to remain in the profession, some states are also planning or implementing teaching residencies following teacher education. These may offer opportunities for new forms of assessment by a designated mentor teacher at the local site, which have yet to be explored. In addition to written tests and classroom observations, evaluation of teachers on the basis of their students' test performance are becoming increasingly common, as discussed by Berk in chapter 8.

The structured performance assessments being developed by the TAP are prototypes for a new type of teacher examination, distinct from all the forms of teacher testing just described. Exercises based on these prototypes may be included in a voluntary examination for practicing teachers, developed and administered by the teaching profession itself. In time, this form of exercise may also find application in assessments of teacher education students, in teacher licensure, and perhaps in the implementation of career ladder, merit pay, or mentor teacher programs.

Assessments for Teacher Certification Versus Licensure

In their role of protecting the public from harm, state governments issue licenses to practice various professions, including teaching. Licensure tests are often required to assure a minimum level of safe and effective practice. In contrast to licensure, the term *certification* generally refers to a form of recognition controlled by organizations representing practicing professionals, for example, the National Board of Medical Examiners. Certification attests to some level of mature and expert practice. Following this usage, the "teaching certificates" issued by most states to beginning teachers would be called "teaching licenses."

One key recommendation of the 1986 report by the Carnegie Task Force on Teaching as a Profession, *A Nation Prepared: Teachers for the 21st Century*, was the creation of a National Board for Professional Teaching Standards, "to establish standards for high levels of competence in the teaching profession, to assess the qualifications of those seeking board certification, and to grant certificates to those who meet the standards" (Task Force on Teaching as a Profession, 1986, p. 62). Board certification would not occur until a teacher had at least several years of classroom-teaching experience, and would be entirely distinct from the state licensure required for beginning teachers. Teacher-certification tests will be used for a different purpose and with more experienced examinees than licensure tests. For these reasons, it is appropriate that the certification process require forms and levels of expertise well beyond those expected of beginning teachers. Structured performance assessments may help to address this broader range of knowledge and skills (Shulman, 1987a).

The TAP is not creating a national teacher examination. Although the Carnegie Corporation of New York has sponsored both the TAP and the creation of the National Board, they are independent of one another. The exercises created by the TAP will serve as a library of prototype performance assessments to assist the Board in developing its teacher-certification tests, but will also be generally available to interested researchers and test developers.

There are no testing applications envisioned for which exclusive reliance on structured performance assessments appears desirable, but such exercises may be used in conjunction with other requirements and forms of examinations to improve teacher licensure tests, as well as in certification testing. The State of Connecticut is at the forefront in developing such exercises as part of its Beginning Educator Support and Training (BEST) program (Pecheone, Baron, Forgione, & Abeles, 1988). Together with California, Connecticut has also taken the lead in forming the New Interstate Teacher Assessment and Support Consortium, which is intended among other functions to share information on performance-based teacher assessments and to coordinate similar development efforts among participating states.

Structured Performance Assessments and Teacher Education

The form and content of high-stakes tests can significantly influence the instructional programs that help examinees prepare for them (Fredericksen, 1984). The use of structured performance assessments in certification tests is expected to have a positive influence on teacher education programs, because these exercises employ tasks directly relevant to teaching. If these exercises come to play an important role in licensure examinations, their influence on teacher-education programs may be even more pronounced.

Preparation for structured performance assessments would involve practice in planning lessons, critiquing textbooks, answering student questions, and actual teaching, as well as discussions of the reasons for approaching these tasks in one way or another. Some activities of these kinds are already present in many teacher-education programs. An increase in this kind of activity would arguably improve teacher education.

DEVELOPMENT OF EXERCISE PROTOTYPES BY THE TEACHER-ASSESSMENT PROJECT

Like other professions, expertise in teaching requires mastery of a distinctive knowledge base (Shulman, 1987b). Indeed, one of the hallmarks of a profession is the possession of specialized knowledge and skill acquired through formal training and usually apprenticeship. No one who has not been trained as a lawyer would have much chance of passing a state bar examination, and persons who have not graduated from accredited medical schools are not even permitted to sit for the National Medical Board Examinations (Lareau, 1985). A certification test for teachers should likewise assess a distinctive knowledge base.

Areas of Knowledge Assessed by the TAP Exercise Prototypes

Teachers must have mastered the subject matter they are to teach, and must be familiar with general principles of sound pedagogy, but in addition, they must develop specific expertise in the teaching of a particular subject matter (Shulman, 1987b). This *pedagogi-*

cal content knowledge includes a repertoire of effective instructional activities, knowledge of common student misconceptions and stumbling blocks, metaphors and analogies that can help students to grasp new ideas, information about available curriculum materials and their appropriateness in different situations, and other matters.

A fifth-grade teacher must understand fractions, for example, differently from a mathematician. The teacher must not only understand how to work with fractions, but must possess a store of analogies, instructional activities, and alternative explanations and solution procedures for various kinds of fraction problems. The teacher must also know when and how to use all this information for instruction. A third-grade teacher must not only know how to read, but must also know how to organize the component skills of reading to impart them to learners. A high school physics teacher must not only understand kinematics, but must also know how to make real for students the connections between mathematical symbols and the real-world objects they can represent, and how to prescribe instructional activities that can force students to confront their naive, or "Aristotelian" ideas about motion (McCloskey, 1983).

The TAP exercises were developed around specific subject matters and topics of instruction in order to permit the examination of this pedagogical content knowledge. In one exercise, for example, teachers are interviewed about algorithms like cross multiplying to determine whether two fractions are equal. (The fractions a/b and c/d are equal if and only if $ad = bc$.) Among other questions, teachers are asked whether they would teach cross multiplication as a method for checking the equivalence of fractions, whether this method could be used to explicate underlying mathematical principles, what other methods they would teach, when they would use each method, and what difficulties the teaching of the cross multiplication method might create for students in their subsequent mathematics instruction. The kind of knowledge required to answer these questions or to justify the answers is distinct from a knowledge of the underlying mathematics, but may be critical for effective teaching of fractions.

Structured performance assessments can also tap a teacher's knowledge of curriculum materials. One exercise developed by the TAP requires a teacher to critique a United States history textbook and to evaluate the soundness of the history presented, the quality of the writing, the book's appeal to students, and its appropri-

2. TEACHER PERFORMANCE ASSESSMENTS

ateness for different kinds of students, among other factors. In addition to a general critique, the examinee must respond to short answer questions about the quality of specific sections of the text.

In addition to pedagogical content knowledge and curriculum knowledge, some of the exercises piloted by the TAP attempted an examination of teacher performance skills and collegial interaction. Skill in performance refers to the teacher's ability to perform in front of a class of students—at a minimum to be articulate and moderately engaging. It was assessed primarily in an exercise in each field test that required teachers to present a lesson of their own choosing, planned in advance, to a group of six students. Collegial interaction refers to the teacher's ability to interact effectively with colleagues. It was assessed primarily in a group planning exercise, in which three or four teachers worked together to plan a unit on American history.

An additional exercise that was piloted but not included in the field test examined the teacher's interpersonal skill in managing a classroom disruption. All of the exercises also tested to some degree the teacher's knowledge of subject matter, and the set of exercises as a whole required adequate communication skills, including listening and speaking as well as reading and writing.

It would be rash to claim that all of these different aspects of teacher knowledge and skill were thoroughly or even adequately examined in the exercises piloted, or even that all of them could in principle be adequately examined using structured performance assessments. The assessment center may be an inappropriate context for the measurement of some of these skills, especially collegial interaction, performance skills, and interpersonal skills in managing classroom disruptions. Nonetheless, these exercises may have the potential to significantly extend the range of different kinds of teacher knowledge and skill that can be measured.

Performance Exercises for Teacher Certification

Structured performance assessments for teachers are still in their infancy. Although models exist in the performance center approaches developed for personnel evaluation in industry, these are generally designed to assess more or less generic managerial and organizational skills. Even the exercises used in performance centers for the selection of principals, operated by the National Association of Secondary School Principles (Hersey, 1986; Landholm, 1986), require relatively little specialized knowledge of school organization or pedagogy (Aburto & Haertel, 1986).

Design of the summer 1987 field tests began with the identification of many more potential exercises than were ultimately included, and with an initial conception of the types of knowledge to be assessed that was somewhat broader than the final conception. From these preliminary ideas, a set of exercises was chosen for development to represent a range of different teaching situations (qualities of schools, communities, and learners), response modes (demonstration, verbal responses, written products of different kinds), and varieties of activities (teaching, preparing to teach, collegial interaction). Considerations of fairness to teacher examinees from different ethnic backgrounds dictated that exercises not depend on detailed knowledge or experience in highly specialized instructional settings, although there was a tension between this concern and the desire to provide examinees with as much context and background as possible for each exercise. For each exercise, points of vulnerability were identified, and an attempt was made to avoid including several exercises that shared a common weakness. Finally, each potential exercise was examined for its representativeness of some larger class of exercises that would be more or less parallel to the prototype. Ideas that appeared to defy replication were not pursued.

Each exercise chosen for development went through a process leading from an initial sketch to a preliminary script, pilot-test materials, pilot by the author of the exercise, supervised pilot by another examiner, preparation of training materials for field test examiners, and finally, inclusion in the field test. Group and individual reviews of each exercise were required at specified points in this process (Wilson, 1988).

The TAP was assisted in this work by exemplary teachers in elementary mathematics and in high school United States history. Some of these were teacher collaborators who served as paid consultants to the project, but a larger number participated in a teacher advisory panel or contributed in other ways. The teacher collaborators were observed in their classrooms teaching the focal content of each assessment; responded to a series of structured interviews about their own background and experience, their pedagogical methods, details of their short-range and long-range instructional planning, their methods of student assessment, and other matters; assisted in developing stimulus materials for the exercises; and served in the field test as examiners. Together with the teacher advisory panel, they also served as subjects for exercise pilots and participated in extensive discussions of specific exercises, which led to numerous improvements.

The classroom observations and interviews involving the teacher collaborators built upon earlier and concurrent studies on the knowledge base of teaching. These were referred to as the *wisdom of practice* studies in the TAP, and helped especially to define the pedagogical content knowledge to be assessed.

Scoring Performance Exercises

In the TAP field tests, dramatic differences were evident among the performances of different teachers, and especially between beginning and highly experienced teachers, but it is one thing to recognize the variability of teachers' performances and another to derive reliable and valid measurements from them. By design, nearly all of the questions posed in the various exercises have several correct answers. In scoring, it is necessary to recognize the validity of alternative responses while maintaining distinctions among different degrees of response quality.

Scoring and interpretation of exercise performance were of concern from the beginning of exercise development, but work on scoring began in earnest after the 1987 field test. In the following months, preliminary scoring schemes for nearly all of the exercises were revised and elaborated, with as many as three successive scoring systems developed and applied for some exercises. The study of scoring culminated during the summer of 1988, when teachers from outside the project were hired to score the exercises using the final scoring systems developed. This final scoring is providing information about interrater reliability and about the strengths and weaknesses of alternative scoring methods. Preliminary information about scoring is available in interim reports (e.g., Haertel, 1988; Shulman, Haertel, & Bird, 1988). Only a brief sketch of the scoring can be presented here.

A set of five "scoring dimensions" has been developed to guide and organize scoring efforts. The most important of these are "content-specific pedagogy" and "subject matter knowledge," together with "professional responsibility," "class organization and management," and "pedagogy, sensitivity, and responsiveness to students." Each exercise is scored only for those dimensions it can inform. Scores are assigned on a six-point scale, from AAA (Distinguished) through C (Questionable). The same six-point scale is used for all dimensions and for all exercises. Most scores range from AA (Commendable) down to B+ (Adequate) or B (Limited). The rating of A (Satisfactory) is considered borderline with respect to a certification decision, although of course the cutting score, the scale, the scoring systems, and even the entire approach taken may be changed by the National Board. Where evidence with respect to a dimension is thin, the rating is enclosed in brackets to distinguish clearly between the strength of the evidence available and the quality of the performance. The ratings are supplemented by brief narrative comments as required to call attention to unanticipated or atypical aspects of performance that might have a bearing on a certification decision.

The dimensions have been useful in organizing the work of scoring development, but their convergent and discriminant validity and their ultimate role in scoring have yet to be determined. It is possible that scores across dimensions will turn out to be highly correlated, in which case the separate scores might be of limited value. It is also possible that scores for the same dimension across exercises will not correlate as highly as scores across dimensions for the same exercise, which might also call the use of separate scores into question.

Two general approaches have been taken to scoring the different exercises. One strategy is "holistic," relying on descriptions of B+ and of AA performances with respect to each dimension scored. An examinee's performance is reviewed and summarized in a standard format specifying particular elements of the performance that should be noted. The performance summary is then compared with the two descriptions for each dimension. If it closely matches one or the other description, the corresponding rating is assigned. If it is between the B+ and the AA descriptions, a rating of A may be used; a performance that surpasses AA can be assigned the AAA rating; and so forth. Alternatively, descriptions were sometimes prepared for all six levels to better define the entire scale.

An alternative to holistic scoring is to identify discrete, scorable elements of the performance. These are presented in a checklist for each dimension, which is used to record those elements present in a given protocol. In some scoring schemes, this identification of elements is augmented with simple ratings for each element, or brief comments. The scorable elements for each dimension are then combined following a more or less explicit rule. Initially, rather than inventing some arbitrary rule, scorers are encouraged to deliberate about each protocol and arrive at a judgment about the preponderance of evidence. Later, after sufficient experience with this kind of system, it may be possible to formulate an explicit rule that captures the sense of these deliberations and makes this step of the scoring procedure more objective.

NEED FOR FURTHER RESEARCH

Educational researchers have used a variety of paradigms to study processes of teaching and learning (Shulman, 1986a; 1986b), and impressive progress has been made, but the knowledge base of teaching has yet to be codified as clearly and completely as that of many other professions. Many existing teacher examinations and observational systems are justified on the basis of findings from process–product research studies, which may show no more than that the teacher behavior to be chosen as "correct" was found to correlate with some learning outcome, in some particular time and place, with some particular teachers and learners. Moreover, research on the kind of content-specific pedagogical knowledge that was the focus of the TAP's structured performance assessments has been especially meager (Shulman, 1986b). This presents an obvious difficulty for developing, scoring, and interpreting tests of teachers' distinctive expertise. There is no case law, or textbook, or published research literature that sets forth generally accepted and empirically grounded answers for every question asked in the TAP exercise prototypes.

One possible conclusion would be that development of structured performance assessments designed to measure content-specific pedagogical knowledge cannot proceed until there is substantial professional agreement on questions of how particular topics in the curriculum should be taught, but I believe that is unduly pessimistic. The work of developing scoring schemes and warrants for asserting the superiority of some answers over others has proceeded concurrently with the development of the exercises, and progress has been impressive. Many decisions about the acceptability of specific answers must be regarded as provisional, and further research will clearly be needed before exercises of this kind are used to reach significant decisions. But for virtually every question asked in any of the prototype exercises, some answers are clearly acceptable, and others are clearly deficient.

Grounds for Judging Answers in Performance Exercises

The answers to performance exercises include responses to direct questions; as well as demonstrations like responding to student questions or presenting a prepared lesson; products like lesson plans; and other scorable responses. It is useful to distinguish two related issues in using these answers to reach decisions about examinees. First is the problem of evaluating answers for correctness or quality. Second is whether these particular, scorable responses ought to be counted in reaching the decision at hand. The first of these issues is logically prior to the second. If there is no basis for distinguishing better from worse answers to a question, it obviously has no place in an examination.

Correctness of Exercise Responses

Granting that there is no one right way to prepare a lesson plan, critique a textbook, or answer a student's question, there are, nonetheless, some clear criteria by which answers can be judged. First is factual correctness. Content-specific pedagogical knowledge is bound up with subject-matter knowledge, and the content conveyed by a teacher's lesson should be consistent with the generally accepted views of subject matter specialists. Correctness and precision are sometimes matters of degree, of course, and it may be proper to teach school children some generalizations to which experts would take exception, but the principle stands that the content of teachers' instruction should be accurate. The TAP exercise prototypes also evaluated teachers' knowledge of curriculum. In constructing their responses, examinees were often expected to draw on their knowledge of how typical elementary mathematics textbooks are organized, for example, or the kinds of manipulatives and other instructional materials typically used to teach basic concepts about fractions. In the next round of TAP exercise development, focusing on literacy in the early grades, teachers will be expected to be broadly familiar with children's literature, and to be able to suggest appropriate readings for different pedagogical contexts and goals. (It bears repeating that all of the TAP prototypes were designed to assess more than subject-matter knowledge or knowledge of curriculum materials per se. If the goal were no more than measurement of information, less costly forms of assessment could be used.)

Second, teachers' scorable responses should comport with accepted general pedagogical principles. Lessons should have some discernible purpose and structure, explanations should be clear, vocabulary should be appropriate to the level of the children addressed. Instruction should proceed systematically, unless there is some definite and probably explicit rationale for proceeding otherwise. If a teacher is asked to present a lesson prepared in advance to a group of six well behaved children, then she or he should in some way monitor the engagement and understanding of all six of them, and not entirely ignore those who fail to raise their hands.

Third, where there are generally accepted answers to questions of pedagogical content knowledge, these provide a standard against which to judge an examinee's answer. In one exercise, teachers are shown a method for checking whether two fractions are equivalent, and asked, among other questions, what other methods they might teach children for checking the equivalence of fractions. The expected answers include algorithms for reducing both fractions to lowest terms, or converting them to decimals. Granting that a teacher might produce some unexpected answer that was neither clearly correct nor clearly incorrect, all of the answers to that question that were in fact obtained during the tryout of the exercise could be scored without difficulty.

It must be acknowledged that generally accepted answers are not necessarily correct. A consensus of teachers, even expert teachers, might represent no more than conventional wisdom, some mixture of truth and folklore. But the best available knowledge, even if imperfect, is appropriately assessed in a certification test. The limitations of a professional consensus are less of a problem for exercise development than the difficulty of *determining* a professional consensus about the proper instructional treatment of particular curriculum topics. The work of teachers is largely private and individual. A masterful lesson might be captured on film or videotape, but this is rarely done. Even within a single school, teachers often fail to discuss their instructional practices with one another. Journals for teachers in particular school subjects offer sensible and promising instructional ideas, but these tend to be fragmentary and to lack broad empirical support. Moreover, the correct answers to pedagogical questions depend on a host of contextual factors. Teachers must tailor their instruction to the needs of different learners, and the TAP staff has discussed at length how to score an examinee's statement that "it works for me," or "this is what I have found with my kids." (The decision has been that such a statement alone is insufficient justification for a questionable answer.)

The involvement of many practicing teachers in developing the TAP exercise prototypes has already been described. In addition, the TAP was guided by "expert panels" in each content area. These included practicing teachers highly regarded by their peers, nationally known teacher educators specializing in the content area, and university-based scholars in the cognate discipline. Each panel was co-chaired by a university faculty member and a classroom teacher. The expert panels reviewed ideas for exercises, critiqued the exercises at several points in their development, and discussed scoring criteria and the levels of performance that should be expected.

The use of these different sources of information provides some assurance that the scoring schemes developed by the TAP would find a degree of support among experienced and successful teachers, and provides a model that may be followed in further exercise development. However, the existing research base and the involvement of a handful of experts and teacher collaborators are not enough to justify expansive claims that the "knowledge base of teaching" has been discovered.

Continued research on teacher testing can accelerate knowledge growth in teaching. Commentary on structured performance exercises and discussion of the merits of different responses can help to bring forth an expert consensus on the solution of the pedagogical problems these exercises pose. Together with other initiatives toward the professionalization of teaching, teacher certification can also help to change attitudes and professional norms that have impeded the sharing and testing of new instructional practices, and can encourage more attention to pedagogical content knowledge in teacher-education programs. The development of an empirical and consensual knowledge base of teaching can and should proceed concurrently with research and development on teacher assessment.

Determining What Should Be Covered by a Teacher-Certification Test

Even after agreement is reached on the scoring of responses to structured performance exercises, the inclusion of these exercises on a teacher certification test remains to be justified. This is part of test validity, and is properly addressed under the conventional rubrics of content-related, criterion-related, and construct-related validity (American Educational Research Association, American Psychological Association, & National Council on Measurement in

Education [AERA, APA, & NCME], 1985). Some of the groundwork for studies of content and construct validity has already been carried out by the Stanford TAP, although of course all aspects of validity will merit careful reexamination once a set of operational examinations has been prepared by the National Board.

With respect to content validity, the structured performance exercises in a certification examination should each be manifestly relevant to the work of teaching. Taken as a whole, the set of exercises used should be representative of some definable domain. It should be clear what areas of knowledge and skill the exercises are designed to cover, and balanced coverage of those areas should be provided.

Criterion-related validity may be difficult to assess, because appropriate criteria against which to validate performance exercises may not exist and may be difficult to construct. Better performance on structured performance exercises ought to imply some capability for better performance in the classroom, but defining and quantifying better classroom performance will be a challenge. A premature insistence on criterion-related validity evidence using inadequate criteria could be unwise. It may be that criterion-related validity will best be addressed at the level of the entire teacher-certification process, with other lines of argument used to support the inclusion of particular kinds of exercises in the overall examination procedure. The design of sound criterion-related validation studies will not be possible until the newly formed National Board has had a chance to consider in much greater detail the form of their examinations, and the nature and level of the status that board certification is meant to confer.

Construct validity is close to the heart of the argument for new forms of teacher examinations. The fundamental justification for the cost of developing and administering these assessments is their potential to measure forms of knowledge and skill critical to expert teaching but difficult or impossible to assess using other forms of examinations. Continuing research is essential to better define pedagogical content knowledge, to establish the capability of structured performance exercises to assess it, and to show that the knowledge and skills measured by these exercises really do matter in the work of teaching.

Future research must also attend to plausible rival hypotheses about what the exercises measure, including hypotheses about cultural, gender, or other forms of bias. A thorough investigation of assessments relying on interview responses must address the possibility that verbal fluency or glibness can exert an undue influence on scores, for example. Subtle effects of interactions between the gender and culture of the examiner and the examinee must also be considered. These issues have been discussed repeatedly as the TAP prototypes have been developed and scored, but conscientious exercise development is no more than a prelude to the empirical studies that will be required.

Reliability, Validity, Efficiency

In designing a certification test for teachers, as in many measurement problems, there is a tension among the three goals of reliability, validity, and efficiency. Reliability refers to the replicability or reproducibility of judgments—across occasions, across raters or judges, and sometimes across forms or versions of a test or other assessment. Validity refers to a number of concerns that bear on the appropriateness of score-based inferences. It encompasses content validity—the extent to which the assessment is representative of the knowledge and skills required of teachers; criterion-related validity—the extent to which scores on the assessment are useful in distinguishing examinees capable of different degrees of proficiency in the classroom; and construct validity—the extent to which claims for the measurement of a distinctive knowledge base of teaching and for the distinctiveness of the dimensions used in rating can be supported. Efficiency refers to the costs of an assessment, in preparing the examination, in examinee time, in examiner time, and in scoring. It is roughly the case that if any one of these three constraints were relaxed, the other two could be satisfied. (Only roughly because an instrument's reliability places a statistical limit upon its criterion-related validity.) Given unlimited time and resources, a complex, rich observation of actual classroom practice over a long period of time, conducted by a panel of carefully trained observers, could probably provide an assessment of high reliability and indubitable validity. Shortening an assessment of this kind (improving efficiency) would compromise reliability, whereas substituting more efficient forms of assessment to satisfy the ends of reliability and efficiency together would likely reduce validity by employing assessment tasks that were less like actual teaching.

Closely related to the tension among reliability, validity, and efficiency is the goal of objectivity in measurement. Different forms of assessments vary in the amount of judgment required in scoring the performance of each individual examinee. At one extreme, an objective multiple-choice test requires virtually no judgment at all on the part of the examiner. At the other extreme, an unstructured, holistic rating of performance following a brief classroom visit allows enormous latitude for the observer. Other things being equal, a more objective measurement is likely to assure more equitable evaluation of all examinees, and is likely to be more reliable than an instrument that calls for more judgment on the part of the observer. However, the single minded pursuit of objectivity can lead to a sacrifice of validity.

Standard Setting

The immediate purpose of teacher-certification testing is to arrive at pass–fail decisions about individual examinees. Setting standards for reaching these decisions will be a complex and difficult task, which properly devolves upon the newly created National Board. The standards established for these first teacher-certification tests will express to the public and the profession the meaning of board certification. If board certification is to contribute maximally to the professionalization of teaching, it must represent a significant level of expertise and attainment, but at the same time, the standard must not be perceived as unrealistic or unattainable. The proportion of candidates who succeed will strongly influence attitudes toward the certification program, as well as both the supply of and demand for board certified teachers.

Teacher performance exercises will provide only one of several different kinds of evidence that are expected to play a part in the certification process, and the board will have to decide what level of performance to require in each area. It will also have to decide whether strengths in one area will be allowed to offset weaknesses in another, or whether separate standards will have to be met for each component of the certification process. Clearly, standard setting for teacher performance exercises cannot be divorced from the purposes and context of the entire certification procedure, but it may be helpful to comment in general terms on a possible approach.

As with present teacher-licensure tests, judgmental methods are likely to play a large part in standard setting. These are methods relying on direct examination of tests by panels representing relevant constituencies (teachers, administrators, the public, etc.). When these methods are applied to multiple-choice tests, panelists are asked to make a large number of narrow judgments about items, sometimes rating their difficulty or importance, or deciding which distractors a minimally competent examinee should be able to eliminate. These small judgments by many panelists are then combined by some arithmetic procedure to yield an overall passing score for the examination. Judgmental methods used for multiple-choice tests include the Angoff method (attributed by Angoff to Tucker), the Nedelsky method, and the Ebel method (Berk, 1986).

Although these methods enjoy some support in the psychometric community (e.g., Berk, 1986; IOX Assessment Associates, 1983a; 1983b), they have also been strongly criticized (e.g., Glass, 1978; Shepard, 1980). Authors taking exception to these methods have questioned the logical basis for assuming that panelists are able to make accurate judgments of the kind required. In the context of teacher licensure, if one argues that the items directly ask about things that classroom teachers need to know, then it follows that classroom teachers may be in a position to say which or how many items prospective teachers should be able to answer. But if the items are conceived as no more than indicators of knowledge or skills that teachers need, then the judgment task called for seems to depend on the panelists' knowing both the minimum level of the underlying knowledge or skill needed for acceptable teaching performance, and the regression of item performance on the underlying skill. In practice, panelists often seem uncomfortable with their ability to make the judgments called for (Shepard, 1980).

The judgmental standard-setting methods used with multiple-choice tests would be unsuitable for use with teacher-performance exercises, for at least two reasons. First, performance exercise protocols do not provide any natural breakdown into discrete, scorable units corresponding to objective test items. This is by design and may be intrinsic to whatever value these exercises have in eliciting distinctive areas of knowledge and skill. Second, no clean distinction can be drawn between scoring and interpretation for these exercises. On a multiple-choice test, scoring is an objective, mechanical procedure, logically and operationally distinct from the interpretive step of arriving at a pass–fail decision by comparison to a cutting score. On performance exercises, the methods of scoring envisioned so far all call for judgments and interpretations as part of the initial quantification of the examinee's responses.

New or modified judgmental standard-setting methods appear highly promising for performance exercises, because the kinds of tasks set and responses elicited are more like actual teaching. A teacher panelist might not know how to judge the probability that a minimally competent teacher would know the answer to a multiple-choice question, but might be far more comfortable reading through examples of textbook critiques, lesson plans, or packets of instructional materials, and deciding which are of sufficient quality to warrant certification. After panelists reviewed, discussed, and rated selected protocols, these could be used to construct a rating scale to which other protocols could then be compared. Alternatively, statistical methods for "policy capturing" might be used to determine those quantifiable features of protocols that distinguished those judged acceptable versus unacceptable, leading to an objective formula for scoring and rating future protocols from the same exercise.

THE FUTURE OF TEACHER PERFORMANCE EXERCISES

Much work remains to be done before teacher-performance exercises are ready for operational use. Work on methods of scoring is ongoing, and reliability and validity are only now being examined. In addition to research and development on the prototypes themselves, the structure of the larger certification process will require further clarification, as will the organization and logistics of test administration. That being said, the task is well begun, and results to date are very encouraging. As the National Board, the State of Connecticut, and other organizations and states proceed with the development of these tests, a clearer picture of their strengths, limitations, and range of potential applications will emerge.

Performance exercises may contribute to the *definition* of teacher expertise, as well as contributing to its *assessment*. Standards for exemplary teaching practice must reflect a consensus of mature teaching professionals, but there have been few major forums for the deliberations necessary to arrive at such a consensus. The activities of developing and scoring performance exercises and designing a National Board examination are providing significant opportunities for reflection and discussion about what board certification ought to represent, and performance exercises can provide concrete cases to focus such discussions. The work of the TAP has already raised a number of issues that the National Board may need to address: Should certification imply that in addition to making sound pedagogical decisions, a teacher is able to explain the rationale for those decisions? To what extent should certification attest to a teacher's specialized knowledge about teaching in different sociocultural settings? How should significant controversies or philosophical differences among teachers be resolved? Teachers who disagree fundamentally whether elementary mathematics instruction should give priority to teaching algorithmic skills or mathematics as a problem-solving process may approach some performance exercises in entirely different ways. The National Board must not espouse some narrow orthodoxy, but neither can it be entirely catholic in its conception of teaching excellence.

The National Board is creating a conception of exemplary classroom teaching, and its performance exercises will embody that conception. A few years from now, it may be possible to show empirically that performance exercises can distinguish between degrees of classroom expertise so defined, but for the present, an emphasis on criterion-related validity evidence would be premature. As stated earlier, appropriate criteria against which to validate these exercises may not yet exist. Just as thermometers were first designed to reflect rough and ready notions of hot and cold, so teacher performance exercises must first succeed in representing rough and ready notions of good pedagogical practice. Just as thermometers came in time to be *definitive* of temperature, so structured performance exercises may help to define teaching expertise.

REFERENCES

Aburto, C., & Haertel, E. H. (1986). *Teacher Assessment Project Study Group on Alternative Assessment Methods: Executive summary of the Assessment Technologies Conference* (Report No. 5). Stanford, CA: Stanford University Teacher Assessment Project.

American Educational Research Association, American Psychological Association, & National Council on Measurement in Education. (1985). *Standards for educational and psychological testing.* Washington, DC: American Psychological Association.

Berk, R. A. (1986). A consumer's guide to setting performance standards on criterion-referenced tests. *Review of Educational Research, 56,* 137–172.

Bridges, E. M. (1986). *The incompetent teacher.* Philadelphia, PA: Falmer Press.

Fredericksen, N. (1984). The real test bias. *American Psychologist, 39,* 193–202.

Glass, G. V. (1978). Standards and criteria. *Journal of Educational Measurement, 15,* 237–261.

Haertel, E. H. (1988, April). *Quantifying the wisdom of practice.* Paper presented at the meeting of the American Educational Research Association, San Francisco.

Hersey, P. W. (1986). Selecting and developing educational leaders. *School Administrator, 43*(3), 16–17.

IOX Assessment Associates. (1983a). *Appraising the legal defensibility of the National Teacher Examinations for the state of Kentucky.* Los Angeles, CA: Author.

IOX Assessment Associates. (1983b). *Appraising the Preprofessional Skills Test for the state of Texas. Report number one: Test suitability and performance standards.* Los Angeles, CA: Author.

Landholm, L. J. (1986). Observations of participants: Center helps one's monitoring of strengths, weaknesses, *NASSP Bulletin, 70*(486), 24–25.

Lareau, A. (1985). *A comparison of professional examinations in six fields: Implications for the teaching profession.* Stanford, CA: Knowledge Growth in Teaching, School of Education, Stanford University.

McCloskey, M. (1983). Naive theories of motion. In D. Gentner & A. L. Stevens (Eds.), *Mental models.* Hillsdale, NJ: Lawrence Erlbaum Associates.

Pecheone, R. L., Baron, J. B., Forgione, P. D., Jr., & Abeles, S. (1988). A comprehensive approach to teacher assessment: Examples from math and science. In A. B. Champagne (Ed.), *This year in school science 1988: Science teaching—Making the system work* (pp. 191–214). Washington, DC: American Association for the Advancement of Science.

Sandufer, J. T. (1986). State assessment trends. *AACTE Briefs, 7*(6), 12–14.

Shepard, L. A. (1980). Standard setting issues and methods. *Applied Psychological Measurement, 4,* 447–467.

Shulman, L. S. (1986a). Paradigms and research programs in the study of teaching: A contemporary perspective. In M. C. Wittrock (Ed.), *Handbook of research on teaching* (3rd ed., pp. 3–36). New York: Macmillan.

Shulman, L. S. (1986b). Those who understand: Knowledge growth in teaching. *Educational Researcher, 15*(2), 4–14.

Shulman, L. S. (1987a). Assessment for teaching: An initiative for the profession. *Phi Delta Kappan, 69,* 38–44.

Shulman, L. S. (1987b). Knowledge and teaching: Foundations of the new reform. *Harvard Educational Review, 57,* 1–22.

Shulman, L. S., Haertel, E. H., & Bird, T. (1988, April). *Toward alternative assessments of teaching: A report of work in progress.* Stanford, CA: Teacher Assessment Project, Stanford University.

Task Force on Teaching as a Profession. (1986, May). *A nation prepared: Teachers for the 21st century.* Hyattsville, MD: Carnegie Forum on Education and the Economy.

Wilson, S. M. (1988, April). *Planning the pedagogical decathlon.* Paper presented at the meeting of the American Educational Research Association, New Orleans.

3
Improving Teaching Through the Assessment Process

Donald M. Medley
University of Virginia

INTRODUCTION

The first opportunity to use teacher evaluation to improve teaching arises when a student applies for admission into an undergraduate teacher preparation program. At this time it is the responsibility of the program faculty to determine whether each candidate possesses those abilities and other personal characteristics that every teacher needs, but cannot expect to acquire in such a program, and to deny admission to those who lack one or more of them. The second opportunity arises when the student has completed the program. At this time it is the responsibility of the state certification agency to find out whether each candidate has acquired the minimum professional knowledge and skill necessary for certification as competent to enter the teaching profession, and deny certification to those who have not. Additional opportunities arise after the teacher enters into practice and either comes up for tenure or becomes a candidate for merit pay. At either point it is the responsibility of the school administration to ascertain whether the teacher is performing well enough to receive tenure or merit pay and deny them to those who are not.

If the evaluation made at each of these times is valid and is followed by appropriate action, the overall quality of teaching in the schools is expected to improve because incompetent teachers would be systematically eliminated from the profession. In order for this theory to work, each incompetent teacher who is eliminated must be replaced by another teacher who is competent. Thus the success of this strategy depends on the assumption that an ample supply of competent teachers is available to replace those we eliminate, an assumption unlikely to prove true.

There is a second strategy for using teacher evaluation to improve teaching, the success of which does not depend on this rather dubious assumption. This alternative strategy is to increase the competence of the incompetent teachers we already have instead of replacing them. The success of this strategy depends, like that of the first, on the validity of the teacher evaluations used. Unless the procedures used to screen out incompetent teachers are valid, all that the first strategy can do is increase teacher turnover. Unless the evaluation procedures used to upgrade the competence of the teachers we have are valid, all that the second strategy can do is prolong the training some teachers receive.

There are two major questions that must be answered before either of these strategies can be applied with any success. The first of these questions is: What should we evaluate? The second question is: How shall we evaluate it? Only when the first question has been answered is it possible to answer the second. Past efforts to use teacher evaluation to improve teaching have failed, largely because they have tended to neglect the first question and concentrate on the second. Before we can answer either question we must make and preserve careful distinctions in the meanings of four terms too often used interchangeably. These terms are *teacher competence, teacher competency, teacher effectiveness,* and *teacher performance.*

Some Important Definitions

In defining these four terms I will use the simple model of the teacher evaluation process shown in Figure 3.1. The diagram presents a kind of inventory of the points in a teacher's professional life at which evaluations designed to improve teaching can be made. It shows five points at which teachers may be assessed on different bases, and four points at which other relevant variables—usually called "context" variables—may be assessed.

3. IMPROVING TEACHING 39

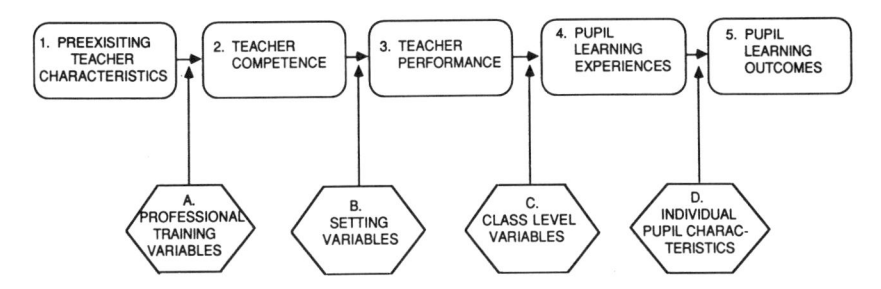

FIG. 3.1. Five Teacher Assessment Points

Preexisting teacher characteristics are assessed at Point 1, the earliest point at which any teacher evaluation is feasible. Evaluations of preexisting teacher characteristics may be used by teacher educators to improve teaching by using them to decide which candidates should be admitted into a preservice teacher preparation program and which should not.

There are a number of abilities and other characteristics that teachers need and are expected to acquire before beginning professional training. One example is the kind of academic ability the Scholastic Aptitude Test is used to measure. Another is the basic general knowledge, sometimes called "general literacy," that all high school graduates are expected to possess. It is generally agreed that any teacher of any grade or subject should be literate in this sense.

What is unique to these characteristics is that their development neither is nor should be part of a professional teacher education program. Hence students who lack such a characteristic when they begin their professional preparation will almost certainly not possess it when when they finish the program. If it is known that possession of the characteristic will be required for certification, then the time to evaluate it is before the teachers enter the program, not when they finish it.

Teacher Competence

Teacher competence is assessed directly at Point 2, usually as a basis for deciding whether the teacher should or should not be certified or licensed to teach. The state certification agency tries to improve teaching in the state by permitting only teachers with some minimum level of competence to become teachers.

Before we can evaluate competence validly and reliably enough to implement either of the two strategies for improving teaching, we must have a precise definition of competence. This requires us first to *specify* exactly what we mean by the term, and then to *define* the knowledge, skills, and so forth, that a teacher must possess in order to be competent.

Specifying Competence. Competence is specified by identifying the teaching tasks or functions that a competent teacher must be able to perform. For some purposes we may need to specify competence rather narrowly, for instance, when specifying competence to administer and interpret individual intelligence tests or competence in using a particular method of teaching reading. For other purposes we may need to define competence more broadly, for example, as in competence to teach kindergarten, competence to teach high school mathematics, or competence to teach pupils with severe emotional handicaps.

Defining Competence. Once competence is specified, the second important step is to identify the knowledge, skills, and other qualities a teacher must possess in order to perform the functions specified. Only then can we say we have defined competence precisely enough to be able to evaluate it objectively, validly, and reliably.

Teacher Competency

Despite some negative connotations that it has acquired over the years, I shall use the term *teacher competency* to refer to any single item of knowledge, skill, or any other specific characteristic we have identified as one that a competent teacher is expected to possess. We can then say that *teacher competence* in performing a function is defined as *the possession of a specific set of teacher competencies* relevant to the performance of that function.

Teacher Effectiveness

Whether or not a competent teacher will be effective on the job depends in part on whether the set of competencies that make up the definition is sufficient to guarantee effectiveness. At the present state of knowledge about the nature of effective teaching this is most unlikely. At best, a definition of competence can and should incorporate all we know plus, perhaps, our best guesses about what we do not know, that will help a teacher perform the specified function.

The least that we can expect a teacher preparation program

3. IMPROVING TEACHING

faculty to do is to equip each graduate with this knowledge—in other words, the faculty should transmit to the teacher what they see as the relevant wisdom of the profession. And the least that we can expect of a valid evaluation of competence is a measure of how much of this wisdom each teacher has acquired.

Teacher Performance

Teacher performance is assessed at Point 3, usually as a basis for one or another administrative decision about teacher utilization. Teachers are hired, tenured, recognized as master teachers on the basis of evaluations of their performance on the job. School administrators can improve the quality of teaching by screening out teachers who fail to perform the specified function successfully and replacing them with teachers who do perform it successfully.

Teacher performance is defined, not in terms of competence nor in terms of what the teacher is able to do, but in terms of what the teacher actually does on the job. Unlike competence, which is evaluated on the basis of teacher behavior in a test situation, performance must be evaluated on the basis of the behavior of the teacher while doing the job he or she was hired to do. Evaluations of teacher performance are therefore based on observations of the processes and procedures the teacher uses in teaching, observations made during one or more visits to the teacher's classroom (not on the results the teacher obtains).

Assumptions. Valid performance assessment is possible only if two assumptions are true. One is the assumption that the teacher behavior observed is a representative sample of the teacher's behavior when he or she is not being observed. The other is that it is possible to specify rules of procedure that a teacher should follow.

The first of these assumptions is almost certainly unjustified and unjustifiable. The request many evaluators make that while the teacher is being evaluated he or she should act as though no observer were present is a request that the teacher is likely to ignore, and indeed has a perfect right to ignore. The right to do one's best when one's performance is being evaluated for employment, tenure, or promotion may well be a basic human right.

The second assumption is also questionable. It depends on the doubtful proposition that there is one way to teach in a given situation which is best for all teachers; and on the even more doubtful proposition that someone who has just walked in the door is a better judge of what a teacher should be doing at any given moment than the teacher who has been there since the beginning of the school year. Both are inconsistent with the assumption that the nature of teaching requires a teacher to function as a professional problem solver.

Performance or Competence? In view of these limitations, it may seem odd that the vast majority of evaluations of practicing teachers are evaluations of this type, and that almost all decisions about teacher personnel are based on performance evaluations. The only explanation I can suggest is that what these evaluators are really trying to evaluate is teacher competence. It is much more difficult to infer teacher competence from teacher performance than it looks; and even if it were not, a teacher's competence is not the appropriate basis for the kinds of decisions that are based on these evaluations. It is not the teacher who is able to do the best job but the one who does the best job who should be hired and retained. The race goes not to the swiftest but to the first to reach the finish line.

Pupil learning experiences are assessed at Point 4. This term will be used to refer to any in-school pupil activity intended to result in pupil learning. Doing a workbook assignment is one example of a pupil learning experience; watching and discussing an instructional film is another. Listening to the teacher is a third, and perhaps the most popular of all. We all know that learning results from activity of the learner. Making sure that pupils engage in productive activities, that is, providing them with learning experiences appropriate to the goals of education is what schools and teachers are for.

Evaluations based on observations of pupil behaviors during visits to a teacher's classroom may provide a desirable alternative basis for the decisions about teacher utilization usually based on performance evaluations. What would be more logical than to evaluate a teacher's performance on the basis of the amount and quality of the learning experiences her pupils have in her classroom, that is, on the use she makes of the time pupils spend under her care?

Assumptions. Two assumptions must be true for evaluations of pupil learning experiences based on classroom observations to be valid. The first is that the pupil activities observed during a visit are representative of those that occur in that same classroom when the observer is absent. The second assumption is that it is possible to define the kinds of learning experiences the pupils in a certain class should be having, regardless of who their teacher is.

3. IMPROVING TEACHING   43

Let us compare these two assumptions with the parallel assumptions that underlie performance evaluations made at Point 3. The assumption that observed pupil behaviors are representative of "normal" pupil behaviors is somewhat more likely to be true than the assumption that observed teacher behaviors are representative of "normal" teacher behavior. For one thing, the pupils are not being evaluated, so their right to do their best is not involved.

The second assumption required at Point 4 is also more justifiable than the second assumption required at Point 3. If we take the point of view that the school system employs th teacher to provide pupils with appropriate learning experiences, it seems reasonable for the school system to define the kinds of learning experiences that are appropriate. Doing so does not mean that the school system must prescribe how the teacher should go about performing this function, as is the case when performance is assessed directly at Point 3. Assessment at Point 4 leaves teachers free to function as professionals and use whatever processes and procedures they think best.

Although some teacher-rating scales contain items that refer to related pupil behaviors (such as level of attention), I know of no instance in which the learning experiences of teachers' pupils have been the explicit and sole basis of evaluations of teacher performance made to support personnel decisions. The best example I know of the use of pupil-learning experiences as a basis for evaluating teachers occurred in a research project (Cf. Berliner, 1979; Denham & Lieberman, 1980).

Pupil-learning outcomes are assessed at Point 5. This term refers to changes in pupil status with respect to educational goals that take place during the period of time a teacher has the pupil in her class. The ultimate purpose of efforts to improve teaching is, of course, to increase pupil learning outcomes.

The amount and quality of learning outcomes in a teacher's classroom depend on a great many important factors. Teachers have a considerable amount of control over some of these, including their own competence and performance while teaching. But teachers have relatively little control over other factors, such as the support available from the school and community, the makeup of the class, and the characteristics of the individual pupils in the class.

Contextual Factors

So far we have discussed only those factors over which the teacher has considerable control, those which are or could be foci of efforts to evaluate teachers. Let us now turn our attention briefly to those factors over which the teacher has relatively little control, represented in Figure 3.1 at Points A through D. Variables of these types are usually called "contextual factors."

A. Professional Training Variables. Type-A factors are characteristics of teacher training that affect teacher competence directly and affect teacher performance, pupil learning experiences and pupil learning outcomes only indirectly. Changing training variables can increase pupil learning outcomes by increasing teacher competence, although a lot of things can go wrong between Point A and Point 5.

B. Setting-Variables. Type-B factors are characteristics of the setting, that is, of the community, the school system, and the individual school in which the teacher is employed. Changes in setting variables, in, let us say, the administrative and supervisory support a teacher receives, can increase pupil learning outcomes by improving teacher performance.

C. Class-Level Variables. Type-C factors are characteristics of the pupils in a teacher's class as a group. Changes in the makeup of a class, in the mix of abilities, ethnic groups, mainstreamed pupils, and so forth, can, by changing the nature of this group, alter the learning experiences a pupil has in it, and increase (or decrease) pupil learning outcomes.

D. Individual Pupil Characteristics. Type-D factors are characteristics of the individual pupil that determine what and how much a pupil learns from a given learning experience. They include such things as aptitude for learning and motivation to learn.

Teacher Effectiveness

The term *teacher effectiveness* refers to the portion of what a pupil learns that is attributable to the performance of his teacher. It is so difficult and expensive to obtain valid measures of teacher effectiveness that they are useless for all practical purposes except research, especially studies of the validity of other ways of evaluating teachers. The technical problems that must be solved in order to obtain valid direct measures of teacher effectiveness are formidable. It is necessary, first to identify and then to measure all of the important factors that affect pupil learning outcomes and then tease out and evaluate the effect of the teacher by statistical means. No less formidable are the difficulties to be overcome in obtaining defensible measures of pupil progress toward the important goals of education.

Even if direct measurements of teacher effectiveness were easy enough to obtain so that they could be used for routine teacher evaluations they would be of limited use in our efforts to improve teaching by either of the two major strategies defined earlier. The information such measurements contain about which teacher should be eliminated comes too late to be of any use. The time to eliminate an incompetent teacher is *before*, not after the teacher has taught long enough to become a candidate for permanent tenure. Nor do direct measures of teacher effectiveness contain any diagnostic information, any clue as to what the ineffective teacher needs to do in order to become more effective.

Needed Research. The principal use of direct measures of teacher effectiveness is in the research we so badly need to improve evaluations of teachers at Points 1 through 4. First of all we need *research in classroom learning*, that is, research correlating pupil learning experiences with pupil learning outcomes, adjusting for important individual pupil characteristics. Such research should tell school administrators what kinds of learning experiences maximize pupil learning outcomes, so they can evaluate a teacher on the basis of the amount of such learning experiences the teacher provides.

Next we need *research in teaching*, that is, research correlating teachers' performance and the learning experiences pupils have in their classrooms, adjusting for important class characteristics. Such research should tell supervisors how teachers should behave in order to provide pupils with the kind of learning experiences that research in classroom learning indicates they should have, so they can diagnose and prescribe ways in which teachers can improve their performance.

Next we need *research in teacher competence*, research correlating teacher competencies and teacher performance, adjusting for important setting variables. Such research should help teacher educators and state certification agencies to improve their definitions of competence and, therefore, improve the performance and increase the effectiveness of the teachers they train and certify.

Finally, we need *admissions research*, research correlating pre-existing teacher characteristics with measures of teacher competence obtained at the end of training, adjusting for important training variables. Such research should tell admissions officers what characteristics to require students to possess in order to maximize the number who will acquire the competencies identified by research in teacher competence as ones every graduate should possess.

Focus of This Chapter

While the educators, certification agencies, and teacher educators of the country are waiting for the findings of all of this research, they have no choice but to continue to try to improve teaching by evaluating teachers as well as they can. The most highly visible efforts to improve teaching by using teacher evaluation are of course those being made by the large-scale teacher-evaluation programs so many states are operating. Most of these programs base their evaluations on conventional paper-and-pencil tests or on expert ratings of teacher performance. There is no evidence that scores on either type of instrument have any appreciable validity as measures of teacher competence, performance, or effectiveness. It is therefore highly improbable that any of these programs is effective in improving teaching.

It is the thesis of this chapter that, although the knowledge of the nature of teacher competence presently available is far from complete, it is sufficient to enable us to develop much more valid and reliable instruments for evaluating teacher competence—that can be administered at little or no greater cost in time or money than the virtually worthless ones in present use.

The first critical step we must take in order to develop such instruments is to define competence explicitly enough so that it can be measured. In order to do this we need, first, to *specify* competence in terms of what a competent teacher is supposed to be able to do. Only then will it be possible to *define* competence, to identify exactly what knowledge, abilities, and so forth, a competent teacher must possess.

Before a state licensure or certification officer (or anyone else) can design a valid system for evaluating teachers he or she must specify the kind of teachers wanted, that is, the teaching functions they should be qualified to perform. Will they be expected to function as elementary teachers, physics teachers, special education teachers? Then what must be decided next is precisely what competencies, what knowledge, skills, and so forth, a teacher should

3. IMPROVING TEACHING 47

possess in order to be declared competent to perform these functions.

At this point the state licensure or certification official should be able to turn to the research for guidance; but in the present state of the art of teaching, not enough is known about the relationship between competence and effective teaching to make it possible to arrive at an authoritative answer, a definition of teacher competence on which there is any general consensus. This fact does not reduce the need for the certification official to be precise in defining competence; if anything, it makes the need for precision more important. If the teachers certified as competent fail to perform satisfactorily it is important to be able to tell why, and revise the definition of competence accordingly.

The rest of this chapter focuses on these problems; on specifying, defining, and evaluating teacher competence.

A FRAMEWORK FOR DEFINING TEACHER COMPETENCE

What I propose to do next is present a kind of model definition or framework for a definition of teacher competence that will facilitate the related task of developing valid, objective, and practicable procedures for evaluating teacher competence. An inspection of almost any definition of teacher competence published in the past reveals a failure to distinguish between the task of *specifying* the functions a competent teacher must perform and that of *defining* the competencies needed to perform those functions. (For an excellent example see Johnson, Okey, Capie, Ellett, & Adams, 1978.) As we have seen, such a specification is a necessary first step in the process of defining teacher competence; but by itself such a specification is of little help in the construction of an evaluation instrument. The framework I present includes both a specification and a definition.

Because the model I propose to describe needs to be applicable to a definition of almost any kind of teacher competence, the function specified must be generic, must be one that any and every teacher is expected to perform. Does such a teaching function exist, and if it does, what is it? I suggest that any profession is defined by some one generic function that all members of that profession must perform; and that competence in that profession must be defined in terms of the knowledge, skills, and abilities needed to perform this generic function.

The Generic Function of the Teacher

I first became aware of the generic function of the teacher when I read the report to the American Association of Colleges for Teacher Education of its Bicentennial Commission (Howsam, Corrigan, Denemark & Nash, 1976). According to this report, the function of teachers in this society is the same as that of any other professional, which is to bring professional knowledge to bear on certain problems the society faces. The report notes that as civilizations advance and encounter more and more complex problems, they turn for solutions more and more often to persons with special competence to deal with such problems.

The people they turn to are members of what are called *learned professions*. These professions are called "learned" because practitioners of each one of them possess specialized knowledge and skill relevant to the solution of a certain class of difficult problems. The role society expects teachers to fulfill, like that of practitioners of other learned professions, is to apply specialized professional knowledge and skill to the solution of problems of a certain type.

Just as society expects physicians to apply the accumulated wisdom or "mystique" of the medical profession to the solution of health problems of their patients, so it expects teachers to apply the accumulated wisdom or mystique of the teaching profession to the solution of learning problems of their pupils. There is no doubt about the need for such knowledge, although there is some question in the public mind whether enough of it exists to make the average teacher any better able to cope with teaching problems than anyone else.

Three Types of Teaching Problems

Which way is the best way to evaluate a teacher's ability to solve a teaching problem depends very much on the nature of the problem. It is therefore useful to group the different kinds of problems teachers must solve according to how a teacher's ability to solve them is most validly—and easily—evaluated. We use the following three categories.

Category 1: Interactive Teaching Problems include teaching problems that arise in the classroom when pupils are present and interacting with the teacher—participating in a discussion, listening to a teacher presentation, working individually under the teacher's supervision, or having learning experiences of some other kind under the teacher's guidance.

Category 2: Preactive Teaching Problems include teaching problems that arise when no pupils are present, while the teacher plans instruction, diagnoses pupil needs, evaluates test papers, or performs some other teaching task that does not involve interacting with pupils.

Category 3: Reflective Teaching Problems include problems teachers recognize while reflecting on or reviewing their own past performance with a view to improving future performances.

The first two categories were originally identified by Jackson (1966). Jackson pointed out that the abilities a teacher needs to make the almost instantaneous decisions required when teacher and pupils are interacting are very different from those needed to make the deliberate decisions made while reviewing past interactive sessions or planning future ones. The third category came to our attention in the work of Cruickshank and Applegate (1981), who have developed procedures for preparing teachers to solve problems of a third type. One of the characteristics of a learned profession is that the process of professional education continues throughout the practitioner's career, that the true professional never ceases to reflect on past performances with a view to improving future ones.

Teacher Competence and Teacher Performance

Let us turn now to the often-neglected step of defining the knowledge and the skills a teacher needs in order be competent to perform the generic teaching function, which is to solve teaching problems.

The problem-solving process can be conceptualized in different ways for different purposes. Because of the purpose this conceptualization is to serve, I have chosen to break up the process into four steps, each of which calls for different competencies, best evaluated by different methods.

The four types of competencies are referred to as: *perceptual skills, professional judgment, professional knowledge,* and *perfor-*

mance skills. The relationships of each of these types of competencies to performance are shown in Figure 3.2.

The four types of competencies are shown at the left of the diagram, with arrows from each leading to diamonds containing question marks, representing "branch points."

Let us agree that a teaching problem arises whenever a pupil does something that he or she should not do, or when something happens to him that should not happen. One pupil copying another's work during a test might be one simple example; a misspelled word on a test paper may be another.

Type 1: Perceptual Skills

It is obvious that a teacher cannot solve a teaching problem unless he or she is aware of the occurrence of the event that gives rise to the problem; the teacher must see the pupil copy or realize that the word is misspelled before he or she can deal with either of the problems just mentioned.

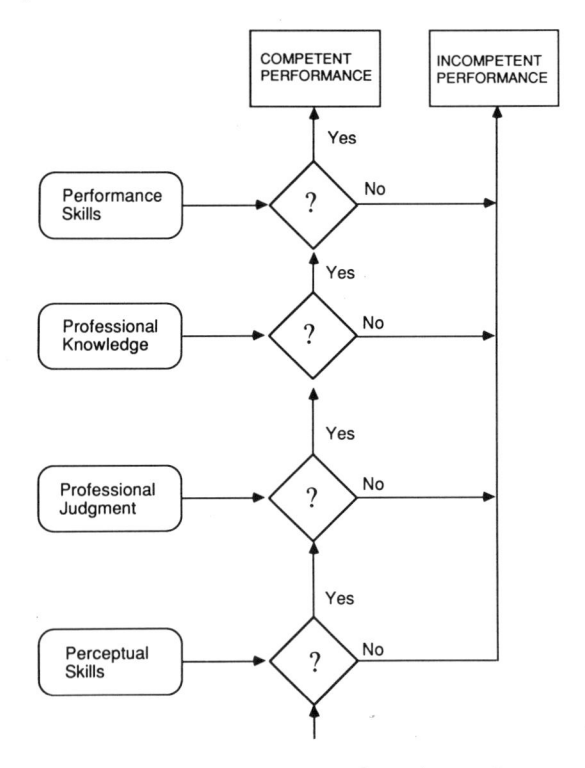

FIG. 3.2. Teacher Competence and Teacher Performance

3. IMPROVING TEACHING

The competencies a teacher needs in order to be aware of what is happening to the pupils will be called *perceptual skills*. Kounin (1970) has enriched the language of teaching by introducing the term *withitness* in referring to the aspect of this competency relevant to interactive teaching, and Berliner (1986) studied differences in what "expert" teachers and novice teachers see when they view the same classrooms. Pupils speak of teachers with high perceptual skills of this type as having eyes in the back of their heads. Possession of this skill enables some teachers to nip certain situations in the bud—to move a pupil to another seat before he or she even thinks of misbehaving.

Smith (1969) identified a somewhat different kind of perceptual skill relevant to interactive teaching—a skill needed to recognize abstract pedagogical concepts when they occur in th "real world," and he also invented "protocol materials" to be used to help teachers develop this skill. Knowledge of reinforcement theory is of little use unless you can recognize when a pupil is being reinforced.

Perceptual skills probably play a no less important role in the solution of preactive teaching problems; the ability to recognize arithmetic errors and misspelled words or to read pupils' handwriting may be examples.

Note that, in the figure, an arrow runs from perceptual skills to a branch point and that two arrows come out of it. If a teacher fails to see a problem behavior, that is, lacks the relevant perceptual skill, we follow the "no" arrow which leads us to "incompetent performance." This means that if the teacher fails to apply the competency, he or she fails to perform the function, that is, to solve the problem.

If the teacher does see the behavior (does apply the competency) we follow the "yes" arrow to the next branch point.

Type 2: Professional Judgment

Competencies of this type involve recognizing the behavior as problem behavior, as something that needs to be changed or corrected. During interactive teaching the most obvious examples have to do with the limits the teacher sets on pupil behavior; for example, how much noise, how much moving about, and so on, the teacher permits. Professional judgment in such matters is a major factor in classroom management. Professional judgment also has to do with teacher expectations, with the kind of pupil response or performance the teacher finds acceptable or praiseworthy from which of her pupils. Professional judgment in preactive teaching also has a lot to do with expectations or standards of pupil performance.

If the teacher is aware of problem behavior but does not recognize that it is problem behavior, we follow the "no" arrow out of the second branch point in the diagram to "incompetent performance." If she does recognize the existence of the problem we follow the "yes" arrow to the next branch point.

Type 3: Professional Knowledge

If the teacher recognizes a problem, the next type of competency needed is knowledge of various possible responses to the problem and their probable consequences. Part of this knowledge may be regarded as "foundational," knowledge presumably acquired in professional courses in psychology, sociology, human growth and development, and so forth, and part of it comes from courses in methods or strategies of teaching; in either case, it must be functional in the sense that the teacher can relate it to the problem behavior he or she faces.

Unless the teacher applies professional knowledge and comes up with a response that solves the problem, we follow the "no" arrow out of the third branch point to "incompetent performance." Otherwise we follow the "yes" arrow to the next (and last) branch point.

Type 4: Performance Skills

Once the teacher has identified a solution to the problem, he or she needs only to implement the solution to solve the problem, as we find by following the "yes" arrow out of the fourth branch point, which leads to "competent performance." If the teacher is unable to implement the solution, we follow the "no" arrow to "incompetent performance."

Note that these four types of competencies are related sequentially; that is, that no opportunity to apply any one competency arises unless all preceding competencies have been applied successfully. Note also that successful performance is possible only if all four types of competencies are successfully applied.

Implications for Improving Teaching. This simple analysis should make it clear why, if we are interested in improving teaching, it is better to evaluate teacher competence than teacher performance. Because teacher performance is defined in terms of success

3. IMPROVING TEACHING   53

in solving teaching problems, all we find out when we evaluate teacher performance is whether or not the teacher solves the problem. This may be useful if the teacher succeeds; but if he or she does not solve the problem, we have no clue as to how or why he or she failed, no indication as to how we can help the teacher improve future performance.

When we evaluate teacher competence instead of performance we still find out whether or not the teacher succeeds in solving the problem; but if the teacher fails we learn a lot more. We learn which of the competencies the teacher needs to acquire in order to solve the problem, and have a clear indication of how to improve the teacher's future performance.

A Competency Matrix

If we combine the three types of problems and the four types of competencies just described, we generate 12 different kinds of competencies. In general, all of the competencies in the same cell may be assessed in the same way, or ways that are quite similar; and competencies in different cells are usually best assessed in different ways. The 12 cells form the skeletal map of the domain of teacher competence shown in Figure 3.3.

	PERCEPTUAL SKILLS	PROFESSIONAL JUDGMENT	PROFESSIONAL KNOWLEDGE	PERFORMANCE SKILLS
INTERACTIVE TEACHING PROBLEMS				
PREACTIVE TEACHING PROBLEMS				
REFLECTIVE TEACHING PROBLEMS				

FIG. 3.3. A Matrix of Teacher Competencies

I call the map "skeletal" because it contains no actual competencies, only empty cells. The matrix was originally designed for use with a set of competencies defined beforehand. The idea was first to assign each competency to one of the 12 cells and then to construct the evaluation instrument or instruments. Experience indicates that the matrix can also prove useful in the process of defining competence. Suppose, for example, that you wanted to define competence to teach one of the primary grades.

Following the structure in Figure 3.3, you might begin by specifying the functions such a teacher would be competent to perform. You would almost certainly specify these functions in greater detail than the matrix shows. You might subdivide interactive teaching problems into those related to classroom management, those related to the delivery of instruction, those related to evaluation, and so forth. Or you might subdivide them into problems that arise in introducing a new activity or lesson, presenting or developing new material, reviewing and summarizing, conducting guided practice, making an assignment, and ending a lesson or activity.

Next you would analyze the process of solving teaching problems (as shown in Figure 3.2) as it applied to problems of each of these kinds, defining in detail the competencies of each type that you considered most important to the performance of each function.

Suppose, for example, that one subdivision of interactive teaching problems you had specified contained problems related to "classroom management." You might consider what kinds of warning signs the teacher should be especially sensitive to (Type 1); what limits the teacher should set on pupil conduct (Type 2); what professional knowledge would be most useful (Type 3); and what techniques or strategies for dealing with pupils the teacher should master (Type 4). Or if a subdivision under "delivering instruction" had to do with teaching reading, a similar analysis might focus on what the teacher should listen and watch for while a pupil reads aloud, what kinds of errors the teacher should or should not interrupt the pupil to correct, and so on.

It should be apparent how much the completion of such a map of the particular domain of competence you wish to measure would simplify the task of constructing instrumentation to measure the precise competence you set out to evaluate.

We have seen that the process of constructing an instrument for measuring teacher competence involves three steps. The first two, specifying the functions a competent teacher must perform and

3. IMPROVING TEACHING 55

identifying the competencies needed to perform them, are by far the most difficult. They have already been discussed. The third step, constructing test exercises that require the use of each of these competencies and assembling them into one or more instruments, is discussed next.

EVALUATING SELECTED TEACHER COMPETENCIES

I deal with this third step by presenting three examples drawn from attempts to evaluate specific competencies for various purposes in which I have been involved. For the sake of brevity I discuss examples related to just one of the three types of teaching problems, those that arise during interactive teaching. Some examples of exercises related to preactive teaching problems have been published elsewhere. (McNergney, Medley, Aylesworth, & Innes, 1983.) Because I have had no experience in evaluating competencies related to postactive teaching problems I do not discuss them here.

Measurement-Based Teacher Evaluation

All three attempts used a general approach to teacher evaluation called *measurement based teacher evaluation*, which was designed to free teacher evaluation from any dependence on the expertise of the person who does the evaluation. The much-debated question, "Who should evaluate the teacher?" disappears when the evaluation is measurement based (Medley, Coker, & Soar, 1984.)

Measurement-based teacher evaluation was designed to emulate the familiar multiple-choice, paper-and-pencil test which, despite its many limitations, represents the most technically advanced methodology yet developed for assessing human characteristics from human performance. From a study of such tests we conclude that there are three essential conditions for objective measurement of human performance, as follows:

1. *All candidates being assessed must perform the same tasks or equivalent tasks.* In the case of a paper-and-pencil test, the tasks set for all candidates are the same: They must all answer same set of test items or questions.

2. *An accurate, quantifiable record of each candidate's perfor-

mance of the tasks must be obtained. In the case of a paper-and-pencil test, the candidate records his own performance by marking an answer sheet that is machine readable.

3. *There must be a procedure for quantifying (or scoring) the performance that can be carried out by a clerk or a computer.* In the case of a paper-and-pencil test, a computer reads and scores the marks on the machine-readable answer sheet.

When these conditions are met, the validity and reliability of the measurements obtained ultimately depend on the degree to which successful performance of the tasks depends on the ability or other characteristic being measured. Given an appropriate set of tasks, the validity and reliability of the measurements obtained depends on how the performance records are quantified or scored.

Powerful analytical procedures have been developed for using empirical data to maximize test validity by refining the tasks (e.g., item analysis) and by refining the scoring procedures (e.g., scaling techniques). These procedures are fully applicable to the refinement of measurement-based teacher evaluation instruments.

Assessing Functional Professional Knowledge

My first example was a response to a request from the developer of a set of inservice teacher training packages, each of which was designed to increase teachers' professional knowledge of techniques for dealing with one type of interactive teaching problems. The developer asked us to construct an instrument that would measure whether teachers who had completed a package were more likely to apply the professional knowledge it contained in solving interactive teaching problems than teachers who had not completed that package. What was needed was what we call "a measure of functional professional knowledge," that is, a measure of the ability to apply professional knowledge to the solution of teaching problems—in this case, interactive teaching problems.

Multiple-choice tests have been widely used to measure knowledge of all kinds, including professional knowledge. But the professional knowledge these tests measure does not seem to be of any use to the teacher in solving interactional teaching problems. If it were of any use, a teacher's scores on the tests would correlate with his or her classroom performance. But repeated efforts to establish correlations between scores on tests of this type and measures of classroom performance have failed, even when the tests used were the best available (cf. Quirk, Witten, & Weinberg, 1973).

The reason becomes clear when we compare the tasks a student must perform to get a high test score with the ones a teacher must perform to succeed in the classroom.

Solutions. The items on a test as well constructed as the National Teacher Examinations are designed to measure the students ability to apply professional knowledge to realistic teaching problems. But every problem a student encounters on such a test has one and only one correct solution, a solution which a panel of experts all agree is the correct solution to that problem. The student's task is to decide which of four or five alternatives is correct. (If there is any doubt about which response to an item is the correct one, the item is discarded.) But when a teacher encounters what may look like a similar problem in the classroom, she is not given four or five alternative responses, one and only one of which is clearly correct. The teacher must think up his or her own alternatives and has no idea how many of them will be correct, if any. Some of the problems that come up have more than one solution, all equally acceptable. Some have none.

Strategies. When a student takes a paper-and-pencil test all of the problems are presented at one time in a neatly printed booklet, and the student is free to attack the problems in any order he or she chooses, to spend as much time as needed on each one, to take extra time to ponder difficult problems, to skip some items and to change his or her mind about some. Interactive teaching problems must be dealt with when they come up; there is no time to ponder, no going back, and to postpone a response is to fail that problem.

Scope. When a student takes a test he or she knows that the solutions to all of the problems on the test will come from a single area of knowledge that the class has had a chance to study; thus the student can forget everything else he or she knows about any other area of knowledge. For example, a student taking a course in educational psychology will not need to apply any previously learned knowledge about the teaching of reading. But a teacher interacting with pupils needs instant access to any knowledge of any subject he or she may possess (or may not possess).

I could go on, but these examples make it quite clear that the skills a student needs to do well on a multiple-choice test have little in common with those a teacher needs to do well during interactive teaching.

A Simulation Exercise. We therefore set about devising a simulation exercise which would require skills more like those the teacher needs. The simulation exercise we constructed confronted teachers with a series of interactive teaching problems similar to those an elementary school teacher might encounter in a normal day in the classroom. Each problem was presented in the form of a brief verbal vignette projected on a screen, with audio. Each vignette was followed by two or more suggested responses the teacher might make to it. The suggested responses to each problem were presented one at a time (in audio only), and the teachers had 5 seconds in which to decide whether or not each response suggested was one they might make in that situation, and to record their decisions by marking the appropriate spaces on machine-readable answer sheets.

The sequence of problems was designed to resemble the normal sequence of events in a classroom, beginning when the first pupils appear in the morning and ending when they board the school bus in the afternoon. For the sake of efficiency in measurement, most (but not all) of the suggested responses presented involved knowledge from one of the instructional packages, but responses reflecting knowledge from different packages were intermingled in a haphazard order.

The complete exercise consisted of 45 vignettes and required teachers to react to almost 200 suggested responses. A sample vignette and the suggested responses that accompanied it follow:

> Margaret and Grace are both docile, well-behaved children who are close friends and who have both been doing well in your class. One day while the children are taking a unit test you see the girls cheating (Grace is letting Margaret copy some of her work).
>
> What might you do?
>
> 101. Confiscate Margaret's paper and send her out of the room.
>
> 102. Walk over and stand near the two girls for the rest of the period.
>
> 103. Do nothing until the test is over; then tell both girls that you are giving them zeros.
>
> 104. Tear up both of their papers.
>
> 105. Move Margaret to a different part of the room.

One point was added to the teacher's score on a package for each response she marked that reflected knowledge of that package. Some suggested responses were inconsistent with the recommendations in a package; one point was subtracted for each of these responses the teacher marked. Those suggested responses that had nothing to do with the training packages (but were included because they are responses that teachers are likely to make) did not count.

Remember that the scores obtained were not intended to evaluate a teacher's overall ability to solve interactive teaching problems, only how well he or she was able to apply specified knowledge to the solution of these problems. In other words, scores were not intended to reflect a teacher's perceptual skill, professional judgment, or performance skills; only professional knowledge.

Measurement Properties. In addition to being inexpensive and easy to administer, this exercise meets all of the conditions for objective measurement of human performance just specified. First, all teachers perform the same tasks; second, they record their own performances, and third, the records they make can be read and scored by a computer. Therefore, as we have noted, the validity and reliability of the measurements depend ultimately on the nature of the tasks that make up the exercise and how responses to them are scored.

I have already presented evidence of content validity in my description of the resemblance between the tasks that make up this exercise and those related to the use of professional knowledge that a teacher faces in the classroom. I do not have any empirical evidence of the validity of this exercise to report.

There is, however, some rather striking empirical evidence of the validity of an exercise constructed by Hayes (1988), which was closely similar to the one described here. The source of the professional knowledge measured was different; Hayes' instrument was designed to measure knowledge of 13 of the 14 BTAP competencies (see Table 3.1)—those relevant to the solution of interactive teaching problems.

Hayes administered her exercise to four intact groups. One group consisted of 46 experienced teachers; one consisted of 30 teacher education students doing their practice teaching; one consisted of 31 college students not preparing to teach; and one consisted of 30 adults who had had no college education.

Although none of these people were aware of the existence of the

TABLE 3.1
Competencies Measured in the Virginia
Beginning Teacher Assistance Program

A. Academic learning time
B. Accountability
C. Clarity
D. Individual differences
E. Evaluation
F. Consistent rules
K. Affective climate
L. Learner self-concept
M. Meaningfulness
P. Planning
Q. Questioning skill
R. Reinforcement
S. Close supervision
W. Awareness

BTAP competencies, the experienced teachers, with a mean score of 199 points, scored significantly higher than the student teachers, whose mean score was 187. Both groups scored significantly higher than the other college students tested, whose mean score was 182, and the noncollege educated adults, whose mean score was 162.

Hayes' instrument is the first and only test of professional knowledge (or of any cognitive ability) I have seen on which teachers in service outperform teachers in training. These findings provide strong evidence of the potential validity of this kind of simulation. And they also provide evidence that some of what teachers learn from experience can also be learned from a study of the findings of research on teaching.

Assessing Multiple Competencies

The second example of the use of measurement-based teacher evaluation to improve teaching was developed for use in a preservice teacher education program. It was designed as a relatively inexpensive way of obtaining diagnostic information about students' progress in acquiring interactive teaching competencies. It yields separate measurements of competencies in three of the cells in the competency matrix: perceptual skills, professional judgment, and professional knowledge.

This is another simulation exercise, administered by projecting brief videotapes of classroom episodes on a screen. Each episode is

3. IMPROVING TEACHING

followed by a series of verbal statements about the episode projected on the same screen (with audio), sometimes one at a time, sometimes in groups. Each statement or group of statements remains visible for a predetermined period of time (usually a matter of seconds). The student's task in each case is to decide whether each statement is true or false and record his or her decision by marking the appropriate space on a machine-readable answer sheet. After the last statement about one episode disappears, another episode appears and the process is repeated. Here is a brief description of one such episode and the statements that follow it:

The film clip shows a teacher standing before a bulletin board picture which shows several people boarding a jumbo jet airplane, discussing the picture with a second-grade class.

83. Most of the students were having difficulty with the main concept the teacher was trying to get across.

84. The teacher should have made contact with the boy in the checked shirt. [R].

85. The learning environment would have been better if the teacher had maintained tighter control.

86. This teacher was using the inductive method.

87. If the teacher had stopped to call for quiet it would have taken even longer to get her main point across.

Each statement is designed to give a student an opportunity to demonstrate a competency of one of the three types being assessed. In most cases, statements relevant to all three competencies follow each episode.

Assessing Perceptual Skills. Statement 83 is intended to give the student who is performing the exercise a chance to demonstrate a perceptual skill of the type Kounin (1970) has called "withitness." Because the pupils are no longer visible when the statement appears, the student would have had to perceive whether or not the pupils were puzzled while the episode was still visible, without any specific prompting to do so.

Statement 86 was intended to assess a perceptual skill of the type described by Smith (1969), the ability to recognize an abstract pedagogical concept as it appears in the "real world" of the teacher. In order to know whether Statement 86 is true or false a student would need not only to know what inductive teaching is but be able to recognize it when he or she sees it.

Assessing Professional Judgment. Statement 84 was intended to give the student an opportunity to demonstrate the ability to apply professional judgment to an interactive teaching problem. The symbol [R] that appears at the end of the statement indicates that while the statement was visible on the screen the relevant portion of the episode (in this instance, the behavior of the pupil in question at the critical moment) was also visible. This is done to minimize the effect of the student's level of perceptual skill as a factor in his or her response to this statement. Otherwise a student whose professional judgment was excellent might fail this task because of a weakness in perceptual skill.

Statement 85 was also meant to assess professional judgment, specifically whether the student was able to assess accurately the level of control maintained by the teacher. It was not deemed necessary to replay any part of the episode in this instance.

Assessing Professional Knowledge. Statement 87 was intended to assess the student's ability to apply professional knowledge to the solution of an interactive teaching problem, in this case, knowledge of the probable consequences of a contemplated teacher behavior. Correct evaluation of this response requires the student to apply what Smith has called "clinical professional knowledge" (Smith, 1983).

Measurement Properties. This simulation exercise, like the first one described, fulfills all of the conditions necessary for objective measurement of human performance. All students perform the same tasks; they record their own performances on machine-readable answer sheets; and the records can be read and scored by a computer. The full range of procedures used to revise paper-and-pencil tests (item analysis, internal consistency analysis, factor analysis, etc.) are available for use in refining this instrument.

The validity and reliability of the scores, therefore, depends on the tasks the students are required to perform. In other words, they depend on what the user builds into the exercise. It should not be difficult for the instructors in a program to select episodes and frame statements that measure students' progress toward the objectives of each of their courses.

If all of the episodes and statements, representing all of the courses in the program, are assembled into one exercise and administered to all students regardless of where they are in the program, the experience will not only be an important learning experience in itself, but will enhance other experiences the students have as well. Students will realize that these realistic teaching problems become easier to solve as they progress through the program, and will see the relevance of their course work to the problems they will encounter as teachers more clearly than students who do not have this experience (cf. Medley, 1988).

Discussions of these and other approaches to the assessment of competencies may be found in Brinkerhof (1978), MacDonald (1978), Medley (1984), Pottinger (1978), and Shearron (1978), as well as in the references cited elsewhere in this discussion.

Assessing Interactive Performance Skills

The third and last example I describe was intended to evaluate interactive performance skills. Interactive performance skills are generally regarded as the most difficult competencies to measure objectively, because they can be demonstrated—and therefore assessed—only while the teacher is interacting with pupils in the classroom. This aspect of teacher competence must therefore be inferred from teacher performance. This not only makes such evaluations relatively costly and cumbersome to obtain; but also makes it particularly difficult to satisfy the first two of the three conditions necessary for objective assessment, that is, to have all of the teachers who are to be evaluated perform identical or equivalent tasks, and to obtain accurate, quantifiable records of each teacher's performance.

For an example of the use of measurement-based teacher evaluation to infer teacher competence from teacher performance I use an evaluation system developed for use in teacher certification. Since July 1, 1985, any teacher who applies for a certificate to teach in the public schools of Virginia receives only a temporary, nonrenewable certificate which is good for 2 years. Before receiving a renewable certificate, candidates must actually demonstrate minimum competence to teach in their own classrooms during their 1st year of teaching.

The *Teacher Performance Record,* or *TPR,* is the instrument used to assess teacher competence in the Beginning Teacher Assistance Program ("BTAP"). The TPR is the best available example of the application of the measurement-based approach to the evaluation of interactive teacher performance skills; therefore, the following description is somewhat detailed but confined as closely as possible to the concerns of this chapter, which are principally methodological. Readers interested on a more complete account of the program and its instrumentation should consult McNergney, Medley and Caldwell (1988) and Medley, Rosenblum and Vance (1989). Let me begin with a brief description of how the program operates.

The Beginning Teacher Assistance Program

Procedures. At the beginning of each teacher's 1st year as a paid, full-time teacher, each one hired in the state of Virginia receives a set of materials which list and describe what are known as the 14 "BTAP competencies" (McNergney, 1988). Three visits to each teacher, each made by a different trained observer, are scheduled during the early fall at a time convenient to the teacher and the observer. The teacher is asked to plan activities during these visits which will enable him or her to demonstrate the possession of each of the 14 BTAP competencies.

Before each visit, the teacher indicates what he or she plans to do during the visit, and describes pertinent characteristics of the class, by responding to an open-ended questionnaire. When the recorder arrives for the visit, he or she collects this document from the teacher and later codes this information onto an Opscan form for use in scoring the teacher's performance. The recorder then spends 30 to 45 minutes recording behaviors in the teacher's classroom and the visit ends.

Only experienced educators not currently employed full time are trained and employed as BTAP recorders. The role of the recorder is very different from that of a supervisor who evaluates teacher performance with a typical rating scale. The BTAP recorder is not expected to evaluate the teacher; the recorder's task is limited to that of making an objective, accurate record of the teacher's performance and sending it to Richmond where it will be read and scored by a computer.

If a teacher fails to demonstrate at least 12 of the 14 competencies during these three visits, three more visits (by different recorders) are scheduled during the next semester. In the meantime the teacher is encouraged to attend special workshops in each area of competence he or she failed to demonstrate, which are offered in every region of the state. If necessary, three more visits may be scheduled during the third semester.

The Teacher Performance Record. The instrument developed to measure the 14 BTAP competencies (the TPR) consists of two Opscan forms. One form, the one the recorder uses in the classroom, is called the *Classroom Process Record*, or *CPR*; it consists essentially of a list of teacher behaviors the recorder is to look for during the visit. The second form is a list of items about the teacher's plans and the setting in which he or she will be observed. The recorder looks for these items in the teacher's answers to the questionnaire filled out before the visit, and indicates which of these items were found by marking the appropriate spaces. The complete record of one classroom visit includes one of these forms and seven CPR forms, properly completed.

During the first 3 minutes of a classroom visit the recorder marks certain teacher behaviors listed on the CPR that are responsive to pupil behaviors (e.g., teacher praises pupil's answer to a convergent question; teacher rebukes off-task pupil) as they occur. At the end of the 3-minute period, the recorder stops observing and marks other behaviors listed on the CPR that occurred during the period, most of which are teacher initiated (e.g., checks understanding; gives overview) and items that describe the situation during that period (e.g., recitation; small group activities).

Before any beginning teachers were observed, data were collected with the TPR in a representative sample of 662 classrooms of practicing teachers throughout the state. These data were used in developing, refining, and standardizing scoring keys for the 14 competencies.

Defining Beginning Teacher Competence

A specification of competence for the beginning teacher is no different than that of any other teacher since, from their first day on the job, beginning teachers are expected to perform the same functions as any other teachers. The difference lies in which of the competencies relevant to the performance of these functions a teacher who has just completed a preservice preparation program offered by a college or university may reasonably be expected to possess.

What colleges and universities are best equipped to do is to communicate knowledge to students; in the case of a professional school or program, this knowledge should mainly consist of functional professional knowledge or, as it is often called, knowledge of "best practice of the profession." Although most professional teacher education programs also try to help students develop performance skills, few such programs, if any, have the facilities necessary to be more than minimally effective in this area.

Considerations such as these suggest that the highest, and most important, level of competence that it is reasonable to expect beginning teachers to possess is functional professional knowledge—professional knowledge that the teacher is able to apply to the solution of teaching problems. The graduate of a professional teacher education program may be expected to know and be able to apply the "best practice of the profession."

There is no consensus in the teaching profession about what this knowledge is, about what is the "best practice of the profession." All we can say at present about what knowledge such a consensus will contain, when and if it is reached, is that it will include knowledge whose relevance has already been established by sound empirical research. We therefore decided to define the competence of the beginning teacher as *the ability to apply the findings of research on teaching to the solution of teaching problems in their own classrooms.*

A first approximation to this knowledge was determined by reviewing the relevant research, as summarized in a number of published critical summaries. (principally Brophy & Good, 1986; Good, 1979).

Indicators of Competence. From our reading of this literature we put together 70 relatively homogeneous clusters of teacher behavior which we called "indicators of competence." These were the behaviors we would expect to observe either more or less frequently in the performance of teachers who were not only familiar with these research findings but able to apply them in their own teaching. Presence of positive indicators and absence of negative indicators would be taken as evidence of *functional professional knowledge* of competencies of the type we wished to assess. Following are four examples (all positive indicators):

C1. Preparing outlines, reviews, and summaries, beforehand
C2. Beginning the lesson or unit with a statement of purposes
C3. Making interrelationships among parts of the lesson clear to learners
C4. Ending the lesson or unit with a summary or review

Competencies. The next step was to group indicators that seemed to the project team to go together into 14 larger clusters of behaviors which we called competencies, shown in Table 3.1. (The four indicators just listed defined *Competency C, Clarity* in the table.)

Although this set of competencies incorporates much of the findings of the research, it was not intended to be, nor should it be regarded as, definitive. It contains some but not all of a body of professional knowledge that every beginning teacher ought to learn, and learn to apply, in preservice training.

Operational Definitions. The operational definition of each of the 14 comptencies, the basis for a scoring key to be used in deriving a measurement of the competency from a TPR record, takes the form of a list of classroom *events* identifiable in a TPR record, each of which exemplifies one of the indicators of that competency. Before defining what I mean by an event let me define three kinds of items that a TPR record contains.

Items. A TPR record shows three kinds of items relevant to a teacher's performance:

- *Teacher behavior items* are things a teacher does, like reprimanding a pupil, asking a question which requires a pupil to recall a specific fact, or checking pupil understanding.
- *Situational items* describe transitory aspects of the situation in which the performance occurred, such as whether a discussion was going on or whether the class was broken up into small groups.
- *Setting items* describe stable aspects of the context in which the performance occurred, such as whether the class was a kindergarten class or a high school algebra class, or whether or not it contained mainstream pupils.

Events. An event is defined basically by the cooccurrence of two items, one behavioral and one situational. One event occurs when a teacher asks a recall question, one which requires a pupil to recall a specific fact, (recorded as a behavioral item) during a drill session (recorded as a situational item). A different event occurs when a teacher asks a recall question during a discussion period (recorded as a situational item). Although the teacher behavior is the same in both instances, the relationship of the two events to teacher competence may be very different because of the differences in the situations in which the behavior occurs. When (in what situation) a behavior occurs may be just as important as what behavior occurs. Although this is not always the case—the effect of some behaviors (like publicly rebuking a pupil) tends to be the same regardless of context—it is true in enough cases that it seems critically important to make this distinction between classroom events and behavioral items.

It seems equally important to have observers record items instead of events. One good reason is that the number of items an observer must be trained to discriminate is much smaller. If we define five kinds of questions, four instructional strategies, and three patterns of classroom organization, the computer will be able to distinguish $5 \times 4 \times 3 = 60$ different events; but the recorder needs to learn to recognize only $5 + 4 + 3 = 12$ items.

Another reason is that items tend to be much easier to discriminate than events, because fewer cues are needed. And a third is that it seems to be easier to record behaviors objectively than events.

Adjusting for Differences in Settings. Setting items could also have been used in defining events, but it seemed more efficient to use the information they contained in a different way. In BTAP they were used to compensate for nonequivalence of tasks due to differences in the settings in which different teachers were evaluated.

First, each setting item was treated as a two-level variable reflecting presence or absence of the condition defined by the item. For example, one setting item was marked if the teacher was observed teaching high school; otherwise it was left blank. Another was marked if the teacher's class contained one or more mainstream pupils, otherwise it was left blank.

Next the raw score of each teacher on each item scored on any of the keys was determined. The raw score on an event initiated by the teacher is its total frequency over all three records. The raw score on an event defined in terms of the teacher's response to a pupil initiation is its frequency relative to the number of opportunities to respond provided by appropriate pupil initiations.

The raw scores on each event in turn were then correlated with all of the setting items in one multiple regression equation, using the scores of the 662 teachers in the norm sample. If the raw scores on an event were not correlated with the presence or absence of any setting item, they were standardized (converted to standard scores) in the whole sample of 662 teachers. A teacher's standard score on such an item indicates whether that event is more or less likely to occur in that teacher's class than in the average teacher's class (and how much more or less likely).

If the raw scores on an event were correlated with any setting variable or combination of such variables, the sample of 662 teachers was subdivided into two or more homogeneous subgroups, and scores on the item were standardized separately in each of the

3. IMPROVING TEACHING

subgroups. In such a case the teacher's standard score on the item indicates whether that event is more or less likely to occur in that teacher's class than in the class of the average teacher *in the same setting* (and how much more or less likely).

For example, how often a teacher uses public praise was found to be correlated with whether or not the teacher was observed teaching one of the "primary" grades. (i.e., kindergarten or one of the first three grades). Primary teachers praised pupils publicly significantly more often than teachers of other grades. The sample of 662 teachers was therefore divided into two groups, one containing only primary teachers, and one group containing all other teachers. The frequency of this event was then standardized separately in each group. Now when a primary teacher's TPR record is scored, the frequency of this item is converted to a standard score in the primary group so that that teacher's score on that event is compared with those of other primary teachers only. And when the record of any other teacher, is scored, the score is converted to a standard score in the group of other teachers so that that teacher's score is not compared with those of primary teachers.

This justifies the assertion that, in any instance in which a teacher's performance is affected significantly by the setting in which it is observed, each teacher's performance is compared only with the performances of other teachers in the same setting. It also makes it unnecessary to set up separate norms for teachers of different grades, subjects, and so forth.

Competency Keys. A temporary scoring key was constructed for each of the 14 competencies by first identifying a set of events that reflected the indicators that defined that competency, and summing the standard scores (with positive or negative weights as appropriate) in each record. Each temporary key went through a number of revisions to maximize its internal consistency, estimated by coefficient alpha. The current versions of the 14 keys have internal consistency coefficients ranging from 0.62 to 0.86 with a median value of 0.71.

Setting Passing Scores. Passing scores were based on estimates of the percent of teachers who were employed in Virginia at the time when the norm data were collected that lacked each of the 14 competencies. The estimates were obtained by sending descriptions of the competencies to a sample of school principals and asking them to estimate these percents. (Most of them were in the vicinity of 10%.) We then set the pass score for each competency at the corresponding percentile in the distribution of scores on that competency in the norm sample. In order to earn a passing score on a competency, then, a beginning teacher had to perform at least as well as an experienced teacher regarded by her principal as possessing that competency. In order to qualify for a renewable certificate of competence, a beginning teacher must earn a passing score on 12 of the 14 competencies.

Meeting the Conditions for Objective Assessment

Let us consider the degree to which these assessments fulfill our three conditions for objective assessment of human performance.

1. Equivalence of Tasks. Nominally, the tasks set for all teachers are the same: to demonstrate as many of the 14 competencies as they can. But the nature and difficulty of the task each teacher faces depends in part on the setting in which the task must be demonstrated, and especially on the kind of pupils in the class. Three stops were taken to compensate for such variations in difficulty.

The first step was inherent in the way competence was defined, competence was defined as functional professional knowledge of certain research findings, that is, as the ability to apply these findings to teaching problems. If, for example, a teacher responds to disruptive pupils in the way the research recommends, he or she is demonstrating competence, even if the disruptive behavior continues or worsens. (If anybody's competence is called into question in such a case, surely it is that of the researcher!) This greatly reduces the effect on task difficulty of differences in the ways different classes respond to the same teacher behavior.

The second step was to use relative instead of absolute frequencies in scoring events defined in terms of teachers' responses to pupil initiations. For example, suppose that one research finding was that effective teachers incorporate unsolicited pupil comments into discussions more often than ineffective teachers do. Because this can only be done if a pupil makes such a comment, the difficulty of the item depends on how common such comments are in the teacher's class. Instead of merely counting how often this happens, then, we also count the number of unsolicited pupil comments, the number of opportunities a teacher has to incorporate such comments, and use the proportion of opportunities in which the event occurs.

3. IMPROVING TEACHING

The third step designed to reduce differences in task difficulties was the adjustment for measurable differences in setting variables already described.

2. Quantifiable Performance Records. A machine-readable record of each performance is made by a disinterested observer trained to observe and accurately record such performances. The accuracy of the record (and ultimately the validity of scores based upon it) depends only on the recorder's skill in recognizing and recording the items listed on the schedule, not on the recorder's expertise as a judge of teacher performance.

3. Machine Scoring. Records made by BTAP recorders appear to the computer exactly like test answer sheets.

I suggest that the TPR meets the conditions for objective measurement of human performance well enough so that the validity and reliability of any score on the instrument depend almost entirely on the items contained in the instrument and on how they are scored.

Because the events scored on the TPR represent only a crude first attempt at a sample of the events that distinguish effective teaching from ineffective teaching, the validities of the 14 scores derived from it must also be limited. Much of this limitation could be removed by revisions in the instrument itself that are perfectly feasible. The approach shows considerable promise, more than any available alternative.

IMPACT OF THE PROGRAM

The Beginning Teacher Assistance Program program is explicitly intended to improve teaching through the use of teacher evaluation. In doing so it proposes to use two major strategies. The principal strategy is to identify teachers otherwise qualified for teaching certificates who lack one or more competencies essential for satisfactory performance and offer them assistance in remedying these deficiencies. As its name implies, the program was conceived of primarily as an assistance program. The second strategy for improving teaching is to screen out, by denying renewable teaching certificates to, those teachers unable to remedy the deficiencies.

By the end of the 1986–1987 school year, the competence of almost 2900 teachers had been assessed at least once; one cohort of 669 teachers had had three opportunities to be assessed; and hundreds of teachers had been offered the opportunity to improve their competence (with or without assistance from BTAP) and be assessed again. From these data we can get some idea of the impact of the program.

Impact on Teacher Education Programs. Perhaps the most important effect of the program is the impact it has had on the way teachers are prepared in the state. Since its implementation teacher education students are being made much more aware of the existence of research on teaching and of some of its findings than ever before, as well as of the importance of learning to apply these findings in their own classrooms. It is unfortunate that so many instructors in the teacher education programs of the state seem to have decided to respond to the program by coaching students to pass BTAP rather than by helping them understand the research and master the functional professional knowledge behind the evaluations. But as their students practice demonstrating the indicators of competence they cannot help becoming aware of and even trying out teaching strategies and tactics they might not otherwise encounter, and becoming aware of the research base for them.

We can get some idea of what has happened from the fact that the first 669 beginning teachers evaluated in the fall of 1985 scored, on the average, 4.4 T-score points higher than the 662 experienced teachers in the norm sample. This happened even though this first group of beginners had no clearer idea in advance of what the instrumentation would measure than the teachers in the norm sample. And yet only 56% of this first group qualified for permanent certification by demonstrating possession of 10 of the 14 competencies.

Since the fall of 1986, teachers have been required to demonstrate possession of not 10 but 12 of the 14 competencies in order to qualify. Despite this increase in difficulty, 69% of the group first assessed in the fall of 1986 qualified on their first attempt. This 13% increase over the 1985 cohort clearly indicates that something has changed in the way teachers are trained in the Commonwealth of Virginia.

Impact on Teacher Competence. A more direct way of gauging the impact of the program on teaching in the state is by examining what happens to teachers who do not qualify for renewable certificates on their first attempt. In order to qualify on their second attempt, such teachers must learn to demonstrate at least one, and usually more than one, of the competencies they failed to demonstrate the first time.

No fewer than 88% of approximately 300 teachers who failed to qualify in the fall of 1985 increased their competence enough to qualify in the spring of 1986. It has been suggested that this first group may not have taken BTAP very seriously until they learned from the press that more than half of them had failed to qualify. If this was true, part of this dramatic improvement in competence may be spurious.

Subsequent experience does not support this idea. A second group was first assessed in the spring of 1986, just after the news broke. About 100 of them failed to qualify, but 96% of them improved enough to qualify in their second attempt (in the fall of 1986). And 88% of the 400 who failed to qualify on their first attempt in the fall of 1986 also improved enough to qualify on their second attempt.

This strongly suggests that, although most teacher education students now take the evaluation seriously, many of them are not acquiring enough competencies during their preservice preparation to qualify for certification without further preparation. This is further confirmed by the fact that 95% of the only group that has completed the program (the group first assessed in 1985) eventually succeeded in demonstrating 12 competencies and qualifying for renewable certificates.

Since the program began operation, the number of graduates of the teacher education programs of the state able to demonstrate 12 of the 14 BTAP competencies has steadily increased. Most of those graduates who do not demonstrate 12 competencies manage to acquire the additional competencies they need after graduation. Thus although the program is not denying renewable certification to many candidates, it does seem to be improving teaching in the state.

SUMMARY AND CONCLUSIONS

Failure to make important distinctions between three aspects of teaching has frustrated most past efforts to use teacher evaluation to improve teaching. These aspects are: teacher effectiveness (defined as the impact of a teacher's performance on her pupils), teacher performance (defined as the deployment of a teacher's competencies on the job) and teacher competence (defined as the possession of repertoire of competencies—knowledges, skills, etc.— relevant to effective performance of a specified teaching function).

Valid evaluation of each aspect requires different procedures, and each has a different role to play in the improvement of teaching. Valid evaluation of teacher effectiveness must be based on pupil performance; valid evaluations of teacher performance must be based on the teacher's own performance on the job; valid evaluations of teacher competence must be based on the teacher's performance under test conditions.

Valid evaluations could be used to improve teaching by identifying and eliminating ineffective teachers and replacing them with more effective ones. But valid evaluations of teacher effectiveness are almost impossible to obtain, partly because it is so difficult to isolate the effect of teacher performance on pupils from the many other powerful factors that also affect it, and partly because of a lack of instruments that measure most of the important outcomes of education.

Valid evaluations of teacher performance could be used to improve teaching by identifying substandard performers and either reassigning or replacing them. But valid evaluations are difficult if not impossible to obtain because they require a better understanding of the teaching-learning process than is currently available.

Valid evaluations of teacher competence can be used to improve teaching by identifying incompetent teachers and either replacing them with competent teachers or by helping them to become competent (by pinpointing causes of incompetence and providing remedial treatment). Valid evaluation of teacher competence is feasible by the use of existing knowledge of the nature of teacher competence and available assessment procedures.

The process of developing valid, reliable and objective procedures for evaluating teacher competence involves three steps: (a) specification of the teaching function the competent teacher is expected to perform, (b) definition of the competencies (knowledges and skills) a teacher needs in order to perform this function, and (c) development of an instrument consisting of tasks designed to elicit demonstrations of these competencies.

Most of this chapter is devoted to a description of procedures for performing the three steps and a presentation of examples of procedures that have been used to evaluate teacher competence.

REFERENCES

Berliner, D. C. (1979). Tempus educare. In P. L. Peterson & H. J. Walberg (Eds.). *Research on teaching: Concepts, findings and implications* (pp. 120–135). Berkeley, CA: McCutchan.

Berliner, D. C. (1986). In pursuit of the expert pedagogue. *Educational Researcher, 15*(7), 5–13.

Brinkerhof, R. O. (1978). Competency assessment: A Perspective and an approach. *Journal of Teacher Education, 29*(2), 21–24.

Brophy, J. E., & Good, T. L. (1986). Teacher behavior and student achievement. In M. C. Wittrock (Ed.). *Handbook of research on teaching* (3rd ed., pp. 328–375). New York: Macmillan.

Cruickshank, D. R., & Applegate, J. M. (1981). Reflective teaching as a strategy for teacher growth. *Educational Leadership. 38,* 553–54.

Denham, C., & Lieberman, A. (Eds.). (1980). *Time to Learn.* Washington, DC: National Institute of Education.

Good, T. L. (1979). Teacher effectiveness in the elementary school. *Journal of Teacher Education, 30*(2), 52–64.

Hayes, L. J. (1988). *A simulation test of teacher competence.* Unpublished doctoral dissertation, Charlottesville, VA: University of Virginia.

Howsam, R. B., Corrigan, D. C., Denemark, G. W., & Nash, R. J. (1976). *Educating a profession.* Washington: American Association of Colleges for Teacher Education.

Jackson, P. W. (1966). *The way teaching is* (pp. 7–27). Washington, DC. Association for Supervision and Curriculum Development and the Center for the Study of Instruction of the National Education Association.

Johnson, C. E., Okey, J. R., Capie, W., Ellett, C., & Adams, P. T. (1978). *Identifying and verifying generic teacher competencies.* Athens, GA: College of Education, University of Georgia.

Kounin, J. S. (1970). *Discipline and group management in classrooms.* New York: Holt, Rinehart & Winston.

MacDonald, F. J. (1978). Evaluating pre-service teachers' competence. *Journal of Teacher Education, 29*(2), 9–13.

McNergney, R. F. (Ed.). (1988). *Guide to teaching.* Boston: Allyn & Bacon.

McNergney, R. F., Medley, D. M., Aylesworth, M. S., & Innes, A. H. (1983). Assessing teachers' planning abilities. *Journal of Educational Research, 77,* 108–111.

McNergney, R. F., Medley, D. M., & Caldwell, M. S. (1988). Making and implementing policy on teacher licensure. *Journal of Teacher Education, 39*(3), 38–44.

Medley, D. M. (1984). Teacher competency testing and the teacher educator. In L. J. Katz & J. G. Raths (Eds.), *Advances in teacher education* (Vol. 1, pp. 59–94). Norwood, NJ: ABLEX.

Medley, D. M. (1988). An outcomes-based teacher preparation program. In W. J. Gephart & J. B. Ayres (Eds.), *Teacher education evaluation* (pp. 58–83). Boston: Kluwer Academic.

Medley, D. M., Coker, H., & Soar, R. S. (1984). *Measurement-based evaluation of teacher performance: An empirical approach.* New York: Longman.

Medley, D. M., Rosenblum, E. P., & Vance, N. C. (1989). Assessing the functional knowledge of participants in the Virginia Beginning Teacher Assistance Program. *Elementary School Journal, 89,* 496–510.

Pottinger, P. S. (1978). Designing instruments to measure competence. *Journal of Teacher Education, 29*(2), 28–32.

Quirk, T. J., Witten, B. J., & Weinberg, S. F. (1973). Review of studies of the concurrent and predictive validity of the National Teacher Examinations. *Review of Educational Research, 43,* 89–113.

Shearron, G. F. (1978). Designing and improving instruments for measuring competence. *Journal of Teacher Education, 29*(2), 18–20.

Smith, B. O. (1969). *Teachers for the real world.* Washington, DC: The American Association of Colleges for Teacher Education.

Smith, B. O. (1983). Closing: Teacher Education in Transition. In D. C. Smith (Ed.), *Essential knowledge for beginning educators* (pp. 140–145). Washington, DC: American Association of Colleges for Teacher Education, ERIC Clearinghouse on Teacher Education.

4

Assessing the Quality of Teacher Assessment Tests[1]

William A. Mehrens
Michigan State University

This chapter discusses some of the types of evidences that are appropriate for assessing the quality of teacher-licensure tests. Licensure tests are used to make dichotomous decisions, so reliability estimates of the consistency of decisions are needed. Because the inference of interest has to do with the minimum competency necessary to prevent harm from coming to the clients, it is argued that content validity is the type of validity evidence most appropriate for licensure tests. However, evidences for criterion-related validity, construct validity and "curricular validity" are also discussed. The issue of whether the cut score on a licensure test should in any way be related to the supply and demand and the requirements for reporting test scores and documenting the quality of the test are also discussed.

It is concluded that teacher-licensure tests allow valid in-

---

[1]Portions of this chapter have been adapted from Validity Issues in Teacher Competency Tests, *Journal of Personnel Evaluation in Education*, 1987, *1*, 2, 195–229 and from *Issues in Teacher Competency Tests* which was prepared for the Commission on Testing and Public Policy, Graduate School of Education, University of California, Berkeley.

ferences for a delimited set of inferences. An effective teacher-licensure test will not eliminate the need for subsequent teacher evaluation; it will not cure all educational ills; and it will not eliminate all ineffective teachers. Nevertheless, it should help ensure that those individuals who are licensed have a minimal level of competence on some important subdomains of knowledge and skills relevant to their profession

ASSESSING THE QUALITY OF TEACHER-ASSESSMENT TESTS

> Scott wont pass in his assignment at all, he had a poem to learn and he fell tu do it. (*Time*, 1980)

> If selection of the most suitable people to be teachers is a matter of importance to the five percent of the population who become teachers, it is no less important a matter to the 100 percent who become students. (Pratt, 1977, p. 16)

> If education is the cornerstone upon which a great nation builds, then teaching is our most important human activity. (Sweeney & Manatt, 1986, p. 446)

It seems so obvious. Quality education is important to the nation. Quality teachers are important for quality education. But historically not all who received licenses to teach were of high quality—or necessarily even competent. We do not want incompetent teachers. Licensure tests are used in over 900 other occupations in an effort to protect the public, and in those occupations the public typically has a choice of whom to go to for services. Teachers have conscripted clients. Licensure tests should be able to weed out prospective teachers with skills at a level such as that demonstrated in the first of the preceding quotations. Isn't it obvious licensure tests should be useful in a profession as important as teaching?

But things are not always as obvious as they seem. What is "teacher competency?" How do we know whether tests really measure it? Such questions should be, and have been, asked. This chapter is intended to take a close look at several issues regarding the quality of teacher-competency tests. A general conclusion of the paper is that if such tests are constructed properly they will be of sufficiently high quality to be valid for a delimited set of inferences.

CURRENT POPULARITY OF TEACHER-COMPETENCY TESTS

Teacher-certification tests are not new. They were first officially endorsed in 1686 (Vold, 1985) and administered as early as the 18th century (Carlson, 1985). However, they are currently enjoying a revival.

Gabrys (1987) reported that "as of June 1, 1986, 46 states had regulations requiring some form of competency assessment of teachers. Three additional states were actively planning programs to test teachers . . ." (p. 27).

The very rapid spread of teacher-testing programs is politically based and supported by the public. Gallup polls (1984)indicate that 89% of the public (and 63% of the teachers) believe that teachers should "be required to pass a state board examination to prove their knowledge in the subjects they will teach" (p. 107). Many educational leaders also support teacher testing. The recent Holmes Group (1986) and Carnegie (1986) reports on teaching both support examinations for prospective teachers. Both the American Federation of Teachers AFL–CIO and the National Education Association (NEA) currently support examinations for licensing new teachers (Cameron, 1985; Shanker, 1985).

WHY TEACHER-COMPETENCY TESTS?

The motivating factor behind teacher-competency tests is that the public and many educators believe that both our colleges and our state-licensing boards have failed as gatekeepers. Although debateable, there is considerable evidence for those beliefs (see Mehrens, 1986a; 1987a; 1987b).

A few educators may discount, or perhaps even support, the deplorable standards (arguing that love, patience, compassion, and so forth, are the important criteria to be a teacher (Hilldrup, 1978, p. 28). The public and professional educators interested in reform, however, do not support low standards. They are dismayed that some teachers communicate with parents in the style quoted earlier in this chapter. They are dismayed that not all elementary school teachers have mastered elementary school arithmetic. The public (and almost all educators) believe that teachers should be able to read, write, and do simple arithmetic. Most would accept the reasonable assumption that you can not teach what you do not know; that if you are to teach the basics you should know them (see Carnegie Task Force, 1986; Holmes Group, 1986; Shulman, n.d.; 1986).

But are *examinations* necessary to establish that applicants for a teacher certificate know the basics? Why not rely on colleges of education or certification agencies? Because the traditional approaches have not worked (see Mehrens, 1986a; 1987a; 1987b). Graduation from one of the 1200 institutions with teacher-education programs simply does not ensure sufficient competence. This is partly due to political considerations (see Scriven, 1979), but even if program approvals were not subject to political considerations, there is no compelling reason to believe they would fulfill their purpose of protecting the interests and welfare of the public. As Freeman (1977) pointed out:

> In general, the development of certification requirements appears to have been dictated, to a large extent, by the intuitive notions of "what a teacher or guidance counselor needs to know" and then using available higher education categories to express the requirement. One might well make out a case that an elementary teacher should have a general knowledge of mathematics. As expressed in rules and regulations, this intuitive judgment becomes "four hours of mathematics." (p. 75)

It is ironic to note that some of the critics of current examinations suggest they are based on inadequate job analyses. What about the course requirements, or the general program requirements established by certification boards? Where are the job analyses that determined "four hours of mathematics" gives elementary teachers sufficient knowledge of mathematics?

DEFINING AND ASSESSING TEACHER COMPETENCE

Not all writers differentiate between the quality of the *teacher*, the quality of the *teaching*, and the outcomes of the teaching (Darling-Hammond, Wise, & Pease, 1983). Medley (1982) made the following useful distinctions between four terms that others have treated as synonyms:

> *Teacher competency:* Any single knowledge, skill, or professional value position, the possession of which is believed to be relevant to the successful practice of teaching. Competencies refer to specific things that teachers know, do, or believe but not to the effects of these attributes on others.

Teacher competence: The repertoire of competencies a teacher possesses. Overall competence is a matter of the degree to which a teacher has mastered a set of individual competencies, some of which are more critical to a judgment of overall competence than others.

Teacher performance: What the teacher does on the job rather than what she or he can do. Teacher performance is specific to the job situation; it depends on the competence of the teacher, the context in which the teacher works, and the teacher's ability to apply his or her competencies at any given point in time.

Teacher effectiveness: The effect that the teacher's performance has on pupils. Teacher effectiveness depends not only on competence and performance, but also on the responses pupils make. Just as competence cannot predict performance under different situations, teacher performance cannot predict outcomes under different situations.

Generally, the definitions of the competency tests designed for teachers are much like the definition Medley used for teacher competency. For example, the Alabama Board stated their test was "to measure the specific competencies which are considered necessary to successfully teach" (Alabama State Board of Education, 1980). *Considered* and *necessary* are the two key words in that statement. *Considered* suggests, correctly, that the decision is a professional judgment and *necessary* suggests that the competency is not sufficient.

This chapter is limited to a discussion of issues in assessing the quality of competency tests used for assessment by licensing agencies. Tests that colleges might wish to use for either entrance or exit purposes are not considered. Tests used for employment purposes are not considered. Furthermore, measures of teacher performance or measures of teacher effectiveness (except for the role they may play in evaluating the validity of the teacher competency tests) are not considered.

LICENSURE, CERTIFICATION, AND EMPLOYMENT EXAMS

The terms *licensure* and *certification* have been used interchangeably by some individuals in education and it is not always clear to educators how employment exams differ from the other two types. But both the legal and psychological professions have made distinctions among the three terms. Thus, some definitions and explanations are in order.

The U.S. Department of Health, Education, and Welfare (1971) defined licensure as follows:

> Licensure: The process by which an agency of government grants permission to persons to engage in a given profession or occupation by certifying that those licensed have attained the minimal degree of competency necessary to ensure that the public health, safety and welfare will be reasonably well protected. (p. 7)

The same agency defined certification as follows:

> Certification: The process by which a nongovernmental agency or association grants recognition to an individual who has met certain predetermined qualifications specified by that agency or association. (p. 7)

One of the major distinctions in the two definitions is whether or not the agency is governmental or nongovernmental. Because, historically, the "certification" of teachers has been done typically by a governmental agency, what the public has typically called "teacher-certification requirements" are actually licensure requirements.

A second distinction is that licensing is a mandatory program designed to protect the public from incompetents. It is a selecting-out process. Licensure procedures are to determine whether or not individuals have *minimal* competence. Certification is typically voluntary and grants special status to the individuals certified. It is a selecting-in process. Certification typically goes beyond the minimum requirements. (The type of examinations Shulman [n.d.] and Shanker [1985] advocated would not appear to be minimal.)

Although there are distinctions in the definitions of the two words, and these distinctions would suggest both different purposes as well as different properties of the examinations, the use of the phrase "teacher certification" probably is not too misleading. However such programs, which are discussed in this chapter, are, in fact, state-licensure programs. Their purpose is to protect the public from incompetents.

Employment tests have a quite different purpose from licensure tests. Employment tests are intended to help identify those applicants for a job who are likely to be the most successful. Whereas licensing exams are designed to further the states' interests, employment exams are intended to further the employers' interests.

The *Standards for Educational and Psychological Testing* (American Educational Research Association, American Psychological Association, & National Council on Measurement in Education [AERA, APA, NCME], 1985) clarified the differences in a succinct manner: "For licensure or certification the focus of test standards is on levels of knowledge and skills necessary to assure the public that a person is competent to practice, whereas an employer may use tests in order to maximize productivity" (p. 63).

Because employment and licensure examinations serve different purposes, they may well be constructed somewhat differently. Whether or not the examinations differ, we make different inferences from the scores of examinations used for employment and licensure and, therefore, the kinds of evidence gathered to support their uses should differ. Because many people confuse the validity requirements of the two types of examinations, they will be discussed in more detail at various points in the chapter, which is primarily devoted to technical measurement issues of relevance for licensure tests.

RELIABILITY

Licensure tests are used to make dichotomous decisions. As the *Standards*[2] pointed out: "Estimates of the consistency of decisions are needed whenever decision rules assign people to categories according to specified test score intervals. An estimate of the standard error of measurement at the cut score is helpful" (AERA, APA, NCME, 1985, p. 20).

Standard 2.12 is quite specific about what the authors believe is conditionally desired. "For dichotomous decisions, estimates should be provided of the percentage of test takers who are classified in the same way on two occasions or on alternate forms of the test. (conditional)" (p. 23).

Other literature (e.g., Millman, 1979) suggests that the Kappa index, which corrects the proportion of agreement for chance effects, should also be computed. Because two different scores per person are not typically obtained in licensure tests it is necessary to estimate the proportion of consistent decisions from the distribution of scores for a single administration. The *Standards* do

---

[2]*The Standards For Educational and Psychological Testing* is a single book and purists may wish to follow reference to it with a singular verb. However, when shortening the reference to just *Standards* the plural form sounds more appropriate and will be used throughout the chapter. The defense, in addition to the sound, is that there are a set of standards within the single book.

not specify any particular formula to estimate this. The literature suggests that "there is no procedure for estimating this quantity that is clearly preferred over all others" (Traub, 1986, pp. 5–6). (See also Subkoviak, 1984.) Certainly, the Subkoviak, Huynh, and Marshall procedures would all be considered acceptable (Subkoviak, 1984).

Standard 2.12 just quoted, by its calling for estimates of the consistency of *decisions,* and Standard 11.3 both show a clear preference for reliability indices that are based on a threshold-loss function. Novick, chair of the *Standards* committee also previously had argued for this approach (Hambleton & Novick, 1973). The threshold-loss function assumes that all misclassifications are equally serious regardless of their size. If misclassifying an individual close to the cut score is a less serious error than misclassifying one far above or below the cut score, then one should use a procedure that involves a squared error-loss function. Examples would be Livingston's (1972) approach or the Brennan and Kane index (1977).

Traub (1986) has recently argued for the threshold loss function for licensure tests because "an error of classification has consequences that are as serious *for the candidate* [italics added] whose true score lies relatively near the cutting score as for the candidate whose true test score lies relatively far from the cutting score" (pp. 5–14). However, not all specialists would wish to use the threshold loss function. Recall that the purpose of licensure tests is to protect the public. Most measurement specialists believe that knowledge measured in a licensure test is a continuous variable and that the cut score artificially divides the variable into two categories. One could argue that a false positive teacher candidate with a true score far below the cut score would be more costly in terms of harm to the *public* than a false positive whose true score was just one point below the cut score. One could make a comparable argument for false negatives. For a more thorough discussion of this issue see Berk (1984a), Subkoviak (1984), and Brennan (1984).

A third approach would be to estimate the reliability of the domain score estimates—consistency across parallel or randomly parallel test forms. The traditional K-R 20 is commonly used if one assumes parallel tests. As Traub (1986) pointed out, although such an estimate is not *required* by the *Standards* for licensure tests, it does provide useful information. It does not replace one of the other estimates discussed earlier.

As indicated in the first quotation from the *Standards* in this section, an estimate of the standard error of measurement at the cut score is helpful (see also Standard 2.10). Again, a variety of formulas could be used. They make slightly different assumptions, and there is no consensus as to what method is best (Feldt, Steffen, & Gupta, 1985).

Of course if one knew the cut score in advance of test construction and had item statistics on a large number of items one could construct a test with a small standard error at the cut score. However this typically would not work in the initial construction of licensure tests because the cut score is based on item judgments—not determined in advance. If one assumed a constant cut score and had dependable item statistics, one might build subsequent test revisions on such a basis. However such tests may not be truly equivalent to the first.

Standards 2.1 and 11.4 (AERA, APA, NCME, 1985) speak of estimating reliability of the subscores that are reported and used. Because subscores are not typically used in teacher licensure decisions they would not need to be reported. If they are reported they might be used as study guides by candidates who failed and thus it would be useful to report their reliabilities and standard errors. The reliabilities are frequently low and candidates should recognize their limitations as study guides. However, it should be stressed that low subscore reliabilities are irrelevant in litigation regarding the legality of using the total score for licensure decisions.

Some individuals like guidelines as to how reliable a test should be. Traub (1986) chose 0.80 as an arbitrary value for an acceptably high decision consistency index. However, he did not suggest discontinuing tests with lower estimates. Rather he suggested they "give cause for concern" (p. 5–23).

VALIDITY: SOME GENERAL NOTIONS

> Validity has long been one of the major deities in the pantheon of the psychometrician. It is universally praised, but the good works done in its name are remarkably few. (Ebel, 1961, p. 640)

The AERA, APA, NCME (1985) *Standards* state that validity,

> refers to the appropriateness, meaningfulness, and usefulness of the specific inferences made from test scores. Test validation is the process of accumulating evidence to support such inferences. (p. 9)

Although validity is a unitary concept, evidence may be accumulated in many ways. Traditionally, psychometricians have categorized the various types of validity evidence into content-related, criterion-related, and construct-related evidence of validity although "rigorous distinctions between the categories are not possible" (AERA, APA, NCME, 1985, p. 9).

"In general, content-related evidence demonstrates the degree to which the sample of items, tasks, or questions on a test are representative of some defined universe or domain of content. Criterion-related evidence demonstrates that test scores are systematically related to one or more outcome criteria" (p. 10–11). Construct-related validity evidence "focuses primarily on the test score as a measure of the psychological characteristic of interest. . . . Such characteristics are referred to as constructs because they are *theoretical* [italics added] constructions about the nature of human behavior" (p. 9).

The lack of a rigorous distinction among the categories of validity evidence is especially true between the categories of content and construct validity evidence. A distinction Tenopyr (1977) preferred is that content validity deals with inferences about *test construction*, whereas construct validity involves inferences about *tests scores*. Others such as Guion (1977) and Messick (1975) would agree with her. Although Cronbach (1980) referenced Guion, Messick, and Tenopyr as if he agreed with them, he worded the point quite differently. As he stated, "content validity is *established* [italics added] only in test construction, by specifying a domain of tasks and sampling rigorously. The *inference back to the domain* [italics added] can then be purely deductive" (Cronbach, 1980, p. 105). This wording holds more appeal to me. We do make deductive *inferences* from the score on the test to the domain. The *defense* of this inference from a score on a sample to a score on a domain is contingent on the test-construction process which includes domain specification and item sampling.

It is unfortunate, but not incapacitating, that measurement specialists do not all use the validity terms the same way. In this chapter the words will be used in what might be called the "traditional" sense. If some type of evidence described under content-validity evidence seems more to some reader like construct validity, that reader is surely capable of handling the internal translation he or she must engage in to comprehend the discussion. In fact, some who argue that licensure tests need construct validity evidence might well feel appeased if some of the evidence here placed under content were recategorized to construct.

The terms *curricular validity* and *instructional validity* are being used increasingly in the educational measurement literature. Al-

4. ASSESSING THE QUALITY

though many would suggest that these terms are *not* categories of validity (and they are not in the index of the new *Standards*), they do have some relevant meaning (Mehrens & Lehmann, 1987; Yalow & Popham, 1983). However, both are generally considered irrelevant in judging the quality of licensure examinations. Reasons for this are discussed later.

INFERENCES FROM TEACHER-COMPETENCY TESTS

Before discussing the kinds of validity evidence needed for teacher-competency tests, it is necessary to consider what inferences we wish to make from the scores. It is important to distinguish the inferences the test builders and test users wish to make from the inferences that others may draw (or claim you cannot draw) from the scores. The builders and users of tests have a responsibility to gather evidence (or use logic) to support their particular inferences. In the process of doing this they may use logic or evidence to rule out the plausibility of some potentially competing inferences. However, they do *not* have any responsibility to gather evidence to support (or refute) all inferences others may make (or claim cannot be made) from the test scores. This point needs to be stressed because a common method of attacking the use of tests is to state that there is no evidence that the scores predict some variable that the users/builders never intended the scores to predict. For example, some educators attack teacher-competency tests used for licensure purposes because the passing of such tests does not guarantee one will be a good teacher. As Mehrens and Lehmann pointed out, "That, of course, is true but totally irrelevant" (1984, p. 582).

This procedure of attacking a test because its scores do not measure something they were not intended to measure has been recognized for decades (Rulon, 1946). Some individuals have been known to criticize tests of teacher subject matter or pedagogical knowledge because they do not measure love, warmth, compassion, or some other characteristic just as, a few years ago, some individuals criticized intelligence tests because they did not measure motivation. It should not take too much sophistication in measurement to recognize that a test designed to measure one variable should *not* be criticized for not measuring another! Wood (1940) made this point over 45 years ago: "The validity of the examinations should be judged by the accuracy with which they measure not the total complex of teaching ability, but those parts which they are designed to measure . . ." (278–279).

Of course, if test builders/users do not wish others to make incorrect inferences from the scores, they have a responsibility to make clear just what inferences they wish to draw, and the evidence or logic supportive of those inferences. Almost all those who write in the professional literature regarding licensure examinations, would agree with Kane (1984) that such exams should "be interpreted as providing evidence of an examinee's present competence on specific abilities that are needed for practice" (p. 2).

CONTENT-VALIDITY EVIDENCE FOR TEACHER-COMPETENCY TESTS

Measurement leaders in the field of licensure generally agree with the position taken in the *Standards* that content validity is the primary concern for licensure tests. (e.g., Bond, 1987, p. 19; Linn & Miller, 1986, pp. 4–3; Shimberg, 1982, p. 62; Vertiz, 1985, p. 97.)

However, the content-validity evidence should differ for licensure and employment purposes. For licensure tests the "focus of test standards is on levels of knowledge and skills necessary to assure the public that a person is competent to practice, whereas an employer may use tests in order to maximize productivity" (AERA, APA, NCME, 1985, p. 63). Further, employment tests may measure *aptitude* to learn a *specific* job, whereas licensure is usually intended to determine current qualifications for a *broad field* rather than a specific job. This has implications for the content to be covered (AERA, APA, NCME, 1985, p. 64).

Another distinction is that although an employment test should cover the totality of the knowledges, skills, and abilities (KSAs) desirable on the job, the content domain of a licensure test should be limited to the "knowledge and skills necessary to protect the public" (AERA, APA, NCME, 1985, p. 64). Note that *abilities* was left out of this quotation. Linn (1984) and Kane (1984) have made the same point. There is at least some legal precedent to suggest that a licensure examination need not evaluate the full range of skills desirable to practice a profession (Eisdorfer & Tractenberg, 1977, p. 119).

Note that the quotation from the *Standards* given earlier suggests that the focus should be on *necessary* knowledge and skills to assure that the person is competent to practice. The problem with the "necessary" requirement is that very, very few specific competencies are probably absolutely necessary to adequately practice any profession, yet if one person has twice as many very important competencies as another person it is certainly prudent to believe that the public is safer with the first person than with the second. Further, if one only tested for necessary skills, it would follow that the cut score should be set at 100% (or whatever other percentage one may arrive at through those "counting backwards from 100%" procedures that Glass, 1978, talked about).

The necessary requirement is probably least debatable in the subject-matter tests of teacher competency. A reasonable argument is that one cannot teach what one does not know. Galambos (1984) suggested that this assumption has been accepted as self-evident by legislators. Critics of licensure examinations also will be likely to accept this assumption as self-evident at the general, abstract level. But even in subject-matter tests there will be questions that ask about specific knowledge that is not absolutely essential. For example, every reasonable person would probably agree that an American History teacher should have some knowledge of American History in order to teach it. However, a specific question that taps a specific portion of the overall domain may test for knowledge that not all would consider absolutely essential. This could be true even though the question matches a fairly specific relevant objective. What needs to be made clear in these situations is that the test samples the domain, and that a single inference is made about the knowledge of the domain rather than a set of inferences about the knowledge of specific questions (or specific objectives). If a test is composed of questions, all of which measure relevant objectives within a relevant domain, then it is reasonable to infer that a person with a high test score over that domain has the minimum necessary knowledge to teach the domain, and to infer that a person with a low test score over the domain does not have the necessary knowledge. These could be reasonable inferences even though one might not believe that the knowledge tapped by any single questions was *absolutely* necessary.

The necessity to have knowledge regarding classroom management, assessment techniques, or developmental psychology is probably less "self-evident" than the necessity to know the subject matter. The same is true for knowledge of basic skills. It is probably least self-evident that a test over general knowledge measures necessary knowledge. Is it necessary for a person to be well educated in a general sense in order to be an adequate teacher?

Tests over pedagogy, basic skills, or general knowledge are almost certain to contain questions testing specific knowledge that is not absolutely essential. For example, most of us would probably agree that teachers should know something about how to measure the knowledge of their students. A test over that subdomain of pedagogy would be considered relevant. We could all probably agree at the abstract level that a teacher could know so little about that subdomain that he or she should not be licensed to teach. That indeed, giving a license to teach to someone who knew almost nothing about measurement techniques could well result in harm to individual pupils. To protect the public from that potential harm one might well decide to build a test covering measurement knowledge. Questions matching relevant objectives within that subdomain might help contribute to a correct inference about whether prospective teachers know the minimum amount necessary about the subdomain to be licensed even if each specific question, standing alone, could not be defended as measuring absolutely essential knowledge. Obviously the same point could be made for the basic skills. For example, we would probably all agree that teachers should have some skill in spelling. We could probably all agree at an abstract level that there exists a level of spelling proficiency so low that people with only that level of proficiency should not be licensed. We might be able to make correct inferences about the inadequacy of necessary spelling skills from a spelling test even though we could not defend the absolute necessity of being able to spell any single word in the test.

Making an inference about the general adequacy of necessary knowledge from a test sampling a domain, without making any assumptions about the absolute necessity of each specific piece of knowledge tapped by each question, should not be something about which the measurement community would disagree.

Content Validity Established Through Test Construction

Content validity is established only in test construction (Cronbach, 1980, p. 105). Thus, it is essential that those who wish to argue the validity of teacher competency tests through content validity evidence must follow appropriate test construction procedures.

The major points of concern in establishing the content validity of a licensure test appear to be (a) developing an original list of competencies, (b) doing some type of job analysis survey, (c) specifying the domain for the test, (d) writing and validating the items, and (e) obtaining an overall judgment of the content validity of the test. These five steps will be discussed in some detail in the following sections plus the additional sixth step of communicating the domain to the test takers and the general public.

Developing an Original List of Competencies

The most general starting point for developing the list of competencies is to appoint a relevant committee to do the task. This committee should be composed of experts within the field. For teacher competency exams these experts may be practicing K-12 teachers, supervisors, university professors, and/or state department personnel. The members of the committee should have the necessary expertise and the committee should have credibility with the appropriate constituencies. It is probably useful to have a variety of perspectives represented on the committee (Yalow & Collins, 1985).

The starting point for the committee should be an understanding of the purpose(s) of licensure tests. The next task should be a thorough review of the relevant literature (Burns, 1985; Kane, 1984). This should include a thorough review of the teaching competencies tested in other states, the scope and content outlines from state departments of education, and the literature on teaching effectiveness. Note that this is not the same thing as trying to establish the "curricular validity" of an examination. The purpose of going to the literature is to find out what is critical, not to find out what is being taught in any particular curriculum. One additional literature source that may be helpful in formulating task statements is the literature reporting how teachers spend their time in the classroom (see Rosenfeld, Thornton, & Skurnik, 1986).

Of course, the literature review would be somewhat different for examinations in pedagogy than for examinations in subject matter fields. As mentioned earlier, for subject matter fields, an assumption considered self-evident is that one cannot teach what one does not know. Therefore, it is critical that teachers know the content they are to be certified to teach. To determine this content, a search of the curricular materials in the appropriate grade levels for which certification will be given is appropriate. However, it is *not* being suggested that teachers only need subject-matter knowledge at the level they are teaching (see Shulman, 1986).

Doing the Job Analysis Survey

Professional standards, logic, and legal precedent all stress the importance of job relevance or job relatedness in both employment and licensure exams. There is no specific Standard on how to do the job analysis. The *Uniform Guidelines* state that "Any method of job analysis may be used if it provides information for the specific validation strategy used" (Equal Employment Opportunity Commission, 1978, p. 38300).

The *Guidelines* do impose two basic requirements for a job analysis to be used in content validation: (a) The analysis must yield an operational definition of the domain and (b) the content of the domain should be necessary for critical or important work behaviors. Two commonly accepted methods of determining job-relatedness are through document review and group discussion. These two methods (sometimes called logical analyses) should be employed by the committee developing the list of original competencies discussed in the previous section. According to the *Principles for the Validation and Use of Personnel Selection Procedures* (American Psychological Association [APA], 1980) this process of using the pooled judgment of experts is a recognized approach to determining job relatedness (or job analysis).

A major advantage of a logical analysis is that "it makes use of the extensive body of existing knowledge and can focus on the main goals of the job or category of jobs" (Kane, Kingsbury, Colton, & Estes, 1986, p. 1.6). The main disadvantage is that it may overlook important aspects of work.

Another common approach to job analysis is observation. But, "some jobs, including many in the white collar occupations, do not lend themselves readily to analysis by observation. Employees in such jobs frequently can describe their work fairly readily" (U.S. Civil Service Commission, 1973, p. 6). Most experts feel this quote is particularly appropriate to the job of teaching, especially for licensure exams where the critical job elements need to be included as opposed to the total domain of job elements. Although a few educational measurement experts would wish the job analyses to include observations, they appear to be in the minority (see Kane et al., 1986, p. 1.7).

Typically a job-analysis survey (or task inventory) of people in the profession is conducted to confirm, disconfirm, or add to the judgments of the committee experts (Pecheone, Tomala, & Forgione, 1986; Yalow & Collins, 1985). (This survey is often referred to as an *empirical* analysis and some have confused this with criterion related validity.) The survey instrument itself can vary in the specifics of the wording, and there are a number of variations in the sampling process.

Almost invariably the surveys ask respondents to rate the importance and/or frequency of use of a set of competencies or objectives gathered by a panel and based, in part, on a literature review. Job analyses for employment exams typically place heavy emphasis on frequency data (Williamson, 1979, as referenced in Kane, 1984). For licensure exams it is common also to gather data regarding the importance or criticality of the job element with respect to the purpose of protecting the public. As Kane suggested, "Given that the purpose of licensure is to protect the public, the 'harmful if missed' category would seem to be especially important for licensure examinations" (1984, p. 12).

Some researchers (Colton, Kane, Kingsbury, & Estes, 1987; Elliot, 1987; Kane et al., 1986) discuss how to examine the construct validity of the job analysis. This is accomplished through setting hypotheses about the dimensional structure of the data; anticipated differential responses (or lack thereof) across different groups of respondents; agreement of responses with the professional literature; and so forth. This testing of the hypotheses about the job analysis data can also be used as indirect construct validity evidence for the test data. It adds credence to the supposition that the test measures teacher competence.

Not much research has been done on who should be sampled by the survey. Generally, the sampling has been done from the domain of practicing teachers in the state who are licensed in the field for which the test is designed. Elliot (1987) found that there were no differences in amount of *time spent* on various job content areas between individuals with and without Masters' Degrees and among individuals of varying years of teaching experience. However, he did find differences across grade levels taught.

If one wished to check the consistency of the survey data due to sampling error, one could divide the participants into two half-samples. This was done in a least one state (Echternacht, 1985). Basically, the evidence suggested that there was considerable consistency across the half-panels.

Obviously, most surveys done to help determine job relevance are *not* done at the item level (exceptions would be for those surveys performed to "validate" existing tests). Surveys are done prior to final determination of the appropriate domain and the table of specifications for the test. All this, of course, is accomplished prior to building items for a test. Nevertheless, some critics have contended that the survey portion of the job analysis should be at the item level. The argument goes something like this: Just because an objective may be determined to be job relevant, it does not follow that an item purporting to test that objective is also job relevant. That is a theoretical possibility given certain flaws that may occur in the item writing procedures. Nevertheless, the determination of the test's domain, which is what the job analysis survey helps do, simply is not done at the item level. One does need to have item review procedures to assess the item validity, and these are discussed later. These procedures are not reasonably considered a part of the job analysis.

Determining the Domain Specifications

As Elliott and Nelson (1984) pointed out: "There is little to guide the developer of teacher licensing tests in making the huge leap from job analysis to domain specifications" (p. 9). This should not surprise us. Experts in the field of achievement testing have for years been unable to reach complete accord on how explicitly the content domain needs to be defined or what algorithms one might set up to weight the subcategories of the domain or to sample within the subcategories. Determining the domain specifications is obviously a judgmental task, and as Cronbach (1980) suggested, "the defense must be prepared to show that the domain is relevant and that weight is properly distributed over it" (p. 105).

Three general points need to be made about the domain of licensure tests: (a) the domain should be fairly broad because a certificate is not for a specific job but for a general kind of job; (b) the domain does not have to cover the total set of tasks determined by the job analysis, and related to that; (c) a licensure test does not need to have, and probably should not have, subcategory weights that are proportionate to the amount of time one spends on that subcategory on the job.

What one should do is cover the domain of *critical* knowledge and skills. The weighting of an area should be based on the degree of its criticality, which in turn is based on both frequency and impact. One should be particularly alert to the "harmful if missed" category for licensure examinations (Kane, 1984).

As mentioned earlier, a fairly common procedure in conducting the job analysis survey is to ask questions both about the amount of time spent in teaching or using an objective, as well as the criticality of the objective. Often, these data are combined in some fashion to determine a single value of "importance" for each objective. There is no single established algorithm for combining the two pieces of information or for arriving at weights for the table of specifications. Some evidence suggests the algorithm used to combine the two variables does not matter a great deal because the correlations between the responses to the two questions is quite high. For example, one unpublished study investigated the intercorrelations among three formulas for combining information. Job analysis information was collected for three different scales: (a) Have you taught directly or utilized this objective during this school year or the past school year? If answered affirmatively, two more questions were asked; (b) How much time was spent teaching or using this objective? (5-point scale); and (c) How essential is it that this objective be included in the curriculum of my entire teaching field or the content of my instructional support field? (5-point scale). Values were computed separately for each participant using the three formulas: $-\sqrt{B^2 + C^2}$; ABC^2; and ABC. These values were averaged across participants. The correlation of the objectives between the first two formulas was 0.93, between the first and third it was 0.91, and between the second and third it was 0.996 (M. A. Lahey, personal communication, 1985). Schmeiser (1987) also found that three different methods of obtaining composite scores produced a very high degree of consistency. However, Kane et al. (1986) in a survey of nursing practices did find some differences across the algorithms they used. More research should probably be conducted in this area.

Once one has information about the objectives (or tasks), it is both appropriate, and common practice, to use it along with any subdomain information to select a proportional number of important objectives within each subdomain. It generally would be considered acceptable practice to give the panel of experts some flexibility in choosing objectives rather than forcing them to use some unflexible algorithm based on the ratings (see Millman, 1986).

Writing and Validating the Items

The most commonly used item format for licensure examinations is the multiple-choice item (Shimberg, 1982). This seems quite appropriate because the purpose of most licensure tests is to see whether or not the applicants have the necessary knowledge. Almost all authors of measurement texts have advocated the use of multiple-choice items (see for example, Bloom, Madaus, & Hastings, 1981; Ebel, 1979; Gronlund, 1985; Hills, 1981; Hopkins & Stanley, 1981; Mehrens & Lehmann, 1984; Nitko, 1983; Sax, 1980). There is a wide body of literature demonstrating that multiple-choice items can measure knowledge. However, some critics have suggested this format is inappropriate. Pottinger (1979) argued against such a format because he believed it does not do an adequate job of protecting the public. That is, multiple choice tests let too many incompetent people get certified. This may be true. Research generally has shown that short answer questions are more difficult than multiple-choice questions. This is particularly true of questions requiring solutions to problems. Apparently generating a solution is more difficult than choosing one. However, the correlation across people between the two types of tests is typically quite high. Further, the cut-score procedure is based on the multiple-choice items so the individuals determining the cut score have taken item format into account.

Other critics have argued that multiple-choice tests keep competent people out. Such critics seem to base their criticism on the notion that some people know a lot of material but are unable to demonstrate it on multiple-choice tests. The available evidence certainly suggests that you cannot be admitted to or graduate from a *reputable* college without having the limited skill necessary to respond to such items. Logic plus previously available evidence of the validity of tests using multiple-choice items suggests that one can adopt this format without having to gain independent evidence of the validity of such a format for this particular type of situation.

The writing of multiple-choice items is basically no different for the purposes of teacher certification tests than for any other test given to educated adults. Some professionals prefer item writers to work from what are commonly called "item specifications" (Popham, 1984). Others prefer to write items directly from objectives. There is no particular reason to prefer either approach although Millman (1986, pp. 3–8) suggested, and I would concur, that more testing experts are in the latter camp. If the job analysis survey was based on some statements of the competencies desired (perhaps as statements of objectives), then translating these into item specifications prior to writing items in no way guarantees that the items will be more valid measures of the original competencies than if the items were written directly from the statements of competencies. It is true, of course, that well-written item specifications tend to ensure that the items match the item specifications, but there may well have been some slippage between the statement of competency and the item specification. This slippage could well be greater than that between the statement of competency and the item written directly from it. Almost all popular measurement texts (such as those referenced a few paragraphs back) do *not* advocate including item specifications as a stage in test construction. The new *Standards* (AERA, APA, NCME, 1985) do not mention item specifications in the index, nor as far as I could determine, anywhere throughout the book. (See Popham, 1984; Roid, 1984, for positions advocating item specifications.)

Whether or not items are written from item specifications, it is necessary to have the items reviewed by a panel of experts. Specific procedures for the item reviews have varied somewhat across states, but the general intent in all cases is to determine the adequacy of the items as measures of the objectives (or statements of competencies). Hambleton (1984) gave an excellent overview of some of the methods of judging item validity. He suggested two general methods for judging items: using empirical techniques and collecting judgments from content specialists. He and most other measurement specialists prefer the second approach. He described several possible judgmental procedures. One of these is a procedure developed by Rovinelli and Hambleton (1977) that results in an index of item-objective congruence. However, as Hambleton (1984) pointed out, this procedure is very time consuming to implement. A second approach mentioned by Hambleton is to have content specialists rate the item-objective match. A third approach would be to have the judges match the test items with the objectives.

In all the procedures mentioned, one could check the expertise or care of the judges by including some "marker" or "lemon" items which did not match the objectives to see if the judges identified these bad items. Hambleton reported that in one study it was found necessary to eliminate one reviewer (out of 20) because that reviewer detected only 2 of 19 bad items. Although I like the notion of marker items, to my knowledge most reviewers have not used them. I would not consider their absence as an indication that the item review was inadequate. If only one out of 20 reviewers turns out to be incompetent or careless, that suggests there are plenty of reviewers who do spot bad items.

An approach developed by Nassif (1978) and commonly used by NES is frequently called a dichotomous judgment model. In this procedure, each member of a panel of content experts indicates for each item whether or not the item is accurate, congruent with the objective, significant, and lacking in bias. For an item to be considered valid it must pass *all four criteria*. To "pass" the judges' results are compared to the binomial distribution to determine the probability, due to chance alone, of obtaining x valid responses for an item from a total of N raters. In essence, this means that for an item to pass *almost all the raters* would have to indicate that the item is valid on *all four criteria*.

Another example of the item review process was the one used by Florida. First, a review panel keyed the items; traced them back (blind) to the subskill and content categories; and then rated the items for appropriateness. Secondly, three separate reviews of the items were conducted: for content, bias, and technical quality. The content reviews were conducted by the content specialists; the bias reviews were conducted by minority persons, women, and experts trained in linguistics; and the technical review panel included both measurement and language arts experts.

Some measurement experts would prefer the approach of using separate groups of experts to make the separate judgments. Others believe that what evidence exists suggests a panel of content experts is sufficient to do all the tasks. In fact, there is some anecdotal evidence to suggest that minorities select fewer items as being biased than do nonminorities (W. Ruch, 1984, personal communication). Berk (1984b, p. 100) suggested that the panels be composed of individuals representative of the appropriate subpopulations (e.g. males, females, Blacks, Whites, Hispanics). Tittle (1982) suggested using "at least two representatives from each group as expert judges" (p. 55), although she suggested that further research was needed with respect to the use of expert judges.

There is also some disagreement as to whether or not the judges should be meeting as a group and forming a consensus, meeting as a group and having the opportunity for discussion but voting independently, or making totally independent judgments. Each method has some potential disadvantages. The first two may suffer from social psychological factors. An assertive, strong-willed person may end up "controlling" the vote. The third approach may suffer due to the lack of opportunity to discuss with others, which may stimulate one's thinking.

Whatever particular methods are used the *Standards* state conditionally that "the relevant training, experience, and qualifications of the experts should be described" (AERA, APA, NCME, 1985, p. 15).

Overall Judgment of Content Validity

Because content validity is established only in test construction the judgment of the adequacy of the content validity should be based on a judgment of the adequacy of the construction process. If the original list of competencies has been developed by experts, if the job analysis (or survey) is accomplished appropriately, if the test specifications have been developed from the results of the first two steps, and if the items have been written and validated in a satisfactory manner, then the test will have appropriate content validity. It will be assessing those competencies that experts in the field thought necessary for beginning professionals to have in order to protect the public. Even if all the steps were not executed perfectly, the use of multiple review groups on multiple occasions should provide "enough safeguards against the inclusion of some out right invalid topic or objective" (Millman, 1986, p. 3–7).

States that adopt the various NTE tests frequently make an overall judgment as to the content validity of those tests in a different fashion than that described here. Typically a thorough review of the test construction process is not made. Rather an analysis of the items within the various NTE tests is made. The approach used is to survey a group of individuals (frequently called the "job relevance panel"). These individuals are asked to make judgments about the degree to which the knowledge or skills tested are relevant to competent performance as a beginning practitioner. The states set some cut off on the degree of relevance ratings to arrive at a decision regarding whether the total test has sufficient content relevance to administer in the state.

Communicating the Domain to the Public

Both the individuals applying for licensure and the general public have a right to know the general content of a licensure examination. No one debates this. However, there is some debate about just what the public is to be told. Generally, the survey of objectives (job analysis) results in a greater number of objectives being rated as essential than it is possible to test in any given test. Thus, the test itself must sample the objectives from the total domain of objectives.

In my opinion, the situation in licensure tests is the same as for any other test where there is a sampling of objectives. One wishes to make an inference from the objectives sampled to the total set of objectives judged relevant. In order to do so, one *must* communicate the total set of objectives rather than the subset, which is sampled for the test.

It is appropriate to tell those who will be taking the test that all objectives will not be tested. This is what is done in many of the licensure tests. For example in the Examination for the Certification of Educators in Texas (ExCET) the *Study Guide* (National Evaluation Systems, n.d.) specifically states that the test measures only a portion of the objectives.

Of course, if the test objectives are broad enough, or the test is long enough, so that the total set of objectives are tested, then there is nothing wrong with communicating to the public the specific objectives tested because the inference does not go beyond those particular objectives. Apparently the Texas Examination of Current Administrators and Teachers (TECAT) covers *all* the basic reading and writing skills that educators need to perform adequately. Thus the list of objectives made public was limited to the objectives actually tested. Shepard and Kreitzer (1987) found that monumental effort went into preparing for the TECAT. "As soon as test specifications were available, the Continuing Education Division of the University of Texas at Austin, in cooperation with the Texas Classroom Teachers Association, developed a review course and a 300 page self-study book" (p. 6). Furthermore, 12 videotapes were prepared and used extensively in preparation for the test. Now this is fine *if* the objectives were all inclusive of the basic skills in reading and writing that teachers should know and *if* the information and preparation helped the teachers develop the skills as opposed to just passing the test. But, as Shepard and Kreitzer (1987) reported, "at some point legitimate teaching to the test crossed over an ill-defined line and became inappropriate. . . . Over and over again, . . . teaching to the test involved exploitation of the test specifications . . ." (p. 9).

I agree with Shepard and Kreitzer that the line between legitimate teaching to the test and illegitimate teaching of the test is not well defined. But there is a legitimate worry that if too much information is released in advance about a test—such as which specific objectives are tested and detailed item specifications regarding how the questions and multiple-choice options are developed—one will no longer be able to infer competence in the domain from a passing score on a test. In the extreme one could give out advance copies of the test; most of us would feel that to be inadvisable for licensure tests where the goal is to protect the public from incompetents.

Not all would agree with my position. An expert witness at one trial testified that he found it misleading to communicate a larger set of objectives to candidates than are actually being tested. Perhaps the measurement issue revolves around the meaning of a "criterion-referenced" test (CRT). Perhaps some feel that one can only infer to the objectives specifically sampled and that an inference to the domain from which the objectives were sampled is not appropriate. In any event, the purpose of a licensure exam is to protect the public and the inference we wish to make is that a candidate does, or does not, have sufficient competence on all the knowledge relevant for that protection. If that domain is reasonably large, as it is almost sure to be in most professions, it will be necessary for the test to sample the domain at both the objective and item levels.

CRITERION-RELATED VALIDITY EVIDENCE

As mentioned earlier, some critics attack teacher competency tests because the passing of such a test does not guarantee that one will be a good teacher. A true, but totally irrelevant point. As Vold (1985) suggested, the promise of teacher exams "is not so much that they can identify competent teachers, but they do seem capable of weeding out incompetent ones" (p. 5). Johnson and Prom-Jackson (1986) pointed out that the cognitive abilities of teachers "constitute a necessary but not nearly sufficient condition" [for teacher success] (p. 279). Certainly, no one who knows anything about validity and testing would suggest a test score can offer any guarantee. But should not such tests have some predictive validity? A few writers would argue yes. Hecht (1979), for example, although admitting that predictive validity studies in licensure tests are rare indeed, suggested that "predictive criterion-related validation studies would be the type most closely fitting the expressed purpose of licensure exams" (p. 21). However her opinion is certainly not the common view held by most measurement experts. Shimberg (1982) stated the more commonly held position quite nicely:

> What Hecht overlooks, however, is a difference between the purpose of a test intended for use in an employment situation and one intended for use in licensing.

...

> Those who believe that it is the purpose of licensing boards to predict job success might think so, but to follow their lead would drastically change the nature and purpose of licensing. It is doubtful that many legislators would agree that predicting job success should be a function of licensing boards. (p. 60)

Kane (1984), in arguing against any reason to expect a correlation coefficient based on data from passing candidates, admitted that a measure of agreement between the pass/fail dichotomy on the licensure examination and a competent/incompetent dichotomy in subsequent practice would have some relevance. However, an index "that would address this issue cannot be estimated without having criterion scores for those who fail the examination as well as for those who pass. Attempts to collect such data might be considered unethical (and probably illegal) in many professions" (Kane, 1984, p. 5).

Even if such data were gathered, a lack of a relationship could well be due to our inability to detect those practitioners who are incompetent and causing harm to the public. Kane (1982; 1984), Linn (1984), Rosen (1986), Shimberg (1982; 1984), and others all have argued that it is both unfeasible and inappropriate to expect criterion-related validity of a licensure examination.

The *Standards* state that

> Investigations of criterion-related validity are more problematic in the context of licensure or certification than in many employment settings. Not all those certified or licensed are necessarily hired; those hired are likely to be in a variety of job assignments with many different employers, and some may be self-employed. These factors often make traditional studies that gather criterion-related evidence of validity infeasible. (AERA, APA, NCME, 1985, p. 63)

One of the major practical problems in criterion-related validity is that there is no clear definition of what it means to be an effective teacher (Webb, 1983). This certainly complicates the criterion problem. Stark and Lowther (1984), for example, listed six different conceptualizations of teaching and gave as examples 10 different criteria for teacher evaluation.

Ebel (1961) and Kane (1984) both discussed the many criterion problems for licensure exams. As Cronbach (1970) stated: "When a test fails to predict a rating, it is hard to say whether this is the fault of the test or of the rating" (p. 127). Petersen (1987) reported that administrative reports were bunched up at the high end of the scale, showed little variance, and did not correlate with other measures used to evaluate teachers. Berliner (1986) discussed the lack of training of judges of teacher competence: "Only a few states provided any training for their judges, and when training was provided it was usually for one-half day" (p. 11). He compares that to the training of other judges "We learned that to become a livestock judge in Arizona you ordinarily have to take a year of livestock evaluation courses at a college. . . . The American Kennel Club's application for a judge requires 10 years documented experience in the field. . . . Written testing and an oral interview are also required. . . . In figure skating it can take 10 to 15 years" (pp. 12, 13).

It is probably safe to suggest that if teachers had high supervisors' ratings on teaching effectiveness but could not pass a test on the content they were supposed to be teaching, most reasonable people would (and should) doubt the ratings. That may not be quite as likely if the test were covering pedagogy. (It is interesting in this general regard to reflect on what the differences might be in public perception if an MD or an attorney practiced "successfully," but had not passed the prerequisite licensure examination and/or not received the prerequisite professional training. In those cases where someone has been caught practicing medicine without a license the general reaction of the public is not that such instances indicate that the person practicing was competent and that licensure of MDs is not needed. Rather, they typically interpret the situation as an instance of an incompetent not getting caught sooner.)

It is important to point out once again, that validity has to do with the inferences one wishes to draw from a score. Few, if any, of the advocates for licensure tests in general, or for teacher licensure tests in particular, wish to infer that the scores will predict degree of success on the job. Consider Ebel's (1977) comment:

> Never, while I was at the Educational Testing Service, did I hear any of the administrators of that organization or the directors of the National Teacher Examination program claim that the test would predict success in the classroom. What we did claim was that it would indicate how much the applicant knew about the job of teaching. We claimed that it was a necessary, but certainly not a sufficient condition for effective classroom performance. We defended this claim on logical grounds. We believed it could not be defended empirically, and did not need to be. That is, none of us believed that a correlation between ratings of classroom effectiveness and NTE scores could shed more than a feeble and uncertain light on how well

the test was doing the job it was intended to do. None of us doubted that knowing how to do a job usually facilitates doing it. (p. 60)

In another article, Ebel (1975) made the following point:

> Often the test itself is as good a criterion of competence to teach as we are likely to get. In such a situation, it makes little sense to demand that the validity of the test be demonstrated unless, of course, *the intent is not to validate but to discourage its use* [italics added]. (pp. 26–27)

In summary, licensure tests are not designed to predict degrees of success among those licensed; it is generally conceded that criterion-related validity studies for licensure tests are unfeasible; and many individuals would rather trust the test scores than the criterion measures if a criterion validity study were done and the test failed to predict. It does not follow from all of the preceding statements that it is inappropriate to attempt to find out what, if any, correlates of teacher-licensure tests exist. Although correlational data are somewhat sparse, they are consonant with the logical inference that knowledge about teaching and the subject matter being taught (competence) should be related to both performance and effectiveness in teaching.

Webster (1984) conducted a study using both a general aptitude test: the *Wesman Personnel Classification Test* (WPCT), and the NTE Common Exam. As Webster pointed out, the *WPCT* was not designed to identify persons who would make excellent teachers.

> It was assumed however, that persons who scored very low on the WPCT would be expected to encounter more-than-average difficulty in a profession that depends so much on one's ability to communicate. In short, it seemed logical that successful teachers should be minimally competent in acquiring, remembering, and transmitting knowledge. (p. 4)

Using a class average residualized composite score (CARCS), Webster found a correlation of 0.47 between CARCS and the NTE Common, 0.47 between CARCS and WPCT-Verbal, 0.37 between CARCS and WPCT-Math, and 0.48 between CARCS and WPCT-Total. All correlations were significant at $p \leq .01$.

Piper and O'Sullivan (1981) had university supervisors rate elementary education majors on a Performance Evaluation Instrument designed to measure classroom competencies. They found that scores on that instrument were significantly correlated (0.43)

4. ASSESSING THE QUALITY 105

to NTE Common Examination scores. Coleman et al. (1966) found that the verbal ability of teachers was the single most important characteristic of teachers in accounting for student outcomes. Other research shows that teacher competency tests are related to admission tests (Ayres, 1983; McPhee & Kerr, 1985).

CONSTRUCT-VALIDITY EVIDENCE

Although some measurement experts believe that all validity is construct validity, other measurement experts worry some about this labeling because "theoretical constructions about the nature of human behavior" (AERA, APA, NCME, 1985, p. 9) often implies hypothetical constructions (Ebel, 1974). Haertel (1987) suggested that in achievement testing either of two positions may be taken.

> A *domain* [italics added] of test items may be considered to operationalize achievement outcomes, so that achievement is defined in terms of test performance, or items may be treated as partial and imperfect indicators of student proficiency, so that achievement cannot in principle be defined in terms of any single operational procedure for its measurement. The former position is consonant with a behaviorist orientation, which treats mental entities as no more than interviewing variables, and the latter with a cognitivist orientation, which treats mental entities as *hypothetical constructs* [italics added]. (pp. 5–6)

Given Haertel's conception of cognitive learning outcomes, he believes they cannot be defined in behavioral terms. However, Ebel (1977), in speaking specifically about educational and employment testing, suggested the following:

> Most of what we teach in educational institutions, and most of what we test for in employee selection are knowledges, skills, and abilities. These can all be defined operationally. They are not hypothetical constructs. . . .
> Why do we continue to talk about construct validity as if it were something we all understood and have found useful? Has any educational or employment test ever been shown to possess construct validity? . . . It should be of no real concern, at the present stage of its development, to those of us engaged in achievement or job testing (p. 61).

Many measurement experts are concerned about any implied necessity for construct validation because it is viewed "as an ill defined and unending process" (Linn, 1984, p. 7). The *Standards* do not *require* construct validity evidence for licensure tests. However, they do state that "Standard 11.2: Any construct interpretations of tests used for licensure and certification should be made explicit, and the evidence *and logical analyses* supporting these interpretations should be reported. (Primary)" (AERA, APA, NCME, 1985, p. 64, emphasis added).

The problem is that a critic may infer a construct the builder/user did not want implied and then criticize the builder/user for not making it explicit! Those measurement experts who think all validity is construct validity would probably suggest that the very term *teacher competency* implies a construct, although the definition by Medley given earlier in this chapter would not necessarily lead to such a conclusion. According to Medley's (1982) definition, competencies refer to specific things that teachers know, do, or believe but not to the effects of these attributes on others. Teacher competence is the repertoire of competencies a teacher possesses. This does not seem like a theoretical construct. It would seem a set of items could *sample* this repertoire rather than being a *sign* of a theoretical construct (see Mehrens & Lehmann, 1987).

Builders/users of teacher competency tests are in somewhat of a dilemma with respect to referring to evidence they gather as construct validity evidence. If they do so, then the critics say "Ah-ha, you do admit competency is a construct." Then, because construct validation is somewhat an ill-defined and unending process the critics can (and do) attack whatever evidence is gathered as being inadequate. The very choice of wording may eventually cause builders/users legal grief. For example, Kane, when talking about licensure tests commonly used the phrase "critical abilities" which may allow some individuals to infer a construct. The writers of the *Standards*, apparently very alert to this issue, wisely used only the terms *knowledges* and *skills* in referring to licensure tests, leaving *abilities* out of the commonly used KSA terminology.

If a builder/user wished to gather evidence labeled "construct validity" evidence (in spite of the illogical but real legal dangers of so doing) how should it be done? There is wide agreement that "Evidence identified usually with the criterion-related or content-related categories ... is relevant also to the construct-related category" (AERA, APA, NCME, 1985, p. 9). Thus, test development procedures, test formating, administration conditions, reading/language level of the test, and internal consistency estimates are all relevant data for inferring the measurement of a construct (AERA, APA, NCME, 1985, p. 10).

Because all such data and procedures are typically well documented for teacher licensure tests, there exists considerable evidence one could call "construct validity" evidence. The comment to Standard 11.2 quoted earlier suggests that

> Good performance on a certification examination should not require more reading ability, for example, than is necessary in the occupation. The job analysis procedures used in establishing the content-related validity of a test can also contribute to the construct interpretation. One may show, for example, that qualified experts helped to define the job, identify the knowledge and skills required for competent performance, and determine the appropriate level of complexity at which these knowledges and skills should be assessed. (AERA, APA, NCME, 1985, pp. 64–65)

Certainly it readily can be inferred that minimally competent professional educators (to keep up in their professional literature, read principals' memos and, indeed, read the material they assign their students) need to be able to read at a level higher than that required of multiple-choice tests. The job-analysis, content-validity evidence discussed earlier in this chapter is usually available for well-developed licensure tests. There are some criterion related validity studies, and internal reliability estimates typically suggest that only one construct is being measured by a test. Possible sources of error such as college graduates not being able to take multiple-choice tests or not being motivated for a licensure examination can be ruled out thus eliminating competing hypotheses for what it is the test is measuring (e.g., test-taking skill or motivation).

If all the aforementioned procedures are acceptable for establishing construct validity, then builders/users of teacher-competency tests can and do provide construct validity evidence. What cannot be provided very easily, is evidence that a teacher competency test measures some broad, general theoretical notion. If one is going to suggest that a test measures a theoretical construct, it would appear necessary to define the construct. Kane (1984) suggested that as *one example* of construct validity the construct at issue, "professional competence, is defined in terms of the network of theoretical and empirical relationships incorporated in the department of learning" (p. 8). However, in another article he pointed out that

> the validation of measurements that are interpreted as dispositions does not depend on theory. Measurements of a disposition are valid

to the extent that they provide accurate estimates of universe scores. The existence of laws or theories involving a dispositional attribute has no direct bearing on the validity of measurement of the attribute. . . . This point of view is generally consistent with the interpretation of measurement in science. . . . Campbell . . .concluded that "measurement is essential to the discovery of laws" but he did not use the laws to evaluate measurement procedures. (Kane, 1982, p. 151)

This latter view suggests that the validity evidence that a certain dispositional attribute has been measured (construct validity?) is not dependent upon evidence of a nomological net. Given the state of theory construction in education that is a good thing!

As has been pointed out by a variety of writers (e.g., Darling-Hammond, Wise, & Pease, 1983), the evaluation of teaching in any generic sense depends on one's conceptions. The Medley distinctions made early in the chapter between teacher competence, teacher performance, and teacher effectiveness must be kept in mind. Whereas teacher competence may be related to teacher performance and effectiveness, licensure tests measure the former, not the latter two. Builders/users should not imply they measure the latter two, and they should not be held responsible for any evidence (or lack of evidence) by those who inappropriately wish to make such inferences.

CURRICULAR VALIDITY

In general, experts on licensure examinations do not discuss what some educators refer to as curricular and/or instructional validity. Licensure tests are designed to protect the public and the appropriate judgment of validity should be based on whether or not the tests cover the knowledges and skills that those licensed should possess. For the purpose of the licensure decision, it is irrelevant and inappropriate to consider curricular/instructional validity in judging the quality of the test.

The confusion that exists among some people regarding curricular validity in educational licensure probably arose for two reasons: (a) confusing the situation in the Debra P. case with licensure decisions (see Rebell, 1986), and (b) forgetting the original purpose of the NTE and the reason for the *NTE Guidelines*. The Debra P. case related to whether it was legal to deprive a high school student of a diploma based on a minimum competency test. An appellate court ruled that it would be considered unfair to withhold a diploma from those who did not learn unless, through the curriculum/instruction, they had been given an opportunity to learn the material. (For those of you not aware of the case, the state won because it demonstrated that the test did have curricular validity.) Of course *that is all irrelevant to the quality of a licensure examination.*

> The criterion of "job-related" validity is different from "instructional" validity as argued in the Debra v. Turlington (1981) case. These two perspectives are opposite in outlook or goal direction. From the licensing examination perspective, job-related validity looks to the *future* or practice-related competence, whereas instructional validity looks at the relationship of the examination with *past* instruction/training . . . a licensing agency that addresses itself to instructional validity instead of job-related validity would be considered somewhat irrelevant to the societal concerns and problems at stake today. (D'Costa, 1985, p. 2).

The *Standards* (AERA, APA, NCME, 1985) implicitly recognize the legitimacy of the distinction between the two uses. Although they do not use the term *curricular validity*, they do address the notion in Chapter 8, "Educational Testing and Psychological Testing in the Schools." Chapter 11, "Professional and Occupational Licensure and Certification," makes no mention of such a standard.

The *NTE Guidelines* state that: "The primary function of NTE tests is to provide objective, standardized measures of the knowledge and skills *developed in academic programs.* . . ." (Educational Testing Service [ETS], 1983b, p. 2). Given that primary function, the guidelines for the proper use of the NTE stated that one component for conducting a validation of the NTE tests for certification is "an assessment of the appropriateness of the tests' content, given relevant teacher-training curricula. . . ." (p. 9). They also suggested that the certifying agency should: "validate the tests to determine that they measure a representative sample of the knowledge and skills required for certification of beginning teachers. . . ." (p. 8). The published *NTE Guidelines* quote the federal district court ruling in the South Carolina case that the tests are

> a fair measure of the knowledge which teacher education programs in the state seek to impart. . . . there is ample evidence in the record of the content validity of the NTE. . . . The NTE have been demonstrated to provide a useful measure of the extent to which prospective teachers have mastered the content of their teacher training programs. (p. 21)

That decision seemed by many to be reasonable. The tests were *fair*, and they did what the *Guidelines* state was the primary purpose of the test—to provide measures of the knowledges and skills developed in academic programs. What that has to do with the *quality* of the test as a *licensure* examination is hard to determine. One could argue that because the academic programs are good programs, covering appropriate knowledges and skills, then a test measuring those knowledges and skills would be a good test. But one of the whole purposes behind licensure examinations is that the public does not wish to depend upon the quality of the educational/training programs. It would make little sense to build a licensure examination based on the curriculum of an inadequate college! Roth (1984) provided a brilliant summary of the South Carolina case.

> In the *United States v. South Carolina* case, the Plaintiffs presented only one alternative, graduation from an approved teacher training program, to the use of the NTE for certification purposes. The trial Court did not feel that the alternative would achieve the State's purpose in certifying minimally competent teachers as well as the use of the NTE. The Court in support of this finding made two points. One, evidence demonstrated that the teacher training programs varied in admission requirements, academic standards, and grading practices. Two, evidence demonstrated that the State approves only general subject matter areas covered by the programs, not the actual course content of the programs. Both of these points would seem to weigh negatively on the Court's position that validation against the teacher training programs was sufficiently reflective of actual knowledge needed for the teaching positions. Here the Court would seem to be admitting that the twenty-five teacher training programs were in fact different and therefore not all would be to the same degree reflective of knowledge needed to competently perform the job. The Court, however, while finding the teaching programs themselves an inadequate measure of teacher competency saw no inconsistency in finding test validation against those same teacher programs acceptable. (p. 4)

Roth went on to argue that the validity question for licensure examinations is job relevance, not training program relevance. This is the commonly—almost universally—accepted position.[3]

---

[3]I would have preferred that Roth not have used the *Uniform Guidelines* as support for his position. There is much other literature, as well as basic logic, available to support his position and many individuals do not feel the *Uniform Guidelines* apply to licensure tests, a subject discussed later in this chapter.

Most states using the NTE tests have "validated" them both for their match to the colleges' curricula and to the requirements of the job. There is certainly nothing wrong with doing a study to determine whether or not students have been given the opportunity to adequately learn what is in a licensure examination. What would be wrong would be to leave questions on essential knowledges and skills out of an exam (or not score them) because they were not in some curriculum.

It seems reasonable to conclude that the methods used by the states for validating the NTE tests (and setting their cut scores) minimize the chances for false rejects and increase the chances for false acceptances. If a prospective teacher has not learned an adequate amount of what is both in the curriculum *and* considered relevant, then the person probably does not have a sufficient amount of the essential knowledges and skills to be licensed. However, a person could have mastered the specific knowledges and skills validated and tested and still not have some other essential but nontested knowledges and skills. (Of course the use of *any* test decreases the number of false acceptances from what one would obtain if no licensure test were required.)

A reasonable argument can be made that if the State Department of Education has oversight responsibilities over both the program approval of colleges of education and the content of licensure examinations, there should be a relationship between them. That relationship will, no doubt, exist in most states for most objectives. But if it does not exist, and if the licensure examination has appropriate content validity as described in an earlier section, the indictment is against the program, not the licensure examination. The relationship of course holds only for tests over knowledge of the profession of education. It cannot and should not occur for licensure exams that cover basic skills such as reading, writing, and basic mathematics. These should not be taught as part of the curriculum of a professional school. The competencies in subject matter such as that taught in secondary schools should also not be covered by the colleges (departments) of education although they, perhaps, have some responsibility for assuring that graduates have competent prerequisite skills in those areas as well as necessary subject-matter college course work somewhere in the university (college).

If colleges graduate individuals who have not been given the opportunity to learn the necessary knowledges and skills required in the profession to protect the public, what should we do? We might consider closing down those colleges or bringing about additional pressure for them to do a better job. A state might even consider giving an inadequately prepared student free remediation (assuming the inadequate preparation is the institution's fault, not the individual's fault). Ekstrom and Goertz (1985) argued that accountability for student failure is often misplaced:

> Although instruction in basic skills and subject matter areas is usually not provided in the schools of education, basic skills and subject matter specialty tests are used to evaluate the teacher education programs. Teacher education departments are held responsible for education students' knowledge of these areas while non-education departments actually providing the instruction have little or no incentive to improve their teaching in ways that will improve teacher quality. (p. 9)

What the state must *not* do is to give an inadequately prepared graduate a license to teach!

At times it has been suggested that a licensure test is an inappropriate measure for assisting in evaluating the professional curricula of colleges if the tests have not been built based upon the college curricula or instructional objectives. That notion is based on a grievous confusion between curricular and instructional evaluation. If one is evaluating the efficacy of the instruction then it is important for the test to match the instructional objectives. However, if we wish to determine whether or not a college is teaching (and/or the students are learning) the material deemed crucial for professionals to know, then the test must be based on that material—not the material that happens to be taught. It would seem this confusion should have ended 25 years ago (see, Cronbach 1963, p. 680).

HOW VALID MUST A TEST BE? IDEALISTIC VERSUS REALISTIC STANDARDS

Two general questions have been debated by measurement experts regarding the validity of teacher competency examinations: How valid should the tests be? And, how valid are they?

Some people would prefer not to give examinations unless they are the best they can possibly be. But if one never used tests unless they were "the best possible thing" one would never use tests. The crucial question is whether or not test data improve the decision making over and above the decisions that would be made without the test data. I would hope that the psychometric community could agree to agree on the question although they may well differ on the answer to it.

Of course, when competency tests are used in a conjunctive model as an additional criterion (not the sole one) to those criteria already used, the result is to decrease the number of false acceptances from the number previously made and to (potentially) increase the number of false rejections. Thus it is the relative costs of these two errors that must be considered. Reasonable people can disagree with respect to those relative costs. But we need to keep in mind that the whole purpose of licensure (whether or not one uses test data) is to protect the public (i.e., to decrease the number of false acceptances into the profession).

Another way of looking at how valid teacher-competency tests should be is to compare them to other licensure examinations. By and large, other licensure tests leave much to be desired. Shimberg (1985) reported on a study he completed with Esser and Kruger which found serious shortcomings in many board-developed licensure tests.

> Few of the tests that they studied were based on an up-to-date job analysis, and rarely was there evidence of a test plan or specifications to govern test content. Many relied on essay and short-answer questions for which even board members could not agree on acceptable answers. Where performance tests were used, test administration conditions were frequently not standardized, explicit rating criteria were not available, and raters were untrained. (p. 9)

Werner (1982) provided us with the following insights.

> Too frequently, test program development proceeds from a picture of occupational practice which is outdated, imbalanced with respect to various practice specialty areas, skewed toward matters of only academic interest, or insufficiently representative of practices which have the greatest potential for public harm. . . .
> And in California, we amaze barber applicants each year by asking them to specify the average number of hairs on the human head while we neglect to assess meaningfully their knowledge of potentially harmful cosmetic chemicals. (pp. 7–8)

Finally, consider some excerpts from an article on the *Examination for Professional Practice in Psychology* (Carlson, 1978), which was first released in 1964.

Test development for the AASPB "National Examination" has always leaned heavily upon the voluntary participation of qualified psychologists throughout the APA. Items are contributed by psychologists recognized in their specialty area. . . . There is no way to pretest new items or to establish norms in advance of publication. . . . The item classification scheme, or list of content area categories, and the distribution of items among those areas are necessarily somewhat arbitrary. . . . Further studies are contemplated comparing test scores with academic background, supervised experience, and certain evidences of satisfactory or unsatisfactory performance in the profession. *The commitment of AASPB to a program of ongoing, thorough, validity study could hardly be stronger* [italics added]. (pp. 491–492)

In fact, the commitment of AASPB was so strong that in 1980 they decided to "initiate a research program to ascertain whether there might be a more objective, empirically based method for determining examination content" (Rosenfeld, Shimberg, & Thornton, 1983, pp. 1–2). In 1983 the results of the formal job analysis were published, 18 years after the test was first given for licensure purposes!

In preparing to write this chapter, I reviewed portions of the construction/procedures for the teacher competency tests used in at least 15 different states. Without exception the care in the test construction process (which determines the content validity) and/or the care in validating the questions (e.g., for the adoption of the NTE examinations) plus the reporting of those procedures exceeded what has typically been done in other licensure examinations.

FURTHER POSSIBLE RESEARCH ON VALIDITY ISSUES

It should be clear to even the most casual reader that I believe current teacher competency tests, in general, are providing us with data that facilitates our current decision-making processes with respect to teacher licensure. (This is not an endorsement of all such tests. I have not seen all such tests.) In simple laymen's language, the tests are valid enough to be used for the purpose for which they are designed. That does not mean that more research on validity issues would not be useful. One can certainly imagine studies that could bolster the validity claims of existing teacher competency tests, just as one could imagine validity studies that could bolster the validity claims of the alternate ways we have typically used in the past to make licensure decisions. Unfortunately, there is in our society a dual standard with respect to validity evidence. We expect more such evidence when the data used to facilitate decision making emanates from tests that when it emanates from alternate sources. Thus, an important preamble to this short section is that current tests provide inferences that are valid enough to justify current test use, and that the validity evidence is far stronger than the validity evidence we have for the other data used for licensure such as "three hours of mathematics," or "thirty credits of methods courses."

It is probably fair to say that all of the five steps discussed in this chapter in the development of content valid teacher-competence tests could benefit from further research. First, what procedures impact the development of the original list of competencies? Do different committees or different instructions or time lines given to the committees result in different lists or competencies? How should we "validate" the competencies the committees produce? Must we accept them on faith? If not, what external criteria would we use?

It is also reasonable to conclude that we would profit from more research in job-analyses procedures. Is a survey of teachers really the best way to conduct a job analysis? Would we get different results if we were to send in teams of observers to observe for hundreds of hours? If so, how should we decide which one of the approaches leads to better data? Can teachers really rate competencies in terms of their criticality? Would there be any better way to determine how critical a competency is? What impact would changes in the directions to teachers have on their judgments regarding the necessity of the competencies? Would a description of a competent teacher attached to the survey impact the results? If the surveys more strongly encouraged teachers to suggest new competencies, would the domains be less likely to exclude those harmful if missed competencies? All of these questions are researchable. At the current time we do not have sufficient evidence regarding how much the domains might change across different job-analysis strategies. Of course none of this research would empirically answer the question of which strategy produces the "best" domain of competencies.

Licensure tests are not designed to predict degrees of relative performance, they are designed to measure necessary competencies. Of course there is an implied "prediction" that individuals *not* having the basic competencies will be more likely to harm the public (students) than those who do have the minimum competencies. This is the basis for claiming the competencies measured in a licensure examination are necessary. How should one support the claim of necessity? If there were no practical design problems and no criterion measurement problems then one could employ a criterion related validity study. Such studies may prove useful in spite of design and measurement problems. However, several things should be kept in mind. The ideal criterion is degree of harm to the children. This is *not* the same as teacher performance. It is a *subset* of what Medley termed *teacher effectiveness*—the effect that the teacher's performance has on pupils. Obviously not all effects can be labeled harmful. Careful consideration would need to be given to what effects are to be considered harmful and what the operational definitions of those effects should be. One might believe, as I do, that it is harmful to students to be exposed to teachers who use incorrect grammar, spell words incorrectly on the board, and/or write poorly worded notes to parents. One might believe, as I do, that it is harmful to students to be exposed to teachers who do not know the specific subject matter they are teaching, or who know it so superficially that they cannot tie it together with previously learned or to-be-learned material, or who do not know the most efficacious methods of teaching the material to students from a variety of backgrounds. One might believe, as I do, that it is harmful to students to be exposed to teachers who do not know how to assess the learning of their pupils, who do not know how to organize learning materials, determine appropriate objectives, maintain classroom control, or recognize the advantages of intermittent reinforcement over continuous reinforcement. The problem is to define and measure the *harmful* effects, and to show that the lack of teacher competence lead to the harmful effects. To me, harm has been inflicted if the student learns less than the optimal amount due to a teacher's lack of knowledge about basic communication skills, the subject matter taught, or the pedagogy of teaching. To measure that harm in a research study would be difficult indeed. Others, of course, may have a much more limited definition of harmful.

Certainly the determination of what is meant by *harmful* and *necessary* could profit from further considerations. The constitutive definitions should precede operational definitions. Once operational definitions were obtained surely one could, at least theoretically, conduct empirical studies to determine whether lack of "necessary" knowledge resulted in "harmful" effects on children. If not, the standard for necessary could be lowered and a new study conducted. As a graduate of a university known as the dustbowl of empiricism I cannot in good conscience argue against the potential value of such studies. Nevertheless, there are countless reasons why such studies may not have enough power to show a relationship between lack of teacher knowledge and harm to the student even if the relationship actually exists. Frankly, if a study fails to reveal an effect of a lack of "necessary" knowledge on pupils the public may well doubt the results, and so might I. Our acceptance or rejection of the empirical results would of course vary depending on our subjective notions of how low or high the standards for "necessary" knowledge had been set!

Other correlational studies could also be conducted. We could continue to investigate whether the knowledge displayed on current tests correlate with a lot of other different measures. The correlations could be based on the actual scores on the test and/or the dichotomous decisions made from the scores. I am inclined to believe these studies would be useful. However, these studies should probably *not* be carried out by the licensure agencies. The reason is that someone may misinterpret the intent of these studies and argue that the agency is using the tests to predict degree of some other variable. Research scholars interested in the relationships between teacher knowledge of basic skills, subject matter, and/or pedagogy, and other variables should be conducting these studies. With years of research and considerable luck we might be able to establish a nomological net among a variety of relevant variables. I would not be inclined to view these studies as telling any more about the validity of the test as a measure of teacher competence than the validity of the measure of the other variable. For example, if a teacher-competency test does not correlate with grades in practice teaching or scores obtained from some teacher-performance scale, that low relationship does not indicate either that the test does not measure competency or that a grade or score on a performance scale does not measure performance. (Recall that performance, according to Medley, depends on teacher competence, the work context, and the teacher's ability to apply his or her competencies at a given point in time.) If I felt some other variable was so logically related to teacher competence that a low measure of relationship was an indicant that one of the measures lacked validity, I might well suspect the other measure. Certainly, on the face of it, one should place as much confidence in an achievement test as a measure of competencies as in a performance scale as a measure of performance.

The point of this brief and very general section on possible further research on the validity issues is that of course we should continue to research how to define and measure teacher competencies and to investigate their correlates. This research will be fraught with difficulties, but potentially valuable to the profession and to the general welfare of the public. While this research is being conducted we should continue to use the best data we have available (which includes test data) to determine who should be licensed.

THE CUT SCORE

The purpose of this section is not to review all the many methods of setting a cut score. They have been reviewed in detail elsewhere (e.g., Berk, 1986; Jaeger, 1986; Livingston & Zieky, 1982). There is considerable debate about what method is "best." In discussing the various drafts of the *Standards*, Linn (1984) stated that while earlier drafts of the *Standards* contained a standard dealing with the cut score of licensure tests eventually "it was concluded that there was not a sufficient degree of consensus on this issue within the area of certification and licensure testing to justify a specific standard on cut scores within this chapter" (p. 12).

Avoiding debates over specific cut score methodologies, there are still some cut scores issues worthy of discussion. They basically center around the issues of supply and demand, the costs of false rejects and false acceptances, and the public perception of cut scores.

Generally, writers in the field of licensure examinations have suggested that supply and demand considerations are not relevant to the cut score decision. There has been particular concern that licensure not be used by those already licensed as a way to regulate supply and thereby economically benefit themselves. Consider the following excerpts:

> Since a major purpose of licensing is to prevent the unqualified from practicing, it follows that licensing should, by definition, be exclusionary: it should exclude from practice those who do not meet a predetermined standard. Those who do meet the standard should be licensed and allowed to practice. But licensing should not be used as a way to regulate the supply of practitioners for the economic benefit of those in a given occupational group. (Shimberg, 1982, p. 35)

> The process of determining a cut score for licensure and certification examinations is different from that in employee and student selec-

4. ASSESSING THE QUALITY

tion. . . . There is not an explicit limit on the number of people that can be considered qualified. Cut scores associated with selection or classification uses of tests, on the other hand, are influenced by supply and demand. . . ." (AERA, APA, NCME, 1985, pp. 63–64)

Except in situations where a licensing board is misusing its licensing powers for monopolistic purposes, there is no fixed number of licenses that may be issued. If all applicants are qualified, all should be licensed. If none are qualified none should be licensed. The fact that no jobs exist should not, in theory, determine the passing rates. (Shimberg, 1984, p. 3)

All of the preceding excerpts state quite firmly that supply and demand are irrelevant. They do not specifically address the issue of the costs of false acceptances and false rejections. Pottinger (1979) addressed that concern as well as several others.

Licenses are often restricted to those whose test scores are higher than minimal levels required for competent performance. This is especially true when cut-off scores are determined by (1) manpower supply and demand in the profession, (2) the desire to minimize false-positive measurement errors, (3) the desire to "upgrade" the profession, or (4) other "arbitrary" decisions about who should be allowed to enter the professions.

Such occurrences discriminate unfairly against those who are competent but are selected out of occupational opportunities by those who believe in the simple equation: Higher test scores mean better job performance. The tacit assumption that superior abilities in all measured skills or characteristics are desirable for performance is highly questionable. (p. 41)

At a theoretical level, there is much in all the preceding excerpts with which to agree. The purpose of a licensure examination is to protect the public from incompetents. It is not, like an employment examination, designed to predict levels of productivity among those who pass the test. Indeed, it has been argued that licensure examinations should not be required to have predictive validity partly because of their purpose and design (and partly because of criterion measurement problems). However, there are degrees of competence or incompetence. There are degrees of danger to the public. Furthermore, tests are never designed perfectly. Many licensure tests, in fact, have many of the same characteristics as employment tests. Schmidt and Hunter (1981) suggested the following about employment tests:

The problem is that there is no real dividing line between the qualified and the unqualified. Employee productivity is on a *continuum* from very high to very low, and the relation between ability test scores and employee job performance and output is almost invariably linear. . . . No matter where it is set, a higher cutoff score will yield more productive employees, and a lower score will yield less productive employees. . . . it means that if the test is valid, all cutoff scores are "valid" by definition. The concept of "validating" a cutoff score on a valid test is therefore not meaningful. (1130)

In theory, employment tests should be positively correlated with the criterion true scores above the cut score and, in theory, licensure tests need not be. However, in actual practice, questions get placed on a licensure test because they are judged to measure important knowledge or skills. Then, some group of people determine that only a certain percent of these need to be answered correctly in order for a person to be licensed. Surely the higher the percent of the items that an individual gets correct, the less danger to the public. Surely, all else being equal, the higher percent of items correct, the more competent the person. In fact, to be totally competent, a person would have to score 100% on a test. Most would agree that competence is a matter of degree rather than kind and there is no single point on the continuum that separates the competent from the incompetent (see Jaeger, 1986, p. 195). Due to the minimum level of many teacher competency tests and the criterion problems, one should not expect to find a great deal of predictive validity with any observed criterion. Nevertheless, logic suggests that knowing more critical skills is better than knowing less; and if one had a measure of the true criterion, one might well expect to find a positive slope for the regression line of true criterion on test score.

Assuming positive slope, a reasonable position to take is that supply and demand, costs of false rejects and false acceptances, and desire to upgrade the profession *should* all be related to the cut-off score. In fact, supply and demand concerns are logically related to costs of false rejects and false acceptances. If a person were quite ill, but no licensed MD were available, that person would probably prefer going to a nonlicensed graduate of a medical college than going to someone with no medical training whatsoever. Particularly if the graduate was a false negative who failed the examination! If there were generally a shortage of doctors, it might make some sense to lower the qualification a bit. If there were generally a surplus, it might make sense to raise the standards.

4. ASSESSING THE QUALITY 121

Whatever the merits of the views just expressed, it is obvious that, in practice, the cut scores on tests for the licensure of teachers have *not* been placed high as a way to regulate the supply of practitioners for the economic benefit of current teachers. In fact, there is evidence to suggest that "qualifying scores may simply represent minimal levels of proficiency that are politically acceptable and that do not threaten to reduce the supply of teachers" (Gifford, 1986, p. 253).

However we currently have a shortage of teachers in some areas and many are predicting a general shortage of teachers in the near future. Some have suggested that teacher-competency exams have exacerbated the problem. Should we lower the cut scores to bring supply and demand into better balance? Some would suggest we should: "Recognition of teacher supply and demand problems is certainly part of the proper exercise of protecting the public. . . . Obviously, having no teacher in a classroom is less preferable than a teacher who has some knowledge" (Boyd & Coody, 1986, Part II, p. 26).

Rebell and Koenigsberg (1986, p. 65) also supported the relevance of supply and demand in setting the cut score and reference two recent court cases where there were rulings specifically citing supply and demand as a consideration in setting a cut score.

Given the already perceived low standards for entering the teaching profession, others would not wish to lower standards to alleviate shortages.

> The standards for entering teachers must be raised. . . . The time-honored response to teacher shortages is to lower standards for entry into the profession. But the only way to make sure the country gets the kind of teachers it needs is to raise them to levels never met before. (Carnegie Task Force, 1986, p. 35)

> If we allow the teacher shortage to become an excuse for staffing classrooms with anything less than the most competent, best trained, and fully certified teachers, public education in the United States could be headed for a real downward spiral. I am purposing, instead, a controversial but educationally honest method of dealing with teacher shortages: leave the classrooms vacant, rather than fill them with lower-quality substitutes (Watts, 1986, p. 723).

Sykes (1986) discussed the tradeoff between standards and amount of services provided as follows:

> For the most part, the elimination of low quality services is reckoned a benefit of standard-setting, but there may be hidden social costs.

Consider, for example, this tradeoff: three persons out of ten have access to high quality service, while the rest receive no service or low quality service: or eight of ten receive middling service. Raising standards to enter professional practice may improve the quality of individual service but reduce access to that service, while excluding lower quality service providers from the market, who might be willing to work in poorly served locales. (pp. 6–7)

There is at least some tentative evidence to suggest that the public does not wish to lower standards in education to relieve shortages. In a Gallup (1986, p. 55) poll the following questions was asked with results as reported:

If your local schools needed teachers in science, math, technical subjects, and vocational subjects, would you favor or oppose those proposals?
Increasing the number of scholarships to college students who agree to enter training programs in these subjects?

Favor	83%
Oppose	11%
Don't Know	6%

Relaxing teacher education and certification plans so more people could qualify to teach these subjects?

Favor	18%
Oppose	74%
Don't Know	8%

Although there is disagreement about the supply/demand issue, it is obvious that the placement of the cut scores *has* been influenced by people's beliefs about the relative costs of false rejects and false acceptances. States, in general, have gone through some procedure (such as Angoff's) to get some judgmental standard regarding what a *minimally* qualified candidate should know in order to be licensed. They have then *reduced* this score by anywhere from one to three standard errors of measurement! For example, Virginia reduced the cut score by "two standard errors below the derived standards in order to minimize the probability of misclassifying an individual as 'incompetent' solely as a result of measurement or sampling error" (Cross, 1984, p. 15). Several states (e.g., Alabama, Mississippi, and Louisiana) have actually set their cut score three standard errors of measurement below the standard obtained from their cut-score study. This means there is a 50% chance of licensing an examinee whose true score is three

4. ASSESSING THE QUALITY   123

standard errors *below* the judged standard, whereas there is less than a probability of 0.0014 that a person whose true score is equal to the standard will not be licensed! Given that a person has repeated opportunities to take the test, there is virtually *no* chance that a person whose true score was above the judged standard would not be licensed. However, after three attempts, 87.5% of those whose true score was three standard errors below the judged standard would pass the test. Obviously, the only legitimate rationale for this approach is that false rejects are considered much more expensive than false acceptances. Neither the public nor I would believe this given a sufficiently large pool of applicants.

The public should rightly be concerned about the profession's apparent concern for false rejects and its lack of concern for false acceptances. We need to consider the purpose behind the movement for teacher competency exams. The public believes that some current teachers are not competent enough. They would like to see procedures implemented to reduce the supply of incompetents. The public is concerned with false positives not false negatives and the purpose of licensure is to protect the public. Would the public be impressed that we have, in several states, intentionally set the cut score three standard errors of measurement *lower* than the standard recommended by a qualified panel of experts? If the general public took our professional exams (the pedagogy exams, not the subject matter exams) would they be impressed at how much we expect our professionals to know? How impressed would they be at the cut scores for those basic skills exams used in some states?

Have measurement experts, who have been advising the policy makers that set the cut scores, made clear the implications of reducing the cut score by some function of the standard error regarding the proportion of false positives and false negatives? If those who have the authority to make the decisions wish to reduce the false-negative error rate to essentially zero and to increase the false-positive error rate, fine. They might, because of their fear of law suits from individuals who fail the tests. Busch and Jaeger (1986) may have been unfortunately correct when they suggested that: It is likely that the courts will view favorably, a standard-setting procedure in which the rights of the individual examinee receive greater deference (p. 17). However, to be faithful to their charge to protect the public the policy makers ought to be more concerned with false positives who teach than with law suits from those who fail. They also should consider "if they are willing to to risk the quality of education and the lawsuits by parents whose children were assigned to teachers scoring 3 standard errors below the minimum standard" (Mehrens, 1986b, p. 10).

Finally, I have a suggestion for those who are concerned that our cut scores are too high. If we consider education a profession, if we believe in standards, have pride, and have a competitive spirit we could try the following. Give the bar examination and the medical-licensure exams to the general public. Determine how many standard deviations the cut score is above the mean performance of the public. Give our pedagogy exams to the public. Set our cut scores the same number of standard deviation units above the public mean as the average that exists for the other two exams. (If we are not competitive, maybe we should set it at the lower of the two.)

In summary, I believe this whole issue of whether cut scores on licensure tests should be influenced by supply/demand, relative costs of misclassifications, and desire to upgrade a profession is deserving of more consideration.

REPORTING RESULTS

Under the section on content validity it was mentioned that one should communicate the domain of the licensure test to the public. If the objectives actually on the test are only a sample of the total set of objectives in the domain, and if one wished to make inferences to the competency of teachers in the total domain, it would impede the accuracy of the inference to communicate the specific objectives sampled by the test. The broader issue of communicating the results of the tests is discussed in this section.

The ETS (1983a) *Standards for Quality and Fairness* state in their Score Interpretation Procedural Guidelines that the testing organization should "provide score interpretation information for all score recipients in terms that are understandable and useful to each category of recipient" (p. 18). As Shannon (1986) suggested, that guideline is somewhat vague. What is meant by "score recipient," "categories," and what criteria should be used to determine what is "useful?" Vorwerk and Gorth (1986) submitted that the examination results should be reported to four parties: individual examinees; the colleges and universities the certification applicants attended; the state which must determine whether certification should be granted; and finally, the public should receive aggregate results.

The categories for the score recipients for licensure tests are "pass" or "fail." However it is generally considered wise to report out using a continuous score scale along with the scaled passing score for failing candidates. Some experts suggest the actual score is not useful for passing candidates (see Shannon, 1986, p. 36). Such scores could lead to inappropriate ranking.

With respect to what is useful information, there is considerable discussion about the necessity or value of reporting subscores. If they are reported, there is considerable discussion about what the format of the subscore reporting should be like.

In general, licensure tests are not primarily designed to be diagnostic. They are designed to categorize individuals into two groups: those sufficiently competent and those not. Because of that, they have been (or should have been) designed to maximize the reliability and interpretability of the total test scores (see Shannon, 1986, p. 7). At the same time, most tests have content outlines that permit the breakdown of the scores into subtest scores. There is a natural press to wish to use subtest results to guide both those who have not passed and wish to retake the test as well as those who have responsibility for the training/education of subsequent candidates. Thus subscores are frequently reported.

Shannon (1986) discussed at length some distinctions between CRTs (he put licensure tests in this category) and diagnostic tests. Although the two types of tests are different he pointed out that CRTs are often used for diagnostic purposes to provide examinees with specific information. He stressed the limitations of this:

> Although CRT subject scores may provide examinees with a general indication of subject matter strengths and weaknesses, they tend to be ineffective at revealing causes underlying failure (e.g., deficiencies in instruction). Subtest scores might indicate which broad skill areas should be emphasized in preparing for retesting but would not indicate specific skill failures or suggest learning strategies. (p. 7)

As Millman (1986, p. 3–38) pointed out, the AERA, APA, NCME (1985) *Standards* do not require subtest score reporting because such subscores are not used in the making the licensure decision. The key Standard is in the chapter on licensure and certification:

> Standard 11.4: Test takers who fail a test should, upon request, be told their score and the minimum score required to pass the test. Test takers should be given information on their performance in parts of the test for which separate scores or reports are produced *and used in the decision process* [italics added]. (AERA, APA, NCME, 1985, p. 65)

If subscores are reported, Standard 2.1 may apply.

Standard 2.1: For each total score, subscore, or combination of scores that is reported, estimates of relevant reliabilities and standard errors of measurement should be provided in adequate detail to enable the test user to judge whether scores are sufficiently accurate *for the intended use of the test* (Primary). [italics added]. (AERA, APA NCME, 1985, p. 20)

Note the emphasis added to the preceding excerpt. It seems possible to argue that the reporting of the subscore reliabilities is not necessary because the intended use of the test is for making licensure decisions. But if that is so, why report the subtest scores in the first place. Is there not an implication that they will be used for something? Probably. Thus, I take the position that if the subscores are reported, their reliabilities ought also to be reported. The danger is that these subscore reliabilities will be smaller than someone's arbitrary cut-off score for reliabilities. One would hope that in any court battles over licensure tests, judges could recognize that a test may have a low subscore reliabilitie and yet be quite useful for its primary purpose—determining the competency of the applicants.

Gifford, (1986, p. 266) takes the strong position that licensing tests should not be used as diagnostic tools because of the low reliability of the subscores. Gabrys (1987), however, suggested that the second goal of teacher competency testing programs "is to provide diagnostic information about candidates' strengths and weaknesses to the candidates and to the teacher training institutions" (p. 85). In actual practice, most states report subscore information to the recipients. The best metric to use for the subscores is beyond the scope of this chapter. See Millman (1986) and Shannon (1986) for some thoughts on that issue.

Although not directly tied to reporting, it should be mentioned that it is fairly common for states to produce support systems including study guides for applicants. See Downs and Silvestro (1987) and Weaver (1986) for brief discussions of such support systems and their effects.

EVIDENCE OF TEST QUALITY

In this chapter I have addressed primarily the issue of validity for licensure tests and have addressed to a lesser degree the issues of reliability and the setting of cut scores. Other issues related to test quality include test administration and scoring procedures, bias considerations, and equating of different forms. These could all be discussed, but the most general conclusion I would draw is that the considerations of such issues for teacher-licensure tests would be the same as for any high-stakes criterion-referenced achievement test.

A final issue to be discussed is the evidence that should exist regarding the quality of the test scores. There should be evidence documenting all stages of test construction, administration, scoring, and reporting. Evidence must be gathered and maintained regarding how the issues of reliability, validity, setting cut scores, equating and determining lack of bias were addressed.

The *Standards* (AERA, APA, NCME, 1985) have a chapter "Test Publication: Technical Manual's and User's Guides" which contains 11 standards. The index to the *Standards* references other standards that pertain to publishers' materials. The background section of the chapter makes the following relevant points: "Publishers should provide enough information for a qualified user or a reviewer of a test to evaluate the appropriateness and technical adequacy of the test. Even when a test (or test battery) is developed for use within a single organization, a brief manual will be useful" (p. 35).

There has not been total agreement either about the degree of detail that should be in a manual or about the kinds of statements that a publisher should be able to document. In the Alabama lawsuit the documentation issue received consideration attention. Plaintiffs' experts argued for the necessity for very complete documentation, whereas Defendant's experts, though obviously not opposed to documentation, felt that a rule of reason should apply. As was stated in the *Defendant's Post-Trial Memorandum:* "Regardless of how much documentation one created or maintained, a reviewer could always find something that was not documented; again a "rule of reason" applies" (Boyd & Coody, 1986, p. 70).

One possible rule of reason is to use what commercial publishers do. Hall (1985) reviewed the technical data of 37 published achievement tests. He reported that only 54% provided information on the manner in which they selected their test items, only 46% reported item discrimination information, 49% item difficulty, 32% logical techniques for race bias, and 11% empirical techniques for race bias. For the criterion-referenced tests within the sample the percentages were even lower. For example while 89% of the norm-referenced tests provided reliability data, only 11% of the criterion-referenced tests reported such information.

However, what has been done is not the same as what should be done. It is obvious that many publishers are less diligent than they should be. Because critics will want to audit the test construction process for high stakes tests such as licensure tests, the publishers would be wise to be particularly diligent in the accuracy and thoroughness of their documentation. Manuals should be quite complete and records should exist to verify the information in the manuals. However, again we should apply a rule of reason. For example, in Texas approximately 200 educators in each of 63 different fields were involved in the job analysis survey. Would it be reasonable to keep the original approximately 12,600 response sheets for years after they had been scored and recorded on computer tapes? A publisher building a variety of tests for a number of different agencies would soon need an exorbitant amount of storage space. Of course some records need to be maintained. For example, it would seem necessary to retain the examination answer sheets for at least some period of time (perhaps 1 year) to allow for verification by those who may wish to challenge the accuracy of the scoring process. To many experts it would seem sufficient to have the item ratings from individuals on validity panels recorded on computer tape. However, others believe the original rating sheets should be maintained.

Most argue that a *detailed* resume on each person on a validity panel need not be placed in a formal report, or even necessarily kept on file. Of course their *names* should be available so that someone who wishes can check their qualifications. Indeed there should be some sort of summary statement about the training, the experience and the qualification of the panel members. But there is room for disagreement among experts about the extent of the documentation required and, as mentioned, publishers would be wise to be diligent. However, it is *not* logical to infer that a test produces scores with low validity because of a lack of documentation. Documentation of the test construction process, per se, does not influence the scores or their validity. The correct inference from inadequate documentation is simply that there is inadequate documentation not that the test scores are invalid.

CONCLUSION

In the past our colleges and state licensing boards have failed as adequate gatekeepers to the teaching profession. Consequently, almost all states have implemented some sort of competency assessment of teachers. In this chapter I have discussed the issues of reliability, validity, setting the cut score, reporting scores, and the necessity to provide documented evidence of test quality.

Even if we have top notch tests of competence and set the "correct" cut score we need to recognize the limitations of the inferences we can make from licensure tests. Such tests do not address the issues of overall teacher performance or teacher effectiveness. A high quality teacher-licensure test will not eliminate the need for subsequent teacher evaluation; it will not cure all educational ills; it will not eliminate all ineffective teachers nor (because of false positives) even all incompetent teachers. It should help ensure that those individuals who are licensed have a minimal level of competence on some important subdomains of knowledge and skills relevant to their profession. That is a step in the right direction.

REFERENCES

American Educational Research Association, American Psychological Association, & National Council on Measurement. (1985). *Standards for educational and psychological testing.* Washington, DC: American Psychological Association.

Alabama State Board of Education. (1980, January 8). *Minutes.* Montgomery, AL. Author.

American Psychological Association. (1980). *Principles for the validation and use of personnel selection procedures.* Washington, DC: Author.

Ayres, Q. W. (1983). Student achievement at predominantly white and predominantly black universities. *American Educational Research Journal, 20*(2), 291–304.

Berk, R. A. (1984a). Selecting the index of reliability. In R. A. Berk (Ed.), *A guide to criterion-referenced test construction* (pp. 199–230). Baltimore: Johns Hopkins University Press.

Berk, R. A. (1984b). Conducting the item analysis. In R. A. Berk (Ed.), *A guide to criterion-referenced test construction* (pp. 97–143). Baltimore: Johns Hopkins University Press.

Berk, R. A. (1986). A consumer's guide to setting performance standards on criterion-referenced tests. *Review of Educational Research, 56*(1), 137–172.

Berliner, D. C. (1986, April). *In pursuit of the expert pedagogue.* Presidential Address of the 1986 Annual Meeting of the American Educational Research Association. San Francisco, CA.

Bloom, B. S., Madaus, G. F., & Hastings, J. T. (1981). *Evaluation to improve learning.* New York: McGraw-Hill.

Bond, L. (1987). The Golden Rule Settlement: A minority perspective. *Educational Measurement: Issues and Practice. 6*(2), 18–20.

Boyd, D. R., & Coody, C. S. (1986). *Defendant's post-trial memorandum.* Margaret T. Allen et al. and Board of Trustees for Alabama State University and Eria P. Smith v. Alabama State Board of Education et al., Civil Action No. 81-697-N.

Brennan, R. L. (1984). Estimating the dependability of the scores. In R. A. Berk

(Ed.). *A guide to criterion-referenced test construction.* (pp. 292–334). Baltimore: Johns Hopkins University Press.

Brennan, R. L., & Kane, M. T. (1977). An index of dependability for mastery tests. *Journal of Educational Measurement, 14,* 277–289.

Burns, R. L. (1985). Guidelines for developing and using licensure tests. In J. C. Fortune & Associates (Eds.), *Understanding testing in occupational licensing* (pp. 15–44). San Francisco: Jossey–Bass.

Cameron, D. (1985). The NEA position on testing in-service teachers. *Educational measurement: Issues and practice, 4*(3), 26–27.

Carlson, H. S. (1978). The AASPB Story: The beginnings and first 16 years of the American Association of State Psychology Boards, 1961–1977. *American Psychologist, 33*(5), 486–495.

Carlson, R. E. (1985). *The impact on preparation institutions of competency tests for educators.* Presented as part of a symposium entitled: The assessment boomerang returns: Competency tests for educators. American Educational Research Association, Chicago, IL.

Carnegie Task Force. (1986). *A nation prepared: Teachers for the 21st century.* The report of the task force on teaching as a profession. Carnegie Forum on Education and the Economy. New York: Carnegie Corporation.

Coleman, J. S. et al. (1966). *Equality of educational opportunity.* Washington, DC: U.S. Department of Health, Education and Welfare, Office of Education.

Colton, D., Kane, M., Kingsbury, C., & Estes, C. (1987, April). *Examining the construct validity of job analysis data: A strategy and an example.* Paper presented at the Annual Meeting of the American Educational Research Association, Washington, DC.

Cronbach, L. J. (1963). Course improvement through evaluation. *Teacher's college record, 64,* 672–683.

Cronbach, L. J. (1970). *Essentials of psychological testing* (3rd ed.). New York: Harper & Row.

Cronbach, L. J. (1980). Validity on parole: How can we go straight? In W. B. Schrader (Ed.), *Measuring achievement: Progress over a decade. New Directions for testing and measurement, Vol. 5* (pp. 99–108). San Francisco: Josey–Bass.

Cross, L. H. (1984). *Validation study of the National Teacher Examinations for certification of entry-level teachers in the Commonwealth of Virginia.* Paper presented at the annual meeting of the American Educational Research Association and the National Council on Measurement in Education, New Orleans, LA.

Darling-Hammond, L., Wise, A. E., & Pease, S. R. (1983). Teacher evaluation in the organizational context: A review of the literature. *Review of Educational Research, 53*(3), 285–328.

D'Costa, A. G. (1985). *Documenting the job-relevance of certification and licensure examinations using job analysis.* Paper presented at the annual meeting of The American Educational Research Association, Chicago, IL.

Debra, P. v. Turlington. (1981). 644 F. 2d 397, 5th Cir.

Downs, S. L., & Silvestro, J. R. (1987, April). *Support systems for teacher certification testing programs.* Paper presented at the annual meeting of the American Educational Research Association. Washington, DC.

Ebel, R. L. (1961). Must all tests be valid? *American Psychologist, 16,* 640–647.

Ebel, R. L. (1974). And still the dryads linger. *American Psychologist, 29*(7), 485–492.

Ebel, R. L. (1975). The use of tests in educational licensing, employment, and promotion. *Education and Urban Society, 8*(1), 19–32.

Ebel, R. L. (1977). Comments on some problems of employment testing. *Personnel Psychology, 30,* 55–63.
Ebel, R. L. (1979). *Essentials of Educational Measurement* (3rd ed.). Englewood Cliffs, NJ: Prentice Hall.
Echternacht, G. (1985). *Report of a study of selected NTE tests for the State of Maryland.* Princeton, NJ: Educational Testing Service.
Educational Testing Service. (1983a). *Educational Testing Service Standards for Quality and Fairness.* Princeton, NJ: Educational Testing Service.
Educational Testing Service. (1983b). *NTE programs: Guidelines for proper use of NTE tests.* Princeton, NJ: Author.
Eisdorfer, S., & Tractenberg, P. (1977). The role of the courts and teacher certification. In W. R. Hazard, L. D. Freeman, S. Eisdorfer, & P. Tractenberg (Eds.), *Legal Issues in teacher preparation and certification* (pp. 109–150). Washington, DC: ERIC Clearinghouse on Teacher Education.
Ekstrom, R. B., & Goertz, M. E. (1985, April). *The teacher supply pipeline: The view from four states.* Paper presented at the annual meeting of the American Educational Research Association, Chicago, IL.
Elliot, S. M. (1987, April). *Validating job analysis survey instruments used in developing teacher certification tests: A construct validity study.* Paper presented at the annual meeting of the National Council of Measurement in Education. Washington, DC.
Elliot, S. M., & Nelson, J. (1984). *Blueprinting teacher licensing tests: Developing domain specifications from job analysis results.* Paper presented at the annual meeting of the National Council on Measurement in Education, New Orleans, LA.
Equal Employment Opportunity Commission, Civil Service Commission, Department of Labor and Department of Justice. (1978, August 25). Uniform guidelines on employee selection procedures. *Federal Register, 43*(166), 38290–38315.
Feldt, L. S., Steffen, M., & Gupta, N. C. (1985). A comparison of five methods for estimating the standard error of measurement at specific score levels. *Applied Psychological Measurement, 9,* 351–361.
Freeman, L. D. (1977). State interest, certification, and teacher education program approval. In W. A. Hazard, L. D. Freeman, S. Eisdorfer, & P. Tractenberg (Eds.), *Legal issues in teacher preparation and certification* (pp. 67–108). Washington, DC: ERIC Clearinghouse on Teacher Education.
Gabrys, R. E. (1987). State reaction to national teacher testing and certification issues. In National Evaluation Systems, Inc. (Ed.). *Trends in teacher certification testing* (pp. 25–29). Amherst, MA: National Evaluation Systems.
Galambos, E. C. (1984). *Testing teachers for certification and recertification.* Paper presented at a Hearing of the National Commission on Excellence in Teacher Education, Atlanta, GA.
Gallup, G. H. (1984). The 16th Annual Gallup Poll of the public's attitudes toward the public schools. *Phi Delta Kappan, 66*(1), 23–38.
Gallup, G. H. (1986). The 18th Annual Gallup Poll of the public's attitudes toward the public schools. *Phi Delta Kappan, 68*(1), 43–59.
Gifford, B. R. (1986). Excellence and equity in teacher competency testing: Policy perspective. *The Journal of Negro Education, 55*(3), 251–271.
Glass, G. V. (1978). Standards and criteria. *Journal of Educational Measurement, 15,* 237–261.
Gronlund, N. E. (1985). *Measurement and evaluation in teaching* (5th ed.). New York: Macmillan.

Guion, R. M. (1977). Content validity, the source of my discontent. *Applied Psychological Measurement, 1*, 1–10.

Haertel, E. (1987, April). *Structuring item domains to map the school curriculum.* Paper presented at the annual meeting of the American Educational Research Association, Washington, DC.

Hall, B. W. (1985). Survey of the technical characteristics of published educational achievement tests. *Educational Measurement: Issues and Practice, 4*(1), 6–14.

Hambleton, R. K. (1984). Validating the test scores. In R. A. Berk, (Ed.), *A guide to criterion-referenced test construction* (pp. 199–230). Baltimore: Johns Hopkins University Press.

Hambleton, R. K., & Novick, M. R. (1973). Toward an integration of theory and method for criterion-referenced tests. *Journal of Educational Measurement, 10,* 159–170.

Hecht, K. A. (1979). Current status and methodological problems of validating professional licensing and certification. In M. A. Bunda & J. R. Sanders (Eds.), *Practices & problems in competency-based measurement* (pp. 16–27). Washington, DC: National Council on Measurement in Education.

Hilldrup, R. P. (1978, April). What are you doing about your illiterate teachers? *The American School Board Journal,* pp. 27–28.

Hills, J. R. (1981). *Measurement and evaluation in the classroom* (2nd ed.). Columbus, OH: Merrill.

Holmes Group, The (1986). *Tomorrow's teachers: A report on the Holmes Group.* The Holmes Group. East Lansing, MI.

Hopkins, K. D., & Stanley, J. C. (1981). *Educational and psychological measurement and evaluation* (6th ed.). Englewood Cliffs, NJ: Prentice Hall.

Jaeger, R. M. (1986). Policy issues in standard setting for professional licensing tests. In W. P. Gorth & M. L. Chernoff (Eds.), *Testing for teacher certification* (pp. 185–199). Hillsdale, NJ: Lawrence Erlbaum Associates.

Johnson, S. T., & Prom-Jackson, S. (1986). The memorable teacher: Implications for teacher selection. *The Journal of Negro Education, 55*(3), 272–283.

Kane, M. T. (1982). A sampling model for validity. *Applied Psychological Measurement, 6*(2), 125–160.

Kane, M. T. (1984). *Strategies in validating licensure examinations.* Paper presented at the annual meeting of the American Educational Research Association, New Orleans, LA.

Kane, M. T., Kingsbury, C., Colton, D., & Estes, C. (1986). *A study of nursing practice and role delineation and job analysis of entry-level performance of registered nurses.* Chicago, IL: National Council of State Boards of Nursing.

Levine, E. L., Ash, R. A., Hall, H. L., & Sistrunck, F. (1981). *Evaluation of seven job analysis methods by experienced job analysts.* Unpublished manuscript. University of South Florida.

Linn, R. L. (1984). *Standards for validity in licensure testing.* Paper presented at the "Validity in Licensure Testing" symposium at the annual meeting of the American Educational Research Association, New Orleans, LA.

Linn, R. L., & Miller, M. D. (1986). Review of test validation procedures and results. In M. Jaeger & J. C. Busch, (Eds.), *An evaluation of the Georgia Teacher Certification testing program* (Chap. 4). Greensboro, NC: Center for Educational Research and Evaluation. University of North Carolina.

Livingston, S. A. (1972). Criterion-referenced applications of classical test theory. *Journal of Educational Measurement, 9,* 13–26.

Livingston, S. A., & Zieky, M. J. (1982). *Passing scores: A manual for setting stan-*

dards of performance on educational and occupational tests. Princeton, NJ: Educational Testing Service.
McPhee, S. A., & Kerr, M. E. (1985). Scholastic aptitude and achievement as predictors of performance on competency tests. *Journal of Educational Research, 78* (3), 186–190.
Medley, D. M. (1982). *Teacher competency testing and the teacher educator.* Charlottesville, VA: Association of Teacher Educators and the Bureau of Educational Research, University of Virginia.
Mehrens, W. A. (1986a). *Validity issues in teacher competency tests.* Gainesville, FL: University of Florida, Institute for Student Assessment and Evaluation.
Mehrens, W. A. (1986b). Measurement specialists: Motive to achieve or motive to avoid failure? *Educational Measurement: Issues and Practice, 5*(4), 5–10.
Mehrens, W. A. (1987a). *Issues in teacher competency tests.* Prepared for the Commission on Testing and Public Policy Graduate School of Education, University of California, Berkeley.
Mehrens, W. A. (1987b). Validity issues in teacher competency tests. *Journal of Personnel Evaluation in Education, 1,* 195–229.
Mehrens, W. A., & Lehmann, I. J. (1984). *Measurement and evaluation in education and psychology* (3rd ed.). New York: Holt, Rinehart, & Winston.
Mehrens, W. A., & Lehmann, I. J. (1987). *Using standardized tests in education* (4th ed.). New York: Longman.
Messick, S. A. (1975). The standard problem: Meaning and values in measurement and evaluation. *American Psychologist, 30,* 955–966.
Millman, J. (1979). Reliability and validity of criterion-referenced test scores. In R. E. Traub (Ed.), *New directions for testing and measurement:* (No. 4): *Methodological developments* (pp. 75–92). San Francisco, CA: Jossey-Bass.
Millman, J. (1986). Review of test development and score reporting procedures. In R. M. Jaeger & J. C. Busch (Principal Investigators). *An evaluation of the Georgia Teacher Certification Testing Program* (Chap. 3). Greensboro, NC: Center for Educational Research and Evaluation, University of North Carolina at Greensboro.
Nassif, P. M. (1978). *Standard-setting for criterion-referenced teacher licensing tests.* Paper presented at the annual meeting of the National Council on Measurement in Education, Toronto, Canada.
National Evaluation Systems. (n.d.). *Study Guide: Examination for the certification of educators in Texas.* Amherst, MA: Author.
Nitko, A. J. (1983). *Educational tests and measurement.* New York: Harcourt Brace Jovanovich.
Pecheone, R. L., Tomala, G., & Forgione, P. D., Jr. (1986). Building a competency test for prospective teachers. In W. P. Gorth & M. L. Chernoff (Eds.), *Testing for teacher certification* (pp. 99–113). Hillsdale, NJ: Lawrence Erlbaum Associates.
Peterson, K. D. (1987). Teacher evaluation with multiple and variable lines of evidence. *American Educational Research Journal, 24*(2), 311–318.
Piper, M. K., & O'Sullivan, P. S. (1981). The National Teacher Examination: Can it predict classroom performance? *Phi Delta Kappan, 62*(5), 401.
Popham, W. J. (1984). Specifying the domain of content or behaviors. In R. A. Berk (Ed.), *A guide to criterion-referenced test construction* (pp. 29–48). Baltimore: Johns Hopkins University Press.
Pottinger, P. S. (1979). Competence testing as a basis for licensing: Problems and prospects. In M. A. Bunda & J. R. Sanders (Eds.), *Practices and problems in competency-based education* (pp. 28–46). Washington, DC: National Council on Measurement in Education.

Pratt, D. (1977). Predicting teacher survival. *The Journal of Educational Research, 71*(1), 12–18.
Rebell, M. A. (1986). Disparate impact of the teacher competency testing on minorities: Don't blame the test-takers—or the tests. *Yala Law & Policy Review, 4,* 2, 372–403.
Rebell, M. A., & Koenigsberg, R. G. (1986). *Post-trial memorandum of law on behalf of amicus curiae National Evaluation System, Inc.* Margaret T. Allen, et al. and Board of Trustees for Alabama State University and Erica P. Smith v. Alabama State Board of Education et al. Civil Action No. 81-697-N.
Roid, G. H. (1984). Generating the test items. In R. A. Berk (Ed.), *A guide to criterion-referenced test construction* (pp. 49–77). Baltimore: Johns Hopkins University Press.
Rosen, G. A. (1986, August). *A perspective on predictive validity and licensure examination.* Paper presented at the 94th annual convention of the American Psychological Association, Washington, DC.
Rosenfeld, M., Shimberg, B., & Thornton, R. F. (1983). *Job analysis of licensed psychologists in the United States and Canada.* Princeton, NJ: Center for Occupational and Professional Assessment, Educational Testing Service.
Rosenfeld, M., Thornton, R. F., & Skurnik, L. S. (1986, March). *Analysis of the professional function of teachers: Relationships between job functions and the NTE Core Battery* (Research Report 86–8). Princeton, NJ: Educational Testing Service.
Roth, R. (1984). *Validation study of the National Teacher Examinations for certification in the State of Arkansas.* Paper presented at the annual meeting of the American Educational Research Association and the National Council on Measurement in Education, New Orleans, LA.
Rovinelli, R. J., & Hambleton, R. K. (1977). On the use of content specialists in the assessment of criterion-referenced test item validity. *Dutch Journal of Educational Research, 2,* 49–60.
Rulon, P. J. (1946). On the validity of educational tests. *Harvard Educational Review. 16*(4), 290–296.
Sax, G. (1980). *Principles of educational and psychological measurement and evaluation* (2nd ed.). Belmont, CA: Wadsworth.
Schmeiser, C. B. (1987, April). *Effects of translating task analysis data into test specifications.* Paper presented at the annual meeting of the National Council on Measurement in Education. Washington, DC.
Schmidt, F. L., & Hunter, J. E. (1981). Employment testing: Old theories and new research findings. *American Psychologist, 36*(10), 1128–1137.
Scriven, M. (1979). *Recommendations for modification in external assessment process.* State of California: Commission on Teacher Preparation and Licensing.
Shanker, A. (1985). A national teacher examination. *Educational Measurement: Issues and practice, 4*(3), 28–31.
Shannon, G. A. (1986, April). *Usefulness of score interpretive information for examinees who fail criterion-referenced tests.* Paper presented at the Annual Meeting of the American Educational Research Association, San Francisco.
Shepard, L. A., & Kreitzer, A. E. (1987, April). *The Texas teacher test.* Paper presented at the annual meeting of the American Educational Research Association, Washington, DC.
Shimberg, B. (1982). *Occupational licensing: A public perspective.* Princeton, NJ: Educational Testing Service.

Shimberg, B. (1984). The relationship among accreditation, certification and licensure. *Federation Bulletin, 71*(4), 99–116.
Shimberg, B. (1985). Overview of professional and occupational licensing. In J. C. Fortune & Associates (Eds.), *Understanding testing in occupational licensing* (pp. 1–14). San Francisco: Jossey–Bass.
Shulman, L. S. (1986). Those who understand: Knowledge growth in teaching. *Educational Researcher, 15*(2), 4–14.
Shulman, L. S. (n.d.). *Knowledge and teaching: Foundations of the new reform.* Paper prepared for the Task Force on Teaching as a Profession. Carnegie Forum on Education and the Economy, New York.
Stark, J. S., & Lowther, M. A. (1984). Predictors of teachers' preferences concerning their evaluation. *Educational Administration Quarterly, 20*(4), 76–106.
Subkoviak, M. J. (1984). Estimating the reliability of mastery-nonmasterly classifications. In R. A. Berk (Ed.), *A guide to criterion-referenced test construction* (pp. 267–291). Baltimore: Johns Hopkins University Press.
Sweeney, J., & Manatt, R. P. (1986). Teacher evaluation. In R. A. Berk (Ed.), *Performance assessment: Methods and applications* (pp. 446–468). Baltimore: Johns Hopkins University Press.
Sykes, G. (1986). *The social consequences of standard-setting in the professions.* Paper prepared for the Task Force on Teaching as a Profession, Carnegie Forum on Education and Economy, New York.
Tenopyr, M. L. (1977). Content-construct confusion. *Personnel Psychology, 30,* 47–54.
Time. (1980, June 16). Help! Teachers can't teach. *Time Magazine,* pp. 54–63.
Tittle, C. K. (1982). Use of judgmental methods in item bias studies. In R. A. Berk (Ed.), *Handbook of methods for detecting test bias* (pp. 31–63). Baltimore: Johns Hopkins University Press.
Traub, R. E. (1986). Review of test reliability assessment procedures and results. In R. M. Jaeger & J. C. Busch (Eds.), *An evaluation of the Georgia Teacher Certification testing program* (Chap. 5). Greensboro, NC: Center for Educational Research and Evaluation, University of North Carolina.
U.S. Civil Service Commission. (1973). *Job Analysis: Key to better management.* Washington, DC: Superintendent of Documents, U. S. Government Printing Office.
U.S. Department of Health, Education and Welfare. (1971). *Report on licensure and related health personnel credentialing.* PHEW publication 72-11. Washington, DC: Author.
USES. (1983). *Overview of validity generalization for the U.S. Employment Service* (USES Test Research Report No. 43). Division of counseling and test development employment and training administration. U.S. Department of Labor, Washington, DC.
Vertiz, V. C. (1985). Legal issues in licensing. In J. C. Fortune & Associates (Eds.), *Understanding testing in occupational licensing* (pp. 87–106). San Francisco: Jossey–Bass.
Vold, D. J. (1985). The roots of teacher testing in America. *Educational Measurement: Issues and Practice, 4*(3), 5–6.
Vorwerk, K. E., & Gorth, W. P. (1986). Common themes in teacher certification testing program development and implementation. In W. P. Gorth & M. L. Chernoff (Eds.), *Testing for teacher certification* (pp. 35–43). Hillsdale, NJ: Lawrence Erlbaum Associates.

Watts, G. D. (1986). And let the air out of the volleyballs. *Phi Delta Kappan, 67*(10), 723–724.

Weaver, J. R. (1986). Study guides and their effect on programs. In W. P. Gorth & M. L. Chernoff (Eds.), *Testing for teacher certification* (pp. 235–251). Hillsdale, NJ: Lawrence Erlbaum Associates.

Webb, L. D. (1983). Teacher evaluation. In S. B. Thomas, N. H. Cambron-McGabe, & M. M. McCarthy (Eds.), *Educators and the law* (pp. 69–80). Elmont, NY: Institute for School Law and Finance.

Webster, W. J. (1984). *Five years of teacher testing: A retrospective analysis.* Paper presented at the annual meeting of the American Educational Research Association, New Orleans, LA.

Werner, E. (1982). *What a licensing board member needs to know about testing.* Paper given at the annual conference on The Clearinghouse on Licensure, Enforcement and Regulation, The Council of State Governments, Chicago, IL.

Willimason, J. W. (1979). Improving content validity of certification procedures by defining competence in specialty practice: Directions, resources, and getting started. In *Definitions of competence in specialties of medicine, conference proceedings* (pp. 61–86). Chicago: American Board of Medical Specialties.

Wood, B. D. (1940). Making use of the objective examination as a phase of teacher selection. *Harvard Educational Review, 10,* 277–282.

Yalow, E. S., & Collins, J. L. (1985). *Meeting the challenge of content validity.* Presented as part of a symposium session "The assessment boomerang returns: Competency tests for Educatory" at the annual meeting of the American Educational Research Association, Chicago, IL.

Yalow, E. S., & Popham, W. J. (1983). Content validity at the crossroads. *Educational Researcher, 12*(8), 10–14, 21.

5

Teacher Evaluation in the Organizational Context

Linda Darling-Hammond
RAND Corporation

Personnel evaluation in an organization provides a powerful metaphor for what is valued in the organization, how roles are construed, and which goals have *de facto* priority in the management of organizational affairs. The importance attached to this function says much about the organization's relationship to its clients, as well as the relationships among organizational members. The same can be said about the importance of evaluation in an occupation whose members share a common service mission. Indeed, evaluation plays a particularly critical role in an occupation that claims to be a profession. This chapter explores the role of teacher evaluation in school organizations and in the teaching profession. It examines how organizational norms, conceptions of teaching, and management strategies influence the design and outcomes of evaluation, and how evaluation practices, in turn, shape the life of the organization and the nature of the teaching occupation.

Teacher evaluation can be a routine, pro forma activity with little utility for shaping what goes on in schools, or it can be an important vehicle for communicating organizational and professional norms and for stimulating improvement. This chapter starts from the proposition that the outcomes of evaluation often depend as much on the conditions under which it is designed and implemented as on the formal design as it exists on paper. Evaluation processes, their outcomes and effects, are a function of many different technical, organizational, and political factors that interact in important ways.

Technical aspects of evaluation include (a) methods, instrumentation, and sources of evidence; (b) the training and expertise of evaluators; and (c) structural features of the evaluation process, such as who evaluates, when and how often, how data are combined and aggregated, what purposes evaluation is intended to serve, how judgments are communicated, and what follow-up is planned. A fair amount of research attention and practitioner energies is devoted to designing singular technical features of evaluation. Less attention has been paid to the combined outcomes of their interaction as a total system of evaluation. Each of these factors is shaped, in turn, by organizational conditions and constraints.

Organizational factors influencing evaluation include school or school-district goals and perceived problems (these may drive the evaluation process or, if they do not, they may contribute to the perception that evaluation is not an important activity to invest in); resources such as time, personnel, and expertise for evaluation; collective bargaining and legal requirements; and structural features of the organization, such as the degree of centralization of school functions, specialization of tasks, and the size and mode of bureaucratic organization. Evaluation practices that are highly successful in some organizations may be absolutely unmanageable in others, unless substantial changes to the organizational environment are made.

Compatibility considerations arise where technical and organizational factors meet. The extent to which an organization's purposes will be achieved by the evaluation processes chosen depends on the degree to which particular methods and instruments provide reliable and valid data *for the primary purpose(s)* for which they are used; the degree to which the process as implemented is sufficiently timely, credible, and efficient to provide usable information; and the degree to which the process supports organizational norms and conceptions of good teaching.

Increasingly, all of these factors are influenced by outside forces in the political system. State policy initiatives, especially, frame not only the goals and procedures for teacher evaluation but also the goals of schooling and the means by which schools organize themselves to perform their mission. As decisions about who will teach and how they will do so are made by state policymakers, a number of evaluation dilemmas have emerged: How do conceptions of good teaching embodied in state certification and teacher education policies match those held by local school districts and professional organizations? How compatible are state- or locally-developed teacher-evaluation practices with conceptions of teaching embodied in curricular, testing, and school management policies? Can a coherent view of teacher knowledge, roles, and teaching functions be forged from the currently disparate views reflected in the plethora of state, local, and professional initiatives intended to shape the act of teaching and its assessment?

The answers to these questions will determine both the shape of teacher evaluation and the nature of teaching as an activity, a job, and an occupation for many years to come.

THE ROLE OF EVALUATION IN AN ORGANIZATION AND A PROFESSION

Evaluation is not only influenced by organizational considerations, it also shapes the organizational context and the conditions of teaching work. Whether intentionally or not, a teacher-evaluation system represents the incentive structure and mode of accountability implicitly adopted by an organization. It communicates conceptions of teaching and expectations regarding performance priorities, norms for behavior, and the nature of the work itself. If a heavy investment is made in applying the key organizational resources of time and expertise to evaluation functions, evaluation communicates that teaching is important to the organizational mission. When this does not occur, the evaluation process communicates an alternate message—that what teachers do is not critical to the functioning of the organization.

Depending on how an evaluation process is designed, and how well it is implemented, it can guide professional and personal development, and influence motivation. If designed appropriately and implemented with sufficient attention, evaluation can provide data for personnel decision making, thus shaping the composition of the teaching force. These functions of evaluation are more likely to occur if evaluation is a "high stakes" activity; that is, one that is used for decision making by the teacher, the evaluator(s), and/or the organization. This is not so much a matter of intent as it is of actual implementation. Usable evaluation is not achieved by exhortation. As we discuss below, an evaluation process must be credible, appropriate for its purposes, and doable within time, personnel, and budget constraints if its results are, in fact, to be used.

In the past, teacher evaluation has generally not been a high stakes activity, in part because improving the quality of teachers has not been seen as key to improving the quality of education. Instead, school-improvement efforts over the past several decades have focused on improving the curriculum, altering school management methods, and developing new programs. Thus, teacher evaluation, where practiced, was largely a routine, paper exercise to which few resources and little organizational attention were devoted. As a consequence it has often had little influence on decisions about personnel, staff development, or the structure of teaching. As more attention is being devoted to evaluation, and as its results are used for a greater range of decisions, its role in shaping teaching will increase. Educators must, therefore, worry more now than in the past about *how* evaluation affects teaching performance, rather than whether it will.

In particular, the increased importance of evaluation holds promise and potential difficulties for the professionalization of teaching. Careful selection and evaluation of practitioners are fundamental to any occupation that seeks to become a profession. The bargain that professions make with society is that only qualified and trustworthy individuals will be admitted and supported in the occupation in return for the monopoly that the public grants over services and the right to hold title to membership in the profession (Sechrest & Hoffman, 1982). Thus, professions invest heavily in the training, licensure, selection, and induction of their members through mechanisms like selective admissions to professional schools, intensively supervised internships and residency programs, professional certification examinations, and ongoing peer review of practice (Darling-Hammond, 1986).

The decision to invest heavily in the competence and expertise of practitioners is due to several factors that characterize professions:

1. Because the clients of the work do not present uniform, routine needs and problems, professionals must be able to use good judgment in applying specialized knowledge in nonstandardized ways.

2. Because of their special relationship to clients—the fact that they possess knowledge and authority that the client does not possess and which they are expected to use in the client's best in-

terest—professionals must adhere to both technical and ethical standards of appropriate practice.

3. Because professionals practice autonomously, the public must rely on the practitioners' internalization of the necessary knowledge, judgment, skill, and code of ethics rather than on inspection systems. This internalization of professional norms and standards of practice is accomplished by the many evaluation mechanisms adopted by professions for defining, transmitting, and enforcing such standards.

In one sense, greater attention to evaluation functions in schools suggests a more professional conception of teaching: a conception in which the need for practitioner competence is recognized, as opposed to one in which teaching work is viewed as the routine implementation of curricula and procedures designed by others. On the other hand, heightened implementation of evaluation conceived as inspection of the performance of routines can contribute to a view of teaching as a rote exercise, divorced from considerations of students needs or teaching knowledge.

The role of evaluation in schools and in the teaching profession is currently being reshaped in important ways. This reshaping is a result of the increased focus on teachers in the policy environment, by the increased sophistication of basic and applied research on teaching and teacher evaluation, and by the willingness of practitioners to engage many of the difficult issues which evaluation poses. These influences on evaluation practice, however, do not always operate compatibly with one another. Indeed, they very often embody entirely different notions of what teaching requires and, hence, what "good" teaching means.

CONCEPTIONS OF TEACHING WORK

Evaluation involves collecting and using information to judge the worth of something. It is an activity that teachers themselves engage in, though often informally (Shavelson, 1973). Different conceptions of teaching work imply different ways by which information is collected and judgments of worth are made. Implied in these different conceptions of teaching work are different notions of educational goals, teacher knowledge and activities, teaching behavior, and self- or other evaluation activities.

Teachers have been compared to craftspersons and professionals (Broudy, 1956; Lortie, 1975), bureaucrats (Wise, 1979), managers (Berliner, 1982), laborers (Mitchell & Kerchner, 1983), and artists (Eisner, 1978). Here we use four ways of looking at teaching work: labor, craft, profession, or art (Mitchell & Kerchner, 1983). These ways of viewing teaching work sharply reveal the assumptions that lie behind different techniques for evaluating teachers. Every technique implicitly rests on assumptions about what teaching is and, hence, what the relation of the teacher to the administrative structure of the school ought to be.

Every teacher-evaluation system must embody a definition of the teaching task and a mechanism to evaluate the teacher. Under the conception of teaching as *labor*, teaching activities are "rationally planned, programmatically organized, and routinized in the form of standard operating procedures" by administrators (Mitchell & Kerchner, 1983, p. 35). The teacher is responsible for implementing the instructional program in the prescribed manner and for adhering to the specified routines and procedures. The evaluation system involves direct inspection of the teachers' work—monitoring lesson plans, classroom performance, and performance results; the school administrator is seen as the teachers' *supervisor*. This view of teaching work assumes that effective practices can be determined and specified in concrete ways, and that adherence to these practices will be sufficient to produce the desired results.

Under the conception of teaching as *craft*, teaching is seen as requiring a repertoire of specialized techniques. Knowledge of these techniques also includes knowledge of generalized rules for their application. In this conception, once the teaching assignment has been made, the teacher is expected to carry it out without detailed instructions or close supervision. Evaluation is indirect and involves ascertaining that the teacher has the requisite skills. The school administrator is seen as a *manager* whose job it is to hold teachers to general performance standards. This view of teaching work assumes that general rules for applying specific techniques can be developed, and that proper use of the rules combined with knowledge of the techniques will produce the desired outcomes.

Under the conception of teaching as *profession*, teaching is seen as not only requiring a repertoire of specialized techniques but also as requiring the exercise of judgment about when those techniques should be applied (Shavelson & Dempsey-Atwood, 1976; Shavelson & Stern, 1981). To exercise sound professional judgment, the teacher is expected to master a body of theoretical knowledge as well as a range of techniques. Broudy (1956) made the distinction between craft and profession in this way: "We ask the professional to diagnose difficulties, appraise solutions, and to choose among them. We ask him to take total responsibility for both strategy and tactics. . . . From the craftsman, by contrast, we expect a standard diagnosis, correct performance of procedures, and nothing else" (p. 182). Standards for evaluating professionals are developed by peers, and evaluation focuses on the degree to which teachers are competent at professional problem solving; the school administrator is seen as an *administrator* whose task it is to ensure that teachers have the resources necessary to carry out their work. This view of teaching work assumes that standards of professional knowledge and practice can be developed and assessed, and that their enforcement will ensure competent teaching.

Under the conception of teaching as *art*, teaching techniques and their application may be novel, unconventional, or unpredictable. This is not to say that techniques or standards of practice are ignored, but that their form and use are personalized rather than standardized. As Gage (1978) explained, the teaching art involves "a process that calls for intuition, creativity, improvisation, and expressiveness—a process that leaves room for departures from what is implied by rules, formulas, and algorithms" (p. 15). He argued that teaching *uses* science but cannot itself *be* a science because the teaching environment is not predictable. In this view, the teacher must draw upon not only a body of professional knowledge and skill, but also a set of personal resources that are uniquely defined and expressed by the personality of the teacher and his or her individual and collective interactions with students.

Because teaching viewed as an art encompasses elements of personal insight (as well as theoretically grounded professional insight), the teacher as artist is expected to exercise considerable autonomy in the performance of his or her work. Evaluation involves both self-assessment and critical assessment by others. Such evaluation entails "the study of holistic qualities rather than analytically derived quantities, the use of 'inside' rather than externally objective points of view" (Gage, 1978, p. 15). It relies on high-inference rather than low-inference measures, on observation of patterns of events rather than counts of specific, discrete behaviors (Eisner, 1978; Gage, 1978). In this view, the school administrator is seen as a *leader* whose work is to encourage the teacher's efforts. The view assumes that teaching *patterns* (i.e., holistic qualities that pervade a teacher's approach) can be recognized and assessed by using both internal and external referents of validity.

Obviously, these four conceptions of teaching work are ideal types that will not be found in pure form in the real world. In fact, various components of teachers' work embody different ideal types (e.g., motivating students, performing hall duty, presenting factual information, establishing and maintaining classroom relationships). Nonetheless, the conceptions of teaching work signal different definitions of success in a teacher-evaluation system.

CONCEPTIONS OF TEACHING IN TEACHING RESEARCH

Although the various conceptions of teaching work are distinct along several dimensions, they can be usefully viewed on a continuum that incorporates increasing ambiguity or complexity in the performance of teaching tasks as one moves from labor at one extreme to art at the other. The role of the teaching environment in determining teacher behavior also increases in importance as one moves along the continuum. The more variable or unpredictable one views the teaching environment as being, the more one is impelled toward a conception of teaching as a profession or art. Gage (1978) used the distinction between teaching as science or art to describe how the elements of predictability and environmental control differentiate the two. A science of teaching is unattainable, he observed, because it "implies that good teaching will some day be attainable by closely following rigorous laws that yield high predictability and control" (p. 17). Using science to achieve practical ends, he argued, requires artistry—the use of judgment, intuition, and insight in handling the unpredicted, knowledge of when to apply which laws and generalizations and when not to, and the ability to make clinical assessments of how multiple variables affect the solution to a problem.

Research on teaching parallels these conceptions of teaching work in the degree to which predictability and environmental controls are assumed or even considered in the design and goals of the research. Some efforts to link specific teacher characteristics or teaching behaviors to student outcomes have sought context-free generalizations about what leads to or constitutes effective teaching. Although this line of research strongly suggests that what teachers do in the classroom does affect students, claims that discrete sets of behaviors consistently lead to increased student performance (e.g., Medley, 1979; Rosenshine & Furst, 1971; Stallings, 1977) have been countered by contradictory findings that undermine faith in the outcomes of simple process-product research (e.g., Doyle, 1978; Dunkin & Biddle, 1974; Shavelson & Dempsey-Atwood, 1976). The most extensive process-product study of teacher effectiveness, the Beginning Teacher Evaluation Study, conducted for California's Commission for Teacher Preparation and Licensing, contributed to the discomforts associated with linking context-free teacher behaviors to student learning. After that monumental effort, "[t]he researchers . . . concluded that linking precise and specific teacher behavior to precise and specific learning of pupils (the original goal of the inquiry) is not possible at this time. . . . These findings suggest that the legal requirement for a license probably cannot be well stated in precise behavioral terms" (Bush, 1979, p. 15; see also McDonald & Elias, 1976).

Some researchers have addressed the problem of inconsistent research findings by reference to interaction effects and attention to other situation-specific variables. This line of research finds that effective teaching behaviors vary for students of different socioeconomic, mental, and psychological characteristics (e.g., Brophy & Evertson, 1974; 1977; Cronbach & Snow, 1977; Peterson, 1976), and for different grade levels and subject areas (Gage, 1978; McDonald & Elias, 1976). Nonetheless, given the particular teaching context, many infer from this research that appropriate behaviors can be specified to increase student achievement.

Problems have been identified even with this more limited approach to linking teaching behaviors with student outcomes. Interaction effects that may be identified from teaching research are not confined to easily translatable two- or even three-way interactions. Thus, their generalizability for establishing rules of practice is severely constrained (Cronbach, 1975; Knapp, 1982; Shavelson, 1973).

A related finding is that teaching behaviors that have sometimes been found to be effective often bear a distinctly curvilinear relation to achievement. A behavior that is effective when used in moderation can produce significant and negative results when used too much (Peterson & Kauchak, 1982; Soar, 1972) or when applied in the wrong circumstances (e.g., Coker, Medley, & Soar, 1980; McDonald & Elias, 1976). This kind of finding also makes it difficult to develop rules for teaching behaviors that can be applied generally.

As the various lines of research on teacher effectiveness ascribe different degrees of generalizability to effective teaching behaviors and different weights to context-specific variables, they embody different conceptions of teaching work. The more complex and variable the educational environment is seen as being, the more one must rely on teacher judgment or insight to guide the activities of classroom life, and the less one relies on generalized rules for teacher behavior.

The conversion of teacher effects research findings to rules for teacher behavior is a cornerstone of many performance-based teacher evaluation models. These models implicitly assume that the rules are generalized because student outcomes are determined primarily by particular uniform teaching behaviors. By implication, the models assume either that other contextual influences on student outcomes are relatively unimportant, or that these other influences do not call for different teaching behaviors for teaching to be effective. Research on nonteaching variables in the educational environment indicates that many factors other than teaching behaviors have profound effects on student learning (Anderson, 1982; Centra & Potter, 1980; McKenna, 1981), and that effective teaching must be responsive to a number of student, classroom, and school variables in ways that preclude the application of predetermined approaches to teaching (Joyce & Weil, 1972).

Researchers who adopt an ecological perspective for investigating teaching also point out that reciprocal causality, particularly with respect to teacher and student behaviors, limits the applicability of process-product research findings (Doyle, 1979). Research grounded in this perspective finds that what students do affects teachers' behaviors and that the complexity of classroom life calls for teaching strategies responsive to environmental demands. As Doyle (1979) noted,

> Traditionally, research on teaching has been viewed as a process of isolating a set of effective teaching practices to be used by individual teachers to improve student learning or by policy makers to design teacher education and teacher evaluation programs. The emphasis in this tradition has been on predicting which methods or teacher behaviors have the highest general success rate, and much of the controversy over the productivity of research on teaching has centered on the legitimacy of propositions derived from available studies. . . . [The ecological approach] would seem to call into question the very possibility of achieving a substantial number of highly generalizable statements about teaching effectiveness. (pp. 203–204)

Research on the stability and generalizability of measures of teaching behaviors lends support to a context-specific view of teaching. Stability refers to the extent that a teacher's behavior as measured at one point in time correlates with measures taken at another point in time. Generalizability refers to the extent that such measures are stable across different teaching situations (e.g., different subject areas, grade levels, student ability levels, etc.). The bottom-line question is, Does a given teacher exhibit the same kinds of behavior at different points in time and within different teaching contexts? In general, the answer is "no," especially with regard to low inference measures of specific, discrete teaching behaviors (Shavelson & Dempsey-Atwood, 1976).[1] Although this finding may be due to poor measurement instruments, it may also be due to the fact that teachers adjust their behaviors to the changing needs of the teaching context.

We see the manifestations of these different points of view in teacher evaluation systems that are based on divergent premises. On one hand, many states are considering or beginning to implement systems of competency-based certification or recertification and performance-based evaluation (Vlaanderen, 1980). These systems often assume the validity, stability, and generalizability of a uniform set of effective teaching behaviors. On the other hand, teacher evaluation systems that rely heavily on approaches like clinical supervision, self-assessment, and interactive evaluation processes have been developed on the premise that situation-specific elements and teacher intentionality must play a role in assessing teacher performance.

These different approaches to teacher evaluation are currently on a collision course, as evaluation has increasingly become the subject of state and local policy making. These policies and their spinoffs—collective bargaining agreements and court decisions—themselves embody notions of teaching that are frequently incompatible with other evaluation goals and with the demands of teaching work.

THE POLICY CONTEXT

The public has come to believe that the key to educational improvement lies as much in upgrading the quality of teachers as in changing school structure or curriculum. Foreshadowing the reforms of the 1980s, the most frequent response to the 1979 Gallup poll's question on what public schools could do to earn an "A"

---

[1]However, high-inference, global ratings that rely on patterns of overall teacher behavior are somewhat more stable than other measures (Shavelson & Dempsey-Atwood, 1976).

grade was improving teacher quality, beating by large margins such reforms as emphasizing the basics, improving school management, lowering class size, or updating the curriculum (Gallup, 1979). Importantly, those other approaches to reform, which often hypothesized a teacher-proof road to educational improvement, had characterized state legislative initiatives throughout the 1970s (Darling-Hammond & Wise, 1981). In response to these new perceptions about the importance of teacher quality, states and local school districts have initiated a wide range of policy changes affecting the certification, evaluation, and tenure of both prospective and currently employed teachers (Darling-Hammond & Berry, 1988).

At least 46 states have adopted teacher competency tests, such as the National Teacher Examinations, as a prerequisite for teacher certification; 25 have required tests for admission to teacher education programs. Most states have replaced lifetime teaching certificates with requirements for continuing licensure. Some have adopted comprehensive programs that include higher admission standards for colleges of education, competency tests for certification and recertification, evaluation of performance, and continuing teacher education (Kleine & Wisniewski, 1981).

Most states have legislated requirements for teacher performance evaluation (Beckham, 1981), and some of the more recent statutes specify which testing instruments or evaluation procedures are acceptable. Increasingly popular are state-mandated beginning teacher programs that prescribe the entire supervision and evaluation process for 1rst-year teachers, including the frequency and nature of evaluation, the sources of data, rating instruments, and the number and type of evaluators. As a licensing activity, these beginning teacher programs are presumably distinct from evaluation for employment decisions; however, they are inextricably entangled with local district procedures for assessing teaching performance (Wise & Darling-Hammond, 1987). Many states have also mandated the use of these or other procedures for merit pay or career-ladder placement determinations.

Clearly, the development of teacher-evaluation practices in local school districts does not occur in a vacuum. State policies often define some of the key features of evaluation; other state and local policies regarding teachers and teaching define the nature of teaching desired, and the means by which it is sought. These include everything from the job roles and tasks assigned to teachers to teacher selection and assignment policies to instructional management systems.

Not surprisingly, teacher-evaluation processes increasingly have become the subject of collective bargaining agreements. A RAND Corporation study found that between 1970 and 1975, the percentage of contracts examined that contained teacher-evaluation provisions increased from 42 to 65 (McDonnell & Pascal, 1979). This proportion has doubtless increased substantially since then. Contracts often specify methods of information gathering, frequency of observations and evaluation, processes for communicating evaluation criteria and results, opportunities for teacher response and remediation in the case of negative evaluations, and due process procedures (Strike & Bull, 1981).

Mitchell and Kerchner (1983) argued that because of collective bargaining, teacher evaluation has become an increasingly rule-based process, linked less to judgments of competence than to evidence about whether teachers have adhered to clearly specified minimum work standards. "The objectification of evaluation standards," they stated, "has had the effect of discoupling the relationship between teaching performance and the behaviors on which teachers are held subject to discipline and discharge" (pp. 19–20). Their observation suggests the difficulty in developing a single teacher-evaluation process that can be used for both formative (improvement-oriented) and summative (personnel decision making) purposes.

Although a survey by the American Association of School Administrators (Lewis, 1982) found that few school districts were using evaluation results as the basis for layoff decisions, there is a growing literature on the legal requirements for using evaluation results for dismissal (Beckham, 1981; Peterson & Kauchak, 1982; Strike & Bull, 1981). Courts have generally required that a school system strictly apply an established formal dismissal procedure with due process safeguards. Further, school authorities must determine minimum acceptable teaching standards in advance, inform the staff of these standards, and, finally, document for the court how a teacher's performance violates these standards (Beckham, 1981). Beckham recommended that to withstand judicial scrutiny an evaluation policy must include: (a) a predetermined standard of teacher knowledge, competencies, and skills; (b) an evaluation system capable of detecting and preventing teacher incompetencies; and (c) a system for informing teachers of the required standards and according them an opportunity to correct teaching deficiencies.

Each of these criteria poses some problems for the design and implementation of a teacher-evaluation system. There are particular difficulties in integrating the requirements of an evaluation policy geared toward job-status decisions with those of a policy aimed at improving teaching. The most obvious problem is that developing a predetermined standard of teacher knowledge, competencies, or skills poses nontrivial controversies about the content, specificity, and applicability of the standards for particular teachers and teaching contexts.

This tension between evaluation goals is in part a reflection of the differences among evaluation constituencies. These stakeholders have divergent views of the primary purpose of teacher evaluation and, hence, of what constitutes a successful evaluation system. Knapp's (1982) articulation of various stakeholders' perspectives is useful. Teachers have a stake in maintaining their jobs, their self-respect, and their sense of efficacy. They want a teacher-evaluation system that encourages self-improvement, appreciates the complexity of their work, and protects their rights. Principals have a stake in maintaining stability in their organizations, allowing them to respond to parental and bureaucratic concerns for accountability while keeping staff morale intact. They want an evaluation system that is objective, not overly time consuming, and feasible in the organizational context. Parents and public officials have a stake in the "bottom-line"—the effects of teaching on student outcomes. They want an evaluation system that relates teacher performance to teacher effectiveness, and that guarantees appropriate treatment of children in classrooms.

These differing priorities make choices about teacher evaluation processes difficult. Processes that seek to attend to the complexities of teaching may be viewed as overly time consuming and practically unmanageable in organizational terms. Processes that seek to maintain school stability may be viewed as inadequate guarantors of appropriate treatment for students. Differing priorities also affect implementation, because even after a policy is adopted, its terms and emphases are renegotiated at every level in the implementation system (Berman & McLaughlin, 1973–1978; Elmore, 1979). This renegotiation may not occur in a formal way, but practices at the school district, school, and classroom levels will be a function of cross-pressures that may alter the formal process in important ways.

All of these factors argue for understanding teacher-evaluation plans in the context of organizational policies and practices. The succeeding sections of this chapter examine evaluation purposes, processes, and methods, and discuss how they shape the implementation and outcomes of evaluation.

PURPOSES FOR TEACHER EVALUATION

As indicated in Table 5.1, teacher evaluation may serve four basic purposes. The table's cells artificially represent these purposes and levels of decision making as distinct. In fact, teacher evaluation may be directed at small or large groups of teachers (rather than simply individuals or whole schools), and may represent hybrid improvement and accountability concerns (as when promotion decisions are linked to improvement efforts).

Many teacher-evaluation systems are nominally intended to accomplish all four of these purposes, but different processes and methods are better suited to one or another of these objectives. In particular, improvement and accountability goals may require different standards of adequacy and of evidence. Focusing on individual or organizational concerns also leads to different processes, for example, bottom-up or top-down approaches to change, unstandardized or standardized remedies for problems identified. Berliner and Fenstermacher illuminated these differences with respect to staff development (the table's improvement dimension), although their observations are applicable to accountability purposes as well. Their definition of staff development encompasses four scales along which approaches may differ:

> Staff development activities may be [a] internally proposed or externally imposed, in order to [b] effect compliance, remediate deficiencies, or enrich the knowledge and skills of [c] individual teachers or groups of teachers, who [d] may or may not have a choice to participate in the activities. (Fenstermacher & Berliner, 1983, p. 5)

They noted that as more differentiation occurs between participant roles and organizational levels, the profile of a staff development activity tends to shift from internal to external initiation, from an enrichment to a compliance focus, from participation by individuals or small groups to standardized programs for large

TABLE 5.1
Four Basic Purposes of Teacher Evaluation

Purpose/Level	Individual	Organizational
Improvement (formative information)	Individual staff development	School improvement
Accountability (summative information)	Individual personnel (job status) decisions	School status (e.g., certification) decisions

groups, and from voluntary to involuntary participation. As the profile of a staff development activity shifts, so does its usefulness for a variety of purposes.

Staff development may be a vehicle for training teachers as technicians to implement policies devised by someone else (Floden & Feiman, 1981). Teacher evaluation in this case would focus on how faithfully the prescribed procedures or curricula are adhered to. This approach is most useful for organizational accountability purposes. Alternatively, staff development may be viewed as a means for helping teachers move from the acquisition of particular skills to applications of their judgment in order for them to play an analytic role in developing curricula and methods. Or staff development may be designed to help the teacher move to higher developmental stages in order to enable him or her to develop multiple perspectives about teaching and learning, to become more flexible, adaptive, and creative (Floden & Feiman, 1981). Teacher evaluation in these cases would focus on teachers' personal stages of development and would be most suited for individual improvement purposes.

Many observers have pointed out that public pressures for summative evaluation affecting teacher job status—selection and promotion, dismissal, and reduction in force decisions—may make formative evaluation much more difficult (Feldvebel, 1980; Knapp, 1982; Peterson & Kauchak, 1982). Increasing the prescriptiveness and specificity of evaluation procedures, particularly the need for extensive documentation of all negative findings in case a termination decision eventually is sought, generates anxiety among teachers and inhibits the principal's role as instructional leader or staff developer (Munnelly, 1979). Summative evaluation criteria must be narrowly defined if they are to be applied uniformly, thus limiting their use for formative purposes. Furthermore, constraints on classroom behavior intended to weed out incompetent teachers may prevent good teachers from exercising their talents fully (Darling-Hammond & Wise, 1981). Knapp (1982) concluded

> The net result of these pressures for more careful summative judgments of teachers is to put administrators under particular strain. Though "better" performance evaluation may appear to make the issues explicit and decisions objective, it may also generate as much heat as light, particularly where the various constituents to the design of evaluation do not agree. The pressure to improve teaching performance may foster more elaborate evaluation systems, but with summative thrusts getting in the way of formative efforts. (p. 10)

In general, teacher-evaluation processes most suited to accountability purposes must be capable of yielding fairly objective, standardized, and externally defensible information about teacher performance. Evaluation processes useful for improvement objectives must yield rich, descriptive information that illuminates sources of difficulty as well as viable courses for change. Teacher evaluation methods designed to inform organizational decisions must be hierarchically administered and controlled to ensure credibility and uniformity. Evaluation methods designed to engender support for individual or school-based change must consider the context within which performance occurs to diagnose reasonable and sensible courses of action.

Thus, a district that is most concerned with identifying incompetent teachers will require an evaluation process that features uniformly applicable criteria that can be applied in a highly specified and reliable manner, with careful attention to the procedural aspects that would be raised in a dismissal proceeding. A district that is most concerned with the professional development of individual teachers will require a more flexible process that features personal goal-setting and planning by the teacher, with individual progress rather than a standard outcome the referent for a judgment of success. The former would not be highly useful for individual improvement goals; the latter would be useless for termination decisions. Both approaches might, however, operate in an overall evaluation *system* that carefully targets specific processes to the purposes they are intended to serve.

Although these purposes and the approaches most compatible with them are not necessarily mutually exclusive, an emphasis on one may tend to limit the pursuit of another if the differential utility of each is not understood and explicitly addressed. Similarly, although multiple methods for evaluating teachers can be used—and many argue, should be used—it is important to consider what purposes are best served by each if teacher evaluation goals and processes are to be consonant. Furthermore, some processes are distinctly inconsistent with others and with some purposes for evaluation. These disjunctures should be recognized before a teacher evaluation system is adopted and put in place.

Recently, there has been a growing recognition of the fact that, as the contexts and purposes for teacher evaluation differ, so should the processes adopted. The most obvious case is the evaluation of beginning teachers. Many states and school districts have altered their traditional evaluation processes by (a) increasing the frequency of evaluation and feedback, (b) defining "beginning" teaching skills to be assessed, and (c) frequently increasing the time and specialized expertise available for evaluation by assigning expert veteran teachers, or mentors, the task of helping and assessing novices. By focusing evaluation resources in a systematic fashion at the beginning of a teacher's career, districts can enhance the probability that beginning teachers will learn to teach competently, avoid the need for band-aid approaches to staff development later on, and allow evaluation of veteran teachers to focus more on individual development than on inspections of basic competence.

In addition, districts that have been able to use evaluation effectively in reaching employment termination decisions have generally created specially designed processes for this purpose (Wise, Darling-Hammond, McLaughlin, & Bernstein, 1984). In these districts, identification of a teacher having serious difficulty triggers a process in which intensive assistance is offered by an expert consulting teacher, and a formal remediation process—usually overseen by a committee of teachers and administrators—is pursued. This process attends to the teacher's due process protections, to the nature of assistance needed, and to the fair application of uniform criteria before determining whether the teacher has improved sufficiently to be retained. Joint management–labor cooperation characterizes the design and implementation of these approaches. As a consequence, districts that have used this type of process have successfully terminated the employment of poorly performing teachers (usually about half of those initially identified for remediation assistance) without long and costly battles over the fair application of due process procedures. Such a process brings the necessary resources, credibility, and objectivity to bear on a personnel decision to make the outcome defensible and, ultimately, useful to both the teacher and the organization.

As discussed in the following section, matching process to purpose can increase the reliability, validity, and utility of evaluation so that organizational benefits are more likely to accrue.

TEACHER-EVALUATION PROCESSES AND METHODS

There have been several recent reviews of teacher-evaluation processes in which the authors identified from 6 to 12 general approaches to teacher evaluation (Ellett, Capie, & Johnson, 1980; Haefele, 1980; Lewis, 1982; Millman, 1981; Peterson & Kauchak,

1982). The reviews reveal that the approaches used to evaluate teachers seek to measure very different aspects of teaching and the teacher. The different approaches rely on different conceptions of what demonstrates adequacy and on diverse notions of how to recognize or measure adequacy. Some seek to assess the quality of the *teacher* (teacher competence); others seek to assess the quality of *teaching* (teacher performance). Other approaches seek to assess the teacher or his or her teaching by reference to student outcomes (teacher effectiveness). Medley (1982) offered useful definitions of four terms often treated as synonyms:

- *Teacher competency* refers to any single knowledge, skill, or professional value position, the possession of which is believed to be relevant to the successful practice of teaching. Competencies refer to specific things that teachers know, do, or believe but not to the effects of these attributes on others.
- *Teacher performance* refers to what the teacher *does* on the job rather than to what she or he *can* do (that is, how competent she or he is). Teacher performance is specific to the job situation; it depends on the competence of the teacher, the context in which the teacher works, and the teacher's ability to apply his or her competencies at any given point in time.
- *Teacher effectiveness* refers to the effect that the teacher's performance has on pupils. Teacher effectiveness depends not only on competence and performance, but also on the responses pupils make. Just as competence cannot predict performance under different situations, teacher performance cannot predict outcomes under different situations.

It is generally most important to seek to assess teacher competence directly when job-specific measures of actual performance or effectiveness are not available or appropriate for the evaluation purpose. Thus, measures that seek to assess the readiness of prospective teachers or their suitability for licensure must generally rely on assessments of what teachers know, believe, or can do in limited settings, such as paper-and-pencil tests or simulated teaching situations. Professional certifying exams also seek to assess competence, although the certification process in many professions may also incorporate testaments to performance in residency or apprenticeship programs. Because performance is affected by many variables other than competence, though—aspects of the work environment, motivation, and commitment, for example—

certification procedures and the kinds of tests used for other assessments of competence do not promise to predict performance in a particular job setting.

Most on-the-job teacher-evaluation systems seek to measure performance, generally with reference to behavioral indicators of what the teacher actually does in specified performance situations. Performance indicators are generally the basis for making job status decisions: whether a teacher should be retained or granted tenure, for example. Although performance indicators may also be used to stimulate individual improvement, they can rarely do so without reference to effects. A teacher is unlikely to be motivated to do more of X or less of Y if there is not some reason to believe that his or her effectiveness will improve as a result. Although organizational accountability purposes may be at least nominally served by ensuring that all teachers perform in certain ways (e.g., set objectives, cover the curriculum), neither organizational nor individual improvement goals are served by assessing performance in isolation from its causes and its effects.

This is one of the critical problems with some of the most widely adopted forms of teacher evaluation in current use. Most rely on behavioral indicators of performance to assess teaching, without reference to the appropriateness or effects of the teaching behaviors being measured. Recent efforts to make these assessments "evaluator-proof," particularly in many state-mandated systems, further weaken the link between performance and effectiveness by making the goal of evaluation the tallying of behaviors and the goal of teaching the performance of these behaviors, whether or not they improve student learning (Wise & Darling-Hammond, 1987).

A concern for the effects of teaching on students need not, indeed should not, imply a narrow construction of means–ends criteria in which specific practices are justified only by their links to specific, limited outcomes. Instead, concerns for the effects of teaching on students—their intellectual success and progress, motivation and confidence as learners, attitudes toward school and learning, and growth as responsible human beings—should encourage teachers and evaluators to consider the implications for student lives and learning of teaching decisions, heightening rather than obscuring attention to questions of goals and trade-offs, differing student needs, and the reciprocal nature of teaching. Ultimately, it is only in the examination of how classroom practices affect students that good teaching can be defined.

The tools and processes that are used to assess teacher competence, performance, or effectiveness are based on assumptions about how these qualities are linked to one another, how they may be measured, and how the measurements may be used to make decisions. Indeed as one moves along the continuum from novice teacher to expert teacher, the emphasis in evaluation ought to shift from concerns about basic competence to concerns about performance capabilities and, ultimately, effectiveness. The capacity of an evaluation process to address these concerns will depend upon organizational resources and goals as they are made manifest through several technical aspects of the evaluation process: the expertise of the evaluator(s), the format of the evaluation, and the application of evaluation criteria.

Evaluator Expertise

If we conceive of teaching proficiency as ranging from inadequate at one extreme to excellent at the other, we can see how the demands of evaluation differ for purposes of basic gatekeeping versus identifying "master teachers" and for goals of organizational monitoring versus organizational improvement.

Minimal adequacy demands at least a working knowledge of subject matter and the ability to perform basic teaching activities. In many schools, the minimum requirement for acceptable teaching is the ability to run a nondisruptive classroom. Low-inference measures are sufficient (and in some ways may be deemed preferable) for judging minimal adequacy; that is, does the teacher plan? set objectives? teach to the objectives? establish and enforce rules for student behavior? A modestly skilled observer can ascertain the answers to these questions in a few relatively brief visits.

Beyond minimal adequacy lie increasing degrees of proficiency. A teacher must not only have mastered subject matter and a repertoire of teaching techniques, but also must make appropriate judgments about when those techniques should be applied. Beyond the ability to make appropriate teaching decisions are the abilities to diagnose unusually difficult learning problems, to effectively address the needs of a wide range of students, and to inspire unusually creative or analytic thinking by students. High-inference measures that incorporate notions of effect—or at least knowledge of likely effectiveness—are necessary for judging relative degrees of greater proficiency; that is, *how well* does a teacher plan, within and across lessons, to impart the structure of knowledge in the discipline, to account for the student's levels of development and prior learning, and to achieve the immediate and long-range goals of instruction? A highly-expert evaluator, skilled in the subject area and pedagogical matters and familiar with the classroom context, is needed to ascertain the answers to these questions.

The Format of Evaluation

Assessment of relative proficiency, beyond judgments of basic adequacy, must take into account both context and effects; hence, it cannot be conducted solely on the basis of a few discrete classroom observations. The format of evaluation must reach beyond observed teaching behaviors on a given day or days. In part, this is because measures of specific teaching behaviors have low generalizability; that is, a given teacher does not exhibit the same kinds of behavior at different points in time and within different teaching contexts (Shavelson & Dempsey-Atwood, 1976). Teaching acts, such as instructional format, pacing, and choice of activities, vary with elements of the teaching context such as subject matter, type of student, instructional goals, and stage of development of a unit or course (Stodolsky, 1984). A teacher's relative proficiency in designing appropriate instruction for very different situations cannot be captured in a few observations.

There are other limitations to classroom observation as an assessment method. Classroom observations reveal little about the coherence of the curriculum, the depth and breadth of content covered, the range of teaching techniques used, the quality and variety of materials employed, the types and frequency of students assignments, the quality of instruments (tests, papers, projects) used for student assessment, the kinds of feedback students receive on their work, or the appropriateness of any of these things for individual students and for the classroom context as a whole. These important aspects of teaching cannot be assessed well without other sources of information beyond classroom observation. A longitudinal assessment of teacher plans, classroom activities, and student performances and products is needed to judge relative competence beyond what might be deemed as minimally adequate.

Evaluation Criteria

Criteria and indicators for making judgments of minimal adequacy must be standardized, generalizable, and uniformly applied. Finer distinctions among good, better, and outstanding teachers require nonstandardized applications of criteria that allow for differential indicators. Teaching research has demonstrated that effective teaching behaviors vary for different grade levels, subject areas, types of students, and instructional goals. Thus, assessments of relative teaching proficiency that seek to assess effectiveness cannot be made on the basis of uniform, highly specific behavioral indicators. A single set of broad criteria may be adopted, but their operational indicators must become differentiated for specific applications. This requires both criteria that can be made context sensitive and the insight of a highly expert evaluator.

Evaluation for improvement, if it is to meet the needs of all teachers, must be flexible, for, like individualized instruction, it must take all teachers where they are and help them improve. It must encourage teachers to develop. Criteria must be broad enough and rating scales must have sufficient range to accommodate all.

To be helpful to the teacher, the evaluation process must take into account the specific teaching context. The outcome of the process is advice to the teacher. It is not important—indeed, it is not necessary, possible, or realistic—for school administrators to expect to be able to compare teachers under this type of evaluation. The flexibility needed to provide useful personalized advice to a teacher precludes comparisons or rankings of teachers. If the purpose were narrowed to helping only those who are judged to need it, the process would begin to acquire some of the characteristics associated with other purposes that, because they compare teachers, require a higher order of reliability and a different kind of validity.

Evaluation for the possible termination of employment has different requirements. The criteria and the ratings must be designed to allow decisions about minimally acceptable teaching behaviors. The evaluation task is to distinguish competent from incompetent teachers. The basis for this distinction must be clear. Hence, the school district must specify the criteria, behavioral bases for ratings, and procedures. The bureaucratic demand is for a common scale on which all teachers may theoretically be compared, but the real need is for a list of teaching behaviors that all teachers except the incompetent will exhibit. In practice, this means that judgments typically rest on assessment of generic teaching skills.

The use of generic teaching skills as the basis for evaluation implies that the evaluator need not know much about the subject matter and grade-level pedagogical demands. Thus, a generalist principal can evaluate all teachers under his or her jurisdiction. Presumptive fairness means that the principal can observe all teachers for relatively short periods of time, noting that most teachers have the minimal skills but that the incompetent do not. Having made this determination, the principal (or district administration) may then concentrate evaluation resources on those who may be judged incompetent.

To spend substantial evaluation resources on all teachers in this approach would be wasteful because, by virtue of the focus on minimum skills (skills that, by definition, most teachers have), the process is irrelevant to the needs of most teachers. The school district can concentrate evaluation resources on helping the probationary teacher master the minimum skills or, if this help fails, on making the final judgment of incompetence. It can offer personalized assistance using context-specific applications of the teaching criteria for improvement or remediation. The final determination of incompetence, however, must be seen as reliable. The teacher must be judged by standardized indicators. Multiple samples of the teacher's behavior must be taken. In sum, the judgment must be reliable enough to stand up in a court of law, where a termination decision might be appealed.

Improvement and termination pose different evaluation demands. They require trade-offs between breadth and depth of coverage and between standardized and context-specific notions of acceptable, good, and better teaching. The failure to clarify the purpose or to match the process to the purpose may undo the effectiveness of a teacher-evaluation system.

Considerations in Designing Teacher-Evaluation Systems

School district administrators and state officials do not always consider what their evaluation goals and options are when they adopt a new process. Quite often they focus on the search for an instrument without much thought to the context and means by which it will be used. In broad terms, a number of features of evaluation are constant across most school districts: (a) generally, a single process is intended to serve all purposes—including personnel decision making for both retention and recognition purposes as well as individual and collective improvement goals; (b) criteria are remarkably similar—including teaching procedures, classroom management, knowledge of subject matter, personal characteristics, and professional responsibility—and are operationalized and weighted in the same way for all teachers; (c) the process adopted generally relies on a preevaluation conference, one or more classroom observations, and a postevaluation conference; (d) the principal is the primary, and often the sole evaluator; (e) the outcome is a rating of the teacher, usually on a 3- or 5-point scale (Wise, Darling-Hammond, McLaughlin, & Bernstein, 1984).

As the preceding discussion indicates, these common features of evaluation may limit its utility in accomplishing some goals. Indeed, school districts have common complaints about their evaluation processes. In a RAND survey of school districts about their evaluation processes, almost all respondents cited the same problem areas: that principals lacked sufficient resolve and competence to evaluate accurately—especially in the case of secondary teachers and other teaching specialists; that teachers were resistant or apathetic; that consistency across the school system in the application of evaluation criteria was difficult to achieve; and that evaluators had insufficient training. The problems of how to appropriately differentiate evaluation criteria, tasks, and functions, how to apply sufficient time and expertise to the process, and how to engender teacher cooperation and support are issues that greatly affect the implementation and outcomes of evaluation activities.

Quite often school districts take as given that any evaluation method can be made to suit any purpose, that school principals will "find" time for whatever evaluation requirements are enacted, that all evaluators will be equally competent, that the nature and level of evaluation needs will not vary from teacher to teacher or from school to school, and that the results of evaluation will be used. These assumptions fly in the face of organizational realities and threaten the reliability, validity, and utility of evaluation. These threats in turn lessen the credibility of evaluation, making the activity susceptible to shirking, avoidance, pro forma compliance, and dissension, sometimes more damaging than helpful to teaching, teacher morale, and the organizational cohesion necessary for improvement.

In particular, an inability to target evaluation resources where they are most needed or to differentiate processes for teachers at different career stages and levels of competence creates enormous inefficiencies and engenders large political costs with low levels of benefit to the organization. Consider, for example, that school principals—who have from 20 to 100 teachers to supervise—cannot provide substantial attention to anyone's needs if they are required to evaluate every teacher in precisely the same way each year. Furthermore, experienced and inexperienced teachers are not evenly distributed across schools, nor are incompetent and highly competent teachers. Some schools, due to teacher turnover and seniority transfer policies, have large numbers of both new and marginally competent teachers who require intensive evaluation assistance. These are generally, as well, the schools which pose the most challenging educational problems (Wise, Darling-Hammond, & Berry, 1987). Thus, the places in need of the most evaluation resources have—if the principal's time is the only resource—the least available, once it is divided among a larger number of pressing needs.

Once evaluation requirements exceed the capacity of the evaluator resources available to meet them, the utility of the process is greatly diminished because insufficient attention means that efforts at improvement are too perfunctory to be effective, and attempts at dismissal are too poorly documented and managed to stand up to scrutiny.

A RAND study of effective teacher evaluation processes identified four elements in the design of such systems that contribute greatly to the resolution of typical evaluation problems: (a) organizational commitment, (b) attention to evaluator competence, (c) collaboration in development and implementation, and (d) strategic compatibility (Wise, Darling-Hammond, McLaughlin, & Bernstein, 1984).

Organizational Commitment. Personnel evaluation discomforts any organization. It contains the potential for misunderstanding, miscommunication, and anxiety on the part of both evaluators and those whom they evaluate. Well-conducted evaluation, however, offers the opportunity to improve organizational morale and effectiveness. It can foster concrete understanding of organizational goals and regularize communication among school personnel about the actual teaching work of the organization. It can also deliver the message that the organization needs these people and their efforts to accomplish its goals.

To make evaluation more than an isolated, peripheral activity, an organization must insist on the importance of evaluation from the top levels of the organization, institute concrete mechanisms for translating that insistence into action, and provide sufficient resources to the evaluation process. Evaluation cannot be considered an add-on function if it is to succeed. It must be a central mission for the organization, and it must be supported by resources that enable its results to be used.

Successful districts develop concrete strategies for focusing organizational attention on the evaluation process. Although their approaches differ in specifics, they all recognize that a key obstacle to successful evaluation is time—or, more precisely, the lack of it—for observing, conferring with, and, especially, assisting teachers who most need intensive help. Time for these functions must compete with other pressing needs unless human resources for the functions are expanded and incentives for using those resources are continuous and explicit.

Evaluator Competence. Valid, reliable, and helpful evaluation requires evaluators who recognize good teaching (and its absence) and who know how to improve poor teaching when they find it. Evaluator competence is probably the most difficult element of the process. The best supported and most carefully constructed process will founder if those responsible for implementation lack the necessary background, knowledge, and expertise.

Evaluator competence requires two qualities: the ability to make sound judgments about teaching quality and the ability to make appropriate, concrete recommendations for improvement of teaching performance. If evaluation processes were designed solely to get rid of poor teachers, the second quality would not be needed. However, most evaluation processes also intend to improve instruction, and even those that strive for accountability must, in the interest of fairness, include a real opportunity for improvement before a teacher is dismissed. Thus, those who evaluate must both judge proficiently and help effectively.

Successful districts recognize this dual function of evaluation, and all, to varying degrees, divide the function between principals and expert teachers.

Several considerations underlie the division of evaluation and assistance between administrators and teachers who have been selected for their teaching and counseling abilities. The first consideration is time. Even a conscientious and competent principal who gives evaluation high priority has other administrative duties that compete for time. He or she certainly lacks the time to help a teacher who requires intensive day-to-day supervision. Someone for whom it is a primary responsibility must provide the help for such improvement.

The second consideration in dividing these responsibilities—

one often cited in the literature on teacher evaluation—involves the possibility that role conflict precludes one person's serving as both judge and helper. According to the theory, the judgmental relationships of evaluation inhibit the trust and rapport that a helper needs to motivate a teacher to improve his or her performance. This tension does not necessarily impair the efforts of all evaluators, but the frequency with which it is mentioned by evaluators suggests that the tension is not satisfactorily resolved in many cases. To the extent that role conflict exists, it does not seem to operate in a simple, straightforward manner but rather depends on the evaluator's temperament, the incentive structure in the school district, and the prevailing ethos of the school. Nonetheless, some separation of evaluation from assistance (by the involvement of a committee rather than a single evaluator in making termination decisions and by the enlistment of expert teachers to provide assistance to those having difficulty) has proved a productive strategy in these districts. Particularly when personnel decisions concerning tenure, dismissal, or special teacher status are to be made, a system that ensures decision making by a team of evaluators and that buffers the assistance function from premature or subjective judgment is more likely to result in good faith improvement efforts and in objective, defensible decisions than one in which a single individual must play all roles.

The final consideration goes to the heart of the evaluator competence issue. Principals are not always chosen for either their evaluation ability or their outstanding teaching ability. In fact, an elementary school principal is not likely to have taught at all levels and in all areas of an elementary school, and a secondary school principal is not likely to have expert knowledge of all areas of the high school curriculum. Although principals may know or be trained to recognize the presence or absence of generic teaching competence, the task of providing concrete assistance to a teacher in trouble often requires more intimate knowledge of a particular teaching area than a principal is likely to possess. The logical solution to this dilemma is to assign the assistance function to one who has already demonstrated competence in an area of teaching expertise.

In addition, successful districts provide some form of in-service training for evaluators on evaluation goals, procedures, and techniques. Ultimately, though, supervision of the evaluation process provides the most important check on evaluator competence. Successful districts have mechanisms for verifying the accuracy of evaluators' reports about teachers. These mechanisms, which involve review of evaluations by supervisors or evaluation committees, force evaluators to justify their ratings in precise, concrete terms. Equally important, they support the development and use of shared conceptions of good teaching across evaluators.

Collaboration in Development and Implementation. In each of the districts, the teachers' organization has collaborated with the administration in the design and implementation of the teacher-evaluation process. The extent and nature of the collaboration varies according to political context and organizational characteristics. It frequently entails the formation of a joint teacher and administrator governing body to oversee implementation of evaluation. School-level collaboration is sometimes provided for as well. The districts have in common, however, means for maintaining communication about evaluation goals, processes, and outcomes so that implementation problems can be addressed as they occur. Consequently, evaluation is not an adversarial process but one in which teachers and administrators work together to improve the quality of evaluation.

Strategic Compatibility. Most school districts function with a mixture of policies and procedures, some of which work together and some of which do not. These case studies support the idea that a process as fragile as teacher evaluation must be compatible with at least those other district policies that define the nature of teaching.

In each case-study district, teacher evaluation supports and is supported by other key operating functions in the schools, including staff development and other vehicles for improving teaching. Evaluation is not just an ancillary activity; it is part of a larger strategy for school improvement. The form and function of evaluation make it compatible with other tactics adopted to accomplish other district goals.

The success of teacher evaluation depends finally on the delimitation of its role in the school system. No single evaluation process can simultaneously serve all the possible goals of evaluation well. Nor can evaluation serve alone as the tactical glue for diverse approaches to school improvement. In a practical sense, appropriate strategies for teacher evaluation explicitly address a high-priority goal of the school organization without colliding with other functions or goals. This means that the purposes of teacher evaluation in the organization context must be carefully defined. It also means that new priorities may require explicit changes in teacher evaluation.

To be useful, district evaluation choices should be context sensitive. Because resources are always constrained, evaluation priorities should seek to address pressing needs and should change with circumstances. For example, a district facing a large influx of new teachers may need to focus resources on the support and evaluation of beginning teachers. A district with a tenured, mid-career workforce may need to emphasize professional development of a different kind. Evaluation should be regarded as an important administrative resource for directing the organization, for solving emerging problems, and for communicating purposes and priorities as they evolve.

The Utility of Evaluation

The extent to which district needs and priorities are reflected in evaluation planning greatly affects the utility of an evaluation system. The utility of teacher evaluation depends in part on its reliability and validity, that is, on how consistently and accurately the process measures minimal competence and degrees of competence. The utility of evaluation depends also on its cost, that is, on whether it achieves usable outcomes without generating excessive costs. The results must be worth the time and effort used to obtain them if the process is to survive competing organizational demands. At least three types of costs—logistic, financial, and political—should be considered in assessing utility.

Logistic Costs. Evaluation procedures, if overly complicated, threaten utility. A process too cumbersome to provide timely results loses its utility. If procedural demands exceed staff capabilities, evaluation is implemented poorly and its results are not usable because they are not reliable or valid. A process that is too complicated or too time consuming to be properly implemented has low utility where teacher organizations can block dismissal attempts on procedural grounds. Equally important, excessively complicated procedures dilute evaluation resources, making them less available for improvement purposes.

Financial Costs. As resources devoted to evaluation increase, so must the perceived, observable benefits of evaluation. If the financial costs of the process exceed its perceived benefits, utility suffers. Sooner or later, the system will commit less time and money to the process so as to accommodate other system demands, and the process will lose its usefulness. The evaluation process must be cost-effective enough to allow for a sustained level of effort over time.

By targeting resources on teachers who most need supervision, for example, an evaluation process can provide a cost-effective means of facilitating the organization's work. Inchoate efforts to handle the problems caused by a small number of incompetent teachers cause institutional confusion and divert considerable professional resources from instruction. In such cases, the organization must deal with the results of the problem rather than its source, and school operations suffer. In contrast, a system that intensively supervised all teachers would waste valuable resources on many who did not require assistance; these resources could be used more profitably for actual instruction rather than the monitoring of instruction. Achieving a proper balance of costs and benefits requires strategic thinking in adopting evaluation methods to suit high-priority goals.

Political Costs. Useful evaluation requires political acceptability. A process may be theoretically valid and reliable, but if it is not endorsed by those who control political power, the use of its results will lead to struggles that divert organizational energies from system goals. Similarly, if the process undermines the ability of important constituents—teachers, parents, or administrators—to legitimately influence the teaching-learning environment, it will breed dissension or low morale that adversely affects the larger organizational mission. Achieving political utility generally requires great attention to constituent views in the design process so that joint ownership of the system creates the possibility of success. If this process is given short shrift, the implementation of evaluation is sure to be compromised.

The design and implementation of teacher evaluation processes depend on these aspects and utility. However, they are rarely considered in the literature, which treats issues of reliability and validity in isolation from real-world complexities and constraints. Many theoretically and technically sound evaluation systems fail in their implementation because they do not take into account the logistic, financial, or political realities that ultimately determine their usefulness.

IMPROVING TEACHING AND EVALUATION IN THE ORGANIZATIONAL CONTEXT

The recent evolution of policy analysis and program evaluation has led to a recognition of the importance of including organizational considerations as an integral part of research that attempts to understand policy effects (Sabatier & Mazmanian, 1979; Sproull, 1979; Wildavsky, 1980). Formal policies and procedures, it has been found, may constrain, but do not construct, the final outcomes of any institutional endeavor. The local implementation process and organizational characteristics—such as institutional climate, organizational structures and incentives, local political processes, expertise, and leadership style—are critical elements in determining the ultimate success of a policy at achieving its intended effects (Berman & McLaughlin, 1973–1978; Mann, 1978; Weatherley & Lipsky, 1977). Effective change requires a process of mutual adaptation in which change agents at all levels can shape policies to meet their needs—one in which both the participants and the policy are transformed by the convergence of internal and external reference points.

The application of research-based teacher-evaluation models to real-life settings must overcome the gap that exists between technically defensible specifications of criteria or methods and politically viable solutions to organizational problems. There is a growing recognition that any kind of evaluation activity involves value choices—and conflicts—at all levels of the operating system (Rein, 1976; Rossi, Freeman, & Wright, 1979; Sroufe, 1977). Evaluation is political because it serves as a tool in a larger policy-making process and because it is inherently directed at making a judgment of worth about something. Any such judgment ultimately rearranges or reaffirms an existing constellation of stakes that individuals or groups have in what is being evaluated (Englert, Kean, & Scribner, 1977). Furthermore, the *process* of evaluation encompasses a continual process of bargaining and goal modification that occurs "because the conditions and effective constituency surrounding goal setting are different from the conditions and effective constituency surrounding implementation" (Stone, 1980, pp. 23–24).

Knapp (1982) described the divergence existing between many teacher evaluation models and actual practices in terms of the differing standards applied by researchers and practitioners to ultimately political value choices.

5. TEACHER EVALUATION

Value choices are nowhere more clearly at issue than in decisions about the aspects of the teacher and teaching to be evaluated. Scholars have tended to make these value choices on scientific grounds: in effect, they are arguing that evaluation systems should be focused on whatever can be operationally defined and demonstrated to contribute to student learning.... A number of proposals for improved teacher appraisal systems have been advanced, but a "better" system tends to be defined in terms of accuracy and links to an established base of teacher effects research. Such systems rest on an idealized image of school management, that ignores the powerful effects of organizational and contextual forces on management activity. (pp. 4–5)

In actual practice, Knapp found that schools follow "the lines of least resistance," evaluating aspects of teachers and teaching in more vague terms so as to simultaneously satisfy diverse constituencies. A defensible teacher-evaluation process is one that allows evaluators to balance several goals at once:

- Sorting teachers
- Maintaining staff morale and collegiality
- Maintaining organizational distance from environmental demands (e.g., for accountability)
- Devising improvements that require modest, incremental change

This does not mean that research-based teacher-evaluation models cannot succeed in the real world, only that adaptations to the organizational context must be explicitly considered and sought if the processes are to be implemented successfully.

Implementation of any school policy, including a teacher-evaluation policy, represents a continuous interplay among diverse policy goals, established rules and procedures (concerning both the policy in question and other aspects of the school's operations), intergroup bargaining and value choices, and the local institutional context. Teacher-evaluation procedures, for example, will be influenced by the political climate that exists within a school system, by the relationship of the teachers' organization to district management, by the nature of other educational policies and operating programs in the district, and by the very size and structure of the system and its bureaucracy. These variables and others are equally potent at the school level.

Many organizational theorists have advanced the notion that school systems are loosely coupled. That is, they do not conform to the rational-bureaucratic model, which assumes consensus on organizational goals and technologies, tight links between vertical and horizontal functions and actors, frequent inspection of work tasks, and consistent and unambiguous lines of communication and authority (Deal, Meyer, & Scott, 1974; March, 1976; Weick, 1976). Weick (1982) went so far as to suggest that "the task of educating is simply not the kind of task that can be performed in a tightly coupled system" (p. 674). He argued that it is wrong to treat evidence of loose coupling as the result of improper management or indecisiveness. Because of the nature of teaching work, the diversity of school constituencies, and the changing nature of demands in the educational system, tightly coupled, standardized responses to identified problems may reduce the organization's capability to respond to future needs or problems and may set in motion actions that conflict with other educational and organizational goals.

On the other hand, districts are responsive to parents and the public for the quality of teaching they offer; hence, they must attempt to "couple" reasonably tightly their intentions for evaluation with the practices that occur in schools. If school affairs tend naturally toward idiographic responses to local circumstances we must ask what change strategies can be effective in such a seemingly confused and confusing milieu. Fortunately, organizational theorists do not stop short of suggesting some approaches that are plausible in loosely coupled, nonconsensual organizations like schools.

Communicating Purpose

The first general area for attention concerns the nature and frequency of communications. Weick (1982) contended that one of the most important jobs of administrators in a loosely coupled system is "symbol management"; that is, the articulation of general themes and directions "with eloquence, persistence, and detail" (p. 675). He distinguished symbols from goals. Symbols tell people what they are doing and why; goals tell people when and how well they are doing it. Because problems, hence goals, change constantly, symbols are the glue that holds the organization together.

The symbol manager "teaches people to interpret what they are doing in a common language" (Weick, 1982, p. 676).

Sproull's (1979) implementation research also directs our attention to the importance of communications and symbol management. The implementation processes that greatly affect policy outcomes include: (a) the processes by which the policy is made visible enough to capture the attention of the organization's members; (b) the processes by which it is made meaningful to the members, that is, how it is understood and interpreted at various levels of the operation system; (c) the processes by which response repertoires (standard operating procedures and practices) are invoked; and (d) the processes by which behavioral directives or guides for action are conveyed from the central office to school sites. Successful implementation processes rely on the existence of cognitive "consistency-producing mechanisms" that relate the policy to interpretations of the organization's history and current work. As we have seen, such mechanisms can be incorporated into the design of teacher evaluation processes by attending to allocation of resources, checks on evaluator performance, collaboration between teachers and administrators, and ensuring the compatibility of the process with other organizational goals and activities.

The importance for teacher evaluation of frequent communication and shared understanding between administrators and teachers is supported in several empirical studies reported by Natriello and Dornbusch (1980–1981). Their findings, like those of other implementation researchers (e.g., Cohen, 1976; Deal et al., 1974), indicate differences in perception between superordinates and subordinates regarding the frequency and substance of communications. Teachers report that they do not know what the criteria for teacher evaluation are, that they are rarely observed, and that evaluation feedback is scarce, whereas their principals report just the opposite.[2] More important, frequency of observation and feedback—even negative feedback—is strongly correlated with teacher satisfaction with the evaluation system. Furthermore, teachers are more satisfied with evaluation systems in which they can affect the criteria on which they are judged. These perceptions also influence the teacher's sense of performance efficacy (Fuller et al., 1982, p. 24).

---

[2]A principal may engage in evaluation behavior a great deal of the time; that behavior will be visible to a given teacher only a fraction of the time.

Motivating Change

This brings us to the second area of concern: the development of a sense of efficacy among those at whom improvement efforts are directed. One of the primary goals of teacher evaluation is the improvement of individual and collective teaching performance in schools. Effectively changing the behavior of another person requires enlisting the cooperation and motivation of that person, in addition to providing guidance on the steps needed for improvement to occur. At the individual level, change relies on the development of two important conditions within the individual: knowledge that a course of action is the correct one and a sense of empowerment or efficacy, that is, a perception that pursuing a given course of action is both worthwhile and possible.

Most teacher-evaluation processes attend to questions of how to identify effective teaching without addressing questions of how to bring about changes in teaching behavior, assuming that having discovered what ought to be done, implementation of recommended actions will naturally follow. However, Fenstermacher (1978) argued that "if our purpose and intent are to change the practices of those who teach, it is necessary to come to grips with the subjectively reasonable beliefs of teachers" (p. 174). This process entails the creation of internally varifiable knowledge rather than the imposition of rules for behavior.

Effective change requires knowledge control on the part of the teacher. As Good and Power (1976) noted:

> [A]t best, generalizations about teaching derived from research act as guides to assessing the likely consequences of alternative strategies in complex educational situations. Such generalizations must necessarily be indeterminate since they cannot predict precisely what will happen in a particular case. But this does not decrease their value for the teacher. . . . Theories can be of value in specifying those dimensions which are relevant to the understanding of classroom phenomena, can extend the range of hypotheses (alternative strategies) considered, and *sensitize* the teacher to the possible consequences of his actions. Indeed, ultimately, the validity and usefulness of theory may rest in the hands of teachers . . . that is, whether it sensitizes them to the classroom context, helps them make more informed decisions, and to monitor their own behavior. (p. 58)

The development of an internally verifiable knowledge base empowers the teacher to apply internal against external referents of validity and to engage in appropriate self-assessment and self-improvement activities.

An understanding of how empowerment enables change is further informed by a substantial body of psychological research on self-efficacy. Perceptions of self-efficacy are an important element of the link between knowledge and behaviors. Research on this topic indicates that perceived self-efficacy better predicts subsequent behavior than does actual performance attainment, and that it influences coping behaviors, self-regulation, perseverance, responses to failure experiences, growth of intrinsic interest and motivation, achievement strivings, and career pursuits (Bandura, 1982; Bandura, Adams, Hardy, & Howells, 1980; Bandura & Schunk, 1981; Betz & Hackett, 1981; Brown & Inouye, 1978; Collins, 1982; DiClemente, 1981; Kazdin, 1979).

The relevance of teachers' self-perceptions of efficacy to their performance has been demonstrated in several studies. Berman and McLaughlin's study of the implementation of innovative projects found that the teacher's sense of efficacy had stronger positive effects on the percent of project goals achieved, the amount of teacher change, and improved student performance than did teacher experience or verbal ability (Berman & McLaughlin, 1977, pp. 136–139). Armor et al. (1976) found that teachers' self-perceptions of efficacy were strongly and positively related to students' reading achievement, unlike teacher education, experience, or other background characteristics. Other studies have reported similar positive relationships between teachers' sense of self-efficacy and student achievement (Brookover, 1977; Rutter, Maughan, Mortimore, Ouston, & Smith, 1979).

More important, substantial research also suggests that an individual's sense of efficacy can be influenced by interactions with others as well as by organizational factors. Individual perceptions of self-efficacy and motivation are influenced by the value of rewards and the expectancy of achieving objectives (Vroom, 1964). However, the goals must be personally valued and must present a challenge to the individual, or the task performance will be devalued (Lewin, 1938; Lewin, Dembo, Festinger, & Sears, 1944). Self-efficacy is not entirely an internal construct; it requires a responsive environment that allows for and rewards performance attainment (Bandura, 1982, p. 140). Furthermore, role designations can enhance or undermine self-efficacy.

> Situational factors that often accompany poor performance can in themselves instill a sense of incompetence that is unwarranted....

> [W]hen people are cast in subordinate roles or are assigned inferior labels, implying limited competence, they perform activities at which they are skilled less well than when they do not bear the negative labels or the subordinate role designations. (Bandura, 1982, p. 142)

A review by Fuller, Wood, Rapoport, and Dornbusch (1982) of the research on individual efficacy in the context of organizations suggests that increased performance and organizational efficacy for teachers will result from:

- Convergence between teachers and administrators in accepting the goals and means for task performance (Ouchi, 1980)
- Higher levels of personalized interaction and resource exchange between teachers and administrators (Talbert, 1980)
- Lower prescriptiveness of work tasks (Anderson, 1973)
- Teachers' perceptions that evaluation is soundly based and that evaluation is linked to rewards or sanctions
- Teacher input into evaluation criteria, along with diversity of evaluation criteria (Pfeffer, Salancik, & Leblebici, 1976; Rosenholtz & Wilson, 1980)

Theories on the exercise of authority in organizations also suggest that recognition of task complexity and preservation of some autonomy for personnel encourage a sense of self-efficacy (Dornbusch & Scott, 1975; Thompson, Dornbusch, & Scott, 1975). In addition, motivation by intrinsic incentives through evaluation that allows self-assessment is more powerful than motivation that relies on external assessment and reward (Deci, 1976; Meyer, 1975). As Bandura (1982) observed:

> In social learning theory an important cognitively based source of motivation operates through the intervening processes of goal setting and self-evaluative reactions. This form of self-motivation, which involves internal comparison processes, requires personal standards against which to evaluate performance. (p. 134)

The importance of self-assessment has begun to achieve recognition in the teacher-evaluation literature (Bodine, 1973; Bushman, 1974; Riley & Schaffer, 1979), as has the importance of allowing teacher input into the determination of evaluation criteria and standards (Knapp, 1982).

Individual change relies on knowledge, self-referent thought, and motivation. These are, in turn, profoundly influenced by the signals and opportunities provided within the organizational environment. The transformatory character of individual change is equally applicable at the organizational level. Thus the success of change efforts is influenced by implementation processes that define opportunities for developing shared knowledge, diagnosing and designing strategies, and promoting collective efficacy.

Creating Commitment

The nature of decision-making and policy-formulation processes, which are closely tied to communications and empowerment, is critical to successful implementation of a teacher-evaluation system. These processes involve coalitions of stakeholders interacting to define problems and solutions under conditions of ambiguity (Cohen & March, 1974). Resolving ambiguity by attempts at tight coupling may not necessarily be as productive as indirect change efforts that preserve the ability of smaller units to adapt to local conditions (Deal & Celotti, 1980; March, 1976). As Knapp (1982) commented,

> The process of developing evaluation systems is an occasion for many things in an organization such as the interaction of constituencies, celebration of important values, and the joint recognition of problems. Whether or not performance objectives are met by a specified proportion of a school district's teachers, the *indirect* results of such efforts may have considerable impact on staff enthusiasm, beliefs, or behavior, with ultimate benefits for students. (p. 18)

These propositions lead to four minimal conditions for the successful operation of a teacher-evaluation system:

• All actors in the system have a shared understanding of the criteria and processes for teaching evaluation.

• All actors understand how these criteria and processes relate to the dominant symbols of the organization, that is, there is a shared sense that they capture the most important aspects of teaching, that the evaluation system is consonant with educational goals and conceptions of teaching work.

• Teachers perceive that the evaluation procedure enables and motivates them to improve their performance; and principals perceive that the procedure enables them to provide instructional leadership.

- All actors in the system perceive that the evaluation procedure allows them to strike a balance "between adaptation and adaptability, between stability to handle present demands and flexibility to handle unanticipated demands" (Weick, 1982, p. 674); that is, the procedure achieves a balance between control and autonomy for the various actors in the system.

CONCLUSION

Teacher evaluation is an activity that must satisfy competing individual and organizational needs. The imperative of uniform treatment for personnel decisions may result in standardized definitions of acceptable teaching behavior. However, research on teacher performance and teaching effectiveness does not lead to a stable list of measurable teaching behaviors effective in all teaching contexts. Moreover, research on individual and organizational behavior indicates the need for context-specific strategies for improving teaching that communicate system goals while allowing for intelligent adaptations to school and classroom circumstances. If teacher evaluation is to be a useful tool for teacher improvement, it must strike a careful balance between standardized, centrally administered performance expectations and teacher-specific approaches to evaluation and professional development.

REFERENCES

Anderson, B. D. (1973). School bureaucratization and alienation from high school. *Sociology of Education, 46*(2), 315–334.

Anderson, C. S. (1982). The search for school climate: A review of the research. *Review of Educational Research, 52*(3), 368–420.

Armor, D., Conry-Oseguera, P., Cox, M., King, N., McDonnell, L., Pascal, A., Pauly, E., & Zellman, G. (1976). *Analysis of the school preferred reading program in selected Los Angeles minority schools.* Santa Monica, CA: The RAND Corporation.

Bandura, A. (1982). Self-efficacy mechanism in human agency. *American Psychologist, 37*(2), 122–147.

Bandura, A., Adams, N. E., Hardy, A. B., & Howells, G. N. (1980). Tests of the generality of self-efficacy theory. *Cognitive Therapy and Research, 4*, 39–66.

Bandura, A., & Schunk, D. H. (1981). Cultivating competence, self-efficacy, and intrinsic interest through proximal self-motivation. *Journal of Personality and Social Psychology, 41*, 586–598.

Beckham, J. C. (1981). *Legal aspects of teacher evaluation.* Topeka, KS: National Organization on Legal Problems of Education.

Berliner, D. C. (1982). *The executive functions of teaching.* Paper presented at the annual meeting of the American Educational Research Association, New York.

Berman, P., & McLaughlin, M. W. (1977). *Federal programs supporting educational change: Vol. 7. Factors affecting implementation and continuation.* Santa Monica, CA: The RAND Corporation.

Berman, P., & McLaughlin, M. W. (1973–1978). *Federal programs supporting educational change.* Santa Monica, CA: The RAND Corporation.

Betz, N. E., & Hackett, G. (1981). The relationships of career-related self-efficacy expectations to perceived career options in college women and men. *Journal of Counseling Psychology, 28,* 399–410.

Bodine, R. (1973). Teachers' self-assessment. In E. R. House (Ed.), *School evaluation.* Berkeley, CA: McCutchan.

Brookover, W. (1977). *Schools can make a difference.* East Lansing: College of Urban Development, Michigan State University.

Brophy, J. E., & Evertson, C. (1977). Teacher behavior and student learning in second and third grades. In G. D. Borich (Ed.). *The appraisal of teaching: Concepts and process.* Reading, MASS: Addison Wesley.

Brophy, J. E., & Evertson, C. (1974). *Process-product correlations in the Texas teacher effectiveness study: Final report.* Austin, TX: Research and Development Center for Teacher Education.

Broudy, H. S. (1956). Teaching—craft or profession? *The Educational Forum,* 175–184.

Brown, I., Jr., & Inouye, D. K. (1978). Learned helplessness through modeling: The role of perceived similarity in competence. *Journal of Personality and Social Psychology, 36,* 900–908.

Bush, R. N. (1979). Implications of the BTES. *The Generator, 9*(1), 13–15.

Bushman, J. H. (1974). Are teachers playing "statue" in the classroom? *NASSP Bulletin, 58,* 386.

Centra, J. A., & Potter, D. A. (1980). School and teacher effects: An interrelational model. *Review of Educational Research, 50*(2), 273–291.

Cohen, E. (1976). *Organization and instruction in elementary schools.* Stanford, CA: Stanford Center for Research and Development in Teaching.

Cohen, M., & March, J. (1974). *Leadership and ambiguity: The American college president.* New York: McGraw-Hill.

Coker, H., Medley, D., & Soar, R. (1980). How valid are expert opinions about effective teaching? *Phi Delta Kappan, 62*(2), 131–134, 149.

Collins, J. (1982). *Self-efficacy and ability in achievement behavior.* Unpublished doctoral dissertation. Stanford University.

Cronbach, L. J. (1975). Beyond the two disciplines of scientific psychology. *American Psychologist, 30,* 116–127.

Cronbach, L. J., & Snow, R. E. (1977). *Aptitudes and instructional methods: A handbook for research on interactions.* New York: Irvington.

Darling-Hammond, L. (1986). A proposal for evaluation in the teaching profession. *Elementary School Journal, 86*(4), 1–21.

Darling-Hammond, L., & Berry, B. (1988). *The Evolution of teacher policy.* Santa-Monica: The RAND Corporation.

Darling-Hammond, L., & Wise, A. (1981). *A conceptual framework for examining teachers' views of teaching and educational policies.* Santa Monica, CA: The RAND Corporation.

Deal, T., Meyer, J., & Scott, R. (1974). *Organizational support for innovative instruc-*

tional programs: District and school levels. Paper presented at the annual meeting of the American Educational Research Association, Chicago.

Deal, T. E., & Celotti, L. D. (1980). How much influence do (and can) educational administrators have on classrooms? *Phi Delta Kappan, 61*(7), 471–473.

Deci, E. L. (1976). The hidden costs of rewards. *Organizational Dynamics, 4*(3), 61–72.

DiClemente, C. C. (1981). Self-efficacy and smoking cessation maintenance: A preliminary report. *Cognitive Therapy and Research, 5,* 175–187.

Dornbusch, S. M., & Scott, W. R. (1975). *Evaluation and the exercise of authority.* San Francisco: Jossey–Bass.

Doyle, W. (1978). Paradigms for research on teacher effectiveness. In L. S. Shulman (Ed.), *Review of research in education* (Vol. 5, pp. 163–198). Itasca, IL: F. E. Peacock.

Doyle, W. (1979). Classroom tasks and students' abilities. In P. L. Peterson & H. J. Walberg (Eds.), *Research on teaching* (pp. 183–209). Berkeley, CA: McCutchan.

Dunkin, M. J., & Biddle, B. J. (1974). *The study of teaching.* New York: Holt, Rinehart, & Winston.

Eisner, E. W. (1978). On the uses of educational connoisseurship and criticism for evaluating classroom life. *Teachers College Record, 78,* 345–358.

Ellett, C. D., Capie, W., & Johnson, C. E. (1980). Assessing teaching performance. *Educational Leadership, 38*(3), 219–220.

Elmore, R. T. (1979). *Complexity and control: What legislators and administrators can do about implementation.* Seattle, WA: Institute of governmental Research.

Englert, R. M., Kean, M. H., & Scribner, J. D. (1977). Politics of program evaluation in large city school districts. *Education and Urban Society, 9,* 425–450.

Feldvebel, A. M. (1980). Teacher evaluation: Ingredients of a credible model. *Clearing House, 53*(9), 415–420.

Fenstermacher, G. D. (1978). A philosophical consideration of recent research on teacher effectiveness. In L. S. Shulman (Ed.), *Review of Research in Education* (Vol. 6, pp. 157–185). Itasca, IL: F. E. Peacock.

Fenstermacher, G. D., & Berliner, D. C. (1983). *A conceptual framework for the analysis of staff development.* Santa Monica, CA: The RAND Corporation.

Floden, R. E., & Feiman, S. (1981). *A consumer's guide to teacher development.* East Lansing: Institute for Research on Teaching, Michigan State University.

Fuller, B., Wood, K., Rapoport, T., & Dornbusch, S. M. (1982). The organizational context of individual efficacy. *Review of Educational Research, 52*(1), 7–30.

Gage, N. L. (1978). *The scientific basis of the art of teaching.* New York: Teachers College Press.

Gallup, G. H. (1979). The eleventh annual Gallup poll of the public's attitudes toward the public schools. *Phi Delta Kappan, 60,* 33–45.

Haefele, D. L. (1980). How to evaluate thee, teacher—let me count the ways. *Phi Delta Kappan, 61*(5), 349–352.

Joyce, B. R., & Weil, M. (1972). *Models of teaching.* Englewood Cliffs, NJ: Prentice Hall.

Kazdin, A. E. (1979). Imagery elaboration and self-efficacy in the covert modeling treatment of unassertive behavior. *Journal of Consulting and Clinical Psychology, 47,* 725–753.

Kleine, P. F., & Wisniewski, R. (1981). Bill 1706: A forward step for Oklahoma. *Phi Delta Kappan, 63*(2), 115–117.

Knapp, M. S. (1982). *Toward the study of teacher evaluation as an organizational*

process: A review of current research and practice. Menlo Park, CA: Educational and Human Services Research Center, SRI International.
Lewin, K. (1938). *The conceptual representation and the measurement of psychological forces.* Durham, NC: Duke University Press.
Lewin, K., Dembo, T., Festinger, L., & Sears, P. (1944). Level of aspiration. In J. Hunt (Ed.), *Personality and behavioral disorders* (Vol. 2). New York: Ronald Press.
Lewis, A. (1982). *Evaluating educational personnel.* Arlington, VA: American Association of School Administrators.
Lortie, D. (1975). *Schoolteacher.* Chicago: University of Chicago Press.
Mann, D. (Ed.). (1978). *Making change happen?* New York: Teachers College Press.
March, J. G. (1976). The technology of foolishness. In J. G. March & J. P. Olsen (Eds.), *Ambiguity and choice in organizations* (pp. 69–81). Bergen, Norway: Universitetsforlaget.
McDonald, F. J., & Elias, P. (1976). *Executive summary report: Beginning teacher evaluation study, phase II.* Princeton, NJ: Educational Testing Service.
McDonnell, L., & Pascal, A. (1979). *Organized teachers in American schools.* Santa Monica, CA: The RAND Corporation.
McKenna, B. H. (1981). Context/environment effects in teacher evaluation. In J. Millman (Ed.), *Handbook on teacher evaluation* (pp. 23–37). Beverly Hills, CA: Sage Publications.
Medley, D. M. (1979). The effectiveness of teachers. In P. L. Peterson & H. J. Walberg (Eds.), *Research on teaching* (pp. 11–29). Berkeley, CA: McCutchan.
Medley, D. M. (1982). *Teacher competency testing and the teacher educator.* Charlottesville: Association of Teacher Educators and the Bureau of Educational Research, University of Virginia.
Meyer, M. H. (1975). The pay-for-performance dilemma. *Organizational Dynamics, 3*(3), 39–50.
Millman, J. (Ed.). (1981). *Handbook of teacher evaluation.* Beverly Hills, CA: Sage Publications.
Mitchell, D. E., & Kerchner, C. T. (1983). Collective bargaining and teacher policy. In L. S. Shulman & G. Sykes (Eds.), *Handbook of teaching and policy* (pp. 214–238). New York: Longman.
Munnelly, R. J. (1979). Dealing with teacher incompetence: Supervision and evaluation in a due process framework. *Contemporary Education, 50*(4), 221–225.
Natriello, G., & Dornbusch, S. M. (1980–1981). Pitfalls in the evaluation of teachers by principals. *Administrator's Notebook, 29*(6), whole issue.
Ouchi, W. G. (1980). Markets, bureaucracies, and clans. *Administrative Science Quarterly, 25*(1), 129–141.
Peterson, P., & Kauchak, D. (1982). *Teacher evaluation: Perspectives, practices and promises.* Salt Lake City: Center for Educational Practice, University of Utah.
Peterson, P. L. (1976). *Interactive effects of student anxiety, achievement orientation, and teacher behavior on student achievement and attitude.* Unpublished doctoral dissertation, Stanford University.
Pfeffer, J., Salancik, G., & Leblebici, H. (1976). The effect of uncertainty on the use of social influence in organizational decision making. *Administrative Science Quarterly, 21*(2), 227–248.
Rein, M. (1976). *Social science and public policy.* New York: Penguin.
Riley, R. D., & Schaffer, E. C. (1979). Self-certification: Accounting to oneself. *Journal of Teacher Education, 30*(2), 23–26.

Rosenholtz, S. J., & Wilson, B. (1980). The effect of classroom structure on shared perceptions of ability. *American Educational Research Journal, 17*, 75–82.
Rosenshine, B., & Furst, N. (1971). Research on teacher performance criteria. In B. O. Smith (Ed.), *Research in teacher education: A symposium*. Englewood Cliffs, NJ: Prentice Hall.
Rossi, P. H., Freeman, H. E., & Wright, S. R. (1979). *Evaluation: A systematic approach*. Beverly Hills, CA: Sage Publications.
Rutter, M., Maughan, B., Mortimore, P., Ouston, J., & Smith, A. (1979). *Fifteen thousand hours: Secondary schools and their effects on children*. Cambridge, MA: Harvard University Press.
Sabatier, P., & Mazmanian, D. (1979). *The implementation of regulatory policy: A framework of analysis*. Davis: CA: Institute of Governmental Affairs.
Sechrest, L., & Hoffman, P. E. (1982). The philosophical underpinnings of peer review. *Professional Psychology, 13*(1), 14–18.
Shavelson, R. (1973). What is *the* basic teaching skill? *Journal of Teacher Education, 14*, 144–151.
Shavelson, R., & Dempsey-Atwood, N. (1976). Generalizability of measures of teacher behavior. *Review of Educational Research, 46*, 553–612.
Shavelson, R., & Stern, P. (1981). Research on teachers' pedagogical thoughts, judgments, decisions and behavior. *Review of Educational Research, 51*(4), 455–498.
Soar, R. S. (1972). *Follow through classroom process measurement and pupil growth*. Gainesville: Institute for Development of Human Resources, University of Florida.
Sproull, L. S. (1979). *Response to regulation: An organizational process framework*. Pittsburgh, PA: Carnegie-Mellon University.
Stallings, J. A. (1977). How instructional processes relate to child outcomes. In G. D. Borich (Ed.), *The appraisal of teaching: Concepts and process* (pp. 104–113). Reading, MA: Addison–Wesley.
Stodolsky, S. (1984). Teacher evaluation: The limits of looking. *Educational Researcher, 13*(9), 11–22.
Stone, C. N. (1980). The implementation of social programs: Two perspectives. *Journal of Social Issues, 36*(4), 13–34.
Strike, K., & Bull, B. (1981). Fairness and the legal context of teacher evaluation. In J. Millman (Ed.), *Handbook of teacher evaluation* (pp. 303–343). Beverly Hills, CA: Sage Publications.
Talbert, J. (1980). *School organization and institutional changes: Exchange and power in loosely-coupled systems*. Stanford, CA: Institute for Research on Educational Finance and Governance, Stanford University.
Thompson, J. E., Dornbusch, S. M., & Scott, W. R. (1975). *Failures of communication in the evaluation of teachers by principals* (No. 43). Stanford, CA: Stanford Center for Research and Development in Teaching.
Vlaanderen, R. (1980). *Trends in competency-based teacher certification*. Denver, CO: Education Commission of the States.
Vroom, V. (1964). *Work and motivation*. New York: Wiley.
Weatherley, R., & Lipsky, M. (1977). Street-level bureaucrats and institutional innovation: Implementing special education reform. *Harvard Educational Review, 47*(2), 171–197.
Weick, K. E. (1976). Educational organizations as loosely-coupled systems. *Administrative Science Quarterly, 21*, 1–19.

Weick, K. E. (1982). Administering education in loosely coupled schools. *Phi Delta Kappan, 63*(10), 673–676.
Wildavsky, A. (1980). *Speaking truth to power: The art and craft of policy analysis.* Boston: Little, Brown.
Wise, A. (1979). *Legislated learning.* Berkeley: University of California Press.
Wise, A., & Darling-Hammond, L. (1987). *Licensing teachers: Design for a teaching profession.* Santa Monica: The RAND Corporation.
Wise, A., Darling-Hammond, L., & Berry, B. (1987). *Effective teacher selection: From recruitment to retention.* Santa Monica, CA: The RAND Corporation.
Wise, A., Darling-Hammond, L., McLaughlin, M., & Bernstein, H. (1984). *Teacher evaluation: A study of effective practices.* Santa Monica, CA: The RAND Corporation.

6
Measuring Performance in Teacher Assessment

Richard J. Stiggins
Northwest Regional Educational Laboratory

In performance assessment, the examinee is called upon to display behaviors or produce products which an observer evaluates in terms of prespecified performance standards. This kind of measurement plays a major role in many school evaluation contexts, including both student and teacher evaluation. The observation and evaluation of a teacher's performance in the classroom represents one of many excellent sources of information on teacher capabilities and the effectiveness of instruction. The purpose of this chapter is to review the various ways performance assessment methodology can serve in teacher-assessment contexts.

The review begins with a summary of the range of settings in which the performance of prospective and practicing teachers might be assessed, identifying the various decisions to be made and the various data sources that inform those decisions. This review of decision contexts provides a sense of the various purposes for teacher assessment and the various measurement methods used to serve those purposes. Further, it frames the role of performance assessment in a very general way.

Next, the discussion turns to a description of the basic ingredients of a performance assessment, detailing the components of such assessments, discussing strategies for ensuring their quality, and reviewing the keys to their successful use. This description provides a sense of the range of performance assessment design alternatives available to the user.

Finally, the various purposes for teacher assessment are combined with the various performance assessment design alternatives to reveal how the two can be integrated to promote sound assessment leading to appropriate decisions in a wide range of contexts. This analysis permits an exploration of the fundamental differences in the kind of assessment methods used to achieve different purposes. In addition, it provides a means of examining strategies for ensuring valid and reliable performance assessment in each decision context.

Throughout the discussion, emphasis is placed on differentiating between sound and unsound assessment practices. The result is a detailed portrait of performance assessment at work in the arena of teacher assessment.

THE RANGE OF TEACHER ASSESSMENT CONTEXTS

There are many reasons why we assess teacher performance. Assessments inform decisions during teacher training, at the time of licensure and throughout the teacher's tenure in the classroom. In fact, we can identify at least eight specific decision contexts where assessment of teacher performance plays a role.

For instance, during preservice teacher education, instructors assess *achievement within the specific courses,* documenting the extent to which students have learned and are able to apply the pedagogical principles covered. Assuming that (a) the content of each course contributes to the development of a competent teacher and (b) course assessments cover the content taught, each course assessment verifies achievement of essential pedagogical knowledge and/or skills. Also during preservice training, faculty evaluate the performance of students as they participate in field experiences, such as their *student teaching experience.* Whether evaluating course achievement or student-teaching performance, the use of sound assessment methodology is very important. In either case, sound assessments are those that sample teacher performance in a representative manner according to clearly specified course outcome and/or classroom performance criteria.

Teacher certification and licensing, another teacher-assessment context, calls for the new teacher to be licensed to practice, often on the basis of course work completed and examination. Such evaluations often are required by state law and are carried out by state licensing boards. States often require that the teacher who has been given an *initial certification* be reevaluated at a later time to receive a *permanent certificate*. Because these are important decisions, it is incumbent upon the assessor to employ the soundest of assessment methods. Those methods should evaluate the important dimensions of good teaching based on (a) completion of an appropriate professional preparation program and (b) observation and evaluation of a representative sample of the teacher's classroom work.

Local school districts also assess teachers for a variety of purposes. For instance, they assess prior performance in some terms for purposes of initial *hiring*. That is, the candidates for particular teaching positions are ranked for selection on the basis of some criteria. Further, districts evaluate teachers periodically to be sure *minimum teaching competencies* are being demonstrated in the classroom. Such evaluations often are required by state law and/or collective bargaining agreements. This assures the public that only competent teachers teach. Because important decisions rest in the balance, both the teacher and the district count on the use of the best available assessment methods to assure appropriate decisions.

Yet another context in which districts assess teacher performance is to promote the *professional development* of teachers. For example, assessment for development is becoming more and more common during the induction of new teachers, when many work with mentors to learn the ropes. Mentors assess performance and provide feedback. Assessment for professional development also comes into play when practicing teachers are judged not to be measuring up to minimums. They are asked to participate in important professional development activities. These activities are accompanied by careful repeat evaluations to be sure the needed changes come about. In addition, a great many teachers who may be outstanding professionals already are keenly interested in pursuing ongoing professional development. As these teachers pursue their growth-producing goals and activities, their professional development can be monitored to document and facilitate improvement.

And finally, it has become more and more common for districts to assess and make decisions about teachers' *career advancement* to higher levels of a career ladder, such as to mentor teacher status, or higher pay levels. In this case, the objective of assessment is to

TABLE 6.1
Relationship Between Teacher Assessment Contexts
and Associated Measurement Methods

Measurement Methods

	Paper & Pencil Test					
Decision Context	Basic Academic Skills	Subject Matter	Pedagogical Knowledge	Course Completion	Interview	Performance Assessment
1. Preservice teacher education						
A. Measuring course achievement	N	T	T	N	P	P
B. Evaluation of student teaching	N	N	N	N	P	T
2. Teacher Licensing						
A. Initial certificate	T	T	T	T	P	P
B. Permanent certificate	P[a]	P[a]	P[a]	T	P	T
3. District evaluations						
A. Selection to be hired	P[b]	P[b]	P[b]	T	T	P
B. Assurance of minimum competence	P	P	P	N	T	T
C. Assessment for professional development	N	P	P	P[c]	P	T
D. Career advancement	N	P	P	P	T	T

Note. T = Typical in this context; P = Possible but rarely used; N = Not appropriate
[a]More appropriately done earlier
[b]If test has been validated to assure job relevance
[c]If courses are intended to contribute to specific professional development goals

focus the assessment far above minimum competence and beyond individual professional development to the identification of those who have attained the highest levels of professional excellence. Because few typically are offered the opportunity to ascend to these levels, it is incumbent upon the assessor to screen candidates very carefully using the highest quality data in teacher performance.

Thus, there are a great many contexts for teacher assessment and a great many decisions to be made on the basis of the results. Some of the assessments can be and typically are based on paper-and-pencil tests of basic skills, subject-matter knowledge, and/or pedagogical knowledge. Others often are based on a review of training program transcripts and records. Still others rely on interviews. But many, in fact most, of these decision contexts rely at least in part on performance assessments; that is, measurement of teacher performance based on observation and evaluation of teachers' classroom behaviors and associated products. The relationship between the various decisions and alternative measurement methods used is outlined in Table 6.1. In five of the eight contexts, performance assessment is the typical measurement method used. In the other three, performance assessment has a potential role to play. For this reason, a basic understanding of performance assessment methodology is essential for those who would assess teachers.

PERFORMANCE ASSESSMENT OVERVIEW

To understand the role performance assessment can play in these teacher assessment contexts, we need to begin with an understanding of the basic ingredients in a performance assessment. Any such assessment can be described in terms of four key components: the purpose(s) for assessment, performance to be evaluated, exercise(s) that elicit performance, and performance rating procedures.[1] Each component contains within it a number of subcomponents, or design alternatives, from which the user can choose. It is through an examination of these design options that we can fully understand the wide range of performance assessment possibilities.

---

[1] For a more detailed treatment of these ingredients, see Stiggins, R. J. (1987). Design and developing performance assessments. *Educational Measurement: Issues and Practice, 6*(3), 33–42.

The Basic Components. As this section unfolds, it will become clear that performance assessments vary greatly in their form. The form of any particular assessment depends on its purpose. Without knowledge of the purpose, it is virtually impossible to design a useful assessment. Consequently, the first step in the design of a performance assessment is *to specify the purpose.* The range of alternative purposes is quite wide. For example, performance assessments can inform decisions about examinee strengths and weaknesses, rank order examinees for selection, certify mastery of minimum competencies, and/or evaluate the impact of some instructional treatment of a group of students. Some of these decisions require the generation and use of criterion-referenced data, whereas others rely on norm-referenced results. The type of data needed, in turn, will influence the type of performance-rating procedures used. Thus, the design of a performance assessment begins with the specification of purpose: What is the decision to be made and who is the decision maker?

Step two in the design of a performance assessment calls for the *description of the performance to be evaluated.* Two aspects of this are important. First, the designer must specify the type of performance to be observed. Three options are available. One can observe examinee behaviors, products created by the examinee, or some combination of these two. The option selected in any particular case is a function of where the best, most conveniently accessible evidence of proficiency can be found.

Second, the designer must specify the performance criteria or the dimensions of performance to be rated—in observable terms. Each key dimension must be specified in two parts: a definition and a performance continuum. Without a clear vision of performance, including a sense of the difference between poor and outstanding performance, it is impossible to judge proficiency. Because these criteria can form the basis of a number of important decisions, no single performance assessment design factor deserves more careful thought than this one. Clearly articulated criteria are an absolute necessity.

Step three in the development of a performance assessment calls for the *design of assessment exercises.* This step includes three design decisions. First, the user must specify the form of the exercises. Three options are available: structured exercises, natural events, or a combination of the two. Structured exercises are specific tasks or problems presented to the examinee to be completed or solved. They are fabricated to simulate part of the actual performance arena and are most useful when (a) the decision context requires that all examinees have an equal and standard opportunity to demonstrate their proficiency or, (b) a natural context for observation simply is unavailable or impractical. Observation of naturally occurring events can serve as the basis of performance assessment when those events contain sufficient observable evidence of proficiency to allow for valid and reliable evaluation. Such naturalistic observations often provide the most valid assessment of performance because they often provide a high-fidelity representation of the real world. However, natural events also are less subject to tight control and standardization. The requirements of performance in natural contexts can vary from occasion to occasion.

Step three in the performance assessment design process also requires the determination of the examinee's level of awareness that an assessment is taking place. A performance assessment can be open and public, unobtrusive or some combination of the two. The option of choice depends on the purpose for the assessment. Unobtrusive assessment, although not common, can be a useful tool. It often requires the observation of naturally occurring events and can be an advantage when (a) the examiner is interested in evaluating typical—not best possible—performance, and/or (b) the examinee is troubled by debilitating evaluation anxiety. Unobtrusive assessment can help alleviate the anxiety.

Finally, step three requires the specification of the number of samples of performance to be observed before making a judgment regarding the adequacy of performance. Choices include one sample of performance at one time, multiple samples at one time, and multiple samples over a period of time. In this case, the option of choice is a function of the seriousness of the decision to be made and the amount of time required to make one observation. The more serious the decision, the more evidence is needed. The more time required per observation, the more expensive will be the assessment. Thus, the context determines the amount of data gathered. In many cases, the choice of options turns on which alternative covers the range of situations in which the examinee might be called upon to demonstrate proficiency in the future.

The fourth and final step in the design of a performance assessment is the development of *performance rating procedures*. The user must determine the nature of the score(s) needed, the identity of the rater(s) and the recording method. With respect to the score, one can opt for a holistic rating (one score covering overall performance), an analytical rating (each performance criterion rated separately), or some combination of the two. This choice is a function of the nature of the data needed to make the decision at hand. For instance, selection decisions often require that examinees be ranked on the basis of overall performance, whereas diagnostic decisions require more detailed analyses of performance. For the former, a holistic score may suffice. For the latter, analytical data are needed.

When selecting the rater(s), the user has four options: independent rating by expert judge(s), peer-rating, self-rating, or some combination of these. Independent expert judges are needed when ratings require specialized knowledge or expertise, a competitive decision requires equal opportunities for all, and/or examinees have a vested interest in results and may be perceived as benefiting unfairly from self- or peer-rating. On the other hand, peer- or self-ratings are viable options when examinees are capable of learning and applying the performance criteria, have nothing to gain from inflating or deflating their ratings, and/or have time to observe and rate performance.

Finally, the recording method can take various forms, such as a checklist (list of attributes to be marked as present or absent in performance), a rating scale (continuum on which poor to outstanding performance is rated), an anecdotal record (verbal description of performance), a portfolio (file of samples of products), an audio or videotape or some combination of these. Another often used, but completely unreliable and unacceptable option is mental record keeping.

Each of the acceptable options has advantages and limitations. Checklists and rating scales provide an efficient means of evaluating and recording but can result in somewhat superficial pictures of performance. Anecdotal records and portfolios provide more detail but are cumbersome. Tapes provide a detailed record of performance, but contain no ratings. The best choice is a function of the use to be made of the results.

In this section, we have reviewed several specific design decisions to be made by the developer of a performance assessment. Each contained a number of design alternatives within it, as summarized below:

1. Specify the assessment purpose
   A. Identify decision(s) to be made
   B. Identify decision makers
2. Define performance to be evaluated
   A. Select the type of performance
      1) Behavior

2) Product
3) Combination of behavior and product
   B. Specify performance criteria
      1) Define each
      2) Develop the performance continuum for each
3. Design exercises
   A. Select the form
      1) Structured exercises
      2) Natural events
      3) Combination of structured exercises and natural events
   B. Determine examinee's level of awareness
      1) Public
      2) Unobtrusive
      3) Combination of public and unobtrusive
   C. Determine number of samples to be observed
      1) One sample, one time
      2) Multiple samples, one time
      3) Multiple samples over time
4. Develop the performance-rating plan
   A. Select the type of score
      1) Holistic
      2) Analytical
      3) Combination of holistic and analytical
   B. Identify the rater
      1) Expert
      2) Peer
      3) Self
      4) Combination of above
   C. Select the recording method
      1) Checklist
      2) Rating scale
      3) Anecdotal record
      4) Portfolio
      5) Audio or videotape
      6) Combination of above

Because these ingredients can be assembled in so many combinations, the range of possible forms of performance assessment is very broad. This is precisely why this kind of assessment is so valuable. In the next section, we explore how it can be molded to fit a wide range of teacher-assessment needs.

Ensuring Quality. Before we go on to explore the specific application of this methodology in various teacher assessment contexts, however, we need to review the keys to successful assessment in general. The quality of our measurement of performance is assured by giving careful attention to the purpose for assessment, communicating effectively, attending to the validity of the assessment and maximizing the reliability of the assessment.

Careful attention to purpose provides a clear sense of the decision to be made and the decision maker. With these factors in mind, the user can tailor exercises, performance criteria and performance records to fit the context. In the absence of a clear sense of purpose, it is impossible to design a meaningful or useful assessment.

Clear communication is central to effective assessment in the sense that examinees must understand the performance expectations or criteria and they must understand the exercises to which they must respond and the feedback provided. Of course, this requires that the assessment developer pay careful attention to these factors during the design process. Clear and thoughtful communication is also central to the effective delivery of feedback to examinees regarding their performance. The most appropriately designed assessment can become completely ineffective if results are poorly communicated.

In order to maximize the validity of the assessment, we must thoroughly articulate the performance dimensions to be evaluated and appropriately sample the range of possible performance arenas. Performance dimensions must be clearly defined to be effectively evaluated, and each dimension must be accompanied by the specification of different levels of performance or a continuum reflecting poor to outstanding performance. These specifications, along with a set of exercises that fairly and thoroughly samples the range of instances when the examinees might be called upon to use their skills, contribute to a valid assessment.

Finally, the keys to a reliable assessment are clear criteria used by thoroughly trained raters in the context of a carefully articulated scoring process. The acid test of the objectivity of performance ratings is for two independent judges to assign the same rating (within a small margin) to the same sample of performance. If such ratings vary greatly, then unclear criteria, rater bias, and/or inadequate rater training are indicated. Also central to reliable assessment are uniform assessment conditions and a large enough sample of performance to lead to confident judgment. The more serious the decision, the more data must be gathered.

Thus, in general, sound performance assessments are those that have a clear purpose, rely on clear communication, and are valid and reliable. Adherence to these quality-control standards can render these assessments more useful in many contexts than any other type of assessment. Let's explore why this is particularly true in teacher assessment.

MEASURING PERFORMANCE IN TEACHER ASSESSMENT

In the introduction, eight specific contexts were identified in which prospective or practicing teachers are assessed for purposes of making specific career-related decisions (see Table 6.1 for review). Further, we pointed out that any of a variety of assessment methods might be used to gather needed information. In five of the eight cases, performance assessment is the typical mode of measurement used. In the remaining three performance assessment represents a viable option. Having defined the active ingredients in a performance assessment and reviewed the wide range of design alternatives, let's explore how those design choices can vary with the teacher assessment context.

To reach this goal, the basic performance-assessment structure (purpose, performance, exercises, and rating procedures) is used to profile assessment practices in each context (course evaluation, student teacher evaluation, initial certification, permanent certification, hiring, minimum competency evaluation, professional development and career advancement). This analysis and profiling process allows us to highlight the keys to conducting valid and reliable assessments in each context.

Measuring Course Achievement. As prospective teachers complete their preservice training and as practicing teachers complete graduate course work, their achievement of course objectives is measured to allow instructors to diagnose student needs and/or determine course grades. Because completion of specific required courses is often a matter that bears directly on later career-related decisions for teachers, these course assessments are very important. Although many such assessments are based on paper-and-pencil tests and performance assessments are rare, they remain an excellent option.

In defining the performance to be evaluated, the instructor needs to consider the intended outcomes of the course. Those outcomes might be reflected in the trainee's ability to demonstrate a particular instructional method in a simulated classroom setting (an observable behavior) or in the trainee's ability to create a specific product, such as a lesson plan or a test developed to reflect a particular unit of instruction. The performance criteria need to be defined in terms consistent with intended course outcomes and in sufficient detail to reflect the specific behavior(s) or product attribute(s) to be demonstrated. Such detailed criteria are central to the teaching of instructional methods. *Without such criteria clearly in mind, it is impossible to teach, let alone measure, mastery of important instructional skills.*

As the instructor develops performance exercises to evaluate college-course achievement, he or she would probably rely on simulations and other college classroom activities to provide needed evidence of proficiency. Assessments in this context probably are announced and may provide only a few samples of the performance of individual students if a large number of students is enrolled in education courses. Naturally occurring classroom events are less likely to be available for the course instructor to use as a basis for evaluating student achievement. However, the more opportunities undergraduates have to demonstrate new skills in real school classrooms, the better will be the diagnostic quality of the performance ratings that may come from classroom performance assessments, and the more effective will be the quality of teacher training. Furthermore, the more opportunities instructors have to watch their students use the skills learned in courses, the better will be the teacher training programs.

Rating procedures used in course assessments will vary as a function of the specific decision to be made. If the reason for assessment is to diagnose the needs of students, then analytic data are required. However, if the reason is to assign a grade, an overall rating of performance may suffice. In most cases, the rater of performance will be the instructor. However, peer- and/or self-rating also remain options that offer the distinct advantage of allowing students to learn and apply the performance criteria to their own and each others performance, which in turn often enhances the performance of the student rater. The choice of record-keeping systems to use is a function of the nature of the depth of information needed. General grading decisions might be based on checklists and ratings, whereas diagnostic decisions may require a detailed analysis of anecdotal events, a portfolio of products or videos of students in action.

The keys to gathering a valid and reliable data on of teacher performance in the context of assessment during teacher training are to:

- be sure to use performance assessment when it represents the best way to measure intended course outcomes,
- translate intended course outcomes into clear and detailed performance criteria, and
- carefully train raters to apply the criteria,
- gather enough observational data to provide a representative picture of the performer's proficiency in all relevant classroom situations.

In other words, validity and reliability problems arise when we:

- use paper-and-pencil tests to measure traits better reflected in student behavior and/or a student product,
- teach and assess on the basis of ill-defined criteria, and
- fail to sample the full range of relevant student capabilities.

Trained raters using clear, course-relevant criteria to rate an appropriate sample of performance can conduct high-quality assessments in teacher training programs.

Evaluating Student Teaching. Within the context of teacher training perhaps the single most important teacher assessment is the evaluation of the students performance during student teaching. In this case, the typical mode of measurement is classroom observation and judgment. Although paper-and-pencil tests, interviews, and the like may play a role, no mode of assessment rivals performance assessment as the means of evaluating success in this context. The decision to be made is a very important one: Is this teacher ready to take responsibility for a classroom? This is the capstone evaluation that reveals whether the student is able to assemble all of the ingredients in sound instruction. But we must also keep in mind the fact that student teaching represents an extension of the preservice teacher-training experience. Trainers have an obligation to observe, diagnose and help improve the practice of those whom they oversee. The decision makers in this context are the supervising teacher and the college coordinator of student teaching.

In defining the performance to be evaluated, the evaluators often rely on an examination of behaviors and products. But in this case, the performance criteria are far more complex than those covered in any single course. In this case, the criteria need to cover all of the important competencies needed to be able to take responsibility for a classroom. They need to reflect dimensions of performance in instructional design (e.g., ability to use technology effectively), classroom management (able to control time on task), assessment and evaluation (apply a range of testing methods), subject-matter knowledge, and other key areas. In a sense, they may represent a compilation of the various course outcomes. In addition, and this is crucial, they may not be the same for all student teachers. Rather, the attributes of a good teacher and good teaching may vary by grade level, subject matter, and school context. If they do, performance assessments must be sensitive to those differences. But whatever the dimensions of good teaching, those dimensions must be thoroughly defined and a continuum of performance must be articulated for each.

In the student-teaching context, the evaluation is based on observation of naturally-occurring events with the student aware that an assessment is underway. Because the field experience is many weeks long, multiple samples of performance are gathered over time. For these reasons, student teaching represents an excellent opportunity for students to learn via detailed feedback from supervisor teachers and to demonstrate their mastery of the skills of teaching.

If the evaluation of performance during student teaching is to fulfill its potential, clear and appropriate performance criteria must be applied by trained supervisors to provide diagnostic (analytical) information leading to a sound overall (holistic) judgment of proficiency. Throughout the field experience, evaluators might use checklists and ratings scales tailored to provide unique information to the student regarding how to improve. In addition, anecdotal records and portfolios might be kept by the student and the supervising teacher as evidence of skill and accomplishment. Audio and videotapes also can be valuable tools in this context.

Thus during student teaching, performance assessments of many types might come into play. But to be valid and reliable, once again, they must be:

- based on clear criteria developed to reflect the full range of appropriate teaching skills
- evaluated through the observation of the full range of classroom events and examination of all relevant documents and artifacts

- by multiple trained observers and raters
- who spend enough time observing and providing feedback to promote the development and appropriate certification of the new teacher.

In the student-teaching context, problems of dependability arise when criteria are vague and/or inappropriate, observations fail to sample enough classroom performance to produce generalizable results, raters are untrained or careless, and/or student teachers receive information that fails to provide guidance as to how to improve.

Initial and Permanent Certification. Upon completion of an accredited program of study, the new teacher is eligible for initial certification to practice. Most often, this is a temporary certificate allowing the teacher to practice for some specified period of time. At the end of that period, if additional training experiences have been completed, a permanent certificate is granted. In this context, then, the first decision is whether to grant a license to teach, and the follow-up decision is whether to allow the teacher to retain that license.

In most cases, these decisions are made by a state bureau based on (a) the analysis of transcripts of courses completed by the teacher and (b) performance on basic academic skills tests. Thus, the assumption is made that the courses taken actually teach required teaching skills and the assessments within those courses test the students' mastery of important skills. If the courses have been carefully developed on the basis of a task analysis of good teaching, the training programs have included a sound student teaching experience, and assessments have been designed to test both knowledge and performance, this assumption may be valid. However, if the basic principles of sound performance assessment have not been adhered to in the evaluation of course and student teaching achievement, transcript analysis will not contribute to valid licensure decisions.

To the extent that certifying agencies are uncertain regarding the quality of undergraduate- and/or graduate-course assessments of teaching skills, supplemental performance assessments might be added to data informing the initial certification decision. These might take the form of precertification internships in which new teachers perform under the watchful eye of an experienced mentor, the successful completion of an employment experience (see minimum competency assessment following), or the successful completion of assessment-center simulations of particular classroom events. In any case, the rules of evidence for sound performance assessment must be adhered to: clear and appropriate performance criteria, a representative set of exercises, and carefully planned and conducted evaluations of performance.

Hiring. When school districts have positions to fill, they must screen candidates, rank order them, make sure the top ranked satisfy minimum acceptance standards, and select the most qualified to be hired. In most cases, the selection process is the responsibility of the district personnel director and the building principal in which the new teacher will be employed. Further, most such decisions are based on the review of placement papers (including transcripts and recommendations) and personal interviews with the teachers. Such decisions rarely are based on the demonstration of teaching skills by the prospective employee. Reliance on records, recommendations, and interviews as information sources for hiring rests on the assumptions that:

- course and student-teaching assessments dependably tested appropriate classroom performance,
- those providing recommendations have observed and evaluated classroom performance in an appropriate manner,
- prior supervisors of experienced teachers have conducted sound performance assessments, and
- the self-reports of performance capabilities presented by candidates during interviews accurately reflect true capabilities.

If these conditions are met, then an independent demonstration of teaching skills prior to hiring is unnecessary.

In short, it becomes obvious at the time of hiring that teacher assessments and decisions build upon one another. Each assumes (often without verification) that the preceding performance assessments were sound. Is this a defensible assumption? In many cases, it may not be. The quality of course and student-teaching assessments is generally unknown. Often, those assessments are designed and conducted by instructors largely untrained in performance assessment methodology. Further, the quality of the performance observations and evaluative judgments of principals and other supervisors has been called into question in the research literature.[2] We know that many of these assessments are conducted by staff untrained in proper methods of observation and evaluation. Finally, we know that self-assessments, although very useful in some contexts, probably are biased in an employee selection situation. Clearly, there is reason to question at least some of the performance assessment methodology that is assumed to support the hiring decision.

Therefore, it may be useful to consider other performance assessment options. The simplest alternative might be to sprinkle interviews with descriptions of typical classroom problems designed to probe the prospective teacher's plan of action in dealing with hypothetical instructional design and classroom management problems. A second option might be to present more complex simulations via video or role play for the candidate to address through the development plans of action. Yet a third choice might be for the teacher to develop products, such as lesson plans or paper-and-pencil tests, which might be evaluated in terms of specific attributes. Another possibility is for the teacher to take over a classroom as a substitute for a day to demonstrate instructional skills. Finally, teacher applicants might prepare videos demonstrating their competence for presentation to personnel officers as part of their application for employment.

In all cases, it will be the responsibility of the assessor to develop a clear and appropriate set of performance criteria, create a range of exercises to sample relevant job-performance situations, train multiple raters to apply criteria appropriately, and conduct the performance assessments in a fair and consistent manner so as to assure all candidates an equal opportunity to be selected. The selection context involves very high-stakes decisions for the teachers involved and for the students in the classes of the teacher hired. For this reason, it is essential that the decision be based on dependably evaluated demonstrations of classroom skill. If records, recommendations and interviews cannot be counted on to provide the needed performance information, alternative performance assessments should be considered.

Assessment of Minimum Competence. Once teachers are hired and begin to practice in the classroom, the assessment of their

---

[2]This literature is summarized in Stiggins, R. J., & Duke, D. L. (1988). *The Case for a commitment to teacher growth: Research on teacher evaluation.* Albany, NY: SUNY Press.

performance via observation and judgment begins in earnest. Supervisors often are required to carry out regularly scheduled evaluation procedures spelled out in state law and local collective bargaining agreements. Their immediate purpose is to make personnel management decisions: Who will be released? Who will be retained? And, ultimately, who will be granted tenure in the district? The immediate goal of these evaluations is to manage incompetence; that is, to see that only competent teachers remain in classrooms. Incompetents must be trained or removed. Such evaluations recur every year or two in most districts. For the teacher who continues to demonstrate minimum competence, these evaluations will not have real impact on the teacher. However, for the teacher who is having difficulty, the evaluation will result in a call for improvement and, if that fails, dismissal.

Because dismissals can be contested, performance assessments used in this context must be legally defensible. Evaluation must be conducted so as to protect the due process rights of the teacher and the district. Therefore, the performance criteria must reflect the competencies that comprise minimally competent teaching. Further, the criteria must be standardized for all to assure equal opportunity for all to succeed. Finally, they must be public and available for all to see and understand in advance of any evaluation.

Sound practice suggests that the performance assessment be based upon observation and evaluation of both classroom practices of the teacher and documents created by the teacher in support of the instructional effort (e.g., lesson plans). Thus, the assessment is based almost completely on the observation of naturally occurring events and products. If the supervisor adheres to the letter of the law and the strict wording of the collective bargaining agreement, the performance assessment often is based on one or two 1-hour observations during the school year, scheduled at mutually agreeable times. Although specific requirements may vary from district to district, observations and evaluations often are made by one person (the supervisor) and ratings reflecting each of the minimum competencies are combined into an overall rating, which is communicated to the teacher in writing. If the judgment is that a particular competency has not been met, a plan of action is developed to overcome the deficiency. If no deficiencies are noted, no action results.

The keys to valid and reliable assessment in the context of minimum competency evaluation are:

- reliance on clearly stated, job-relevant minimum competencies,
- evaluation of performance in terms of a broad range of naturally occurring classroom events and artifacts
- evaluation of performance by observers trained to apply the performance criteria in a systematic and consistent manner,
- the delivery of feedback on performance with an opportunity to overcome any deficiencies, and
- the maintenance of records detailing the teacher's performance rating on all relevant competencies.

Difficulties arise when the performance expectations are not specified at all, are stated in broad, vague terms, or fail to reflect the specific task demands placed upon the teacher. Further, the dependability of assessments based on one or two prearranged samples of teacher performance over the span of a year or two or three must be questioned. The extrapolation from such scant and possibly biased data to the thousands of hours of teaching conducted by the teacher is indefensible. In addition, the danger of bias is great when an evaluation of teacher performance is based on the observations and judgments of only one person. These problems are compounded when that person is untrained or inadequately trained in performance assessment methodology. Finally, the immediate impact of assessment on the quality of instruction is greatly reduced when the feedback given to the performer is not communicated effectively and/or when the teacher is not given adequate opportunity to overcome weaknesses.

In fact, any one of these problems is enough to render an assessment of teacher performance indefensible in a technical and legal sense. But more importantly, poorly conducted performance assessments in the minimum competency evaluation context can lead to profoundly inappropriate impacts on teachers' lives and careers. Such high-stakes decisions demand only the best quality performance assessment.

Assessment for Professional Development. There are at least two instances when teacher performance might be assessed primarily for purposes of professional development. The first is at the time the teacher enters the profession. More and more, teacher induction is coming to mean a time when new staff members are given the time and professional support needed to become accustomed to the school and classroom environment. Often this means the principal and/or senior staff will work with the new teacher to ensure the ongoing development of the teacher's instructional skills. Such support requires that the mentor rely heavily on observation and evaluation of classroom performance.

A second time when performance assessment for professional development becomes relevant is when the experienced and competent teacher decides to develop new professional capabilities—not because the district or a supervisor demands improvement, but because the teacher has high personal professional expectations. Under these circumstances, the teacher might well benefit from observation of and feedback on instruction, as he or she attempts to define new and important professional development goals. Further, that same teacher might continue to benefit from ongoing observation, evaluation and feedback, as she or he strives to improve. This kind of growth-oriented evaluation, although rarely the focus of teacher evaluation policy or publicity, represents one of the keys to the ongoing national efforts aimed at school improvement.

Performance assessment in the professional development context presents unique and interesting challenges. First, the objective is to provide information that will allow the teacher to move far beyond minimum competence toward excellence. For this reason, the performance criteria must reflect the teacher's personal commitment to improving. There is no requirement that criteria be standardized or public. Rather, the criteria can be individualized and very private if the teacher so wishes. In short, the criteria must relate directly to the professional development goal of the individual teacher.

Beyond the performance criteria, the assessment methodology available for use in this context is much more flexible than in the assessment of minimum competence. Observers may view naturally occurring events and documents, or the aspiring teacher may participate in courses and workshops that include structured exercises of various types. Depending on the situation, public or unobtrusive observations may be used and the amount of data gathered may range from a single observation to many observations over a period of time as long as several years. These will vary with the goal. Evaluation procedures are not constrained by law or contractual agreements. They are constrained only by the needs and desires of each individual teacher.

The rating of performance will need to be analytical so the developing teacher can track progress. The list of possible raters is long, including supervisors, peers, students (achievement and evaluations of teaching), and self-ratings. The list of possible recording strategies is similarly long, including checklists, rating scales, anecdotal records, and portfolios and tapes, again, depending on the teacher's professional development goal.

In this context, the keys to quality assessment are:

- selection of performance criteria that match the teacher's individual goal,
- the thoughtful observation of behavior and products that are similarly related to the teacher's goal,
- reliance on multiple trained observers, each of whom commands the respect of the teacher, and
- the careful delivery of enough detailed feedback to allow the teacher to adjust growth activities as needed to reach the goal.

Problems arise when the criteria fail to match the goal, the performance sampled fails to provide the needed information, observers lack credibility for the teacher, and/or feedback is delivered ineffectively.

When the purpose for performance assessment is the development of the professional competencies of an experienced and successful teacher, that teacher must be in charge of the evaluation. The teacher must lead the design of the assessment, identify the observers, review all data, and share results only if and when they wish to. But to take charge, teachers must be skilled in the use of performance assessment methodology on their own behalf.

Career Advancement. This decision context is like the others, in that it presents some unique challenges and requires very thoughtful use of assessment methodology. In this context, unlike the others, the task is to identify those who have attained the very highest levels of the performance continuum. They are tabbed to advance up the career ladder or to receive additional remuneration for outstanding performance. This decision often is made by a supervisor or a district management team.

The major challenge faced in this context is the development of appropriate performance criteria. Under some conditions, this may represent an insurmountable challenge. The potential problem is this: When we deal with minimum competencies, these can be defined and universally applied to all. That is, minimally acceptable performance for one teacher is generally the same as that of most teachers. But at the very high end of the performance continuum this may not be true. There can be many nitions of outstanding performance, depending on the performance context. Thus, there is no universally appropriate set of performance criteria. For instance, outstanding performance in an inner-city high school science classroom may differ fundamentally from outstanding performance in a suburban kindergarten. These differences may not simply be matters of degree. They may reflect differences in the kind of performance required to succeed.

This becomes a serious problem when we frame a decision context that requires that all teachers be measured against the same standard. Decisions as to who will receive merit pay and who will not require this, for example. Equality of opportunity demands that scarce merit-pay resources be made attainable to all on the same terms. But there may be few generalizable and job-relevant performance criteria upon which to base such a far-reaching competition. At the very least, the development of a universally applicable set of high-level performance criteria represents a formidable task that will demand considerable talent, time, and effort. One potential solution to this problem might be to group teachers into categories, such as grade levels, within which a common set of criteria can be applied and to award merit within categories only (i.e., allowing no cross-category comparisons based on differing, noncomparable criteria).

Other kinds of career-advancement decisions may not present such a difficult challenge. For instance, if a career ladder includes a position as a mentor teacher and a clear set of responsibilities is developed for the person who ascends to that level, then the performance criteria can be designed to assess attributes and skills relevant to that job (e.g., the ability to train adults). In any case, the primary key to success in conducting a valid and reliable performance assessment to identify outstanding performers lies in the difficult task of developing the right performance criteria.

In designing exercises for these assessments, either structured simulations or naturally-occurring events will serve. Most such assessments are based on the latter. Assessments often are public and rarely are unobtrusive. And they are most defensible when based on multiple observations of performance by qualified experts gathering data over a period of time. Qualified experts are those who have been trained rigorously to apply carefully developed performance criteria.

ASSESSMENT PURPOSE AND THE KEYS TO SUCCESS

It is clear that different purposes require different kinds of assessment and different kinds of performance assessment. To bring this point home in very clear terms, let me summarize the foregoing discussion in a slightly different way. In the literature on teacher assessment, it is common for scholars and practitioners alike to draw the distinction between formative and summative uses of teacher-assessment results. Formative assessments, for example, serve to promote the professional development of teachers, whereas summative serve the district's personnel management needs. As a conclusion, let's contrast the keys to effective performance assessment in each of these general contexts.

Summative Assessments. Of the decision contexts previously discussed, several are summative in nature. These include final course and student-teaching assessments, certification, hiring, minimum competence assessment, and career advancement. In each of these cases, the first requirement is that the performance criteria be based on a thorough task analysis of the teaching process. This analysis will ensure the job relevance of the standards and will maximize the validity of the performance assessment. Further, sound assessment practice holds that teachers be told of the criteria by which they will be evaluated before the assessment takes place.

The second requirement is that the performance of the examinee be evaluated in the context of actual or simulated classroom settings. The sample of exercises—whether naturally occurring or structured exercises—must reflect in a representative manner the full range of situations in which the student or teacher will be expected to demonstrate proficiency when teaching. This too contributes to valid assessment.

The third requirement is that the raters of performance be thoroughly trained to apply the performance criteria in a systematic and consistent manner. This will minimize bias and increase the chances that a teacher's rating will reflect true capabilities rather than the idiosyncrasies of a particular judge. To further control for bias it is advisable to have summative decisions be based on the observations and judgment of more than one judge whenever possible.

The fourth requirement of sound summative evaluation is that the teacher be given appropriate feedback on performance ratings and that the teacher have the opportunity to act upon that feedback to improve if necessary. This will afford the teacher the opportunity to complete professional development activities and repeat the performance assessment hopefully in a successful manner.

These four requirements are crucial because they protect the due process rights of teachers and provide the district with legally defensible evidence of proficiency for use in personnel actions. These are the standards by which we judge the quality of summative teacher assessments.

Formative Assessments. However, the standards by which we judge the quality of growth-oriented teacher assessments are quite different. Of the assessments just discussed, those that are of the formative variety are interim course and student teacher assessments, and professional development assessment at the time of induction or later in the competent teacher's career. In each of these cases, the test of the quality of the assessment is not its legal defensibility, but whether or not it contributes to the improvement of teacher performance. The keys to achieving this goal are fundamentally different than the keys to effective summative evaluation.

The first key is the teacher (for a more detailed discussion see Duke & Stiggins, 1986). To the extent that the teacher is knowledgeable about effective instruction, has high personal professional expectations, is open to criticism, is willing to change, and is comfortable with the material to be taught, the probability that a particular evaluation will result in growth for that teacher is greatly increased.

The second key to effective formative evaluation is the evaluator, or more specifically, how the teacher perceives the evaluator. The chances of a positive impact of evaluation increases when the teacher sees the evaluator as a credible source of ideas

---

*For a more detailed discussion of these, refer to Duke, D. L., & Stiggins, R. J. (1986). *Teacher evaluation: Five keys to growth*. Washington, DC: American Association of School Administrators, National Association of Elementary School Principals, National Association of Secondary School Principals, & National Education Association.

with persuasive rationale for those ideas. Furthermore, this evaluator must be perceived as patient and worthy of personal trust. Chances of a successful interchange are enhanced if the evaluator has a track record of helping people improve and is seen as sufficiently competent in his or her own right to take over the class and demonstrate the needed changes.

The third key to growth through assessment is the use of sound information gathering procedures. Performance criteria must be clear and perceived by the teacher as relevant in her or his specific classroom context. In addition, appropriate data sources need to be tapped including classroom observations, classroom document analysis, and student records. Finally, all relevant observers need to be tapped to ensure the reflection of a range of perspectives in classroom performance, including supervisors, colleagues, students, and self-assessments.

The fourth key to success in promoting teacher growth through assessment is the feedback provided to teachers. Feedback should be rich enough to act upon, but not so extensive that it overwhelms. It should be primarily descriptive, not only or harshly judgmental; sensitive to agreed upon professional development goals; formal and informal as the situation dictates; and, timed to promote effective communication (i.e., at a time when the teacher can listen and attend).

The fifth and final key to growth-oriented teacher assessment is that it be conducted in a district atmosphere in which teachers know that growth and improvement are valued and where resources (time and money) are appropriated to follow up the assessment with professional development activities and ongoing assessment.

Thus, the keys to successful performance assessment differ greatly as the overall purpose for assessment changes. This is precisely why one cannot carry out successful teacher assessment without a keen sense of purpose and a detailed knowledge of performance assessment methodology structure and design alternatives.

ACKNOWLEDGMENT

This chapter is based on work sponsored in part by the Office of Educational Research and Improvement (OERI), U.S. Department of Education under contract number 400-86-0006, with the Northwest Regional Educational Laboratory, Portland, OR. The content does not necessarily reflect the views of the department or any agency of the U.S. government.

7

Legal and Professional Issues in Teacher-Certification Testing: A Psychometric Snark Hunt

George F. Madaus
Boston College

> But the Snark is at hand, let me tell you again!
> 'Tis your glorious duty to seek it!
> To seek it with thimbles, to seek it with care;
> To pursue it with forks and hope;
>
> But the Judge said he never had summed up before;
> So the Snark undertook it instead,
> And summed it so well that it came to far more
> Than the Witnesses ever had said
>
> But the valley grew narrow and narrower still,
> And the evening got darker and colder,
> Till (merely from nervousness, not from goodwill)
> They marched along shoulder to shoulder
>
> —Lewis Carroll (1975)
> *The Hunting of the Snark; An Agony in Eight Fits*

The validation of teacher-certification tests has become a snark hunt. The snark pursued by test contractors however, is not nearly as elusive, nor fanciful as Carroll's shadowy beast. Their snark is a "legally defensible" test. Test contractors are—merely from nervousness (not from goodwill)—marching along shoulder to shoulder with jurists. I will argue that hunting the shadowy snark through the dark wood of the court room cheapens the conceptualization of validity and delimits the conduct of validation studies to minimalist exercises designed to obtain a positive result.

I start from the basic premise that the most important feature of any test is the accuracy of the inferences or decisions made from the score. Countless generations of measurement students have been taught the old saw: A test can be reliable but not valid, but if it's valid, it has to be reliable. Here I argue that a test can be legally defensible *but not valid*. However, if the results from a well-designed validation process, on balance support the inferences or decisions made on the basis of the test, legal defensibility should be satisfied. Legal defensibility is important. Tests must be able to stand court scrutiny. However, I contend, we have the cart before the horse—whatever courts will accept drives current validation practices. Legal precedent is circumscribing inquiry about the essential question underlying all testing—"how correct are the inferences made from a person's score?"

The vulnerability of testing companies engaged in this legal snark hunt consists in their readiness to view their task no more broadly than that of satisfying the desire of state agencies for legally defensible certification tests. Some contractors are in danger of becoming ambidextrous yes men for states.[1] Testing companies, of course, insist on test validity. However, faced with the exigencies of the applied world—legal precedent, contract obligations, tenacious timelines, and budget limitations—they offer excuses to absolve themselves from gathering construct and criterion-related evidence related to their products. They have built a tunnel through a mountain of precepts about validity which are regularly taught students in test and measurement classes. They take the law of validity literally, but argue that the letter is elastic, plead-

---

[1] There are notable exceptions. ETS refused to bid on the lucrative Texas and Arkansas recertification testing program because, as Gregory Anrig publicly pointed out, the NTE tests should not be used for decisions regarding retention or termination. *The Guidelines For Proper Use of NTE Tests*, states that such decisions: "about in-service teachers should be based on teaching competencies as determined directly by the supervisory and evaluation procedures of the employing school district" (NTE Policy Council, 1985, p. 7).

ing for leniency from basic precepts and strictures. The companies deny that their product purports to measure a complex construct—a subset of competence in the classroom.

This behavior of test contractors is a reaction to the following factors:

- the mandates of policy makers for a quick, visible, quantifiable, and administratively convenient fix to a perceived problem with the quality of the teaching corps
- a naive confidence on the part of policy makers and the public that multiple-choice tests can improve the quality of the teacher corps
- a lack of understanding on the part of policy makers and the public, concerning the kinds of evidence needed to support the inferences they wish to make about teacher candidates
- the bureaucratic nature of the state agencies charged with implementing the mandate of policy makers
- the funding level and lead time available to implement a systematic validation effort
- the applied, commercial nature of the testing industry
- the selection of contractors through the competitive, low-bid RFP process
- the allegiance of testing companies to the state agency that awards the contract, rather than to examinees who later pay to sit the exam, or the general public who often base their perceptions of educational quality on test scores
- the evolution of a set of tried and true procedures for gathering content validation evidence that redounds to confirmation rather than disconfirmation
- the vested interest of policy makers in vigorously defending their programs when legally challenged
- the competitive, adversarial nature of litigation that colors arguments on both sides about scientific-technical issues
- the existence of legal precedent about what is sufficient to justify the use of employment tests

I was asked to address the professional and legal implications of teacher-certification testing. This chapter, therefore, consists of two distinct sections. In the first section, I examine the legal challenges to teacher-certification tests. I offer examples of how testing experts operate within the legal arena. In this first section validity issues are interpreted from the legal rather than psychometric tradition. I begin by describing two types of legal challenges to teacher-certification tests and illustrate the part experts from the psychometric community play in these legal challenges. I conclude the first section with a description of the formula for a legally defensible teacher-certification test that has emerged from court decisions.

In the second section I leave behind the legal tradition and examine the validity issues surrounding teacher certification testing from the professional point of view. I begin by offering examples of the inferences and decisions made by various publics from scores on teacher certification. I then develop the psychometric implications for validation that flow from these inferences, and the problems associated with them in the applied situation. Next, I discuss issues related to the mix of content, construct, and criterion-related evidence that I feel is necessary if we are to understand what we are measuring and basing important certification decisions on. Finally, because the cut-score is the trigger for any inference or decision about teachers, I raise issues related to its validity.

Before I begin, two caveats. First, my treatment of litigation is strictly that of layman. My credentials consist of a single week in law school before leaving for the army, a decision I've never regretted. Second, I have a bias about high-stakes tests. If the use of a test has the potential to harm, or has serious consequences for individuals, the test should be subjected to a thoroughgoing validation *before* it is used operationally. Teacher-certification tests certainly trigger this bias. Large numbers of examinees are affected, particularly large numbers of minorities. From my perspective, the protection of the individual takes precedent over the state's interests until the state can demonstrate that the test, although not error free, does a reasonably good job of identifying individuals who in all likelihood lack the necessary skills or knowledge to be minimally successful in the classroom. The last clause anticipates my later argument that teacher certification tests are really about a candidate's competence in the classroom.

THE BASIS FOR LEGAL CHALLENGES

I shall concentrate on two theories under which teacher-certification tests are challenged: (a) the Fourteenth Amendment to the Constitution; and (b) Title VII of the Civil Rights Act of 1964. I do not attempt to analyze the extensive case law on which these theories are based. Instead, I will use plaintiffs' briefs in *Allen v. The Alabama State Board of Education*, (1985), and *The Georgia Association of Educators v. State of Georgia* (plaintiffs' brief, 1987) to illustrate the way they were recently used to challenge two teacher certification-testing programs.[2]

The Fourteenth Amendment to the Constitution

The Equal Protection and Due Process clauses of the Fourteenth Amendment to the Constitution provide the first grounds for legal challenges to teacher-certification tests. Either can be used on behalf of an examinee to challenge the use of a test for entry to the profession as an arbitrary, irrational, or unreasonable governmental action. Thus, for example, in *Schware v. Board of Bar Examiners* (1957) the court ruled that "A state cannot exclude a person from the practice of law or from any other occupation in a manner or for reasons that contravene the Due Process or Equal Protection Clause of the Fourteenth Amendment" (p. 238–39).

The Equal Protection Clause

The Equal Protection clause applies when the government engages in any form of grouping to determine differential government treatment of individuals. Once grouping occurs, courts ask, "What is the composition of the group?" and "What is done to the individual as a result of being placed in the group, that is to say, does it result in the person being stigmatized or denied a basic right such as freedom of speech or the right to vote?" Answers to these questions determine which of three forms of scrutiny of evidence the court will consider in examining the case: (a) If a racial group is affected adversely, or if a fundamental right guaranteed under the constitution is denied on the basis of being placed in a particular group, the claim receives *strict scrutiny*. Where racial grouping occurs it is necessary for plaintiffs to show that grouping was intentionally race based. Further, the court looks to see that the government is pursuing a compelling state interest and that no

---

[2]The reader is warned that I have worked for the Plaintiffs on both of these cases and that although I have tried to report objectively on the "facts" my possible bias should be noted. I have used the following documents in what follows. *Allen v. The Alabama State Board of Education Plaintiffs"* and Plaintiff-Interveners' Joint Proposed Findings of Fact and Conclusions of Law, Civil Action 81-697-N in the United States District Court for the Middle District of Alabama Northern District.

reasonable alternative is less discriminatory. (b) If there is grouping not based on race, or if no fundamental right is denied, the case receives a relatively simple scrutiny. The question the court addresses under this analysis is whether the government is pursuing a legitimate governmental interest and doing it in a rational, nonarbitrary, noncapricious way. (c) Intermediate judicial scrutiny falls between simple and strict. It is used in cases where a well-defined nonracial group is affected or where a fundamental right isn't involved, and the issue has important social significance. Courts have applied the intermediate scrutiny criterion in sex-discrimination and school-finance cases.

The Due Process Clause

The Due Process Clause applies when there is governmental deprivation of a life, liberty, or a property interest. For example, veteran teachers have a property interest in maintaining their jobs. Recertification testing could deprive them of this property interest. There are two types of due process: *substantive* and *procedural*. Substantive due process asks whether a governmental action is just, or fundamentally fair. Arguing that substantive due process has been violated in a teacher-testing case involves demonstrating that the use of the test is so arbitrary and so capricious that it bears no relationship to the state's objective. This is obviously extremely difficult to prove. Procedural due process asks whether the government went about its decision making in a systematic manner designed to minimize mistakes. Procedural due process also affords citizens an opportunity to have advance notice of, and an opportunity to influence, important government decisions that affect them.

Allen v. The Alabama State Board of Education (1985) is illustrative of a Fourteenth Amendment challenge. Alabama required that candidates for initial teacher certification pass a test of professional knowledge and a test specific to their certification area. Plaintiffs challenged the state's testing regulation by arguing that the tests employed:

> were fundamentally flawed, varied from sound psychometric guidelines, and violated basic principles of fairness. Consequently, defendants' classification of teacher applicants who have failed to achieve their cut-off score on these examinations is irrational and violates the equal protection and due process rights of the class. (p. 31)

The plaintiffs, relying heavily on precedent from *Debra P. v. Turlington* (1979),—the Florida minimum competency graduation testing case—challenged the testing program in part on procedural due process grounds:

> [the] defendants hastily concocted and implemented these tests as an absolute requirement for teacher certification in a period not exceeding 18 months. *The tests were in fact used as a requirement for certification only some three months after their construction, the first opportunity to provide students notice of their content* [italics added]. Under these circumstances defendants' implementation schedule of the test provided the plaintiff class insufficient notice, thereby violating their rights to due process under the fourteenth amendment to the Constitution of the United States. (Plaintiffs & Plaintiff-Intervenors', 1986 p. 39).

Plaintiffs in Allen vs. State Board developed their Fourteenth Amendment claim further using opinions from *Debra P.* (1981). First, they asserted that:

> Just as successful completion of a high school program creates a "state-created understanding" that one will receive a diploma, successful completion of a state-approved teacher training program creates such an understanding that one will receive a teaching certificate. (Plaintiffs' & Plaintiff-Intervenors', 1986, p. 33–34)

Second, using language directly from *Debra P.* plaintiffs asserted that a state-required examination used to deny persons a classification to which they have a property right or a limited interest must be "a fair test of that which is taught in its classrooms." (644 F.2d 408) Third they cited the following ruling from *Debra P.* to argue that Alabama had violated due process: "If the test covers material not taught the students, it is unfair and violates the Equal Protection and Due Process clauses of the United States Constitution." (644 F2d 408). Plaintiffs argued that because the testing program had a disparate racial impact, their Fourteenth Amendment claim should receive strict scrutiny. Finally, given disparate impact the defendants have the burden of proving that the examination was in fact a fair test of matters actually taught in the classrooms of their State-approved teacher-training programs and that there was no reasonable alternative that would have a lesser discriminatory impact.

By now readers will recognize the argument for curricular-related validity evidence (Madaus, 1983). Whether the Alabama tests had curricular validity or not isn't nearly as interesting as the argument that what is taught in teacher-training institutions and measured by multiple-choice items is, in fact, necessarily related to performance in the classroom. I examine this line of argument in more detail later.

Title VII of the Civil Rights Act of 1964

The most widely employed and powerful legal theory used to challenge teacher-certification tests is a claim under Title VII of the Civil Rights Act of 1964. Title VII mandated nondiscrimination in employment by reason of race, sex, or national origin. The Act also created the Equal Employment Opportunity Commission to enforce Title VII. It is important to remember that Title VII is an *employment* statute and, therefore, covers only *employment testing*. (The bulk of testing in this country cannot be challenged under Title VII.)

There are two threshold criteria that must be met by plaintiffs to mount a successful Title VII challenge. First, plaintiffs must establish that the State is an *employer*. (Although state employment issue has no direct psychometric implications, unless this first criterion is met, testing issues simply will not get heard.) Defendants in teacher-certification–testing cases argue that the State is merely a licensing board, not an employer; that teachers are employed by local school districts. Therefore, they contend that the State's certification tests can't be challenged under Title VII. However, in *United States and North Carolina Association of Educators v. North Carolina* (1977) and *The Georgia Association of Educators v. State of Georgia* (1987) the courts ruled that the state plays a pervasive role in the operation of the schools and in the employment of teachers. For example, in the Georgia case the court ruled that:

> Although the public schools in Georgia are operated by local school boards, the activities of the local boards are part of a state-wide educational program which is administered by the State and by the Georgia State Board of Education. The State and, in particular, the Board of Education, exercises authority over the local school board in matters that range from curriculum and program requirements to funding, construction of facilities, and long-range planning by local school systems. Under these circumstances, it cannot be determined as a matter of law that defendants are not "employers" for purposes of Title VII. (C86-2234A at 3)

If the defendant is an "employer" under Title VII, the plaintiffs must meet the second precondition to Title VII coverage. They must show that the tests have substantial adverse racial impact. The importance of this second test cannot be over emphasized. A shoddy, invalid teacher-certification test that fails minorities and nonminorities at essentially the same rate as nonminorities cannot be challenged under Title VII. Further, without a Title VII claim it is extremely difficult to challenge a defective, but nondiscriminatory, test under a Fourteenth Amendment due process or equal protection theory.

Once plaintiffs demonstrate adverse impact, the burden of proof shifts to the defendants to show the tests are "job-related" (*Albemarle Paper Co. v. Moody*, 1975). Finally, if the tests are shown to be properly validated, the plaintiffs have an opportunity to prove that "other tests or selection devices without a similar undesirable racial effect, would serve" the defendants' purpose. (*Albemarle Paper Co. v. Moody*, 1975)

DETERMINING ADVERSE IMPACT

The determination of adverse impact is made by comparing the selection rate for the minority group with that of the nonminority group. There are two ways of showing disparate impact: (a) the "80% rule" and (b) the "two or three standard deviation rule." There is, of course, extensive case law interpreting these rules, and learned treatises about them (e.g., Baldus & Cole, 1980; Kaye & Aickin, 1986). I do not attempt to review that literature. Instead, I use a recent challenge to a teacher-certification–testing program—*Georgia Association of Educators v. State of Georgia* (1987)—to illustrate the role testing experts played in the determination of disparate impact. The Georgia case affords the reader a concrete glimpse of how testing experts operate in the adversarial world of law.

The 80% Rule

The "80% rule" was adopted by the EEOC as a "rule of thumb" for assessing adverse impact. *The Question and Answers on Uniform Guidelines on Employee Selection Procedures* (UGESP) states:

> A selection rate for any race, sex, or ethnic group which is less than four-fifths (4/5) (or eighty percent) of the rates for the group with the highest rate will generally be regarded by the Federal enforcement agencies as evidence of adverse impact, while a greater than four-

fifths rate will generally not be regarded by Federal enforcement agencies as evidence of adverse impact. *Smaller differences in selection rate may nevertheless constitute adverse impact, where they are significant in both statistical and practical terms* [italics added] or where a user's actions have discouraged applicants disproportionately on grounds of race sex, or ethnic group. [U.S. Equal Employment Opportunity Employment Commission 29 C.F.R. § 1607.4D]

The 80%, or 4/5 rule, was not intended as a legal definition of discrimination but as a practical device to guide the EEOC in the use of their enforcement resources (Schlei & Grossman, 1983). Further, as the italicized section reveals, the 80% rule is not a hard and fast requirement.

In *Georgia Association of Educators v. State of Georgia* (1987), plaintiffs pointed to data over an 88-year period, in which Whites took the Teacher Certification Test (TCT) a total of 57,503 times and passed 48,986 times, for a pass rate of 85.2%. Blacks took the TCT 19,826 times and passed 8,329 times, for a pass rate of 42.0%. Because the Black pass rate was only 49.3% of the White rate (42 ÷ 85.2 × 100)—considerably less than 80%—plaintiffs argued that their Title VII claim was justified (Plaintiffs' Brief In Opposition, 1987, p. 45). Thus, in Georgia the 80% rule seemed at first glance, straightforward. But looks are deceiving. Two issues muddy the waters; both involve the testing community.

The first issue revolves around the formulation of the comparison groups. Two groups were affected by the Georgia TCT: (a) the "Renewal Certificate Group," consisting of experienced Georgia teachers seeking recertification; and (b) the "Initial Certificate Group," consisting of candidates applying for Georgia certification for the first time. Robert Rentz, an expert for the State Department of Education, reported that his calculations showed that the pass rate for Blacks in both groups was more than 80% of the pass rates for Whites. He concluded, "no 'substantially disproportionate racial impact' is evidenced" (1987a, p. 4). On the basis of the Rentz analysis, defendants argued that plaintiffs had no claim under Title VII.

Plaintiffs countered that an analysis by their expert, John Poggio (1987a) showed that Rentz's numbers were substantially incorrect because of "egregious multiple counting of records" (Plaintiffs Brief in Opposition, 1987, p. 35). In other words, a single person who passed a single test was counted more than once by Rentz; often five or more times. Poggio also challenged Rentz's inclusion of other cases in forming his groups.[3] Rentz (1987b) in reply, argued that the multiple counting was the result of a single person using the test result to apply for more than one certificate, and therefore was legitimate.[4]

Poggio used different inclusion rules to formulate his groups—a single person taking a single test was counted once—and found for all examinees irrespective of initial or renewable status, a ratio of Black pass rate to White pass rate of 74.6%; less than the magic 80% criterion for a Title VII claim. He then calculated the ratio of Black to White pass rates for the Initial and Renewable groups separately and found the ratios to be 69.6% and 82.8%, respectively.

This interchange between testing experts over the 80% rule isn't offered to resolve either claim,[5] nor as a second edition of *How To Lie With Statistics* (Huff, 1954). Instead it illustrates how an important legal trigger can color an expert's approach to an otherwise apparently "objective" set of data.

The second issue surrounding the 80% rule is closely related to the group-definition issue. Given multiple retakes, when do you calculate your ratios to go to court? The ratio will slide with each retake. Because Georgia Blacks failed the TCT in greater numbers than Whites, the pool retaking the test for recertification became more and more Black over time. And with each Black passing a retake the 80% rule becomes harder to meet. The State, of course, would include as many retakes as possible before going to court. Plaintiffs would like to establish a temporal base line beyond which retakes are not considered in the calculations.

Before leaving the '80% rule, one additional observation is in order. It takes no genius to recognize that the 80% rule is a function of where in the distribution the agency sets the passing score. Field-test data, or data from the first or second administration of

---

[3]Poggio's analysis shows that 5,782 matches in the Rentz Initial Certificate file were the result of multiple counting; the comparable figure for the Renewable Certificate file was 5,715 matches. Poggio, offered as one example of thousands of cases of multiple counting a Black who took the TCT Science test on only one occasion and passed it and was counted as a "pass" six times. (Poggio, 1987, p. 5)

[4]Thus Rentz (1987b) argued that the person counted six times as a pass for the science test cited by Poggio could be used by an "otherwise qualified individual in applying for 15 different certificates, any one of which might subsequently qualify that person for different job openings" (p. 1).

[5]My belief is that the Poggio analysis best reflects the situation of how Blacks are affected by the TCT.

the test, permit fine tuning the cut score so that the ratio of the minority pass rate to the nonminority pass rate is greater than 80%. No one admits to this practice, but several plaintiff lawyers I have talked to believe that available data on the minority and nonminority pass rates are used to adjust the cut score after the fact in order to avoid a Title VII claim.

What's wrong with adjusting the cut score to raise the pass rate for minorities? Nothing, if the program is viewed cynically as nothing more than a public relations exercise to assuage a distrustful public that "incompetent" teachers will not be allowed in the classroom. After all, why get involved in very costly litigation if it can possibly be avoided by judicious choice (no pun intended) of a cut score from the known distributions of the two groups? However, if the question of the correctness of the inferences, decisions, or descriptions made from candidates' test performance is taken seriously, then clearly the operational cut-off score should be based on empirical considerations rather than on the vagaries of the 80% rule. I shall return to the question of validity and the cut score later.

The Two or Three Standard Deviation Rule

As we saw in the preceding section, the 80% rule is merely a guideline which admits of exceptions. The courts also consider tests of statistical significance in determining whether a selection device has a disparate impact. The Fifth and Eleventh Circuits have adopted the "two or three standard deviations" test first employed in 1977 by the Supreme Court in *Castaneda v. Partida* (1977). In recent cases these Circuits have approached the question of disparate impact solely from a standard deviation analysis (Plaintiffs Brief in Opposition, 1987).

Castaneda was a case involving jury selection. The Supreme court ruled that a difference of two or three standard deviations (in reality standard errors) between the percentage of the minority group in a large population (the general population) and the percentage of minorities actually selected for jury duty is generally indicative of discrimination.

Let's examine how this rule was operationalized by the experts in the Georgia case. Rentz (1987a) reported that Blacks in the Initial group constituted 12.7% of the larger population who attempted the TCT, but only 10.8% of the smaller sample who passed: a difference of 1.9 percentage points. He then argued that

7. LEGAL AND PROFESSIONAL ISSUES 221

If the differences obtained here (1.9) were translated into standard deviations based on the sample size for the sample passing the TCT (20,660), the result would be 8.26; but if that same difference were translated using the same sample size as *Castaneda v. Partida* (e.g. 870), the result would be 1.68. (p. 4)

For the Renewable group the difference was 2.4, or 8.77 SDs using an N of 21,370, but only 1.76 SDs if adjusted to a sample size of 870. In other words, Rentz considered the N of 870 in *Castaneda v. Partida* as normative. He reasoned that "almost any difference can be found to be statistically significant if the sample size is large enough. The question of whether or not 1.9 is reflective of 'substantially disproportionate racial impact' is not a statistical question" (Rentz, 1978a, p. 4) Rentz was certainly correct on two points: (a) large samples can ensure statistical significance, and (b) the question of what value constitutes substantial racial impact is not statistical. However, his conclusion that for both initial and renewable groups there was "no statistical evidence that persuades me that there is a substantially disproportional racial impact resulting from the requirement to pass the TCT, within the framework of . . . *Castaneda v. Partida*" (p. 5) is itself a value judgment.

Poggio (1987a) countered Rentz's acceptance of the N of 870 as sacrosanct:

> it makes absolutely no sense in statistical terms . . . to take the number of standard deviations computed on the basis of disparities for a sample of over 20,000 test-takers, and "translate" them into the number of standard deviations that would result if the same percentage difference has been observed in much smaller samples. . . . In as much as the difference in black/white pass rates on the TCT was in fact *established* on the basis of the performance of over 20,000 persons, the meaning of that difference properly *must be assessed* in terms of the performance of over 20,000 people. (pp. 12–13)

The sample size issue apart, Poggio criticized Rentz for making the wrong comparison. He argued that the TCT is a selection procedure, and that the EEOC's *Uniform Guidelines on Employee Selection Procedures* defines adverse impact for such procedures in terms of the difference between the selection rate of a particular racial group (in Georgia, Blacks) and the selection rate of the group with the highest selection rates (in Georgia, Whites). Poggio argued that the issue in *Georgia* was different from the issue in *Castaneda*. In *Castaneda* the issue was whether the percentage of minorities selected for jury duty was representative given the percentage of minorities in the general population. In the *Georgia* case Poggio identified "the extent to which the black pass rate differs from the white pass rate" as the central issue (Poggio, 1987a, p. 13). In other words, Poggio argued that the basic question in employment testing is not one of representation but of whether the test treats the two groups more or less equally. On closer examination the representation and the comparative selection methods are identical if the total population of examinees is made up only of Blacks and Whites. However, if the total population includes members of other racial or ethnic groups, the results from the two approaches can differ.

Poggio computed the number of standard deviations between the Black and White pass rates (Table 7.1) to answer what he saw to be the relevant statistical question, that is, "how likely is it that if selection were unbiased as to race, the Black pass rate would be as far below the white passrate as the data show it is in this case?" (p. 14). Poggio pointed out that his comparative pass rates are well in excess of the Supreme Court's *Castaneda* rule and are indicative of discrimination. He argued that even for the Renewal group, where the pass rate is slightly above the 80% rule (82.8%), the disparity between the two pass rates is statistically significant. Finally, he pointed out that even using the Rentz representation comparison (but without the 870 transformation) the number of standard deviations obtained is never less than 9.71.

Rentz (1987b) countered Poggio's critique with an assertion that an analysis of proportional representation is the appropriate comparison. He did not, however, develop the argument of why it was appropriate. Instead he argued that the important statistic to consider is the absolute size of the difference between the population percentage (in this case Blacks taking the test) and the same group's proportional representation in the sample selected (i.e., passing the test), *not* the translation of this difference to standard deviations.

Rentz's argument is worth closer examination. From a review of four cases similar to *Castaneda* he extracted differences between

TABLE 7.1

• All administrations	119.70 SDs
• All Examinees; cumulative pass rate	84.12 SDs
• Initial certification group; cumulative pass rate	77.12 SDs
• Renewal certification group; cumulative pass rate	38.86 SDs

Note. Derived from data in Pozzio 1987a

7. LEGAL AND PROFESSIONAL ISSUES

TABLE 7.2

Case	Population %	Sample %	Difference
Turner v. Fouche	60.0%	37.0%	23.0
Whitus v. Georgia	27.1%	9.1%	18.0
Sims v. Georgia	24.4%	4.7%	19.7
Jones v. Georgia	19.7%	5.0%	14.7

Note. From *Supplement to Affadavit of Dr. Robert Rentz* (p. 3) by R. Rent, 1987b, Georgia Association of Educators v. State of Georgia, Civil Action No. C86–2234A.

population percentages and the sample selected percentages. These are shown in Table 7.2 He concluded that an absolute difference of 19—give or take a few percentage points—is what the courts should be sensitive to. That this absolute difference is a better criterion than an arbitrary "standard deviation rule" which fluctuates with sample size.[6]

Rentz then computed the equivalent differences in population and sample percentages for the Initial, Renewable, and All Examinee groups. These data are presented in Table 7.3 along with the percentage difference from *Castaneda*. The samples Rentz used in computing his differences for the Initial and Renewal groups were substantially different from Poggio's samples.[7] From these data Rentz argued that

> None of the results in the present case are close to the magnitude of the results in *Castaneda v. Partida*. The differences I obtained for certificate applicants are quite small, 1.9 for Initial and 2.4 for Renewal applicants; . . . *The difference in representation for Dr. Poggio's test takers is 11.1, not as small as that for applicants, but below the average of 19 for the four examples cited in the Supreme Court opinion. The 11.1 difference is even below the lowest result of the four cases cited* [italics added]. (Rentz, 1987b, p. 7)

Notice Rentz's use of the difference of 19 as a criterion.

---

[6]Rentz pointed out that a difference of 40.1 obtained in Castaneda translates to 29 standard deviations but if the sample size were to increase ten fold from 870 to 8,700 the standard deviation would be 92. He then asked, rhetorically, if the degree of underrepresentation is more in the second case than the first, and answers no; the number 40.1 represents the degree of "underrepresentation" not the size of the standard deviation.

[7]For example for the Initial group Poggio (1987a) reported 7,557 Blacks took the test and 5,003 passed (p. 20), whereas Rentz (1987b, p. 5) recorded 2,735 Blacks in the population of test takers of which 2,214 passed. The two experts where working from different tapes, with different inclusion rules.

TABLE 7.3

Group	Population %	Sample %	Difference
Initial certification	12.7%	10.8%	1.9
Renewal certification	20.0%	17.6%	2.4
All Examinees	25.6%	14.5%	11.1
Castaneda	79.1%	39.0%	40.1

Derived from data in Rentz (1987b)

The problem with Rentz's absolute percentage difference criterion is that it is an altogether relative, population-dependent index.[8] It is somewhat analogous to the test dependence of the traditional item-discrimination index. The percentage of the minority group in the overall population always sets the upper bound for the difference between the population percentage and the sample selected percentage. Thus if you were to adopt Rentz's "difference of 19" proposal, once the percentage of Blacks in the population falls below 15% you are automatically out of the *Castaneda* ball game. Table 7.3 dramatically illustrates this population dependence; for the Initial certification group the highest difference you could possibly achieve is 12.7—and then only if no Black passed the test.

Taking the ratio of the sample selection percentage to the population percentage removes the population dependence inherent in the Rentz criterion. Table 7.4 presents these ratios for *Castaneda*, the four related cases, and the All Examinee group which Poggio developed and Rentz used in his argument. Ratios for the Initial and Renewable groups are not shown in Table 7.3 because of the large discrepancy in the sample size between the Poggio and Rentz versions. Examination of the ratios in Table 7.4 reveals that in *Castaneda* for every two Mexican Americans in the population only one was selected for jury duty; for the All Examinees group in *Georgia* the ratio is also close to 2 to 1. Both in *Castaneda* and *Georgia* the ratio is lower than that in *Turner v. Fouche*. This analysis, of course, begs the question of whether the representation approach or the comparative selection approach is the correct comparison to make, a question ultimately for the courts, not for measurement experts, to decide.[9]

---

[8]I am greatly indebted to John Poggio for the analysis that follows of the Rentz difference of 19 criterion.

[9]Using the All Examinee figures you can show that this ratio technique is identical to the 80% rule when there are only two groups. Both Rentz and Poggio reported

The analyses and arguments in the Rentz and Poggio affidavits offer us a glimpse into the world of the expert witness. We see two respected, highly qualified professionals attempt to interpret, in the best possible light, what appears at first blush to be simple court guidelines on what constitutes disparate impact. The stakes are extremely high in this interchange. Make no mistake! It is not an academic debate over what statistic to use. Without disparate impact, there is no Title VII claim, and questions about the validity of the test cannot be raised. And as things stand now, absent a Title VII claim, the contractor and agency are home free. There is no other forum, or independent auditing agency to which examinees can bring questions about test validity. I return to this issue later.

Can the profession arrive at a consensus on some of the issues posed in the Rentz/Poggio interchange? There could probably be agreement on the effect of sample size on statistical significance and power associated with the "standard deviation rule." We could probably agree on the correct definitions for the population and the sample selected given more than two racial groups in the overall population. We might even be able to agree on whether the absolute difference criterion of Rentz, or the ratio of sample selected to population criterion described in Table 7.4 is appropriate. But how large the difference or ratio should be is clearly a value question. Similarly, although the 80% rule is free of the population size problem associated with the standard deviation rule, the actual percentage constituting disparate impact is also a value question, particularly when the ratio of selection is close to 80%.

In the final analysis, a judge using his or her own personal calculus—colored by legal precedent, his or her training, temperament, history, intellect, personality, and predilections—must interpret the disparate impact data from contending experts, and decide if an employment test is treating minorities in essentially the same way as it treats Whites. How did the district judge in Georgia interpret the Rentz/Poggio data? Although not ruling on the disparate impact issue directly, he denied the State's motion for partial summary judgment because "the plaintiffs have raised numerous genuine issues of material fact regarding the statistical analysis performed by Dr. Rentz and relied upon by the defen-

---

that for this group the selection ratio of Blacks to Whites is 49.31%. The ratio of Blacks selected to Blacks in the population of test takers is .566. The ratio for the Whites is 1.145 (85.5/74.4). Dividing .566 by 1.145 gives you 49.31%.

TABLE 7.4

Group	Population %	Sample %	Sample/Pop.
Castaneda	79.1%	39.0%	.493
Turner v. Fouche	60.0%	37.0%	.617
Whitus v. Georgia	27.1%	9.1%	.336
Sims v. Georgia	24.4%	4.7%	.193
Jones v. Georgia	19.7%	5.0%	.253
All Examinees	25.6%	14.5%	.566

Derived from data in Rentz 1987a & b

dants" (*Order of Court*, 1987, p. 4). In other words, he still had questions in his mind about disparate impact that have to be argued further. (The Georgia case was subsequently settled out of court.)

THE EMERGENCE OF THE LEGALLY DEFENSIBLE TEST

So much for legal theories used to litigate teacher-certification testing. I turn now to the impact of litigation on test validation. Reviews of employment-testing litigation in general (Novick, 1982; Wigdor, 1982) and teacher-testing litigation in particular (McCarthy, 1985; NTE Policy Council, 1985) are available elsewhere. Therefore, what follows is *my rendering* of the emergence from court rulings of the recipe for "legally defensible" teacher-certification tests and the ingredients of the recipe. To reiterate, it's my contention that the precondition of "legal defensibility" drives applied validation efforts to the detriment of a careful consideration of the evidence needed to sustain the inferences and decisions made from the test scores. The form and technique to construct a "legally defensible" test has almost completely overshadowed the essential question of the meaning behind the test score. What is the form and technique of "legal defensibility"?

A legally defensible test is the product of the quasi-legal, quasi-scientific approach of the court to employment-testing litigation (Schlei & Grossman, 1983). The Second Circuit in *Guardians Association of the New York City Police Department v. Civil Service Commission* (1981) observed that while Title VII forces courts to consider employment testing, it is not primarily a legal subject:

7. LEGAL AND PROFESSIONAL ISSUES 227

[Employment testing] is part of the general field of educational and industrial psychology, and possesses its own methodology, its own body of research, its own experts, and its own terminology. The translation of a technical study such as this into a set of legal principles requires a clear awareness of the limits of both testing and law. It would be entirely inappropriate for the law to ignore what has been learned about employment testing in assessing the validity of these tests. At the same time, the science of testing is not as precise as physics or chemistry, nor its conclusions as provable. While courts should draw upon the findings of experts in the field of testing, they should not hesitate to subject these findings to both the scrutiny of reason and the guidance of Congressional intent. (pp. 169-79)

It seems jurists and legal scholars are as uncomfortable as many of us in testing are with courts ruling on issues of test validity. However, unfortunately, by default the court has become the arbiter of the EEOC *Guidelines* and the *Standards for Educational & Psychological Testing* (American Educational Research Association, American Psychological Association, & National Council on Measurement in Education [AERA, APA, & NCME], 1985).

Two paths to the validation of teacher-certification tests have emerged from this quasi-legal, quasi-scientific crucible of the court room. Both must show that the test is job related. The first, which I call the curricular validity approach, comes out of the *United States v. South Carolina* (1978) case involving the use of the NTE. As we saw plaintiffs in Alabama challenged that state's teacher tests partly on the grounds that it lacked curricular validity. The second approach, which I label the content validity route, has evolved from a number of court decisions interpreting the concept "job relatedness" in employment testing. The two approaches are not qualitatively different. Both involve judgments by panels about the match between test items and a domain. The approaches differ in domain definition.

The Curricular-Validity Approach

In *United States v. South Carolina* (1977) the Justice Department and others challenged South Carolina's use of the NTE program tests for initial teacher certification, and for determining, in part, the salary schedule of experienced teachers. Plaintiffs proved disparate impact, shifting the burden under Title VII to the defendants to demonstrate validity (i.e., job relatedness). To meet this burden of proof, the South Carolina commissioned ETS, the developers of the NTE, to conduct a validity study. The study sought to demonstrate "content validity by measuring the degree to which the content of tests matches the content of the teacher training programs in South Carolina" (*United States v. South Carolina,* 1977, p. 1112). The ETS study involved 456 faculty members from twenty-five colleges and universities in South Carolina. The participants, convened as members of panels and looked at the tests under controlled conditions and made judgments about the relationship between the tests and the curricula of teacher-training institutions in the state. (United States v. South Carolina 1977)

Relying on the following passage from *Washington v. Davis* (1976), a police employment case, the lower court endorsed in principle the ETS decision to validate the NTE against the academic training program rather than actual job performance:[10]

> [A] positive relationship between the test and training-course performance was sufficient to validate the former, *wholly aside from its possible relationship to actual [job] performance as a police officer* [italics added]. . . .
> Nor is the construction foreclosed by either Griggs or Albemarle Paper Co. v. Moody, 422 U.S. 405, 95 S.Ct. 2362, 45 L.ed.2d 280 (1975); and it seems to us the much more sensible construction of the job-relatedness requirement. (426 U.S. at 205–251, 96 S.Ct at 2053, p. 1113)

The Supreme Court affirmed the lower court decision without comment. As I read this ruling, a contractor wishing to build a legally defensible teacher-certification test simply has to show that the test items correspond to skills and knowledge found in the state's teacher-training curricula. This isn't particularly difficult to do. The composition of the panels, and the techniques used to solicit from them the match between test items and teacher-training curricula are straightforward. Further, the methodology is relatively cheap, fast, and—if the test contractor had any foresight at all—confirmatory.[11]

---

[10]The court also cited *Washington v. Davis* (1976) to dismiss the plaintiffs constitutional challenge under the 14th Amendment: "The Supreme Court has held that a substantial relationship between a test and a training program—such as is found here [S. Carolina]—is sufficient to withstand challenge on constitutional grounds" (p. 1108).

[11]It is interesting to note that in the mid 1940s for financial reasons the NTE probably at the request of teacher educators increased the professional information

However, I know of no recent defense of a teacher-certification test that relies solely on this approach. Now when the curricular-validity approach is used it is generally folded into the content-validity approach described in the next section. Nonetheless, it is worth looking more closely at the legal reasoning about validity found in *United States v. South Carolina.*

In *Washington v. Davis* (1976) a test of verbal skills and communication ability was used to screen applicants for a 17-week police academy training program. The Supreme Court accepted the lower court's reasoning that "the lack of job performance validation does not defeat the test, given its direct relationship to recruiting and the valid part it plays in [the training regimen]" (426 U.S. 229 at 236).

The court seemed to brush aside the fact that the South Carolina examinees taking the NTE for initial certification had already successfully completed their teacher training. Instead, the court observed that the NTE, although not measuring teaching skills, "was a measure of the extent to which prospective teachers have mastered the content of their teacher training programs" (p. 1108). The court also pointed to the plaintiffs acknowledgement of the importance of teacher-training programs when they proposed that graduation from "an approved program alone is sufficient to protect the public interest" (United States vs South Carolina, 1987).

The court also opined it was proper to use the NTE scores of experienced teachers for salary purposes. In doing so the court chose to ignore the NTE Policy Board's position that their program tests should not be used for such purposes:

> The current NTE Program tests were developed to provide information about candidates' academic knowledge and skills, typically acquired through a teacher-training program. They do not provide a direct evaluation of teaching performance. For this reason, NTE tests should not be used . . . directly or indirectly, for decisions regarding retention or termination. Such decisions about in-service teachers should be based on teaching competencies as determined directly by the supervisory and evaluation procedures of the employing school district.
>
> Similarly, with the exception of master teacher or career ladder plans, NTE tests should not be used for decisions regarding compensation.

---

to 40% of the common exam total score, and the advisory council shifted from local school administrators to teacher training personnel. For a complete history of the development of the NTE, see Wilson (1984).

> The current NTE tests measure knowledge and skills needed by the beginning teacher; more is required of the teacher in service. (NTE Policy Consul 1985, p. 7–8)[12]

I applaud as eminently sound and fair ETS's position on the use of the NTE program tests with in-service teachers. Nonetheless, there is a curious logical problem with the reasoning behind it that might explain the court's ruling. Why should the knowledge and skills measured by the NTE be job-related for preservice teachers but not for in-service teachers? The court made no such distinction in terms of the degree of knowledge possessed. As far as the court was concerned what was good for the goose was good for the gander: "[T]he State could reasonably conclude that the NTE provided a reliable and economical means for measuring one element of effective teaching—the degree of knowledge possessed by the teacher" (United States v. South Carolina, 1977 p. 1109).

It seems to me that the court did not go far enough in its analysis of the *Washington v. Davis* precedent. The reasoning found in the dissenting opinion makes several very telling points. First, the defendants in *Washington v. Davis* at least offered a correlation between the admissions test and the final examination grades from the police training course to support their validity claim. There is no reference in *United States v. South Carolina* to any correlation between NTE scores and scores in either professional education courses, or in specific subject related academic courses.

Second, even if such correlations had been offered, the ruling seems to take for granted that teacher-training curricula are relevant to one's later teaching performance. The dissenting justices in *Washington v. Davis* noted that: "Sound policy considerations support the view that, at a minimum, petitioners should have been required to prove that the police training examinations either measure job-related skills or predict job performance" (Quoted in Schlei & Grossman 1983, p 126) They argued further that a correlation between the admission test and the grades in training is supportive evidence only if: "(1) the training averages predict job performance or (2) the averages are proven to measure performance in job-related training" (Dissenting opinion *Washington v. Davis*, quoted in Schlei & Grossman 1983, p 124)

Grades in teacher training, like grades in other professional

---

[12]Although I have quoted the most recent NTE guidelines, similar statements can be found in earlier versions and would have been policy at the time of the South Carolina case.

training programs, do not correlate highly with later job performance. (see Haney, Madaus, & Kreitzer, 1987, for a review of this literature) Further, we simply take for granted that the curricula of teacher-training programs are related to teaching performance. I believe that aspects of teacher training may very well be relevant to job performance. Nonetheless, the question of whether those relevant aspects of the training experience can be captured by a secondary indicator—a multiple-choice test—remains unanswered. And, this is precisely the validity issue.

The dissenters in *Washington v. Davis* also had an excellent intuitive recognition the underlying construct at issue in that case: "[T]here is a substantial danger that people who have good verbal skills will achieve high scores on both tests due to verbal ability, rather than "job-specific ability." (426 U.S. 270)[13]

In my opinion, in *United States v. South Carolina* the ruling simply side stepped job-relatedness and the job-specific ability issue raised by the dissenters in *Washington v. Davis*. Nonetheless, the South Carolina decision has provided contractors with one clear line of legally defensible "validity" evidence.

The Content-Validity Approach

A second, and more common route to a legally defensible teacher-certification test is to show job relatedness through content validation. First, I review the essentials of the major cases from which this approach to validation has emerged to describe for the reader the essentials of the approach. To illustrate how the approach was actually implemented and then challenged in court, I outline the steps taken by the test contractor National Evaluation Systems in validating Alabama's teacher certification tests, and briefly list the plaintiffs objections to each step in that process.

Unless plaintiffs can show *intentional* discrimination in the use of a test, the test will not be an issue in constitutional actions. (Schlei & Grossman, 1983). Thus, as we have mentioned earlier, the cornerstone of most challenges to an employment test is a Title VII claim. The first important case was *Griggs v. Duke Power Co.* (1971), where the Supreme Court ruled that "If an employment

---

[13]Interestingly Mitchell (1985) reviewing the NTE also raise a similar construct-related question about parts of the Core Battery. He suggested that different parts of the test may measure, "general intelligence, scholastic aptitude, overall academic achievement, and multiple-choice test item reasoning skills" rather than "mastery of particular domains of curriculum such as professional education" (p. 1066).

practice which operates to exclude Negroes cannot be *shown to be related to job performance* [italics added], the practice is prohibited" (p. 178). The Court went on to interpret the intent of Congress in enacting Title VII:

> Nothing in the Act precludes the use of testing or measuring procedures; obviously they are useful. What Congress has forbidden is giving these devices and mechanisms controlling force *unless they are demonstrably a reasonable measure of job performance* [italics added]. (p. 180).

The key question in subsequent cases became "what constitutes acceptable evidence that the test is job related?" In *Albemarle Paper Co. v. Moody* (1975) the Supreme Court ruled that "[a discriminatory test must be] *predictive of or significantly correlated with* [italics added] important elements of work behavior which comprise or are relevant to the jobs or jobs for which candidates are being evaluated" (422 U.S. 431). Phrases like "predictive of" and "correlated with" imply criterion-related validation, at least for someone like myself with an educational measurement background. But as I experienced first hand in *Allen v. Alabama*, defendants in teacher-certification–test cases argue that criterion-related validity evidence is not necessary; that content-related evidence is sufficient to show job relatedness.[14]

Two 1981 cases seem to be the source of the content-validity approach to job relatedness: (a) a Ninth Circuit ruling in *Contreras v. City of Los Angeles* (1982), an employment case involving accountants; and (b) a Second Circuit ruling in *Guardians Association of the New York City Police Department v. Civil Service Commission* (1981). I shall use the *Guardians* case to illustrate the reasoning underlying the content-validation approach.

What does the content-validity approach to showing job relatedness entail? The Second Circuit, after an interesting discussion of content and construct validity, distilled from the EEOC *Guidelines*

---

[14]After a 6-week trial the district court did not rule because a prior settlement that the State, under intense political and media pressure attempted to disown, was upheld by the Eleventh Circuit (No. 86-7215, 1986). The settlement is now in effect, and experts from both sides will attempt to build a test within its framework. Among other things, both sides agreed to a stricter version of the Golden Rule Settlement in terms of item inclusion on subsequent tests. (Recently the state dropped the teacher exam entirely)

7. LEGAL AND PROFESSIONAL ISSUES 233

five attributes of an exam that, notwithstanding its disparate racial impact, had sufficient content validity to be used for employment decisions:

> The first two concern the quality of the test's development: (1) the test-makers must have conducted a suitable job analysis, and (2) they must have used reasonable competence in constructing the test itself. The next three attributes are more in the nature of standards that the test, as produced and used, must be shown to have met. The basic requirement, really the essence of content validation, is (3) that the content of the test must be related to the content of the job. In addition, (4) the content of the test must be representative of the content of the job. Finally, the test must be used with (5) a scoring system that usefully selects from among the applicants those who can better perform the job. (from employment Practices Decisions, p. 16979)

To understand how contractors in teacher-certification cases have employed these guidelines to build legally defensible tests it is necessary to examine more closely the steps in the job-analysis phase of the content-validation process just described.

The EEOC Guidelines call for an assessment "of the important work behavior(s) required for successful performance and their relative importance" (§ 14(C)(2)). In the *Guardians* case, the Civil Service Commission went through a five-step procedure designed to meet this job-analysis requirement. First, the work behaviors were identified by extensive interviewing of job holders and supervisors. Second, the list was reviewed by another, smaller panel of job holders and supervisors to add any tasks omitted, or to eliminate duplicate tasks, or those so specialized that an entry-level person would not be expected to perform them. Third, a questionnaire was widely distributed to job holders asking them to rate each of the tasks on the basis of its frequency of occurrence, its importance, and the amount of time spent in performing it.[15] The tasks were then clustered into related activities. Finally, each cluster was analyzed by a separate panel of job holders to identify the knowledge, skills, and abilities for the cluster as a whole. This final step defined the test domain and formed the blueprint for item

---

[15]In *Guardians*, 49 police officers and 49 supervisors were interviewed in step one; 7 of each reviewed the list in step two. 5,600 police officers were sent the questionnaire.

writing. These five steps are the skeleton of the job-analysis phase of the content-validity approach to job relatedness.[16]

Given the framework provided by *Guardians*, let us examine the seven steps the contractor in the *Allen v. Alabama* case went through to implement the content-validity approach, and the objections plaintiffs raised. Needless to say, the defendants strenuously contended each objection. The steps and the objections are taken directly from Plaintiffs' and Plaintiff-Intervenors' Joint Proposed Findings of Fact and Conclusions of Law (1986).

1. *Outline Development:* To begin to identify the content of each the 35 certification fields, the contractor reviewed state department guidelines and school based curriculum materials for grades K to 12. This review lead to the generation of a topic outline for each certification area. Each outline included 100 to 200 topics.

Plaintiffs argued that the contractor failed to review curricular material from the state's teacher-training institutions when generating topics for the Basic Professional Studies test (BPS). The BPS was a generic test of professional knowledge and skills which all teachers had to pass regardless of certification area. Thus, plaintiffs argued that the BPS topics lacked any relevant curricular basis. Plaintiffs also argued that the lack of records of any part of any of the topic reviews made an audit of the process impossible.

2. *Objective Development:* To define the limits of each topic and clarify its intent, each topic was rewritten by the contractor as an objective. Curriculum committees composed of eight to ten Alabama educators reviewed and modified the contractor's list of objectives to make them accurate, comprehensive, sufficiently specific, and unbiased.

Plaintiffs argued that although the members of the panels were described as "experts" in their respective fields, the criteria for their expertise were unavailable. Plaintiffs also contended that the verbs used to define many of the objectives were broad and not operational. Therefore, many of the objectives that survived this stage were ambiguous. Further, the committees did not review the objectives relative to teacher-training curricula. Finally, no information was provided on the racial composition of the panels.

---

[16]It is worth noting that the plaintiffs in *Guardians* challenged the care in which each step of the job analysis was conducted and the Court observed that "With a job analysis of questionable sufficiency, the City then proceeded to the test construction stage."

7. LEGAL AND PROFESSIONAL ISSUES

3. *Job Analysis:* To further determine the job-relatedness of each objective that emerged from step 2, a list of the objectives for each certification area was mailed to current job holders (e.g., teachers, principals and support staff) throughout the state. They were asked whether they had taught or used the content of the objective during the current year or in the past year. They were asked the amount of time they spent using the objectives and the extent to which they considered the objectives to be essential to their teaching or instructional support area. From the "time spent" and "essentiality" scales the contractor derived a composite index for each objective. Based on this index, the objectives were characterized as "Preferred" (P) "Accepted" (A) (moderately job related), and "Not-as-Job Related" (NJR).

Plaintiffs spent a great deal of time assailing the rationale and methodology of the job analysis. They argued that a job analysis should have focused on the functions and tasks teachers are expected to perform, not simply the subject matter objectives perceived to be needed on the job. They argued that the contractor employed two incorrect rating scales; no opinions were sought from teacher educators, supervisors, administrators etc.; many of the objectives were too broad to rate properly; nine of the reviews were based on a response sample under fifteen, six under ten and one as low a two; the composite index was flawed for a number of conceptual and methodological reasons; minority opinions were ignored.

4. *Objective Selection:* The results from step 3 were presented to the subject-area curriculum committees to select the final set of objectives for which test items would be written. The committees chose 35 to 54 objectives per exam.

Plaintiffs argued that the objective-selection process was vague and undocumented; hence, the process could not be audited. Plaintiffs pointed out that all the objectives were presented as job-related to some degree; objectives with an NJR composite ratings were presented to the committee as *not as* job related rather than as non-job-related. Since some of these NJR objectives survived the selection process and were included on the test, the job analysis was meaningless because it failed to identify and isolate non-job-related objectives.

5. *Item Writing:* The contractor developed a pool of approximately 150 multiple choice items for each content area; from this pool 120 items were to be included on the test, of which 100 were

to be scorable. The contractor checked the items for content validity, accuracy, sufficiency, clarity, and consistency. An item review conference then gave the curriculum committees an opportunity to review and revise the items in the pool.

Plaintiffs argued that the quality of the item writing and the editorial review was poor; the size of the pool was inadequate forcing the inclusion of questionable items; the item review process did not allow sufficient time for a careful consideration of all items; some changes recommended by the curriculum committees were not made; the items were not field tested; separate bias review panels were not convened to screen the items for potential stereotyping or offensiveness; and no statistical item bias analyses were carried out.

6. *Content Validity Review:* New review panels were formed to determine the content validity of each item and to set the cut-score for each test. Each panel member, working independently, was asked to rate each surviving item in the pool as "valid" *i.e.*, an adequate measure of the objective in question, or "not valid." If the item was rated "not valid," the panelist was asked to indicate one of four reasons for the rating (inaccurate content; not a measure of the stated objective; tricky, ambiguous or misleading; or bias). The panelist had the option of not rating an item that contained unfamiliar content by choosing the "I don't know" response. For each item rated "valid," cut-score data were generated by having the panelist decide whether or not entry level teachers should be able to answer the item correctly. Plaintiffs argued that the original rating forms and the data tapes from this review were not available for auditing; and that simply because an item was judged to measure an objective categorized as job related did not make the item itself job related. They attacked the contractor's cut-score methodology, arguing that among other things, it lacked support in the research literature, and that it produced artificially higher cut-scores than established methods.

7. *Test Assembly:* Data from the previous step guided the assembly and preparation of the tests for the first operational administration.

Plaintiffs contended there were a large number of flawed items on the final test (i.e., the stem did not set a clear problem, the distracters were ambiguous, more than one distracter was correct); there were a large number of negatively stated items; items appeared that measured NJR objectives; items appeared that were never reviewed by subject matter panels; that there were a number of miskeyed items; and item statistics from the first eight administrations signaling possible problems were ignored.

What's wrong with this legal-defensibility approach? Nothing, as long as satisfying the courts is the only objective. However, the essential question is whether the inferences, decisions, and descriptions made about a candidate from his or her performance on the test are inadequately supported by this legalistic approach to validation. Following this tradition of validation in fact defines the kinds of explanations of a score that are sought.

In the remainder of this chapter I examine the inferences that policy makers, the media, and the courts make from teacher certification tests. Second, I describe the mix of evidence needed to support such inferences and critique the shortcomings of present validation techniques. Third, I discuss the tension between exigencies of the applied situation and the need for more thorough validation efforts before the test is used. Fourth, I outline the three types of validity evidence that must be collected during the validation process. Finally, because the cut score triggers the inference or decision, I examine the issue of the validity of the cut score.

THE VALIDITY OF TEACHER-CERTIFICATION TESTS

According to the 1985 *Standards for Educational and Psychological Testing*, "Validity is the most important consideration in test evaluation. The concept refers to the appropriateness, meaningfulness, and usefulness of the specific inferences made from test scores" (AERA, APA, NCME, 1985, p. 9). Any analysis of validity, therefore, must begin with a description of the actual inferences that people make from a person's score on a teacher certification test.

Inferences and Decisions From Teacher-Certification Tests

How do people interpret a candidate's performance on a teacher certification test—what inferences do they make about the person? Consider the following:

- From an editorial in the *Mobile Register:*[17]
  U.S. Middle District Judge Myron Thompson has sentenced hundreds of Mobile public school students to an inferior education with his incredible order that the local school board give regular teaching posts to 51 teachers who had failed to pass a basic competency test. . . .
  Thompson said, in effect, "No! It doesn't matter if they can teach or not. Put them in the classrooms!" ("Filling Classrooms," 1983, p. 4–A).
- From a news story in the *Montgomery Advertiser* concerning the State Board's rejection of a settlement it had earlier agreed to in the *Allen v. Alabama* case:
  Wednesday, Attorney General Charles Graddick[18] blasted the settlement, saying it would lead to "the dumping of 650 incompetent school teachers into the state's public education system" (Cork, 1985, p. 2A).
- From an editorial in the (Montgomery) *Alabama Journal* on the Eleventh Circuit's reinstatement of the settlement in *Allen v. Alabama:*
  The settlement was an utter sell-out of the teacher competency testing program, which sought to do nothing more than keep incompetents—regardless of race—out of the classroom. There is nothing wrong—and nothing discriminatory—about the state's expecting those who would teach to show certain levels of expertise in their particular fields and a degree of general knowledge. ("Living with error," 1987 p. 14)
- From the Austin (Texas) *American-Statesman:*
  Requiring competency tests for teachers, the [Perot] committee estimated, would rid the public schools of 20,000 incompetent teachers. (Copelin, 1984)
- From a letter to the editor of the *Montgomery Advertiser:*
  Putting incompetent teachers into the classroom could prove to be education's Vietnam. Just as the United States could not win a war with only a half-hearted effort, neither can Alabama win a war on illiteracy with incompetent teachers. (Trotter, 1985, p. 12A)
- From the Amarillo (Texas) *News-Globe:*
  Teachers would have to pass a test by June of 1986 to show that they were competent to teach. ("School Reform," 1984, p. 2A)

---

[17]This editorial refers to the use of the NTE by the Mobile Alabama public schools to fire experienced teachers who failed to achieve the cut score of 500 or above. In an out-of-court settlement in *York v. Mobile* the use of the NTE was discontinued. ETS went on record as opposing the school board's use of the NTE for termination decisions.

[18]Graddick, a candidate for Governor in the Democratic primary, made the settlement and the certification testing program an issue in his campaign.

7. LEGAL AND PROFESSIONAL ISSUES 239

- From the decision in *United States v. South Carolina* (1977) discussing the issue of false positive and false negative classifications:
  If there is a teacher shortage, a relatively high minimum score requirement may mean that some classrooms will be without teachers, and it may be better to provide a less than fully competent teacher than no teacher at all. But to the extent that children are exposed to incompetent teachers, education suffers. (445 F..Supp. 1094 at 1115)

- From a January 8, 1980 Alabama State Board of Education resolution:
  [T]he State Superintendent of Education and the State Department of Education staff proposed to develop for Board approval . . . criterion-referenced . . . exit professional competency tests in each of the teacher certification areas specified by Board policy, to measure the specific competencies which are considered necessary to successfully teach in classrooms in Alabama schools. . . . (Plaintiffs' and Plaintiff-Interveners' 1986, p. 15)

- From the test contractor's *Registration Bulletin* for the Alabama Initial Teacher Certification Testing Program:
  An individual's performance on a test is evaluated against an established level of competence. . . . As stated above, the test items were reviewed for minimum content knowledge competence that (a) practicing Alabama teachers must have in order to successfully teach in the classroom, or (b) if in an instructional support personnel position, must have in order to be successful in the position. The pass/fail scores clearly define those individuals demonstrating sufficient competence in the teaching or instructional support field (Plaintiffs' and Plaintiff-Interveners' 1986, p. 53).

- Last, but far from least, from an August 23, 1987 news story in the *Savannah News-Press* headlined **School Firings Praised**:
  Although five Chatham County teachers are among the ranks of 327 teachers state-wide unable to continue teaching in Georgia, U.S. Education Secretary William Bennett assured the state Saturday that it is setting a good example by barring the teachers from the classroom because they failed a new certification test.
  "It is a great thing for the state of Georgia," Bennett said. "It is a declaration that the state is not willing to have incompetent teachers in the classroom." (p. 1C)

There is no shortage of analogous examples. What's clear is that people make inferences from teacher-certification—test scores about a teacher's *competence*. Editorial writers, newspaper reporters, politicians, blue-ribbon committee members, State Board members, judges, ordinary citizens, even test contractors, and yes, the then U.S. Education Secretary all seem to agree that teacher-certification tests measure some aspect of teacher *competence*. Further, this *competence* has a referent—*classroom performance*. Whatever it is, it's necessary for *successful teaching*.

Additionally, note the implicit—sometimes explicit—a priori conviction that the test in fact *correctly* distinguishes between *competent* and *incompetent teachers*. People accept the test as valid without ever seeing or taking it. As feminists have come to realize, whoever names the world owns it (McFague, 1982) Many people have a literalistic mentality and consequently, the test is simply what the contractor or agency says it is. Naming the test reifies it. If it's called a teacher-certification test, a priori it's an indicator of competence. When people reify a test they are no longer like the Wizard of Oz who knew green glasses made Oz green, they believe that Oz *is* green (Turbayne, 1962). Naming something can also affect attitudes at a profound level. This affective component explains why many people find it difficult to understand why plaintiffs challenge a teacher-certification test that "obviously" weeds out "incompetents."

Proponents of teacher-competency testing are quick to point out that the competence being measured is necessary, but not sufficient, for successful classroom performance. Passing the test does not mean the teacher will be successful; the test simply doesn't purport to measure all of the knowledge and skills necessary to teach. These tests only measure certain aspects of the job. However, this argument leaves something important unsaid. If the test is a *valid* measure of some subset of necessary, but not sufficient, knowledge, skills, and abilities, and a person fails it, then it follows that the probability is high that the person is incompetent. Therefore, the person *cannot* be minimally successful in the classroom. In other words, at least for those labeled *incompetent*, successful classroom performance is still the ultimate criterion. I now turn to lines of evidence that are needed to substantiate inferences about competence.

Lines of Validity Evidence

Court decisions apart, what kind of evidence is needed to sustain an inference that a candidate is incompetent to perform successfully in a classroom and, thereby, to justify the subsequent decision not to certify the person? The 1985 *Standards* point out that traditionally there are three categories of validity evidence: content-related, criterion-related, and construct-related evidence. The *Standards* also state that rigorous distinctions between categories are not possible, and that

> An ideal validation includes several types of evidence, which span all three of the traditional categories. Other things being equal, more sources of evidence are better than fewer. However, the quality of the evidence is of primary importance, and a single line of solid evidence is preferable to numerous lines of evidence of questionable quality.[19] (p. 9)

Validation can no longer be a question of one predominant type of validity evidence nor of one predominate method to gather that type of evidence. Rather, the question should be how the three types of validity and various methods of gathering evidence about them should be joined so as to produce a solid, overall line of evidence in support of whatever particular type of inferences or decisions is under consideration.

As we saw, contractors presently are arguing for the single line of content validity evidence to justify the use of teacher-certification tests. How is this all consuming line of evidence gathered? The approach constitutes a closed system of soliciting teacher judgments at key steps in the test construction process (i.e., job analysis, content validation, standard setting). Content-related evidence of job relatedness ultimately comes down to what panels of teachers—about whom we know very little—consider or feel are the skills, knowledge, and abilities needed to function successfully in the classroom (Madaus 1986; Madaus & Pullin, 1987).

The question then becomes "How strong is this judgmental line of evidence?" As far back as 1934, Tyler, describing the practice of

---

[19]Defendants in *Allen v. Alabama* (1985) emphasized the last clause and linked it to the following sentence from the Professional and Occupational Licensure and Certification chapter to argue that criterion-related evidence wasn't needed and a strong single line of content related evidence was sufficient; "Investigations of criterion-related validity are more problematic in the context of licensure or certification than in any employment settings" (p. 63).

validating IQ tests against teacher's judgments of student intelligence, pointed out that using this judgment approach exclusively means that the test is never more valid than the teachers' judgments. More recently, Haney, Madaus, and Kreitzer (1987) pointed out that item bias is the only area of testing where judgmental methods have been closely compared with empirical methods. They pointed to Jensen's (1980) conclusion based on an extensive review that, "claims of test bias cannot be supported by subjective judgments regarding the item content" (p. 371). They concluded that the literature on judgmental versus statistical methods of bias detection is a real source of disquiet when one tries to justify the judgmental approach *exclusively* to establish test validity. It is interesting to note that defendants in *Allen v. Alabama* used this same item bias literature to justify *not* convening separate panels to examine items for bias, offensiveness, and stereotyping.

Granted, teacher judgments carefully elicited form an important line of validity evidence. However, a single line of evidence based exclusively on opinions is, I submit, insufficient to sustain the types of inferences just described (Madaus & Pullin, 1987). I believe that the validation of teacher-certification tests must include evidence from all three traditional validity categories. The inference made from a teacher-certification test is too complex, the decision *not* to certify too important, and the potential harm to individuals too great, to be supported by a single line of validity evidence. Validation if done properly is hermeneutic, and to arrive at the meaning behind a test score, all three kinds of evidence are needed. Further, for any of the three lines of evidence there is no one best method for collecting the data; instead multiple methodologies must be employed to better illuminate the question being investigated.

Validation and Applied Testing

Before developing further the reasons for three distinct lines of evidence, I need to raise one other very important point about validation. Validation is an ongoing, additive process of accumulating evidence, not a single study. However, the open endedness of validation and the necessity for multiple lines of evidence using multiple methodologies immediately pose very real problems for contractors. Contractors, after all work in the applied, commercial, competitive, litigious, nonregulated, business world of testing.

As just noted, a fundamental characteristic of validation is a search for the meaning behind a test score. Validation is ultimately a scientific enterprise. It calls for iconoclastic speculation, suspicion, doubt, autonomous judgment, deliberate hard mindedness, open-ended tensive enquiry, and a willingness to follow the evidence wherever it may lead. Contractors, however, are basically technicians, not scientists. They are forced to have can-do mentalities, which focus more on delivering a product that will stand up in court than on searching for meaning behind a test score. Contractors have to deliver an *operational* test by a fixed date, sometimes as quickly as 6 to 8 months from the award of the contract. To make good contractual obligations they rely on a standard, stereotyped technology that they know the courts have accepted. There simply isn't time to implement an integrated, multifaceted, ongoing validation strategy. Furthermore, contracts are not funded for comprehensive, ongoing validation efforts. Contractors are also acutely aware that pursuing certain lines of evidence is a risky business given the possibility of a legal challenge (Yalow, Collins, & Popham, 1986). Finally, because contractors must produce a product that is "valid" to get paid, they avoid studies that are open to disconfirmation. Simply put, asking disconfirming hypotheses about their product poses a real conflict of interest for contractors. Consequently, habit always triumphs over novelty and they cling to proven techniques and institutionalized formulations that deliver a positive result.

Obviously, in the real world of applied testing, validation cannot be altogether open ended. That's not the issue. Nor is it an issue of whether to test or not. Tests are potentially too valuable a source of important information about individuals and institutions. The critical practical issues are: (a) How much validity evidence is enough before the test can be used *operationally?* and (2) How do we get around the conflict of interest inherent in validation in the applied situation?

Determining that a teacher-certification test is ready for use involves balancing ethical and practical issues as well as individual and social interests. On the one hand, contractors and agencies have an ethical duty to provide the proper kinds of evidence to support inferences of competence in the classroom. There is also little doubt that people can be harmed by a test contractor's product. On the basis of a test score a person is permitted to teach or not; can be stigmatized with the label *incompetent;* can have his or herself concept diminished; can be hurt psychologically and financially. Similarly, teacher-training institutions can be damaged by decisions made about them on the basis of test information. On the other hand tests can provide valuable information about individuals and institutions. Policy makers and the public have come to expect that test information be used to help protect society from incompetent teachers and inferior institutions. Finally, there is no such thing as a perfect test. Even the most thoroughly validated test will produce false positive and negative classifications. Inferences are always problematic. Validation offers a reasoned defense for inferences, not proof.

Given these competing factors, the question then becomes, "What mechanism should be used to decide if the test is ready to be used to make high-stakes inferences and decisions?" One analogy, albeit incomplete, is to drug testing. At what point is it safe to permit the operational use of a new drug? The decision isn't left up to the drug company. There are guidelines from the FDA on the studies that need to be done; and the results are evaluated by the FDA before approving the product for commercial use. Testing has no analogous review mechanism. When the contractor delivers the test, it is used to make important decisions. The profession needs to come to grips with this value-laden, political question of when a test is ready to be used operationally. No resolution, I submit, is to be found in the *Standards*, the EEOC *Guidelines*, the courts, nor the contractor's proclamation of validity.

The profession must also come to grips with the knotty issue of the conflict of interest contractors find themselves in when validating their own test. Of course the contractor must be involved in validation. The test construction process itself is an integral part of the process. However, test validation must continue well beyond the test-construction phase, and must actively pursue disconfirming hypotheses. The answer to this dilemma is, I believe, an independent test-auditing agency analogous to the FDA. Such an agency would provide contractors with guidelines for leaving a proper audit trail during the test construction phase and would audit this phase. It would provide state agencies with guidelines for validation study designs to test disconfirming hypotheses after the test construction stage, and it would audit this phase as well. These audits would guide the agency in making recommendations to the contracting agencies about whether the test is ready for operational use. The profession must take the lead here or legislatures eventually will. New York's "Truth in Testing" legislation is but an initial shot across testing's bow. An independent, profes-

7. LEGAL AND PROFESSIONAL ISSUES 245

sionally sponsored, nongovernmental agency is preferable to the governmental FDA model.

Currently, the closest thing to what I have in mind is the ETS internal auditing process. On assuming the presidency of ETS in 1981, Gregory Anrig initiated an audit process to assure that each of the company's products was in compliance with the ETS *Standards of Quality and Fairness*.[20] An Officer of Corporate Quality Assurance was established to oversee the audits and the implementation of any recommendations coming out of an audit. Each ETS program is reviewed at least every 3 years. A Visiting Committee annually reviews the audit process itself and examines the findings from the yearly audits. The Visiting Committee reports directly to the ETS Trustee Committee on Public Responsibility.

Interestingly, this past year the NTE program was audited. The Visiting Committee observed that

> The role of the tests that comprise the NTE Programs—in qualifying candidates for admission to colleges of education, certification into the profession, and the identification for career ladder and master teaching programs—along with increasing public concern for the quality of our teaching force, guarantees them a place as one of the more controversial testing programs within ETS. (Report of the 1987 ETS Visiting Committee, 1987, p. 3)

The Visiting Committee then raised a series of questions about the NTE programs tests:

- Are the NTE Programs contributing to the improvement of teacher education and practice?
- Do the NTE Programs have a negative effect on the recruitment of minorities into the teaching profession?
- Are the NTE Programs tests valid for the inferences commonly drawn from their uses?
- Can ETS continue to rely on studies undertaken by state-level clients using the NTE Programs tests as their primary source of validity? (p. 9)

The Committee went on to recommend that:

> In light of [its] concerns, and those of others, regarding current NTE Programs tests, along with the changes occurring in teacher educa-

---

[20]The *Standards of Quality and Fairness* are a set of standards that, in my opinion go beyond the 1985 *Standards* in outlining criteria for test development and use.

tion and the teaching profession, . . . the talents, technical expertise, and resources of ETS be directed toward researching and developing new methods of teacher evaluation. [That] would: (1) *respect the complexities of the work of teachers at different grade levels and in different subject or specialty areas, (2) be valid measures of the knowledge and skills teachers need to perform competently* [italics added], and (3) not discriminate against minorities (p. 9)

The audit process is taken very seriously at ETS and is a commendable effort at public responsibility. However, it is not the answer for the entire industry. It lacks the authority of an external independent auditing body. Unfortunately, it certainly would be perceived by some critics of testing as self-serving. Further, it is beyond the resources of smaller contractors. Nonetheless, it provides an excellent model for what an independent agency might do.

I now turn to a closer examination of the need for construct, content, and criterion-related evidence, problems with current validation efforts, and the issue of the validity of the cut score.

Construct-Related Evidence

Inferences people make about a teacher's competence are inferences about a construct. Competence is a construct, and therefore construct validation is essential for any teacher certification test. The construct, competence in the classroom, must be "embedded in a conceptual framework, no matter how imperfect that framework may be" (AERA, APA, NCME, 1985, p. 9). Development of a conceptual framework for teacher competence must involve a functional analysis of what minimally competent teachers actually do in their classrooms. This analysis must start from below with the work of teachers and move then to construct definition. Further, a functional analysis must be specific to the certification area in question. Teaching is not a generic profession. Only by functionally analyzing the different certification areas can the subset of skills, knowledge, and abilities common to all teaching areas be identified. A functional approach would also answer the question of whether a generic professional-skills test required for certification of all teachers makes any sense. I feel that extant generic, multiple-choice teacher-certification tests make little sense, and are simply not valid (Madaus & Pullin, 1987).

Although a theoretical, or structural analysis can also be helpful, the functional, area-by-area approach to defining job competencies should shed more light on the critical ingredients needed to

7. LEGAL AND PROFESSIONAL ISSUES 247

be minimally successful in the classroom. Not all of the ingredients that emerge—in fact probably very few—can be measured by the current, administratively convenient multiple-choice technology. However, by illuminating what's possible within the limits of this technology the first step in the construct validation of such tests has begun.

The functional approach goes beyond the current practice of mailing lists of objectives to teachers for them to rate, although, if done carefully, a survey of teachers' opinions on the aspects identified from the functional analysis contributes to the web of construct-related evidence. Content- and criterion-related evidence, although contributing to construct validation, is insufficient. The 1985 *Standards* remind us that: The process of compiling construct-related evidence for test validity starts with test development and continues until the pattern of empirical relationships between test scores and other variables clearly *indicates the meaning of the test score* [italics added]. (AERA, APA, NCME, 1985, p. 10) The 1985 *Standards* describes the process of compiling construct-related evidence, along with possible sources of, and techniques for collecting such evidence. These suggestions must be taken seriously when validating teacher certification tests.

Content-Related Evidence

As just noted, content validation is the favorite, exclusive approach of contractors building teacher-certification tests. Content-related evidence is a necessary but not sufficient ingredient in validating teacher-certification tests. However, if we are searching for the meaning behind a score on a such a test, then we need to reexamine the techniques currently used to solicit this evidence.

Cronbach, writing in the context of program evaluation, calls for "a bundle of studies [using] different techniques to examine subquestions" (Cronbach & et al 1980, p. 73). Within the same evaluation context Cooley and Bickel (1986) pointed out that multiple approaches to examining a question deepen an understanding of the phenomenon under investigation. This is certainly good advice for those validating teacher-certification tests. Current content validation methodology has become institutionalized, a cocoon for confirmation. Disconfirming hypotheses about content relevance are not examined. To the degree that expert opinion varies as a function of the way it is elicited or quantified, inferences made from scores are suspect.

For content-related evidence to be believable, we need to learn a lot more about things we now take for granted such as: how well panel members understand the tasks they are asked to do; how much response set influences the process as panel members become absorbed in the process; how much the meaning of directions are interpreted and prejudged by individuals according to their own framework; how easily panel members recognize flaws in items; and how time constraints affect the task. We need to learn more about how teacher opinion varies as a function of the composition of the panels, of the wording of the judgment question put to them, and of the way the results are quantified. The final set of items chosen to measure successful job performance should be robust enough to emerge consistently under different conditions of gathering judgments about their relevance. Madaus and Pullin (1987) offered a sample of "what if questions" that test the robustness of teacher judgments about test content.

There is an interesting paradox associated with the current content-validation approach. Many teacher certification test items that successfully survive the content-validation panel review are roundly criticized by test reviewers. This contradictory phenomenon spans the decades and cuts across a number of different tests. (e.g., Buros, 1938; 1953; 1959; 1965; 1972; 1978; Darling-Hammond, 1986; Koerner 1963; Madaus, 1986; Madaus & Pullin, 1987; Melnick, 1987; Melnick & Pullin, 1987; and if it is ever released the trail transcript in *Allen v. Alabama;* see Haney et al., 1987, for former examples and a more detailed discussion). Further, this criticism isn't limited to one or two bad items that may have slipped by accidently. It blankets a host of items. Mitchell's comments on the item quality of the 1976 NTE captures the flavor of this history of criticism:

> The items on the Professional Education test should be carefully scrutinized by potential users. Some of the items seem to smack of professional shibboleths, others have shaky research foundations, others seem to reflect the values of the writer more than the substance of the field, others are simplistic, others are combinations of these. Some items of course, are wholly acceptable. But if the items are taken as a whole, it is in fact difficult to believe that these items adequately sample from the professional preparation provided by most teacher training programs. (p. 517)

The regularity and similarity of this item criticism, across the years and across different contractors' tests calls into question current content-related evidence, and illuminates the need for a careful evaluation of the traditional techniques used by contractors. At the very least this history of item criticism is indicative of the fact that typical content review panels simply aren't sensitive to many problems inherent in the objectives and multiple-choice items they are reviewing.

Questionable items are a serious threat to validity when the inferences about a person are triggered automatically by a cut score on the test. Each item—good, bad, or indifferent—contributes one point to a person's score. To illustrate the damage done by the presence of questionable items, plaintiffs in *Allen v. Alabama* constructed what became referred to in the trial as failure charts for each test.[21] Persons who failed the test were identified. Their answers to the questionable items were then recorded. This gave a crude estimate of the extent to which answering a questionable item incorrectly contributed to falling below the cut score. A considerable number of candidates who were denied certification fell below the cut score due in part to answering a subset of the questionable items incorrectly. For those close to the cut score one or two questionable items may have made the difference between passing and failing. Of course we don't know how these candidates would have answered flawless items measuring the same objective had they appeared. That's not the point. The point is that the inference of incompetence made about these candidates was corrupted by the presence of questionable items.

In summary, content-related evidence is essential in the overall validation of teacher-certification tests. However, the track record for content-validation studies of teacher-certification tests to date is poor. The meaning behind a test score is not enhanced from results obtained using present content-validity techniques. The results do not contribute to construct validation. The methodology endorses many dubious items as job related. We need to begin to carefully reassess the methodologies that have evolved to collect such information. We must ask the extent to which the results, on which everything hinges at the present time, are method dependent. To obtain sound overall content-related evidence we need to begin to employ different techniques with different types of panels.

Criterion-Related Evidence

If teacher-certification tests measure important aspects of successful classroom performance, scores on such tests should corre-

---

[21]Items were labeled *questionable* if there were judged ambiguous, miskeyed, having no best answer, measuring trivial content, or context dependent for an answer. Because the items are protected by court order, and the testimony was in Camera, I am unable to offer concrete examples. Defendants challenged some of the items characterized as questionable, but not the majority.

late with criterion measures of such performance. The record here isn't good either. Reviews of attempts to correlate scores on teacher-certification exams and performance in the classroom show that "teacher tests have little if any power to predict how well people perform as teachers, whether that performance is judged by ratings of college supervisory personnel, ratings by principals, student ratings or achievement gains made by students taught" (Haney et al., 1987, p. 199).

In the 1930s Ralph Tyler reminded the measurement community that indirect (multiple choice) indicators must be validated against direct indicators of the construct of interest. Contractors building teacher-certification tests seem to have forgotten this advice or dismissed it as impractical. Instead, they argue that adequate criterion measures of successful classroom performance simply aren't available. Although this may be true, it is an admission that contractors know next to nothing about the construct that they are trying to measure. This admission also undercuts the accuracy of the so called job analysis portion of the content-validity approach. A proper functional analysis of the job at the outset should produce direct indicators of the construct and also suggest ways to measure them.

The national movement to hold teachers accountable should eventually lead to the development of better, more systematic techniques to evaluate educational personnel. Decisions about such things as merit pay, tenure, and career ladders cry out for such criteria. What emerges from new efforts to evaluate teachers may offer a subset of criteria against which performance on teacher-certification tests can eventually be validated.

Another argument proffered as to why criterion-related evidence isn't needed for teacher-certification tests is that such evidence isn't collected for licensure tests in other professions such as law, medicine, or nursing. One reason for this absence is that candidates in those other professions go into a wide range of very different types of jobs. For example, a candidate who passes the bar exam might practice real estate law, corporate law, criminal law, and so forth. There are so many job paths open to the new lawyer that the criterion problem is simply insurmountable. Or so the argument goes.

The situation in education is different. A teacher applies for a very specific certification; one tied to a grade level, subject field, or speciality area. Unlike lawyers or doctors, teachers don't get a generic license to practice. Thus, for each test particular to a certification area, individualized criteria of competence are needed and should be possible to obtain. With 30 or more separate certification areas this won't be an easy task. However, we have to begin. And despite the difficulty, I feel that criterion-related evidence, whether predictive or concurrent, is absolutely necessary to validate properly the commonly made inferences about minimally successful classroom performance. Without such evidence we are locked into the closed circle of judgmental evidence of content-relevance.

The Cut Score

Essential to any validation of teacher-certification tests are studies of the validity of the cut score. It is the cut score, after all, that triggers both the inferences about a person's competence, and the decision to certify or not. However, to the best of my knowledge, there have been no attempts to validate the cut scores used with teacher-certification tests. Presently cut scores are set by having panels make judgments about the expected performance of minimally competent teachers on each item. The results are then aggregated to arrive at a cut score. We have already discussed problems associated with the closed system of relying exclusively on panel plebiscites about objectives or items. Those same problems apply with equal force to the cut-score process.

We already know that cut scores on teacher-certification tests are method dependent (Berk, 1986, p. 163; Goertz & Pitcher, 1985; Poggio, Glasnap, Miller, Tollefson, & Jaeger, 1986). (This body of literature is a further reason to investigate the method dependence of current content-validation practices.) The practical implications of this dependence is far from trivial. Using the Goertz and Pitcher data, Haney et al. (1987) calculated the proportion of examinees in the 1982–1984 national sample of NTE candidates who would pass or fail using the highest and the lowest cut scores found across the various states using the tests. The figures ranged from 75% to 95% passing the Communication Skills subtest, 67% to 91% passing the General Knowledge subtest, and 78% to 98% passing the Professional Knowledge subtest. These data caused Haney et al. (1987) to ask "Is there really this much variation from one state to the next, in the skills and knowledge level needed to be a minimally successful teacher?" (p. 201–202) Despite questions like these about the underlying construct of teacher competence, judgmental cut-score methodology presently rules the roost. We need to validate any cut score through an empirical examination of the *degree* to which it correctly separates those with insufficient knowledge and skill from those with adequate prerequisites (Madaus, 1986).

It is undeniable that at some point a judgment has to be made about where to set the cut score. However, such a judgment should be informed by data on the number of possible false positives and false negatives associated with the selection. Mass screening techniques in medicine provide an analogy for what is needed. To screen hospital blood-bank donors for possible anicteric hepatitis, measures of serum enzyme are employed (Colton, 1974). To set a cut score for decisions about the blood's acceptability pathologists plotted the distributions of the serum glutamic pyruvic transaminase (SGPT) (transformed to the logarithm to base 10) of healthy individuals and those with hepatocellular damage. Informed cost-benefit judgments can then be made about where in the overlap zone to place the cut score to minimize either of these unavoidable misclassifications.

The medical example just described is, of course, nothing more than the contrasting-groups method used in some minimum competency graduation testing programs. Such a technique could be used for teacher certification tests. Naturally, the underlying scale of the construct teacher competence will not be physical. But the contrasting-groups method for cut-score setting could be employed if serious construct and criterion-related evidence were available.

There is also an analytical approach to the problem of setting a cut score on a teacher certification test. It is based on the fact that a relatively small number of persons tested are actually incompetent. Haney et al. (1987) found that estimates of the percentage of incompetents in the teacher corps are similar to estimates of incompetence associated with other professions—about 10%. When base rates of incompetence are low, even using a screening test that is highly accurate, you run the risk of doing great damage to candidates falsely labeled *incompetent*. I describe three examples that illustrate the point.

Recently in the *APA Monitor* John Bales (1987) reported on the testimony of psychologist Edward Katin to a congressional panel investigating the use of the polygraph in employment settings. Katin pointed out that a relatively small number of people tested by a polygraph will be dishonest or deceptive. Using available estimates of 85% accuracy for the polygraph, and a 10% "dishonest" estimate, he provided an example of what happens under these conditions when 1,000 employees are screened. The polygraph would identify 85 of the 100 dishonest employees, but would misidentify as dishonest 15% or 135 honest employees. Of the 220 "suspects" (85 + 135), 61% are innocent. He concluded that it is a

7. LEGAL AND PROFESSIONAL ISSUES

mathematical reality that the majority of suspects are, in fact, innocent. Nonetheless, a cloud of suspicion blankets these innocents.

Light (1987) offered another provocative example from widespread screening for drugs or AIDS. He asked the simple question "Of all the people that the drug test (or an AIDS test) classifies as having drugs (or AIDS) what proportion *really has it?*" (p. 51). He used the following three figures to answer it: (a) an estimate of 1% for the proportion of people who actually have AIDS or routinely take drugs; (b) an estimate of 95% for the accuracy of a screening test to detect drugs or the AIDS virus when a person really has them; and (c) an estimate of 95% for the accuracy of the test to detect the absence of drugs or the AIDS virus. Using these three estimates he found that "of all the people the test categorizes as having drugs (or AIDS), *only 15% really do!*" (p. 51). Even a test that is 100% accurate in detecting people who do take drugs (or have AIDS) hardly changes the situation. Under this assumption, 17% would be misidentified; 83% of all those labeled as *positive* would be falsely accused. Needless to say, a false accusation in such a matter can seriously harm a person.

But what have hepatitis screening, polygraphs, and drug testing, all involving physical measures, to do with teacher-certification testing? The situations are analogous in that the potential for harm to those falsely labeled *incompetent* is great, and the proportion of teacher candidates who are actually incompetent is probably low—10%. This is particularly true when you consider the fact that few people in testing or education could claim anything near the accuracy for teacher tests ascribed to the polygraph, urine, or blood tests.

Haney, et al. (1987) simulated what might be happening in the teacher-certification–testing situation. They assumed that 10% of the candidates are, in fact, incompetent. Based on a review of the literature they estimated a correlation of .20 between present certification tests and a measure of teacher quality corrected for unreliability. They then used the Taylor and Russell (1939) tables to estimate a 1% increase in selection efficiency in using the test over random selection.

From the state's point of view, such a small increase in selection efficiency might appear worthwhile. However, it hides the balance of correct and incorrect decisions made using the test. To clarify this balance, they carried out a simulation. They assumed an estimate of incompetence of 10%, and a correlation of 0.20 between the test and criterion measure. Further, they assumed both the test and the measure of teacher quality were normally distributed. Next they set the cut score on the test and the measure of teacher quality at 1.28 standard deviations below the mean. Using a Monte Carlo simulation they estimated: (a) the correct acceptances (above the cut score on both variables); (b) the correct rejections (below the cut score on both variables); (c) the false acceptances (above the cut score on the test, but below on the criterion); and (d) the false rejections (below the cut score on the test, but above the cut score on the criterion). As expected, about 10% of the cases were below the cut score on the test and on the criterion. However, only 1.8 out of 100 cases were below the cut score on both measures. Moreover, they found that more than 80% of the cases below the cut score on the test were above the cut score on the criterion. In other words, more than 80% of the rejections based on the test *would be false ones*. The use of a test for widespread screening of teachers (given the previously described assumptions) identifies less than 20% of the candidates who truly fall below the cut score on the real criterion of interest, competence in the classroom. A success rate of 20% must be balanced against the staggering cost of an 80% false negative rate.

These three examples, I think, argue for the need for both analytic and empirical investigations of the validity of any cut score used for the widespread screening of teacher candidates. We can't continue to rely exclusively on teacher judgments about individual items as the exclusive basis for setting a cut-score—not if we are serious about making inferences about competence in the classroom.

CONCLUSION

The courts are a world unto themselves, a world that gives contractors a relatively simple formula for validating teacher certification tests. Although contractors need to be cognizant of judicial opinions about employment tests, they should acknowledge that a legal definition of validity is inadequate. A legally defensible certification test is presently obtained at the expense of a proper search for the meaning behind scores on these tests. It isn't easy to properly validate certification tests in the applied situation. But in the end, if the test survived a proper validation effort, it would be legally defensible.

It is an inescapable fact of life that all manner of people use the tests to make inferences about potential competence in the class-

7. LEGAL AND PROFESSIONAL ISSUES

room. On the basis of these inferences, state agencies make decisions that can adversely affect the careers of numerous candidates. The nature of these inferences demands construct, content, and criterion-related evidence for support. If we are serious about keeping incompetents out of the classroom then we must get a lot more serious about comprehensive test validation. Otherwise, teacher-certification testing is nothing more than a slick public relations ploy.

The dilemma of the ongoing nature of validation and the exigencies of the applied situation must be addressed—and quickly. Guidelines for when a test has been validated sufficiently for operational use must be developed. The profession must come to grips with the conflict of interest that is present when test contractors are the only validators of their own secure products, particularly when they approach validation exclusively from the perspective of defending their product in court. Some independent, mutually respected agency is needed to audit contractors' work during test construction and to apply professional standards for validation after test construction is over.

I opened the chapter with the validation metaphor of the snark hunt from Lewis Carroll. I'd like to close with a paragraph from the preface to *The Hunting of The Snark* as metaphor for what the quest for a legally defensible test is doing to teacher certification testing:

> The Bellman, who was almost morbidly sensitive about appearances, used to have the bowsprit unshipped once or twice a week to be revarnished; and it more than once happened, when the time came for replacing it, that no one on board could remember which end of the ship it belonged to. They knew it was not of the slightest use to appeal to the Bellman about it—he would only refer to his Naval Code, and read out in pathetic tones Admirality Instructions which none of them had ever been able to understand—so it generally ended in its being fastened on, any how, across the rudder. The helmsman used to stand by with tears in his eyes: *he* knew it was all wrong, but alas! Rule 42 of the Code, *"No one shall speak to the Man at the Helm,"* had been completed by the Bellman himself with the words *"and the Man at the helm shall speak to no one."* So remonstrance was impossible, and no steering could be done till the next varnishing day. During these bewildering intervals the ship usually sailed backwards. (p. 8–9)

Teacher certification testing currently is a rudderless enterprise, sailing backwards through a legal sea of codes and court opinion.

It's time to repair, and put in its correct place the rudder of test validity.

ACKNOWLEDGMENTS

My thanks to my generous colleagues at Boston College, Walt Haney, Diana Pullin, Joseph Pedulla, and Amelia Kreitzer for their help, ideas, suggestions, and reactions. My thanks also to Lee J. Cronbach for his insightful reactions. Errors of fact or interpretation and the opinions expressed are solely my responsibility.

REFERENCES

Albermarle Paper Company v. Moody. 422 U.S. 405, 10 FEP 1181 (1975).
Allen V. The Alabama State Board of Education. Civil Action No. 81-697-N (M.D. Ala. 1985).
American Educational Research Association, American Psychological Association, & National Council on Measurement in Education (1985). *Standards for educational and psychological testing.* Washington, DC: American Psychological Association.
Baldus, D. & Cole, J. (1980). *Statistical proof of discrimination.* New York: McGraw–Hill.
Bales, J. (1987, May). Polygraph called invalid job screen. *APA Monitor, 18,* 28.
Berk, R. A. (1986). A consumer's guide to setting performance standards on criterion-referenced tests. *Review of Educational Research, 56*(1), 137–172.
Buros, O. K. (Ed.). (1938). *The nineteen-thirty-eight mental measurements yearbook.* Highland Park, NJ: Gryphon Press.
Buros, O. K. (Ed.). (1953). *The fourth mental measurements yearbook.* Highland Park, NJ: Gryphon Press.
Buros, O. K. (Ed.). (1959). *The fifth mental measurements yearbook.* Highland Park, NJ: Gryphon Press.
Buros, O. K. (Ed.). (1965). *The sixth mental measurements yearbook.* Highland Park, NJ: Gryphon Press.
Buros, O. K. (Ed.). (1972). *The seventh mental measurements yearbook.* Highland Park, NJ: Gryphon Press.
Buros, O. K. (Ed.). (1978). *The eighth mental measurements yearbook.* Highland Park, NJ: Gryphon Press.
Carroll, L. (1976). *The hunting of the Snark: An agony in eight fits.* New York: Clarkson N. Potter.
Castaneda v. Partida, 430 U.S. 482 (1977).
Colton, T. (1974). *Statistics in medicine.* Boston: Little, Brown.
Commerce Clearing House, Inc. (1980). *Employment Practices Decisions, Vol. 23.* Chicago: Commerce Clearing House, Inc. (Guardians ref is page 16979, paragraph 33154) (Library ref #HD6508.C35)
Contreras v. City of Los Angeles, 656 F.2d 1267, 25 FEP 866 and 29 FEP 1045 (9th Cir. 1981), cert. denied, 455 U.S. 1021 (1982).

Cooley, W. & Bickel, W. (1986). *Decision-oriented educational research.* Boston: Kluwer Nijhoff.
Copelin, L. (1984, March 15). Reform plans by Perot panel starting at top. *Austin American-Statesman,.*
Cork, B. (1987, May 15). BOE rejects teacher-test settlement. *The Montgomery Register,* p. 1–2A.
Cronbach, L. & Associates. (1980). *Toward reform of program evaluation.* San Francisco: Jossey–Bass.
Darling-Hammond. L. (1986, Fall). Teaching knowledge: How do we test it? *American Educator,* pp. 18–21, 46.
Debra P. v. Turlington, 474 F. Supp. 244 (M.D. Fla. 1979), affd, in part, revd, in part, 644 F. 2d 397 (5th Cir. 1981), petition for rehg, and petition for rehg, en banc denied, 644 F.2D 397 (5th Cir Sept 4, 1981).
Educational Testing Service. (1983). *ETS standards for quality and fairness.* Princeton, NJ: Educational Testing Service.
ETS Visiting Committee. (1987, June). Report of the 1987 ETS Visiting Committee. (Lyle F. Schoenfeldt, Chair. Submitted to Educational Testing Service Trustee Committee on Public Responsibility.
Filling classrooms with bad tutors. (1983, September 23). [Editorial]. *Mobile Register,* p. 4A.
Georgia Association of Educators v. State of Georgia, Civil Action No. C86-2234A (U.S D.C Atlanta.)
Goertz, M. E., & Pitcher, B. (1985, January). *The impact of NTE use by states on teacher selection.* (RR-85-1). Princeton, NJ: Educational Testing Service.
Griggs v. Duke Power Company, 401 U.S. 424, 3 FEP 175 (1971).
Guardians Association of New York City Police Department v. Civil Service Commission, 630 F.2d 79 FEP 909 (2nd. Cir. 1980), cert. denied, 49 U.S.L.W. 3932 (June 15, 1981).
Haney, W., Madaus, G., & Kreitzer, A. (1987). Charms Talismanic: Testing teachers for the improvement of American education. In E. Rothkopf (Ed.), *Review of research in education, 14,* 169–238. Itasca, IL: Peacock.
Huff, D. (1954). *How to lie with statistics.* New York: Norton.
Jensen, A. (1980). *Bias in mental testing.* New York: Free Press.
Kaye, D. H., & Aickin, M. (Eds.). (1986). *Statistical methods in discrimination litigation.* New York: Marcel Dekker.
Koerner, J. D. (1963). *The miseducation of American teachers.* Cambridge, MA: Riverside.
Light, R. (1987). Estimating the outcome of screening programs: A role for evaluation. *Evaluation Practice, 8*(1), 50–54.
Living with error. (1987 April 19). [Editorial]. *The Alabama Journal,* p. 14.
Madaus, G. F. (1983). Minimum competency testing for certification: The evolution and evalution of test validity. In G. F. Madaus (ed.), *The courts, validity, and minimum competency testing* (pp. 21–62). Boston: Kluwer-Nijhoff.
Madaus, G. F. (1986). Measurement specialists: Testing the faith—A reply to Mehrens. *Educational Measurement: Issues and Practice, 5*(4), 11–14.
Madaus, G. M., & Pullin, D. (1987, September). Teacher certification tests: Do they really measure what we need to know? *Phi Delta Kappan,* 31–38.
McCarthy, M. M. (1985). Competency tests in public employment: A legal view. *Journal of Educational Equity and Leadership, 5*(3), 250–262.
McFague, S. (1982). *Metaphorical theology.* Philadelphia, PA: Fortress.
Melnick, S. L. (1987). *Teacher competency testing.* Paper presented at the annual meeting of the American Educational Research Association, Washington, DC.

Melnick, S. L., & Pullin, D. (1987). Testing teachers' professional knowledge: Legal and educational policy implications. *Educational Policy. 1*(2), 215–228.

Mitchell, J. V., Jr. (1978). [Review of the National Teacher Examinations]. In Buros (Ed.) *Mental Measurement Yearbook* (pp. 516–518). Highland Park, NJ: Gryphon Press.

NTE Policy Council. (1985). *Guidelines for proper use of NTE tests.* Princeton, NJ: Educational Testing Service (Peter LoPresti, Chair)

Novick, M. (1982). Ability testing: Federal guidelines and professional standards. In A. K. Wigdor & W. R. Garner (Eds.), *Ability testing. Uses, consequences, and controversies* (Part II, pp. 70–98). Washington, DC: National Academy Press.

Order of court. (1987). Filed in Georgia Association of Educators v. State of Georgia, Civil Action No. C86-2234A.

Plaintiffs and Plaintiff Intervenors' Joint Proposed Findings of Tact & Conclunors of Law (1987). In Allen v. The Alabama State Board of Education Civil Action No 81-697-N [M.D. Ala. 1985]

Plaintiffs' brief in opposition to motion for partial summary judgment. (1987). In Georgia Association of Educators v. State of Georgia, Civil Action No. C86-2234A.

Poggio, J. P. (1987a). *Declaration of Dr. John P. Poggio.* In Georgia Association of Educators v. State of Georgia, Civil Action No. C86-2234A.

Poggio, J. P. (1987b). *Second declaration of Dr. John P. Poggio.* In Georgia Association of Educators v. State of Georgia, Civil Action No. C86-2234A.

Poggio, J. P., Glasnapp, D. R., Miller, M. D., Tollefson, N., & Burry, J. A. (1986, Summer). Strategies for validating teacher certification tests. *Educational Measurement: Issues and Practice, 5*(2), 18–25.

Rentz, R. (1987A). *Affidavit of Dr. Robert Rentz.* In Georgia Association of Educators v. State of Georgia, Civil Action No. C86-2234A.

Rentz, R. (1987b). *Supplement to affidavit of Dr. Robert Rentz.* In Georgia Association of Educators v. State of Georgia, Civil Action No. C86-2234A.

Schlei, B. L., & Grossman, P. (1983). *Employment discrimination law* (2nd ed.). Washington, DC: The Bureau of National Affairs.

School firings praised. (1987, August 23). *Savannah News-Press,* p i.e.

School reforms to White. (1984, July 1). *Amarillo News-Globe,* pp. 1–2A.

Schware V. Board of Bar Examiners, 353 U.S. 232 (1957).

Taylor, H. C., & Russell, J. T. (1939). The relationship of validity coefficients of tests in selection: Discussion and tables. *Journal of Applied Psychology, 23,* 565–578.

Trotter, G. (1985, April 18). Incompetent teachers hurt kids [Letter to the editor]. *The Montgomery Advertiser,* p. 12A.

Turbayne, C. M. (1962). *The myth of metaphor.* New Haven, CT: Yale University Press.

U.S. Equal Employment Opportunity Commission, Civil Service Commission, U.S. Department of Justice. (1978). Uniform Guidelines on Employee Selection Procedures. *Federal Register, 25,* 38290–38315.

United States and North Carolina Association of Educators v. North Carolina, 400 F. Supp. 343, 11 FEP 257 (E.D.N.C. 1975), vacated and remanded, 425 F. Supp. 789, 14 FEP 971 (E.D.N.C. 1977)

United States v. South Carolina, 445 jF. Supp. 1094, 15 FEP 1196 (D.S.C. 1977) affd without opinion sub nom. National Education Association v. South Carolina, 434 U.S. 1026, 16 FEP 501 (1978).

Washington v. Davis, 426 U.S. 229, 12 FEP 1415 (1976).

Wigdor, Alexandra. (1982). Psychological testing and the law of employment discrimination. In Alexandra K. Wigdor & W. Garner (Eds.), *Ability testing: Uses, consequences, and controversies.* (Part II, pp. 39–69). Washington, D.C.: National Academy Press.

Wilson, Ann Jarvela. (1984). *Knowledge for teachers: The National Teachers Examinations program, 1940 to 1970.* Unpublished doctoral dissertation, University of Wisconsin, Madison, WI.

Yalow, E., Collins, J., & Popham, W. J. (1986, April). *Content validity conundrums.* Paper presented at the annual meeting of the American Educational Research Association, San Francisco, California.

8

Limitations of Using Student-Achievement Data for Career-Ladder Promotions and Merit-Pay Decisions

Ronald A. Berk
The Johns Hopkins University

INTRODUCTION

A study of U.S. school districts conducted 70 years ago reported that 48% of the districts sampled used merit pay (Evendon, 1918). Since then, the quantity as well as quality of teacher-compensation systems has fluctuated markedly (for details, see Cohen & Murnane, 1985; Murnane & Cohen, 1986; Porwoll, 1979). At present, 29 states are implementing large-scale teacher-incentive programs (a.k.a. career ladder, merit pay, pay for performance), funding local plans, piloting testing models, or using state board of education or legislative mandates to develop programs for teachers and administrators (Southern Regional Education Board, 1986) The status of these programs is summarized in Table 8.1.

Teacher performance is at the core of all of the programs in operation or those being considered. Determining who will receive the pay bonuses, which typically range from $1,000 to $3,000 per year, or be promoted up the career-ladder hinges on the methods used to evaluate teacher performance. The current trend in measurement procedures is to deemphasize supervisory ratings by the building principal and instead to emphasize peer evaluation,

TABLE 8.1
Survey of Teacher Incentive Programs

State	Local Initiative Only	Pilots with State Funding and/or Assistance	Full Implementation of State Program	State Program Under Development	Discussion No Legislative Action Pending	Type of Program
Alabama						Career ladder
Alaska						
Arizona		X				Career ladder
Arkansas		(Not Funded)				Career development
California			X			Mentor teacher
Colorado		X				Teacher incentive/career ladder
Connecticut		X				Teacher incentive
Delaware		X				Career development
Florida			X(1)	X(2)		(1) School incentive; (2) Career ladder
Georgia						Career ladder
Hawaii					X	
Idaho				(Not funded)		Career compensation
Illinois		X				Teacher incentive
Indiana		X				Teacher incentive
Iowa						
Kansas	X					Teacher incentive
Kentucky		X				Career ladder
Louisiana		X				Career ladder/school incentive
Maine		X				Tiered certification incentive
Maryland	X					Career development incentive
Massachusetts			X			Teacher incentive
Michigan					X	
Minnesota	X					Teacher incentive
Mississippi			X			Teacher incentive

Missouri		Career ladder
Montana		Career ladder
Nebraska	X	
Nevada		Teacher incentive
New Hampshire	X	
New Jersey		Teacher incentive
New Mexico		Teacher incentive
New York	X	Career ladder
North Carolina	X	
North Dakota		
Ohio		Career ladder
Oklahoma	X	Teacher incentive
Oregon	X	Teacher incentive
Pennsylvania		Teacher incentive
Rhode Island	X	Teacher incentive
South Carolina	X(1) X(2)	(1) Teacher incentive; (2) School incentive
South Dakota		
Tennessee	X	Career ladder
Texas	X	Career ladder
Utah	X	Career ladder
Vermont	X	Teacher incentive
Virginia		Career ladder/teacher incentive
Washington	X	Mentor teacher
West Virginia		Teacher incentive
Wisconsin	X	
Wyoming	X	Career ladder/teacher incentive

Note. Reprinted with permission of the Southern Regional Education Board (1986, p. 9).

classroom observation, student-achievement outcomes, and questionnaire data from principals, teachers, and students (for details, see Southern Regional Education Board, 1986).

Use of Student-Achievement Data

One particular procedure that seems to be gaining acceptance increasingly by legislators and the professionals who are designing the programs is the use of student-achievement data (cf. Robinson, 1983; 1984). These data provide information different from the other measurement tools previously noted. Where classroom observation and ratings by principals, teachers, and students measure a teacher's behavior on the job, student achievement relates to the outcomes of that behavior. That is, the former methods are direct measures of teacher performance; the latter is an indirect measure. Student outcomes are perceived as evidence of a teacher's effectiveness. Because superior teacher performance is the criterion in teacher-incentive programs, the psychometric issue becomes how best to measure that performance—use direct measures, indirect measures, or a combination of both.

Teacher-incentive programs that rely on student-achievement gains have been referred to as "new style merit pay" (Bacharach, Lipsky, & Shedd, 1984), as opposed to "old style merit pay," which bases teacher pay bonuses on principals' evaluations. In 1983, a national survey of merit-pay programs reported that nine school districts in seven states (Arizona, New Hampshire, North Carolina, Oklahoma, South Dakota, Texas, Utah) used student-test scores as evaluative criteria in determining merit pay for classroom teachers (Calhoun & Protheroe, 1983). In all but two of the districts (Dallas and Houston) student achievement served as the only evidence of teacher performance. Today student achievement is a criterion of teacher performance in one third of all statewide teacher incentive/school incentive/career ladder programs. Those programs have been fully implemented in four states (Florida, South Carolina, Tennessee, Utah), are at the pilot stage in four states (Arizona, Kentucky, Maine, South Carolina), and are under development in three states (Alabama, Florida, Georgia). A school incentive program based on student achievement is also under consideration in Alaska, and several career-ladder or merit-pay programs based on student performance have been implemented by local districts (e.g., Campbell County and Danville, Virginia).

Although the results of these surveys do not indicate that the use of student-achievement data is a dominant characteristic or even a trend in most teacher-incentive programs (cf. Moore, 1984), those states where student performance is stressed as the indicator of superior teaching should seriously reconsider the choice of that criterion. Such teacher incentive programs require that students have to perform well on selected achievement tests in order for their teacher to be promoted and/or receive a pay bonus. The teacher's performance on the job may or may not be measured directly. If it is measured, the data are not weighed as heavily in the promotion decision because they are considered "subjective," as compared to the students' achievement data, which are regarded as "objective" evidence of a teacher's performance and effectiveness.

In a more serious application of student-outcome data, student-achievement gains have been used as a major criterion for evaluating teachers as "satisfactory" or "unsatisfactory" in St. Louis. An unsatisfactory classification results in probationary status and can lead to termination. A class action suit was filed in 1986 by the St. Louis Teachers Union (AFT) against this method of teacher evaluation. A U.S. district court decision has not yet been rendered.

Computation of Achievement Gain

When student achievement is adopted as a criterion of teacher performance, it may be expressed as a level of "expected achievement" at the school level to provide school-based awards (e.g., Florida), or as an average pretest-posttest gain score. The last approach, which is most frequently employed in the teacher incentive/career-ladder programs cited previously, is perceived as the simplest, most efficient, and most cost-effective model. It involves a pretest-posttest design where a student-achievement test is administered twice: once at the beginning of the school year (September or October) and once at the end of the year (May or June). One test form or parallel forms may be used. The differences in student performance between the pretest and posttest are computed, and the resulting mean gain score is used to infer the level of teacher performance. Alternatively, the percentage of students in a class who gained "10 or more months in achievement," as measured in grade-equivalent scores, also serves as an index of teacher performance.

Rewarding superior teacher performance on the basis of student-achievement gains is derived from the notion that such gains represent the most concrete product of effective teaching. Proponents of this approach often compare the measurement of a teacher's performance to that of a factory worker's performance; both can be evaluated according to his or her productivity.

Factory Worker–Teacher Productivity Analogy

What's wrong with basing promotions and pay bonuses for teachers on student-achievement gains? Isn't student gain the most important product or work outcome of the job of teaching? After all, if a factory worker's performance can be measured in terms of productivity by the number of widgets he or she produces over a given period of time, why not evaluate a teacher's performance in terms of effectiveness or productivity by his or her students' achievement gains at the end of the school year (cf. Medley, Coker, & Soar, 1984, p. 33)?

The arguments for this factory worker–teacher productivity analogy are derived from the principles of a piece-rate compensation system (Murnane & Cohen, 1986). Piece-rate contracts, where a worker is paid according to the number of widgets produced, is the most common form of "payment by results" (Pencavel, 1977). About 30% of the workers in U.S. factories are employed under piece-rate contracts (Seiler, 1984). These contracts provide a strong incentive for workers to produce, because high productivity results in immediate rewards.

When this piece-rate compensation system is applied to teachers, it breaks down because of the nature of the teaching process and the classroom environment. First, a factory worker uses the same materials (e.g., plywood and chewing gum) to make each product (e.g., widgets). Teachers must work with students whose individual characteristics vary considerably within a single class. This variability precludes all of the students from achieving the same amount at the same rate over 10 months. Second, the characteristics of a factory worker's materials rarely influence his or her skills and rate of production. The worker's ability to build a widget is not affected by the plywood or chewing gum; the quality and quantity of widget production can be attributed solely to the worker. These properties do not generalize to the teaching-learning process. Certain key characteristics of students, such as intelligence and home environment, markedly influence the quality and quantity of their academic achievement, irrespective of what the teacher does in the classroom. Consequently, a teacher's effectiveness is directly affected by the characteristics of the class, which are beyond a teacher's control.

Objectivity of Student-Achievement Data

Students' achievement-test–score gains are often preferred to administrators' ratings of performance and classroom observations because the measurement is perceived to be more objective. This objectivity, however, is illusory. Although students' responses to multiple-choice test items can be scored objectively, the inferences drawn from their scores are subjective. All scores are interpreted, and judgments about student performance are inescapable. When the students' scores are used to infer their teacher's performance, that inference can be erroneous, inasmuch as student achievement is not attributable solely to the teacher. Numerous factors affect the students' performance, only one of which is the teacher's performance.

Assessing superior teacher performance in order to make promotion decisions and award pay bonuses requires a plan that is fair and equitable to all teachers. Establishing such a plan on the basis of achievement-test gains is fraught with difficulty. The difficulties stem primarily from limitations in the testing technology, from factors that influence a teacher's effectiveness beyond his or her control, and from the unfeasibility of executing rigorous experimental-design procedures in the natural school setting (see Haertel, 1986).

This chapter identifies the major limitations of using student achievement as a criterion of teacher performance. It is organized according to four topics: (a) professional and legal standards, (b) factors that influence a teacher's effectiveness beyond his or her control, (c) analysis of achievement gain, and (d) criterion for superior teacher performance.

PROFESSIONAL AND LEGAL STANDARDS

Are there any standards that professionals can use to guide measurement practices in teacher incentive programs? Yes, there are four sources that should be consulted on this question: (a) *Standards for Educational and Psychological Testing* (American Educational Research Association et al., [AERA, APA, NCME], 1985); (b) *Personnel Evaluation Standards* (Joint Committee on Standards for

Educational Evaluation, 1988); (c) *Uniform Guidelines on Employee Selection Procedures* (U.S. Equal Employment Opportunity Commission et al., 1978); and (d) court cases that have relied on the *Guidelines* for the decisions rendered. Although these sources furnish detailed criteria on what should be done, this section concentrates on whether there are any standards that address the use of student-achievement data in the context of teacher evaluation. In addition, it will attempt to extract from those sources the most professionally and legally defensible strategy to evaluate teacher performance.

Standards for Educational and Psychological Testing

Among the four sources, the first set of standards contains one standard that directly attacks the issue. Standard 12.7 states:

> Evaluations of service providers (e.g., teachers and health and social service staff) and administrators should not rest exclusively on the test scores of those people that they serve. (*Primary*)

> *Comment:*

> Test scores of individuals served (e.g., students) will be affected by a great many factors not directly related to the quality of service they receive. (AERA, APA, NCME, 1985, p. 69)

This standard stipulates that student test scores should not be used as the only criterion to evaluate teachers due to numerous uncontrolled factors that do not relate to teacher performance. (These factors are described in detail in subsequent sections of the chapter.)

Because standardized norm-referenced tests as well as criterion-referenced tests are being considered as the measures of "teacher performance," Standard 6.3, which relates to the validity of test score use, is pertinent:

> When a test is to be used for a purpose for which it has not been previously validated, or for which there is no supported claim for validity, the user is responsible for providing evidence of validity. (*Primary*)

8. LIMITATIONS OF USING STUDENT ACHIEVEMENT DATA 269

Comment:

The individual who makes the claim for validity is responsible for providing the necessary evidence. Evidence of validity sufficient for test use may often be obtained from a well-documented manual. If previous evidence is not sufficient, then additional data should be collected. (AERA, APA, NCME, 1985, p. 42)

This standard raises the issue of using a student-achievement test to measure teacher performance. An inference about teacher performance is being drawn from the scores on a test designed to measure student achievement. In the test manuals of the major standardized achievement-test batteries published by CTB/McGraw Hill, The Psychological Corporation, Riverside Publishing, and Science Research Associates, not only is no validity evidence provided for using the scores to infer teacher performance, but there is no mention of any intent that the results of the test should be used to evaluate teachers. Consequently, according to Standard 6.3, the burden for gathering appropriate validity evidence rests with the user—the state or local district. The states and districts identified previously have made no visible effort to obtain that evidence.

Other standards germane to the topic of teacher-performance evaluation fall under the sections entitled "Employment Testing" and "Professional and Occupational Licensure and Certification." The technical procedures for evaluating teachers for career-ladder promotion decisions or for retention, demotion, or termination decisions are derived from the same foundation—a comprehensive job analysis that describes the knowledge, skills, abilities, or other personal characteristics necessary to perform the job. The level of performance desired (e.g., average or superior) or expected (e.g., minimum) can be designated in this definition of the job-content domain. The importance of this first step in establishing the content validity of a test that measures teacher performance is expressed in Standards 10.4, 10.5, and 10.6 (AERA, APA, NCME, 1985):

Standard 10.4

Content validation should be based on a thorough and explicit definition of the content domain of interest. For job selection, classification, and promotion, the characterization of the domain should be based on a job analysis. (*Conditional*) (p. 60)

Standard 10.5

When the content-related validation evidence is to stand as support for the use of a test in selection or promotion, a close link between test content and job content should be demonstrated. (*Primary*) (p. 61)

Standard 10.6

When content-related evidence of validity is presented, the rationale for defining and describing a specific job content domain in a particular way (e.g., in terms of tasks to be performed or knowledge, skills, abilities, or other personal characteristics) should be stated clearly. The rationale should establish that the knowledge, skills, and abilities said to define the domain are the major determinants of proficiency in that domain. (*Primary*)

Comment:

When content-related evidence of validity is presented for a job or class of jobs, the evidence should include a description of the major job characteristics that a test is meant to sample, including the relative frequency and criticality of the elements. (p. 61)

These standards state clearly that a test that measures job performance should be derived from a job analysis and that a close link should exist between the content of the test and the content of the job.

How then would an achievement test of student performance satisfy these standards as a measure of teacher performance? It would be inadequate, because the *Standards* require that job performance be measured *directly* by a test of job content. Students' achievement cannot be used to measure the knowledge, skills, and abilities of a teacher; it does not directly assess a teacher's performance on the job.

Personnel Evaluation Standards

These standards focus exclusively on *personnel evaluation*, defined as "the systematic assessment of a person's performance and/or qualifications in relation to a professional role and some specified and defensible institutional purpose" (Joint Committee on Standards for Educational Evaluation, 1988, pp. 7–8). A standard is "a principle commonly agreed to by people engaged in the professional practice of evaluation for the measurement of the value or the quality of an evaluation" (Joint Committee on Standards for Educational Evaluation, 1981, p. 12). In other words, the *Standards* is the product of a broad search for consensus on what is good and desirable in the evaluation of educational personnel.

Interestingly, among the 21 standards and guidelines for conducting evaluations of teachers, counselors, administrators, and other professional personnel which appear in this document, there is no mention of student-achievement tests. The approach to evaluation advanced in these *Standards* is consistent with the strategy required in Standards 10.4, 10.5, and 10.6, described previously.

The job analysis is the first step. Standard A1 on "Defined Role," with its rationale and guidelines, lays the foundation for the measurement process (Joint Committee on Standards for Education Evaluation, 1988):

Standard
The role, responsibilities, performance objectives, and needed qualifications of the evaluatee should be clearly defined, so that the evaluator can determine valid assessment criteria. (p. 85)

Rationale
This standard specifies the crucial foundation step in any personnel evaluation process. A carefully developed and sufficiently detailed and delineated description of the role, responsibilities, performance objectives, and qualifications is prerequisite to specifying relevant assessment criteria. (p. 86)

Guidelines
A. Develop job descriptions based on systematic job analysis.
B. Obtain position description information from as many knowledgeable sources as possible.
C. Define duties that reflect the needs of students, constituency, and the employing institution.
D. Specify in detail significant role behaviors, tasks, duties, responsibilities, and performance objectives.
E. Make clear the relative importance and performance level of each standard used to define success in the position.
F. Investigate and resolve any discrepancies in the position description.
G. Make clear the relationship between performance indicators and the standard with which each indicator is associated. (pp. 86–87)

The teaching environment and the factors that can influence or constrain teacher performance are considered in Standard A2 on "Work Environment":

Standard
The context in which the evaluatee works should be identified, described, and recorded so that environmental influences and constraints on performance can be considered in the evaluation. (p. 90)

Rationale
Holding educators accountable for the effects of variables they cannot control or influence is likely to lead to resentment and low morale. Failure to take account of environmental factors may also threaten the validity of the evaluation process. (p. 90)

Guidelines
A. Identify and record contextual variables that might affect the work environment.
B. Consider available resources, working conditions, community expectations, and other context variables that might have affected performance. (p. 91)

The validity issue in personnel evaluation is given attention in Standard A4 on "Valid Measurement":

Standard
The measurement procedures should be chosen or developed and implemented on the basis of the described role and the intended use, so that the inferences concerning the evaluatee are valid and accurate. (p. 98)

Rationale
Validity is the single most important issue in the assessment of any evaluation process. If the evaluation is to serve its intended purpose, then the inferences and judgments that are made must be defensible. The selection, development, and implementation of the instruments and procedures for collecting information, as well as the basis for synthesizing the information and drawing inferences from it, must be clearly linked to the purposes for which judgments, inferences, and decisions are made. Further, these linkages must be documented and made public. (p. 99)

One of the common errors listed in relation to the guidelines for Standard A4 is "using a measurement procedure for multiple purposes when it is valid for only one, for example, using students' scores on a nationally standardized test to assess the performance of a teacher or administrator when the test has not been validated for the latter purpose" (Joint Committee on Standards for Educational Evaluation, 1988, p. 100)

Reliability is assigned similar weight in Standard A5 on "Reliable Measurement":

> Measurement procedures should be chosen or developed and implemented to assure reliability, so that the information obtained will provide consistent indications of the performance of the evaluatee. (p. 104)

The preceding standards plus many others in the document stress appropriate, technically defensible, and professionally acceptable practices for evaluating teacher performance. These up-to-date standards do not recommend the applicability of student test scores in this context.

Uniform Guidelines on Employee-Selection Procedures

In addition to the sets of professional standards cited in the first two sections, there are government regulations that protect individuals against any form of employment discrimination. Title VII of the 1964 Equal Employment Opportunity Act is enforced by the Equal Employment Opportunity Commission (EEOC) based on a set of guidelines, entitled *Uniform Guidelines on Employee Selection Procedures* (U.S. Equal Employment Opportunity Commission et al., 1978). These *Guidelines* apply to every kind of personnel-assessment technique used to make an employment decision. This includes "any measure, combination of measures, or procedures used as a basis for any employment decision" (p. 38308).

The purpose of the *Guidelines* is described in Section 1B:

> These guidelines incorporate a single set of principles which are designed to assist employers, labor organizations, employment agencies, and licensing and certification boards to comply with requirements of Federal law prohibiting employment practices which discriminate on grounds of race, color, religion, sex and national origin. They are designed to provide a framework for determining the proper use of tests and other selection procedures. (p. 38296)

One primary concern of the EEOC is whether an assessment procedure results in adverse impact against members of a racial, ethnic, or sex group. The EEOC would consider that a test that has no adverse impact complies with Title VII. If adverse impact is found, it would have to be justified in terms of appropriate validity evidence.

Suppose a disproportionate number of Black teachers in a local district were denied career-ladder promotions or were placed on probation because their evaluations were unsatisfactory compared to those of the White teachers. The determination of adverse impact and compliance with the *Guidelines* by the EEOC would hinge on the validity evidence that supports the use of the particular measurement tools for those "employment decisions."

What types of validity evidence must be documented? The *Guidelines* indicate the same types of evidence as those needed to satisfy the validity standards cited previously, where the most crucial step is the job analysis. The *Guidelines* (U.S. Equal Employment Commission et al., 1978) specify validity studies for (a) content validity—"an analysis of the important work behavior(s) required for successful performance and their relative importance and, if the behavior results in work product(s), an analysis of the work product(s)" (sec. 14C [2]); (b) construct validity—"the job analysis should show the work behavior(s) required for successful performance of the job, . . . the critical or important work behavior(s) in the job or group of jobs being studied, and an identification of the construct(s) believed to underlie successful performance of these critical or important work behaviors in the job or jobs in question" (sec. 14D [2]); and (c) criterion-related validity—"to determine measures of work behavior(s) or performance that are relevant to the job or group of jobs in question" (sec. 14B [2]).

Because student-achievement gain is perceived as an outcome of teaching, that is, work outcome, why not use achievement as a criterion variable? The *Guidelines'* definition of criteria for criterion-related validity studies is as follows:

> Whatever criteria are used should represent important or critical work behaviors(s) or work outcomes. Certain criteria may be used without a full job analysis if the user can show the importance of the criteria to the particular employment context. These criteria include but are not limited to production rate, error rate, tardiness, absenteeism, and length of service. A standardized rating of overall work performance may be used where a study of the job shows that it is an appropriate criterion. (pp. 38300–38301)

Notice that all except one of the preceding criteria stated are objective, single measures of the person being evaluated. Achievement gain, however, is a collective (class) index representing the performance of individuals with diverse academic (and usually demographic) characteristics, which is then applied to the teacher being evaluated. Despite the common interpretation of student-achievement gain as the direct product or outcome of teaching, as noted in the previous section, gain is an indirect measure of teacher performance.

Court Cases

The court cases that have implications for teacher evaluation and for the use of student achievement data to assess teacher performance can be classified into general employment decisions and teacher employment decisions. The purpose of this section is to extract from the court decisions the key factors or issues that are germane to the student test-score approach to teacher evaluation.

General-Employment Decisions

There are numerous court cases involving the use of tests and other measurement techniques in a variety of employment applications that may have a bearing on future litigation on teacher evaluation (see Madaus, chap. 7). Excellent reviews of these cases have been completed by Bernardin and Cascio (1984) and Nathan and Cascio (1986). Their reviews suggest that the courts have been guided by a number of factors in assessing personnel-evaluation systems; some relate to technical standards such as those stated in the *Guidelines*, whereas others pertain to proper personnel practices that help to safeguard against discriminatory employment decisions (Nathan & Cascio, 1986). Four particular factors have emerged from the reviews of Cascio and Bernardin (1981) and Bernardin and Beatty (1984):

1. Standards for performance should be based on a *job analysis*.
2. Evaluation should be based on *specific job dimensions*, not on a global or overall measure.
3. Ratings should be made on behaviorally based *performance dimensions* rather than on personality traits.

4. *Documentation* should be kept and should be accurate. Kleiman and Durham (1981) also emphasized the evidence essential to demonstrate that a performance evaluation is valid or job related. Further, they recommend presenting evidence that the evaluation procedures do not discriminate.

Consistent with the *Standards* and the *Guidelines*, the courts have affirmed the importance of a thorough job analysis. In the teacher-evaluation literature, empirically based schemes have been developed to identify specific job dimensions and behaviorally based performance dimensions (see review by Medley et al., 1984, chap. 4). The methods for assessing these dimensions, however, should be direct rather than indirect. The courts have supported the use of ratings of behavior as the basis for performance evaluation. There is no precedent for the use of student-test scores to measure teacher performance.

Teacher-Employment Decisions

Strike and Bull (1981) surveyed federal law and state regulations governing teacher evaluation, especially personnel policies and actions that relate to termination, salary determination, and promotion and demotion. They recommended that teacher-evaluation procedures focus "only on those aspects of a teacher's performance, behavior, and activities that are directly or indirectly relevant to the teacher's ability to execute the legitimate responsibilities that attach to the job" (p. 336). Their conclusions regarding the principle of *evaluative relevance*, however, are most appropriate to the issues of interest:

> The relevance requirement for . . . external information is . . . connected with the legal core of meaning of teaching competence: external information must be plausibly indicative of the teacher's capacity to fulfill central instructional responsibilities. . . . [C]ertain indirect measures of teaching ability, such as student test results, teacher tests, or research-based instruments, may be held legally relevant to judgments of competence under a variety of conditions. (p. 337)

This principle indicates that student-test scores may be legally relevant to the evaluation of teaching competence. The most recent test of evaluative relevance is *St. Louis Teachers Union v. Board of Education of St. Louis*, described previously, for which a decision has not yet been rendered.

Summary

The themes that recur in both sets of *Standards*, the *Guidelines*, and the court cases are as follows:

1. A comprehensive job analysis is crucial.
2. Evidence of job relatedness for all evaluation instruments must be provided.
3. Appropriate evidence of validity and reliability of test or scale scores used for employment decisions must be obtained.
4. Evidence that instruments are unbiased and nondiscriminatory of racial, sex, and ethnic subpopulations should be available.

As these themes are applied to teacher-incentive programs, it is clear that teacher performance should be measured directly in terms of on-the-job behaviors. An indirect measure such as student-achievement performance may be legally relevant and appropriate as one among several evaluative criteria, although not defensible according to the *Personnel Evaluation Standards* (Joint Committee on Standards for Educational Evaluation, 1988, p. 100).

FACTORS THAT INFLUENCE A TEACHER'S EFFECTIVENESS BEYOND HIS OR HER CONTROL

In the preceding section, it was noted that one of the intractable problems of using student achievement to measure teacher performance is isolating teacher performance as the primary explanation for changes in student performance. This issue is addressed specifically by Standard 12.7 (AERA, APA, NCME, 1985, p. 69) and Standard A2 (Joint Committee on Standards for Educational Evaluation, 1988, p. 114).

There are several factors that can influence a teacher's measured effectiveness that are beyond his or her control. These factors can account for a sizable proportion of the gain that may be exhibited in student achievement. Many of the factors have been identified previously by Berk (1984c; 1988), Haertel (1986), and Medley et al. (1984). In addition, several reviews of research on input-output analyses of schools by Bridge, Judd, and Moock (1979), Centra and Potter (1980), Cohn and Millman (1975), and, especially, Glasman and Biniaminov (1981) provide valuable insights into the impact of numerous variables on achievement. The last review is the most comprehensive to date.

The factors examined in this corpus of literature cluster into three categories: (a) student characteristics, (b) school characteristics, and (c) test characteristics. The work of Glasman and Biniaminov (1981) addresses most of the characteristics that fall into categories a and b; the issues that relate to category c have been discussed by Berk (1988).

Student Characteristics

There are at least seven types of student characteristics that can positively or negatively affect student achievement: (a) intelligence, (b) attitude, (c) socioeconomic level, (d) race/ethnicity, (d) sex, (e) age, and (f) attendance. These are attribute variables. Students possess these characteristics when they enter the classroom; most of them cannot be manipulated by the teacher. Under experimental conditions it might be possible to change intelligence and attitudes to some degree, or to improve attendance. However, under normal nonexperimental conditions, a teacher is assigned a class of students with a given set of characteristics.

The aforementioned student characteristics are described briefly in this section to determine the degree and direction of their effect on student achievement.

Intelligence. Intelligence or academic aptitude typically correlates from 0.40 to 0.70 with achievement, as measured by standardized test batteries. When the correlations are based on class means, they may be as high as 0.90 (Soar & Soar, 1975). As Medley et al. (1984) pointed out, "a correlation of .90 means . . . that about 80 percent of the differences in the pupil achievement scores used to evaluate a teacher were present before [he or] she had any chance to influence them" (p. 34). Furthermore, the interaction of intelligence with other student characteristics and school characteristics can affect achievement levels (Cronbach & Snow, 1977).

Attitude (three variables). Three types of student attitude have been investigated: (a) locus of control—the extent to which outcomes are attributed to self-action (internals) or to fate, chance, and powerful others (externals), (b) self-concept—the beliefs about one's personal characteristics, and (c) academic aspiration—the motivation to achieve in school. Glasman and Biniaminov's (1981) synthesis of the research indicates consistent findings that internal control, high self-concept, and high academic aspirations positively influence reading and mathematics achievement. Locus of control and self-concept tend to have a much stronger effect on achievement than academic aspirations, and these attitudes are stronger determinants of verbal achievement than of socioeconomic variables (Mayeske & Beaton, 1975).

Socioeconomic level (six variables). Six family-background variables have been used in combination to define socioeconomic level, including family size, family income, family occupational status, family possessions, parental education, and family's educational environment. The results of 17 studies were consistent: All of these components of socioeconomic level except family size were strongly and positively correlated with reading, mathematics, verbal, and composite achievement (see Glasman & Biniaminov, 1981). Family size was negatively correlated with achievement (e.g., Hanushek, 1972; Wiley, 1976).

Race/ethnicity. Racial composition of elementary and secondary schools defined either as percentages of White, Black, or non-White students or as a dummy coded variable (Black = 1, others = 0) was negatively correlated with reading, mathematics, and verbal achievement where there was a majority of Black or non-White students. Only one study by Winkler (1975) found a positive association. Interestingly, Mayeske et al. (1973) reported that race/ethnicity accounted for 24% of the variance in achievement when socioeconomic factors were uncontrolled, and only 1% when those factors were controlled.

Sex. Several studies of the relationship between sex, coded as female = 1 and male = 0, and achievement have found consistently positive correlations with reading and composite achievement and negative correlations with mathematics (e.g., Michaelson, 1970; Summers & Wolfe, 1977). In other words, females perform better in reading and males better in math.

Age. Three studies that examined the variable of age in grade, coded as over-age = 1 and not over-age = 0, at the elementary and secondary levels reported negative correlations with reading and mathematics achievement (Boardman, Davis, & Sanday, 1974; Levin, 1970; Michaelson, 1970). Consequently, the age composition of a class can affect achievement gains negatively to the extent that over-age students are in the majority.

Attendance (four variables). Student attendance has been expressed as student turnover, days present, quantity of schooling index, and student unexcused absences and lateness. Only three studies have explored this issue. Their findings at the elementary level indicate that poor attendance negatively affects reading, mathematics, and composite achievement (Murnane, 1975; Summers & Wolfe, 1977; Wiley, 1976).

School Characteristics

Beyond the characteristics of students which can affect achievement gains, there are numerous variables of school conditions and instructional personnel that exhibit similar effects. These variables have been analyzed by Glasman and Biniaminov (1981) and Haertel (1986).

School Conditions. More than 25 studies have investigated variables that relate to school services, facilities, expenditures, staff, and climate. They include the following:

1. school library (number of books per student)
2. class size (number of students per classroom)
3. size of a type of class (e.g., mean school class size in math)
4. age of building
5. size of school site
6. size of school enrollment
7. size of staff
8. turnover of staff
9. expenditures
10. quality of instructional materials and equipment (e.g., desks, chalkboards, textbooks, computers)
11. schoolwide learning climate
12. instructional support (e.g., aides, resource teachers, team teaching)

Glasman and Biniaminov's (1981) review of research on variables 1 through 8 led to their conclusion that the direction and significance of those variables' effects on achievement were inconsistent; the results were positive, negative, and mixed. However,

8. LIMITATIONS OF USING STUDENT ACHIEVEMENT DATA 281

there were consistent negative correlations between class and school size and reading and mathematics achievement; school library size was also positively associated with reading achievement.

Expenditures (variable 9) for administration, instruction, and extracurricular activities were positively correlated with reading and composite achievement (Benson et al., 1965; Cohn & Millman, 1975; Kiesling, 1969; 1970). Research on variables 10 through 12 was examined by Haertel (1986). He concluded that (a) quality of instructional materials may influence achievement (Wiley & Harnischfeger, 1974); (b) teachers can be more effective in schools with favorable learning climates (Bridge et al., 1979; Brookover, Beady, Flood, Schweitzer, & Wisenbaker, 1979); and (c) instructional support at the elementary and secondary levels can affect student performance.

Instructional Personnel. There are several teacher-background and personal characteristics and teacher-assignment and attitude variables that influence student achievement. These variables include:

1. education degree
2. undergraduate education type
3. teaching experience
4. verbal achievement
5. race
6. sex
7. teaching load
8. time in discipline
9. job satisfaction

In their review of more than 20 studies of these variables Glasman and Biniaminov (1981) concluded: (a) higher levels of education, verbal achievement, and experience affected reading and mathematics achievement positively, (b) increased teaching loads and time in discipline produced negative effects on reading, mathematics, and verbal achievement, and (c) greater job satisfaction was positively correlated with reading, mathematics, and verbal achievement.

Test Characteristics

Although the 17 student characteristics and 21 school characteristics identified thus far should suggest the difficulty of attributing student-achievement gains to teacher performance, just how that achievement is measured is equally important to the teacher-evaluation process. The characteristics of the achievement test selected can have a profound effect on what is actually measured, how it is interpreted, and the extent to which student performance reflects teacher effectiveness. In this section, pertinent test characteristics are described under three topics: (a) type of achievement test, (b) curricular and instructional validity, and (c) test score metric.

Type of Achievement Test. The first decision that must be made is the type of achievement test(s) to be used to measure teacher performance. The choices often reduce to standardized norm-referenced tests and criterion-referenced tests. The selection of any single test should be based on its technical adequacy in terms of norms, validity, and reliability. Standards and criteria for judging adequacy are set forth in the *Standards for Educational and Psychological Testing* (AERA, APA, & NCME, 1985). Special attention should be given to the characteristics of curricular and instructional validity. It is important that the items on the test match the objectives of the local curriculum and the instruction that actually occurs. Tests that are insensitive to what is taught in any subject area are inappropriate measures of student achievement as well as teacher performance.

Because standardized norm-referenced tests, such as the Iowa Tests of Basic Skills, California Achievement Tests, Comprehensive Tests of Basic Skills, Metropolitan Achievement Tests, Stanford Achievement Test, and Survey of Basic Skills, typically survey broad domains of content, they rarely "mirror a particular curriculum." In fact, the tests are expressly designed to minimize local, state, and regional content biases (Green, 1983; Mehrens, 1984). If the achievement-test scores do not accurately measure achievement in the program, their validity is weakened. The degree of invalidity is contingent upon the match between what the test measures and what the curriculum covers.

In contrast to standardized tests, criterion-referenced competency tests are tailored to measure the instructional objectives of a school-based program (Berk, 1984a). Such tests, however, must be developed by the local or state educational agency, or in collaboration with a professional test-development contractor. Unfortunately, the experiences with minimum-competency test construction over the past decade indicate that the products of local efforts are far from technically adequate (Berk, 1986). Commercially developed criterion-referenced tests have also been plagued by technical deficiencies (Hambleton & Eignor, 1978) related to item characteristics, mastery–nonmastery cut-off scores, and decision consistency.

Curriculum and Instructional Validity. Although content, criterion-related, and construct validities are applicable to achievement-test scores in general, there are specific types of validity evidence that must be obtained to consider drawing inferences about teacher performance. Such evidence relates to curricular and instructional validity.

Curricular validity refers to the extent to which the items on the test measure the content of a local curriculum (cf. McClung, 1979, p. 682). Although conceptually similar to content validity (Madaus, 1983; Schmidt, Porter, Schwille, Floden, & Freeman, 1983) and even viewed by some experts as synonymous with content validity (Cureton, 1951; Hopkins & Stanley, 1981, chap. 4; Madaus, Airasian, Hambleton, Consalvo, & Orlandi, 1982), curricular validity is operationally very different. In the case of standardized norm-referenced tests, it does not focus on the content domain the test was designed to measure; it deals with a specific domain to which the test is later applied. The relevance of the test in a specific application is being evaluated. Rarely would perfect congruence between the two domains ever occur (e.g., Bower, 1982; Gramenz, Johnson, & Jones, 1982; Jenkins & Pany, 1978; Madaus et al., 1982; Porter, Schmidt, Floden, & Freeman, 1978).

Evidence of curricular validity is obtained by determining the degree of congruence or match between the test items and the curriculum. This is based on a systematic, judgmental review of the test against the curricular objectives or materials by content experts. These experts may be classroom teachers or curriculum specialists; they are the only professionals in a position to judge curricular validity. The review can vary as a function of the following: (a) single grade versus cumulative grade content, (b) specificity of objectives or content/process matrix, (c) internal versus external determination, and (d) curricular materials versus actual classroom activities (for details, see Schmidt, 1983a; 1983b; Schmidt et al., 1983). What emerges from this process are several estimates of content overlap, including the amount of content in common, the percentage of the local curriculum measured by the test, and the percentage of items on the test not covered by the curriculum. The second estimate in particular can furnish evidence of the curricular validity of the test.

When a standardized test is found to have low curricular validity, alternative testing procedures should be considered. One procedure involves customizing the test by developing supplementary items to fill in the identified measurement gaps. These items would be administered and scored in conjunction with the standardized test. Technical problems arise in evaluating the validity and reliability of the "supplementary test" and in equating its scores to the appropriate national norms. Another procedure is to choose an out-of-grade-level test that provides a better curricular match.

An important issue related to curricular validity is whether achievement tests measure what is actually taught in the schools. Very often it is simply assumed or implied that evidence of curricular validity means that the objectives guided the instruction and the curricular materials were used in the classroom. This does not necessarily follow, as several studies have demonstrated (Hardy, 1984; Leinhardt & Seewald, 1981; Leinhardt, Zigmond, & Cooley, 1981; Poynor, 1978; Schmidt et al., 1983). What is measured by the test is not always the same as what is taught, especially with regard to standardized tests. Hence, a distinction has been made between these different domains to which the test items can be referenced (Schmidt et al., 1983). When the domain is the instruction actually delivered, a "measure of whether schools are providing students with instruction in the knowledge and skills measured by the test" (McClung, 1979, p. 683) is called instructional validity.

Instructional validity refers to the extent to which the items on the test measure the content actually taught to the students. Several techniques have been proposed for assessing the overlap between the test and the instruction. Popham (1983) identified four data-sources for describing whether students have received instruction that would enable them to perform satisfactorily on a test: (a) observations of classroom transactions, (b) analyses of instructional materials, (c) instructor self-reports, and (d) student self-reports. Although he views these sources as methods for determining the adequacy of test preparation (Yalow & Popham, 1983), they can be considered as techniques for gathering evidence of instructional validity. Unfortunately, Popham's (1983) evaluation of those techniques suggests that the process of estimating the percentage of a standardized test that has been covered by teaching has numerous methodological problems related to executing the data-gathering procedures (see Leinhardt, 1983; Schmidt et al., 1983). They stem, in large part, from the variability of instructional content, not only among different classes, but within a single classroom.

The evidence from an instructional validity study can reveal "content taught but not tested" and "content tested but not taught." Both types of evidence have significant implications for inferring teacher effectiveness from student-achievement gains. In the case of the former, if the evidence indicates that there is a considerable amount of content being taught but not covered by the achievement test, then the students' performance gains may only partially reflect the teacher's performance. Instruction on skills at the higher levels of cognition (e.g., application, analysis), which are the levels rarely measured by standardized norm-referenced tests (Soar & Soar, 1983), might not be assessed. In that case, an inference about a teacher's performance from the achievement test scores would need to be qualified in the context of what was not measured by the test.

Conversely, if there is validity evidence that a proportion of the test items measures content that was not taught to the students, then inadequate achievement gains on that test cannot be attributed to the teacher's performance, unless that particular content was supposed to be taught. The most common strategy to address this type of test content–instruction mismatch is for teachers to teach the objectives measured by the test. If teachers are to be evaluated according to their students' test performance, then it is highly probable that a sizable portion of the instruction will be driven by the test content. Because most achievement tests tend to measure simpler objectives, as opposed to complex or higher-order objectives, teaching will attempt to maximize student progress on those objectives to produce large achievement gains (Medley et al., 1984, chap. 3).

Test-Score Metric

In order to perform basic arithmetic calculations, such as computing the difference between pretest and posttest scores and group-average scores, equal-interval scales are essential. The most frequently used derived-score scale for norm-referenced tests is the *grade equivalent*. It is not an interval scale and has several other serious deficiencies (see Angoff, 1971; Berk, 1984b; Flanagan, 1951;

Horst, 1976; Horst, Tallmadge, & Wood, 1974; Linn, 1981; Williams, 1980). Those deficiencies have been summarized by Berk (1984b):

> Grade equivalents
> 1. invite seemingly simple but misleading interpretations;
> 2. assume that the rate of learning is constant throughout the school year;
> 3. yield different growth rates at different score levels;
> 4. are derived primarily from interpolation and extrapolation rather than from real data;
> 5. are virtually meaningless in the upper grade levels for subjects that are not taught at those levels;
> 6. exaggerate the significance of small differences in performance;
> 7. are affected by changes in educational customs regarding promotion from grade to grade;
> 8. vary markedly from publisher to publisher, from test to test, from subtest to subtest within the same test battery, from grade to grade, and from percentile to percentile. (pp. 94–96)

Consistent with these deficiencies are the cautions cited for interpreting grade equivalents in relation to Standard 4.1 of the *Standards for Educational and Psychological Testing* (AERA, APA, NCME, 1985):

> Test publishers and users can reduce misinterpretations of grade-equivalent scores, for example, by ensuring that such scores are (a) reported only for grades in which actual growth can be expected, (b) reported only for grades for which test data are available, and (c) accompanied by instructions that make clear that grade-equivalent scores do not represent a standard of growth per year or grade and that 50% of the students tested in the standardization sample should by definition fall below grade level, that if a student scores above grade level it does not necessarily mean that the student has mastered the content material of the higher grade level, and that interpretations of differences between grade equivalent scores on separate subtests should be avoided. (p. 33)

Because grade equivalents can distort a student's actual achievement levels on both the pretest and posttest, there is no technically sound reason to justify their use in the estimation of gain scores. As Angoff (1971) noted, "their simplicity is far more apparent than real" (p. 525); however, the adverse consequences of their continued use will be far more real than apparent.

Percentile ranks are also unacceptable for gain-score analysis inasmuch as they comprise an ordinal scale. Although their interpretation is direct and readily understood, the inequality of percentile units on different parts of the scale render them inappropriate for computing pretest-posttest gains.

The preferred metric for gain-score analysis is simple *raw scores*. They are appropriate when the same test form is administered both times. If parallel forms are employed or it is desirable to compare performances from one subtest to another or from class to class, *scaled scores* should be used. These scores possess the property of equal intervals and permit comparisons of tests within and across grade levels.

For criterion-referenced tests, raw score or proportion correct is an appropriate metric to estimate gain. Linn (1981) recommended that if the content domain of the test is explicitly defined and random or stratified random samples of items can be generated, the estimate of proportion correct on each item sample can be used to obtain growth curves.

Summary

This section presented 17 student characteristics, 21 school characteristics, and 4 achievement test characteristics that can influence the evaluation of teacher performance. In other words, there are more than 40 factors that affect student achievement, its measurement, and its interpretation, irrespective of teacher performance. Despite the interrelationships among many of these factors and the efforts to control or eliminate some of them (see Haertel, 1986), an individual teacher whose performance is being measured via achievement gains is rarely in a position to manipulate those factors in order to neutralize their effect on his or her performance. According to the research literature cited previously, most of the factors have a positive effect on achievement and, consequently, could account for a large proportion of the overall gain over 10 months. A few of the factors had negative effects, and other factors could be positive or negative.

ANALYSIS OF ACHIEVEMENT GAIN

In addition to the aforementioned factors that affect student achievement and inferences about teacher performance, the pretest-posttest database for computing gain scores and the inferences drawn from those scores possess other limitations. Typically, the achievement-test database used in some incentive programs focuses on the difference in the students' performance on a standardized achievement test between September (or October) and May (or June) during the same school year; alternatively, the two testings can occur in May of one school year and again in May of the succeeding year. In either case only two measurement points (pretest and posttest) are used.

As noted in the introduction to this chapter, the states and particular school districts who rely on achievement data for promotion and pay bonus decisions compute the difference between the two testings using three methods:

1. Subtract a student's posttest score (X_2) from the pretest score (X_1), or $X_2 - X_1$.
   Calculate the percentage of students who gained (10 months to be "on or above grade level").
2. Average the $X_2 - X_1$ gain scores for a single class (i.e., mean gain score).
3. Average the $X_2 - X_1$ gain scores for an entire grade level in a school.

Methods 1 and 2 are intended to measure teacher performance; method 3 focuses on school effectiveness. A few of the current teacher-incentive programs employ one or any combination of those methods.

This section examines the adequacy of the preceding methods as measures of gain and the validity of inferences from gain scores.

Measurement of Gain

Traditional Deficiencies

During the past 40 years a considerable amount of research has been devoted to the study of how to measure change or gain over time (see Bereiter, 1963; Cronbach & Furby, 1970; Linn & Slinde, 1977; Lord, 1956; 1963; O'Connor, 1972; Webster & Bereiter,

1963). Much of this work has cited two major deficiencies of pretest-posttest gain scores: their low reliability and their negative correlation with pretest scores.

The formula for the *reliability of a gain score* (r_{GS}) can be expressed in terms of the reliabilities of the prescores (r_{11}) and postscores (r_{22}), considered separately, and the correlation between them (r_{12}), or

$$r_{GS} = \frac{r_{11} + r_{22} - 2r_{12}}{2(1 - r_{12})}.$$

Low reliability can result from this formula under certain observable conditions. First, if the alpha reliability coefficients are identical and equal to the test-retest coefficient, the reliability of the gain score is zero. Second, a high test-retest correlation tends to produce a low gain-score reliability. For example, a test with a common variance and a reliability of 0.80 would have a gain score reliability of 0.60, 0.50, 0.33, and 0 when the correlation (r_{12}) was 0.50, 0.60, 0.70, and 0.80, respectively (Linn, 1981, p. 87). Interestingly, these low gain-score reliabilities would rarely occur because the assumption of common variance is not usually upheld in practice.

This low reliability of gain scores has been regarded as a serious concern in individual student decision making and in decisions based on aggregates of individual gain scores (Method 1). The reliability of a mean gain score (Methods 2 and 3) has been viewed as problematic in terms of stability coefficients from one year to the next. From several studies of the stability of class mean gain, it was found that the median stability coefficient was approximately 0.30 (Brophy, 1973; Rosenshine, 1970). This instability of gains occurred across years, teachers, grade levels, subtest-subject areas, and Title I versus non-Title I schools.

The second deficiency of gain scores is their *negative correlation with pretest scores*. This negative bias has been cited as an important reason to avoid gain scores (Linn & Slinde, 1977; O'Connor, 1972). If the pretest- and posttest-score variances are equal, the correlation between the pretest scores and gain scores is necessarily negative because r_{12} will be less than 1.0. This means that students with low pretest scores will tend to have larger gains than students with high pretest scores. However, the converse is possible. If the posttest variance is considerably larger than the pretest variance, r_{12} may be positive, in which case the initially higher scoring students have a built-in advantage (see Linn, 1981; Zimmerman & Williams, 1982).

Deficiencies as Misconceptions

The findings of investigations comparing numerous strategies for estimating gain (e.g., Corder-Bolz, 1978; Overall & Woodward, 1975; 1976; Richards, 1976) and the reanalyses of these issues by Rogosa (1980; Rogosa, Brandt, & Zimowski, 1982; Rogosa & Willett, 1983; 1985) and others (Nesselroade, Stigler, & Baltes, 1980; Willett, 1988; Zimmerman & Williams, 1982) strongly indicate that the aforementioned deficiencies are not serious. Low reliability and negative correlation with initial status are misconceptions rather than deficiencies.

On the problem of low reliability, Rogosa et al. (1982) pointed out: (a) "low reliability [of gain scores] does not necessarily mean lack of precision," and (b) "the difference between two fallible measures can be nearly as reliable as the measures themselves" (p. 744). Overall and Woodward (1975) also demonstrated that the unreliability of gain scores should not be a cause for concern in determining an instructional effect between two testings. A true effect can be evidenced using a t-test for paired observations "irrespective of the zero reliability of difference scores upon which *all* calculations are based" (p. 86). In fact, the power of tests of significance is maximum when the reliability of the difference scores is zero.

The negative bias of the correlation should be interpreted as an artifact of measurement error on the estimation of the correlation. Rogosa et al. (1982) argued that the bias is not a fundamental difficulty with the use of the gain score as a measure of change.

Alternative Methods

A variety of methods have been proposed for estimating gain, including raw gain, gain adjusted for pretest error, gain adjusted for pretest and posttest error, the difference between true posttest and pretest scores (Lord, 1956), raw residual gain, estimated true residual gain, a "base-free" procedure (Tucker, Damarin, & Messick, 1966), and posttest score adjusted for initial academic potential. None of these procedures provides a satisfactory solution. Three other approaches supplement the information on the two data points (X_1 and X_2) with between-person information (e.g., reliabilities and measurement error variances): (a) weighted reliability measures, (b) Lord–McNemar regression estimates, and (c) Bayes growth-curve estimates (for details, see Rogosa et al., 1982).

New Directions

Despite all of the research cited in this section, which has addressed the technical problems in measuring gain, the most important deficiency of the pretest-posttest gain score is the meager information it yields based on only two measurement points. This issue was virtually ignored in the research literature until the 1980s. The use of *multiwave data,* where three measurements (September-January-May), four measurements (September-December-March-May), or more are obtained, vastly improves the measurement of change over time simply because additional information on each student is available (Rogosa et al., 1982). Multiple measurements provide greater precision in estimating gain than just two measurements (see Bryk & Raudenbush, 1987; Rogosa & Willett, 1985; Willett, 1988).

Validity of Gain-Score Inferences

The validity of gain-score inferences pertains to the underlying pretest-posttest design. The several possible factors jeopardizing the internal validity of the one-group pretest-posttest design have been discussed extensively in the research methodology literature à la Campbell and Stanley (1966) and Cook and Campbell (1979). They have also been emphasized in reviews of the RMC Research Corporation's Title I evaluation model A (Horst, Tallmadge, & Wood, 1974; Linn, 1979; 1980b; 1981; Linn, Dunbar, Harnisch, & Hastings, 1982; Tallmadge, 1982; Tallmadge & Wood, 1976). Among the factors of history, maturation, testing, instrumentation, statistical regression, selection, mortality, and interactions with selection, only those germane to the inference of teacher performance are described in this section.

The gain score computed from the pretest and posttest administrations is to be attributed to the teacher's performance. The score is one indicant of his or her effectiveness. The validity question asks: What other plausible explanations could account for the gain score? If the gain score is invalidated, such that there are many reasons for the improvement in the students' performance, only one of which may be teacher effort, then promoting a teacher or awarding a pay bonus would be unjustified. The relevance of the alternative explanations for gain may vary across classes, grade levels, subject areas, and schools.

History

Gain may be due to history in the sense that events outside of the school setting could have occurred over the 9 to 10 months between the testings which, in turn, affect student achievement. Home and community resources (e.g., books, computers), which may vary as a function of socioeconomic level, educational and cable television programs, and the like, could influence a student's progress in reading, mathematics, and other subjects, irrespective of what happens in the classroom.

Maturation

As the students grow older, wiser, and more experienced over the school year, their learning and measured achievement will be affected to some degree.

Statistical Regression

Students who have low pretest scores will score higher on the posttest, and students who score high on the pretest will score relatively lower on the posttest. That is, the most extreme scores on the pretest tend to "regress toward the population mean" on the posttest. The regression effect operates (a) to increase obtained pretest-posttest gain scores among low pretest scores, (b) to decrease obtained change scores among students with high pretest scores, and (c) to not affect obtained change scores among scores at the center of the pretest distribution (for details, see Cook & Campbell, 1979, pp. 52–53). These changes that occur due to regression cannot be attributed to the teacher. The magnitude of the changes depends on the test-retest reliability coefficient and the ability distribution in the class at the time of the pretest. The higher the reliability and the more average the students, the less will be the regression effect.

Mortality

In the course of a school year, students can leave a given class for any number of reasons. As the composition of the class changes—some students leave and others transfer in—a selection artifact results. The students taking the posttest may be different from those who took the pretest.

Interactions with Selection

When mean gain scores are compared across classes in one school or across schools to determine which teacher(s) or school(s) deserves a financial award, there are additional factors such as selection-history and selection-maturation that could account for differential gains in the classes or schools. *Selection-history* results when the schools being compared are located in different geographic and socioeconomic areas. The students in each school could experience a different local history that might affect achievement gains. *Selection-maturation* occurs when the students in different classes or schools are maturing at different rates due to differences in socioeconomic background or other variables. As noted previously, socioeconomic level is related to achievement growth rates.

Multiple Sources of Invalidity

Ideally, it would be desirable to partial out of the total gain that proportion of gain attributable to extraneous (noninstructional) factors. Suppose that the observed gain scores by students in a class were expressed in terms of variance components, or

$$\sigma^2_{OG} = \sigma^2_{TG} + \sigma^2_{E};$$

that is, the variance of the observed gain scores (σ^2_{OG}) equals the variance of true gain scores (σ^2_{TG}) plus the variance arising from errors of measurement (σ^2_{E}). Unfortunately, although all of the factors mentioned previously can be viewed as systematic error variance, only a few can be quantified by experimental or statistical procedures, such that a factor's specific effect on the gain scores can be estimated and removed from σ^2_{OG}.

Based on the many years of experience with Title I program evaluations and the invalidity issues examined in this section, there appear to be 11 factors that can increase pretest-posttest gain scores from September to June in any given school year:

1. history
2. maturation
3. statistical regression
4. small class size ($n < 30$)
5. overall school effects

6. test-wiseness
7. score conversion errors
8. "minor" variations in test administration
9. teaching to the test
10. coaching on test-taking skills
11. random error

A few studies of regression effect with classes composed primarily of low achievers (Linn, 1980a; Roberts, 1980; Tallmadge, 1982), small class size (Horst, 1981), score conversion errors (Elman, n.d.; Finley, 1981), and random error (Tallmadge, 1982) indicate that these factors alone could account cumulatively for as much as a half standard deviation in gain. The degree to which the other factors could spuriously inflate the average gain is difficult to assess. Furthermore, the impact of the 11 factors in one classroom can also be very different from the impact in other classrooms within the same school.

When these 11 factors are considered in conjunction with the 42 student, school, and test characteristics described previously, the net effect is to produce a sizable gain in the students' achievement which is independent of the teacher's performance or classroom instruction. The cumulative effect of the factors that positively bias estimated gain appears large enough to overstate the amount of teacher effect by a substantial margin. Currently, this "margin" cannot be determined exactly. As a consequence, it would be difficult to set a criterion for superior teacher performance that exceeds both normally expected gain and the gain due to the various sources of invalidity and error in each classroom.

Summary

The preceding analysis of achievement gain suggests eight conclusions in the context of teacher evaluation:

Measurement of Gain

1. The low reliability of gain scores and their negative correlation with pretest scores do not appear to be serious deficiencies of gain scores, as previously believed.
2. Low reliability does not necessarily mean lack of precision,

8. LIMITATIONS OF USING STUDENT ACHIEVEMENT DATA

and the negative bias of the correlation is an artifact of measurement error on the estimation of the correlation.
3. Improved approaches to measuring gain supplement pretest-posttest data with between-person information.
4. The major limitation of the pretest-posttest gain score is the meager information it yields.
5. Multiwave data based on three, four, or more data points are preferable to two-wave data.

Validity of Gain-Score Inferences

6. The sources of invalidity of the pretest-posttest design include history, maturation, statistical regression, mortality, and interactions with selection.
7. There are 11 factors that can increase achievement gain.
8. The net effect of about 50 identified sources of invalidity is to produce a sizable gain in achievement that is independent of a teacher's performance.

CRITERION FOR SUPERIOR TEACHER PERFORMANCE

The career-ladder movement is designed to reward excellence in teaching. Ultimately, the incentive programs are intended to make the teaching profession more attractive in order to encourage the best and brightest to become and remain teachers (Southern Regional Education Board, 1986, p. 6). If excellence or outstanding teaching is the grounds for promotion and pay-bonus decisions, this standard for a teacher's performance must be expressed in concrete, operational language. If gains are to be used to identify the "superior teacher," then a criterion mean-gain score must be specified. What makes this task particularly difficult is the term *superior*. The implication is that the mean gain score of a class (or school) must be well above average or above the level of gain that could normally be expected from 10 months of teaching.

There are at least three major approaches one can pursue in an attempt to provide an operational definition for the criterion of superior teacher performance: (a) statistical significance, (b) educational significance, and (c) normative significance. The appropriateness and feasibility of these approaches are examined in this section.

Statistical Significance

One approach to assessing the degree of pretest-posttest achievement gain is to compute the t-test for paired observations. If the resulting t statistic reaches significance, it can be said that the gain is a "real" rather than a chance occurrence. Degree of gain is, therefore, defined as the magnitude of gain necessary to be found statistically significant.

Statistical significance is an unsatisfactory definition for two reasons. First, no graduated scale of gain is possible to differentiate normal from superior. Either a real gain is found or it is not. And second, because the power of a statistic is so dependent on sample size, teachers with relatively small classes would probably have insignificant gains and those with larger classes would have a better chance of obtaining significant gains. For example, for a class composed of 30 students, there would be greater than a 90% chance of attaining significance for a large gain; whereas for classes of between 10 and 20 students, there would be a 50% to 80% probability, respectively, of detecting similar gains (see Cohen, 1977, chap. 2).

All of these estimates of power could be decreased after considering the unreliability of the test(s). The appropriate pooled within-class reliability estimate for test-retest or parallel forms data has been developed by Subkoviak and Levin (1977, formula 3). Adjustments for unreliability are especially important in view of the fluctuation in power estimates for classroom size samples.

Educational Significance

The question remains as to just how much gain is indicative of superior teacher performance. One index that measures magnitude of gain is *effect size*. For pretest-posttest data, effect size is equal to the average gain score divided by the standard deviation of the test scores, assuming equal pretest and posttest variance (for details, see Cohen, 1977, chap. 2). Gain is simply expressed in standard-deviation units so that a magnitude of gain of, say, 0.5 or 1.0 standard deviation, can be specified as a standard for educational or practical significance. Criteria for what is deemed small, medium, and large gains can also be set.

Despite the availability of this meaningful index for defining "how much gain," determining the criterion for "superior" remains problematic. First, an analysis of class-by-class performances over several years would be required to ascertain the magnitude of gain that can normally be expected from 9 or 10 months of teaching. This analysis is complicated by the variability of class composition by grade level and subject area. Title I evaluation results, for example, suggest that marked differences in gain can occur between grades at the lower levels (Tallmadge, 1982). If it were found that a 0.5 standard deviation is a reasonable expectation for reading gain at a given grade level in a particular school, then at least a baseline has been established for setting a criterion for superior gain.

Second, one must wrestle with the multiple sources of invalidity and measurement error described in the preceding pages. It should be apparent by now that if a gain of 0.5 were found for a single class, it would be imperceptive to attribute that total gain to the teacher's performance. There are too many contaminating factors that could contribute to the estimate of gain. These factors must be addressed in order to isolate the amount of gain only due to in-class instruction.

Normative Significance

The statistical and educational significance criteria for superior teacher performance can be viewed as *absolute;* that is, a designated criterion can be met by one teacher irrespective of how other teachers perform. In fact, it is conceivable that no teacher may satisfy the criterion for "superior" at a particular point in time.

In contrast, the normative significance approach utilizes *relative* criteria, so that "superior" is defined in relation to a norm group of teachers. In one grade level at one school, for example, teachers may be ranked according to their estimated class gain scores. The teacher in the norm group with the largest gain may be identified as superior, relative to the other teachers in the norm group. The magnitude of gain necessary to be classified as superior may vary by grade level, subject area, and school. The implication is that *superior* has no absolute meaning as far as performance; it has relative meaning only.

Embedded within this relative meaning of superior are numerous sources of unfairness and inequity. Unless classes are comparable or matched on the factors discussed throughout this chapter, there are no defensible grounds for assuring a fair and equitable determination of superior performance. The between-class, between-grade, and between-student variability of the student, teacher, and test characteristics interacting with the sources of invalidity and error listed previously render any such determination as nearly impossible.

Summary

Three procedures for defining the criterion of superior teacher performance were examined. Statistical significance and educational significance provide absolute criteria based on probability and magnitude of gain, respectively. Normative significance establishes relative criteria, so that *superior* is defined in relation to a norm group of teachers. All of these approaches are unsatisfactory due to the problems inherent in defining *superior*, specific sources of bias (e.g., class size), and the multiple factors of invalidity and error that preclude the inference of superior teacher performance from achievement gain.

CONCLUSIONS

The four major sections of this chapter have described the difficulties one would encounter in developing a career-ladder or merit-pay program based on pretest-posttest student-achievement gain. These sections reviewed pertinent professional and legal standards, factors that influence a teacher's effectiveness beyond his or her control, the measurement and validity of gain, and, finally, approaches for determining the criterion of superior teacher performance. It is now possible to deduce several conclusions from the issues discussed:

1. There are no professional standards or court decisions to support the use of student-achievement data for any type of teacher evaluation.
    a. Standard 12.7 of the *Standards for Educational and Psychological Testing* (AERA, APA, & NCME, 1985) states that student test scores should not be used as the sole criterion for evaluating teachers or administrators.
    b. The *Personnel Evaluation Standards* do not recommend the use of student-performance data to evaluate teachers, administrators, or any other educational personnel.

8. LIMITATIONS OF USING STUDENT ACHIEVEMENT DATA 299

   c. There are no standards that indicate student achievement should be one among several criteria for measuring teacher performance.
   d. All relevant technical standards, guidelines, and court decisions focus on the direct measurement of a teacher's performance.
2. An inference of superior, mediocre, or poor teacher performance from student achievement gains (or losses) can be contaminated by about 50 other factors.
   a. There are more than 40 student, school, and test characteristics that cannot be controlled by the teacher.
   b. There are 11 sources of invalidity of the pretest-posttest design that can increase achievement gain.
   c. The net effect of all of these factors is to produce a sizable gain in achievement that cannot be attributed to teacher performance or to classroom instruction.
3. Despite the traditional deficiencies of the low reliability of gain scores and their negative correlation with the pretest, the major limitation of gain scores is the meager information they provide based on only pretest and posttest measurements.
   a. Improved approaches to measuring gain supplement pretest-posttest data with between-person information.
   b. Multiwave data based on three, four, or more data points are preferable to two-wave data.
4. Between-class, between-grade, and between-student variability of the 50 sources of invalidity and error render the setting of a meaningful criterion for superior teacher performance nearly impossible.

Although there does not seem to be any single source of invalidity or error (systematic or random) that is large enough to invalidate the pretest-posttest gain-score model, the combination of multiple sources analyzed cumulatively does prove fatal to warrant its rejection as a primary strategy for measuring teacher performance in a career-ladder or merit-pay program. Even if student gains were to be considered as one among several evaluative criteria, the intractable problem of how they should be weighed in conjunction with other criteria must be tackled.

The professional standards, research evidence, and psychometric issues examined in this chapter strongly indicate that student performance on any test should not be used to measure teacher performance. Instead, that measurement should be guided by the *Personnel Evaluation Standards*. Teacher incentive programs should be designed according to those *Standards* and reflect the current state of measurement technology.

ACKNOWLEDGMENT

The author gratefully appreciates the helpful suggestions of John B. Willett and Kim Hoogeveen on an earlier version of this manuscript.

REFERENCES

American Educational Research Association, American Psychological Association, & National Council on Measurement in Education. (1985). *Standards for educational and psychological testing*. Washington, DC: American Psychological Association.
Angoff, W. H. (1971). Scales, norms, and equivalent scores. In R. L. Thorndike (Ed.), *Educational measurement* (2nd ed., pp. 508–600). Washington, DC: American Council on Education.
Bacharach, S. B., Lipsky, D. B., & Shedd, J. B. (1984). *Paying for better teaching: Merit pay and its alternatives*. Ithaca, NY: Organizational Analysis and Practice.
Benson, C. S., et al. (1965). *State and local fiscal relationships in public education in California*. Sacramento: Senate of the State of California.
Bereiter, C. (1963). Some persisting dilemmas in the measurement of change. In C. W. Harris (Ed.), *Problems in measuring change* (pp. 3–20). Madison: University of Wisconsin Press.
Berk, R. A. (Ed.). (1984a). *A guide to criterion-referenced test construction*. Baltimore: Johns Hopkins University Press.
Berk, R. A. (1984b). *Screening and diagnosis of children with learning disabilities*. Springfield, IL: Charles C Thomas.
Berk, R. A. (1984c, March). *The use of student achievement test scores as criteria for allocation of teacher merit pay*. Paper presented at the 1984 National Conference on Merit Pay for Teachers, Sarasota, FL.
Berk, R. A. (1986). Minimum competency testing: Status and potential. In B. S. Plake & J. C. Witt (Eds.), *The future of testing* (pp. 89–144). Hillsdale, NJ: Lawrence Erlbaum Associates.
Berk, R. A. (1988). Fifty reasons why student achievement gain does not mean teacher effectiveness. *Journal of Personnel Evaluation in Education, 1,* 345–363.
Bernardin, H. J., & Beatty, R. W. (1984). *Performance appraisal: Assessing human behavior at work*. Boston: Kent–Wadsworth.
Bernardin, H. J., & Cascio, W. F. (1984). *An annotated bibliography of court cases relevant to employment decisions (1980–1983)*. Boca Raton, FL: Florida Atlantic University.
Boardman, A. E., Davis, O. A., & Sanday, P. R. (1974). A simultaneous equations model of the educational process: The Coleman data revisited with an emphasis upon achievement. In *1973 Proceedings of the American Statistical Association, social statistics section*. Washington, DC: American Statistical Association.

Bower, R. (1982, March). *Matching standardized achievement test items to local curriculum objectives.* Symposium paper presented at the annual meeting of the National Council on Measurement in Education, New York.

Bowles, S. S. (1970). Towards an educational production function. In W. L. Hansen (Ed.), *Education, income, and human capital.* New York: Columbia University Press.

Bridge, R. G., Judd, C. M., & Moock, P. R. (1979). *The determinants of educational outcomes.* Cambridge, MA: Ballinger.

Brookover, W., Beady, C., Flood, P., Schweitzer, J., & Wisenbaker, J. (1979). *School social systems and student achievement: Schools can make a difference.* New York: Praeger.

Brophy, J. E. (1973). Stability of teacher effectiveness. *American Educational Research Journal, 10,* 245–252.

Bryk, A. S., & Raudenbush, S. W. (1987). Application of hierarchical linear models to assessing change. *Psychological Bulletin, 101,* 147–159.

Calhoun, F. S., & Protheroe, N. J. (1983). *Merit pay plans for teachers: Status and description* (ERS Report No. 219-21684). Arlington, VA: Educational Research Service.

Campbell, D. T., & Stanley, J. C. (1966). *Experimental and quasi-experimental designs for research.* Chicago: Rand McNally.

Cascio, W. F., & Bernardin, H. J. (1981). Implications of performance appraisal litigation for personnel decisions. *Personnel Psychology, 34,* 211–216.

Centra, J. A., & Potter, D. A. (1980). School and teacher effects: An interrelational model. *Review of Educational Research, 50,* 273–291.

Cohen, D. K., & Murnane, R. J. (1985, Summer). The merits of merit pay. *The Public Interest, 80,* 3–30.

Cohen, J. (1977). *Statistical power analysis for the behavioral sciences* (rev. ed.). New York: Academic Press.

Cohn, E., & Millman, S. D. (1975). *Input-output analysis in public education.* Cambridge, MA: Ballinger.

Cook, T. D., & Campbell, D. T. (1979). *Quasi-experimentation: Design and analysis issues for field settings.* Chicago: Rand McNally.

Corder-Bolz, C. R. (1978). The evaluation of change: New evidence. *Educational and Psychological Measurement, 38,* 959–976.

Cronbach, L. J., & Furby, L. (1970). How should we measure "change"—or should we? *Psychological Bulletin, 74,* 68–80.

Cronbach, L. J., & Snow, R. E. (1977). *Aptitudes and instructional methods: A handbook for research on interactions.* New York: Irvington.

Cureton, E. E. (1951). Validity. In E. F. Lindquist (Ed.), *Educational measurement* (pp. 621–694). Washington, DC: American Council on Education.

Elman, A. (n.d.). *Quality control in Title I: Manual versus computer conversions of test scores.* Palo Alto, CA: American Institutes for Research.

Evendon, E. S. (1918). *Teachers' salaries and salary schedules in the United States, 1918–19.* Washington, DC: National Education Association.

Finley, C. J. (1981, September). *What can state education agencies do to improve upon the quality of data collected from local education agencies?* Palo Alto, CA: American Institutes for Research.

Flanagan, J. C. (1951). Units, scores, and norms. In E. F. Lindquist (Ed.), *Educational measurement* (pp. 695–763). Washington, DC: American Council on Education.

Glasman, N. S., & Biniaminov, I. (1981). Input-output analyses of schools. *Review of Educational Research, 51,* 509–539.

Gramenz, G. W., Johnson, R. C., & Jones, B. G. (1982, March). *An exploratory study of the concept of curriculum-referenced norms using the Stanford Achievement Test, sixth edition.* Paper presented at the annual meeting of the National Council on Measurement in Education, New York.

Green, D. R. (1983, April). *Content validity of standardized achievement tests and test curriculum overlap.* Symposium paper presented at the annual meeting of the National Council on Measurement in Education, Montreal.

Haertel, E. (1986). The valid use of student performance measures for teacher evaluation. *Educational Evaluation and Policy Analysis, 8,* 45–60.

Hambleton, R. K., & Eignor, D. R. (1978). Guidelines for evaluating criterion-referenced tests and test manuals. *Journal of Educational Measurement, 15,* 321–327.

Hanushek, E. A. (1972). *Education and race: An analysis of the educational production process.* Lexington, MA: Lexington.

Hardy, R. (1984). Measuring instructional validity: A report of an instructional validity study for the Alabama High School Graduation Examination. *Journal of Educational Measurement, 21,* 291–301.

Hopkins, K. D., & Stanley, J. C. (1981). *Educational and psychological measurement and evaluation* (6th ed.). Englewood Cliffs, NJ: Prentice-Hall.

Horst, D. P. (1976). *What's bad about grade equivalent scores, ESEA Title I evaluation and reporting system* (Tech. Rep. No. 1). Mountain View, CA: RMC Research Corporation.

Horst, D. P. (1981, March). *Title I evaluation and reporting system: Examination of the models at the project level.* Mountain View, CA: RMC Research Corporation.

Horst, D. P, Tallmadge, G. K., & Wood, C. T. (1974, October). *Measuring achievement gains in educational projects* (RMC Report UR–243). Los Altos, CA: RMC Research Corporation.

Jenkins, J. R., & Pany, D. (1978). Curriculum biases in reading achievement tests. *Journal of Reading Behavior, 10,* 345–357.

Joint Committee on Standards for Educational Evaluation. (1981). *Standards for evaluations of educational programs, projects, and materials.* New York: McGraw–Hill.

Joint Committee on Standards for Educational Evaluation. (1988). *The personnel evaluation standards: How to assess systems for evaluating educators.* Newbury Park, CA: Sage.

Kiesling, H. J. (1969). *The relationship of school input to public school performance in New York State.* Washington, DC: Office of Education, U.S. Department of Health, Education, and Welfare.

Kiesling, H. J. (1970). *The study of cost and quality of New York school districts: Final report.* Washington, DC: Office of Education, U.S. Department of Health, Education, and Welfare.

Kleiman, L. S., & Durham, R. L. (1981). Performance appraisal, promotion, and the courts: A critical review. *Personnel Psychology, 34,* 103–121.

Leinhardt, G. (1983). Overlap: Testing whether it is taught. In G. F. Madaus (Ed.), *The courts, validity, and minimum competency testing* (pp. 153–170). Hingham, MA: Kluwer–Nijhoff.

Leinhardt, G., & Seewald, A. M. (1981). Overlap: What's tested, what's taught? *Journal of Educational Measurement, 18,* 85–96.

Leinhardt, G., Zigmond, N., & Cooley, W. W. (1981). Reading instruction and its effects. *American Educational Research Journal, 18,* 343–361.

Levin, H. M. (1970). A new model of school effectiveness. In A. Mood (Ed.), *Do teachers make a difference?* Washington, DC: Office of Education, U.S. Department of Health, Education, and Welfare.

Linn, R. L. (1979). Validity of inferences based on the proposed Title I evaluation models. *Educational Evaluation and Policy Analysis, 1*, 23–32.

Linn, R. L. (1980a). Discussion: Regression toward the mean and the regression-effect bias. In G. Echternacht (Ed.), *New directions for testing and measurement (No.8)—Measurement aspects of Title I evaluations* (pp. 83–89). San Francisco: Jossey–Bass.

Linn, R. L. (1980b). Evaluation of Title I via the RMC models. In E. L. Baker & E. S. Quellmalz (Eds.), *Educational testing and evaluation: Design, analysis, and policy* (pp. 121–142). Beverly Hills: Sage Publications.

Linn, R. L. (1981). Measuring pretest-posttest performance changes. In R. A. Berk (Ed.), *Educational evaluation methodology: The state of the art* (pp. 84–109). Baltimore: Johns Hopkins University Press.

Linn, R. L., Dunbar, S. B., Harnisch, D. L., & Hastings, C. N. (1982). The validity of the Title I evaluation and reporting system. In E. R. House, S. Mathison, J. A. Pearson, & H. Preskill (Eds.), *Evaluation studies review annual* (Vol. 7, pp. 427–442). Beverly Hills: Sage Publications.

Linn, R. L., & Slinde, J. A. (1977). The determination of the significance of change between pre and posttesting periods. *Review of Educational Research, 47*, 121–150.

Lord, F. M. (1956). The measurement of growth. *Educational and Psychological Measurement, 16*, 421–437.

Lord, F. M. (1963). Elementary models for measuring change. In C. W. Harris (Ed.), *Problems in measuring change* (pp. 21–38). Madison: University of Wisconsin Press.

Madaus, G. F. (1983). Minimum competency testing for certification: The evolution and evaluation of test validity. In G. F. Madaus (Ed.), *The courts, validity, and minimum competency testing* (pp. 21–61). Hingham, MA: Kluwer–Nijhoff.

Madaus, G. F., Airasian, P. W., Hambleton, R. K., Consalvo, R. W., & Orlandi, L. R. (1982). Development and application of criteria for screening commercial, standardized tests. *Educational Evaluation and Policy Analysis, 4*, 401–415.

Mayeske, G. W., & Beaton, A. E. (1975). *Special studies of our nation's students.* Washington, DC: Office of Education, U.S. Department of Health, Education, and Welfare.

Mayeske, G. W., et al. (1973). *A study of the achievement of our nation's students.* Washington, DC: Office of Education, U.S. Department of Health, Education and Welfare.

McClung, M. S. (1979). Competency testing programs: Legal and educational issues. *Fordham Law Review, 47*, 651–712.

Medley, D. M., Coker, H., & Soar, R. S. (1984). *Measurement-based evaluation of teacher performance: An empirical approach.* New York: Longman.

Michelson, S. (1970). The association of the teacher resourceness with children's characteristics. In A. Mood (Ed.), *Do teachers make a difference?* Washington, DC: Office of Education, U.S. Department of Health, Education, and Welfare.

Moore, B. C. (1984). *The effects of merit pay on selected secondary school teachers in terms of alienation and motivation.* Unpublished doctoral dissertation, Indiana State University.

Murnane, R. J. (1975). *The impact of school resources on the learning of inner city children.* Cambridge, MA: Ballinger.

Murnane, R. J., & Cohen, D. K. (1986). Merit pay and the evaluation problem: Why

most merit pay plans fail and a few survive. *Harvard Educational Review, 56,* 1–17.
Nathan, B. R., & Cascio, W. F. (1986). Introduction. Technical and legal standards. In R. A. Berk (Ed.), *Performance assessment: Methods and applications* (pp. 1–50). Baltimore: Johns Hopkins University Press.
Nesselroade, J. R., Stigler, S. M., & Baltes, P. B. (1980). Regression toward the mean and the study of change. *Psychological Bulletin, 88,* 622–637.
O'Connor, E. F. (1972). Extending classical test theory to the measurement of change. *Review of Educational Research, 42,* 73–98.
Overall, J. E., & Woodward, J. A. (1975). Unreliability of difference scores: A paradox for measurement of change. *Psychological Bulletin, 82,* 85–86.
Overall, J. E., & Woodward, J. A. (1976). Reassertion of the paradoxical power of tests of significance based on unreliable difference scores. *Psychological Bulletin, 83,* 776–777.
Pencavel, J. H. (1977). Work effort, on-the-job screening, and alternative methods of remuneration. In R. Ehrenberg (Ed.), *Research in labor economics* (Vol. 1, pp. 225–258). Greenwich, CT: JAI Press.
Popham, W. J. (1983, April). *Issues in determining adequacy-of-preparation.* Symposium paper presented at the annual meeting of the American Educational Research Association, Montreal.
Porter, A. C., Schmidt, W. H., Floden, R. E., & Freeman, D. J. (1978). Practical significance in program evaluation. *American Educational Research Journal, 15,* 529–539.
Porwoll, P. J. (1979). *Merit pay for teachers.* Arlington, VA: Educational Research Service.
Poynor, L. (1978, April). *Instructional dimensions study: Data management procedures as exemplified by curriculum analysis.* Paper presented at the annual meeting of the American Educational Research Association, Toronto.
Richards, J. M., Jr. (1976). A simulation study comparing procedures for assessing individual educational growth. *Journal of Educational Psychology, 68,* 603–612.
Roberts, A. O. H. (1980). Regression toward the mean and the interval between test administrations. In G. Echternacht (Ed.), *New directions for testing and measurement (No. 8)—Measurement aspects of Title I evaluations* (pp. 59–82). San Francisco: Jossey-Bass.
Robinson, G. E. (1983). *Paying teachers for performance and productivity: Learning from experience.* Arlington, VA: Educational Research Service.
Robinson, G. E. (1984). *Incentive pay for teachers: An analysis of approaches.* Arlington, VA: Educational Research Service.
Rogosa, D. R. (1980). Comparisons of some procedures for analyzing longitudinal panel data. *Journal of Economics and Business, 32,* 136–151.
Rogosa, D. R., Brandt, D., & Zimowski, M. (1982). A growth curve approach to the measurement of change. *Psychological Bulletin, 92,* 726–748.
Rogosa, D. R., & Willett, J. B. (1983). Demonstrating the reliability of the difference score in the measurement of change. *Journal of Educational Measurement, 20,* 335–343.
Rogosa, D. R., & Willett, J. B. (1985). Understanding correlates of change by modeling individual differences in growth. *Psychometrika, 50,* 203–228.
Rosenshine, B. (1970). The stability of teacher effects upon student achievement. *Review of Educational Research, 40,* 647–662.

Schmidt, W. H. (1983a). Content biases in achievement tests. *Journal of Educational Measurement, 20*, 165–178.

Schmidt, W. H. (1983b, April). *Methods of examining mismatch.* Symposium paper presented at the annual meeting of the National Council on Measurement in Education, Montreal.

Schmidt, W. H., Porter, A. C., Schwille, J. R., Floden, R. E., & Freeman, D. J. (1983). Validity a variable: Can the same certification test be valid for all students? In G. F. Madaus (Ed.), *The courts, validity, and minimum competency testing* (pp. 133–151). Hingham, MA: Kluwer–Nijhoff.

Seiler, E. (1984). Piece rate vs. time rate: The effect of incentives on earnings. *Review of Economics and Statistics, 66*, 363–375.

Soar, R. S., & Soar, R. M. (1975). Classroom behavior, pupil characteristics and pupil growth for the school year and the summer. *JSAS Catalog of Selected Documents in Psychology, 5*(200), (ms no. 873).

Soar, R. S., & Soar, R. M. (1983). Context effects in the teaching-learning process. In D. C. Smith (Ed.), *Essential knowledge for beginning educators.* Washington, DC: American Association of Colleges for Teacher Education.

Southern Regional Education Board. (1986, December). 1986—Incentive programs for teachers and administrators: How are they doing? *Career Ladder Clearinghouse.*

Strike, K., & Bull, B. (1981). Fairness and the legal context of teacher evaluation. In J. Millman (Ed.), *Handbook of teacher evaluation* (pp. 303–343). Beverly Hills: Sage Publications.

Subkoviak, M. J., & Levin, J. R. (1977). Fallibility of measurement and the power of a statistical test. *Journal of Educational Measurement, 14*, 47–52.

Summers, A. A., & Wolfe, B. L. (1977). Do schools make a difference? *American Economic Review, 67*, 639–652.

Tallmadge, G. K. (1982). An empirical assessment of norm-referenced evaluation methodology. *Journal of Educational Measurement, 19*, 97–112.

Tallmadge, G. K., & Wood, C. T. (1976). *User's guide: ESEA Title I evaluation and reporting system.* Mountain View, CA: RMC Research Corporation.

Tucker, L. R., Damarin, F., & Messick, S. (1966). A base-free measure of change. *Psychometrika, 31*, 457–473.

U.S. Equal Employment Opportunity Commission, U.S. Civil Service Commission, U.S. Department of Labor, & U.S. Department of Justice. (1978). Uniform guidelines on employee selection procedures. *Federal Register, 43*(166), 38290–38309.

Webster, H., & Bereiter, C. (1963). The reliability of changes measured by mental test scores. In C. W. Harris (Ed.), *Problems in measuring change* (pp. 39–59). Madison: University of Wisconsin Press.

Wiley, D. E. (1976). Another hour, another day: Quantity of schooling, a potent path for policy. In W. H. Sewell, D. L. Featherman, & R. M. Hauser (Eds.), *Schooling and achievement in American society.* New York: Academic Press.

Wiley, D. E., & Harnischfeger, A. (1974). Explosion of a myth: Quantity of schooling and exposure to instruction, major educational vehicles. *Educational Researcher, 4*(3), 7–11.

Willett, J. B. (1988). Questions and answers in the measurement of change. In E. Z. Rothkopf (Ed.), *Review of research in education* (Vol. 15, pp. 345–422). Washington, DC: American Educational Research Association.

Williams, T. B. (1980, April). *The distributions of NCE, percentile, and grade equiv-*

alent scores among twelve nationally standardized tests. Paper presented at the annual meeting of the American Educational Research Association, Boston.

Winkler, D. R. (1975). Educational achievement and school peer group composition. *Journal of Human Resources, 10,* 189–205.

Wolf, R. M. (1977). *Achievement in America.* New York: Teachers College Press.

Yalow, E. S., & Popham, W. J. (1983). Content validity at the crossroads. *Educational Researcher, 12*(8), 10–14, 21.

Zimmerman, D. W., & Williams, R. H. (1982). Gain scores in research can be highly reliable. *Journal of Educational Measurement, 19,* 149–154.

9

Teaching Assessment: The Administrator's Perspective

John R. Hoyle
Texas A&M University

School administrators, especially principals, are under great pressure to insure high levels of teacher competence. Because the school effectiveness research has demonstrated convincingly that effective schools begin with effective principals, Peterson and Finn (1985) drew a less than surprising conclusion by stating that "Practically never does one encounter a good school with a bad principal" (p. 42). A less pedantic east Texas superintendent put it this way, "Bad principals are like fish; you either can 'em or smell 'em for a long time." It is in the complex area of teaching assessment or teacher evaluation that principals draw the most criticism from classroom teachers and particularly from university pundits. As McLaughlin (1986), a longtime student of teacher evaluation, put it: "Teachers seldom respect principals as experts on classroom practice or as skilled classroom observers, and in the absence of principal credibility, teachers consider the evaluation an illegitimate comment on their performance and ignore the findings (p. 163). Teacher evaluation, in short, is an activity that most principals have little interest in or capacity to carry out" (p. 170). Epstein (1985) said that "Critics of current evaluation schemes complain that most are based on the principal's ratings on teachers that result from infrequent (sometimes just one) observations in teachers' classrooms; on cronyism, patronage, or other prejudicial decisions; or on seniority, credentials, and accumulated credits that do not involve the evaluation of teaching skills" (p. 3).

Principals and teachers vary greatly in how they perceive the principal's performance as an evaluator, according to a survey of teachers and principals in Massachusetts (Tirrell, 1986). The respondents were asked to rate the role of the principal in evaluation according to their current perceptions and ideal expectations. Principals and teachers disagreed on 28 of 37 statements concerning current perceptions. They disagreed whether or not the principal

> clearly communicates the philosophy of the evaluation program to the staff; clearly states the purpose of the evaluation in writing to the teachers; ensures that the teachers know and understand the caliber of their work; ensures that teachers are not threatened by evaluation practices; and encourages teachers to experiment with new behaviors designed to address weaknesses indicated in previous evaluations. (pp. 31, 32)

Other studies raise questions about the accuracy of measurement instruments and their criteria to distinguish the truly outstanding teacher from the average or even minimally competent one. Young (1986) identified five major faults in most observation instruments. They are as follows: (a) high inference items, (b) too many items, (c) judgments based on teacher actions, (d) low interrater reliability, and (e) lack of research support. Other research suggests that various groups disagree on the criteria they use to judge teachers. Epstein (1985) found that parents judge teachers on the basis of the degree to which the teacher communicates with the child's family, whereas principals give much less weight to this factor.

In attempting to determine whether people evaluate teaching excellence with the same criteria as they use to evaluate incompetence in teaching, Carey (1986) found that,

> Unlike minimal competence ratings, it might be more difficult to achieve consensus in judgments of excellence in teaching. If this contention is supported in further research it may be that merit pay and mentor teacher plans suffer an Achilles heel that will be difficult to remediate. (p. 10)

The use of student scores on standardized achievement tests has become the major criterion used by some evaluators to judge teacher competence. St. Louis, Missouri, teachers were told by the superintendent in 1985 that they would be rated unsatisfactory and lose their jobs unless their students reached specific levels of achievement or improvement on standardized achievement tests (Shanker, 1986, p. 3c). Other authorities, while urging evaluators to have multiple data sources for more accurate teacher evaluations, are calling for more testing to determine teacher effectiveness. According to Manatt (1986), evaluators are going to have to go,

> deeper than inferences based on research on teaching. We want to look at student test data broken out by classrooms. . . . That way and only that way, can you really narrow it down to a teacher rather than saying in general that the school got these achievements for these boys and girls. (p. 12)

Most researchers and practicing administrators agree that the better teacher evaluation systems can discriminate good teachers from dreadful teachers, and adequate teachers from bad teachers. However, few knowledgeable educators believe that they can segregate the master or clearly outstanding teacher from the really good teacher. This fine line appears to be the source of much of the heat and criticism generated by teacher groups and researchers about the state-of-the art in teacher evaluation.

ADMINISTRATOR TRAINING

Graduate programs in educational administration generally require course work in staff personnel, program evaluation, and curriculum and instruction. However, few programs devote major portions of time to training in teacher evaluation. The hands-on training is left to the school districts or state departments of education after a person is appointed to a principalship. Teacher evaluation is merely one of the many knowledge and skill areas taught in graduate programs that causes critics to claim that the training is "too rigid and rule bound, on the one hand and too soft and ineffective on the other" (Peterson & Finn, 1985, p. 42). Similarly, Hoyle (1985) called attention to the shortcomings of many training programs by inferring that professors often advise students into fragmented individual courses with extreme content overlap or into courses that seem unrelated. Also, most inservice programs, institutes, and academies for administrator training make little pretense at systematic learning. The content is often fragmented, "quick fix" information and makes little attempt at building a sequential accumulation of knowledge or skills. Hoyle also implied that some university preparation programs and training academies make better use of research evidence and examples of successful practice, but it is difficult to isolate preservice and inservice training factors from other socialization factors that determine successful administrative performance. The preparation puzzle makes it clear that principals in many instances do not have specialized knowledge of all the areas that they are expected to evaluate. The limits on their time and expertise and the haphazard way many are trained to evaluate teachers mean that principals face sizable odds in their efforts to distinguish the best from the rest.

PRESSURES FACING ADMINISTRATORS

It is obvious that many critics of principals and their training reveal considerable naivete about the increased demands, pressures, and paperwork brought in by state education reforms and demands for accountability. This naivete is most evident when evaluation reformers recommend that principals spend excessive amounts of time conducting classroom observations. Harried principals find these recommendations troubling and at times offensive. First, many principals dislike and distrust mandated procedures that give them sole control over teachers' salary increases and advances (Burke, 1982; Johnson, 1984). Second, the time it takes to evaluate each teacher according to best practice is enormous. The North Carolina State Department of Public Instruction (1986) studied this time problem and presented the following scenario. If, for example, a preobservation conference requires 30 minutes, an observation requires 60 minutes, a postobservation conference requires 45 minutes with an additional 45 minutes for the required data analysis, and the actual evaluation requires 60 minutes, the following formula will result:

```
Observation #1 (announced)      180
Observation #2 (unannounced)    150
Observation #3 (announced)      180
Evaluation:                      60
                                570 minutes
```

"If a school has 50 teachers and only one administrator who supervises teacher personnel, then about 60 days of 8 hours will be required to complete all observations and evaluations" (North Carolina State Department, 1986, pp. 20, 21). Because these 60 days should properly fall within a 150-day time span, because observations early and late in the year will be impractical, the principal would have no time for any other management duty.

Less naive scholar critics are more attuned with the real world of principals and are aware of the many hats they wear during every school day, week, and year. Acheson (1986) recognized that not all principals can do all things and believes that it is time to redefine the roles of beleaguered principals and teachers. He believes that not all principals have the necessary range of managerial, human relations, and instructional leadership competencies to lead their schools in ways suggested by school effectiveness research and state evaluation reforms. In addition they do not have the time to perform all of these functions and roles in an exemplary manner. He acknowledged that when principals are surveyed, they list instructional leadership as their most important role, but other demands on their time relegate active leadership of the instructional program to a minor role.

Even if the principal devotes 570 minutes a year to each teacher, there is no clear evidence that it does any good. Pundits applaud the "clinical supervision" model which combines a democratically humane approach to supervision with a methodologically sound process (Cogan, 1973). The issue most raised is the question of the amount of time required to implement the process. What most pundits fail to realize is that 570 minutes to complete the clinical supervision cycle amounts to only one day in the life of a teacher. One day of the best instructional leadership displayed by the principal is hardly enough time to influence a teacher to improve instruction or increase effectiveness.

Lack of time is not the only problem. Most observers realize that the principal has the difficult task being both the evaluator of teachers and also a clinical supervisor in a collegial, constructively critical mode. Some principals are able to carry out both functions and are trusted and respected by the teachers, but most principals struggle with the evaluation versus supervision roles. Principals ask how they can evaluate teachers in order to make decisions about retention, promotion, tenure, and selection for career ladders and then turn around and work with them as a friendly critic or colleague to help develop the skills the teachers want and need to become better professionals. In some ways this is the same dilemma a parent faces when serving as both a loving counselor and a stern disciplinarian. It is indeed a delicate balance that few principals or parents perfect (Acheson, 1986).

Principals need love and respect like other professionals. They believe in family, democracy, mom, baseball, and apple pie. Most of them know that there is much rich empirical evidence derived from research in schools that indicates that schools that emphasize collaboration, good leadership, creativity, high expectations, clear goals, and open communication usually out perform schools that develop strict rules, create competition, have unclear goals, and conformity. The administrator is taught in graduate classes and workshops that the key to understanding and building an organizational culture is strengthening relationships and finding the concealed talents and inner motivations of people. The administrator is told to build trust and confidence and to create high morale in the teaching staff but is then required to pit one teacher against another by assessing their teaching effectiveness in order to determine their employment status or to dispense meager financial rewards. These small rewards, better known as merit pay or a rung on a career ladder, go only to a select few who are evaluated as "clearly outstanding" and, as a result, divisiveness builds and the "family" unity is threatened. Thus, the role conflict becomes a source of confusion for administrator and teachers.

English (1985) reported that members of an ASCD-appointed Task Force on Merit Pay and Career Ladders concluded that merit pay by itself:

1. Will not solve problems now facing schools in their efforts to reach higher levels of excellence.
2. Has shown to be ineffective and self-defeating and in fact may be a disincentive for improved performance.
3. Does not have a good track record in the private sector.
4. Represents a simplistic popular approach to the very complex problem of trying to recognize, motivate and utilize talent in schools. (p. 34)

The Task Force members also believe that the current emphasis on career ladders and merit pay contains paradoxical elements that lead to political confrontation rather than productive solutions. For example:

> One view from within and without the profession indicates that since most of the profession indicates that it is impossible to pay all teachers a decent salary (because of economics and perceived public resistance to such cost increases), only some teachers should or can

be paid a respectable wage. This assumes that merit pay is a means to pay just a few teachers, preferably the best or superior ones, a competitive salary.

The opposing view is that the education profession lacks a fair and acceptable means to differentiate between teachers, given the state of present teacher evaluation systems. All attempts to differentiate are therefore considered unworkable and the result is a stalemate. (English, 1985, p. 34)

Principals then are required to use questionable carrot-and-stick methods to reward or punish teachers (punishment is not receiving merit pay or the next step on the career ladder) based on the state-of-the art evaluation systems not suited to be used for both rewarding merit to the best teachers and improving all of the rest.

Even the casual observer can recognize the intense pressure on school principals to become "slave drivers" or "strawbosses" of teachers. Legislatures, corporations, and governors are pressuring school boards and superintendents to improve our failing school systems. The principal becomes the tool for the central administration to fix the school. The answer is to tighten the "Technical Core" (Peterson, Murphy, & Hallinger, 1987), sometimes called "teaching to the test." The principal oversees this convoluted search for excellence and is forced to tighten the lines of authority over teachers and grab control of the curriculum to drive up scores on state minimum-skills tests and standardized achievement tests. This model based on bureaucratic theory can neuter teacher creativity and initiative. As Frymier (1987), a long-term student of humane education and school climate, put it: "In the main, the bureaucratic structure of the workplace is more influential in determining what professionals do than are personal abilities, professional training, or previous experience. Therefore, change efforts should focus on the workplace, not on the teacher" (p. 10).

Most administrators acknowledge that a positive open workplace can promote a positive climate or "feeling" in a school district and in each school in the district. Administrators alone cannot create an open school climate. At best they can set the tone for their staffs to create an open climate. This tone may be described best as morale and work motivation for teachers and students. Positive morale and work motivation promotes an "ethos" that promotes higher achievement by teachers and students. Bureaucratic reform mentality, including misapplied teacher evaluation systems, has little chance of improving schools. Again Frymier (1987) said,

> there are many people in policy making roles and administrative positions who mouth pat phrases about the importance of teachers and teaching—and then proceed to undercut teachers by creating conditions of work that blunt their enthusiasm and stifle their creativity. (p. 9)

THE "ONE BEST MODEL" PROBLEM

The students I teach and the practicing administrators I know want good schools and happy teachers. School improvement is high on their professional and personnel agendas. They dislike the term *school reform* because it implies removing abuses or giving up sin or error. Administrators support school improvement and believe that almost all teachers desire to be productive and to be treated as professionals. This belief leads administrators to support a popular "One Best Model" teacher-evaluation system that rewards all teachers who reach mutually agreed upon professional growth goals. However, applying the One Best Model to all teachers and classrooms becomes problematic. Scores based on classroom observations of the teacher's performance and student gains are only two of the ingredients to use in the "Mutual Benefit" model for judging professional competence. Peterson (1987) reported that the current practice of principal visits and reports alone, "does not promise to promote reforms for teachers or teacher educators" (p. 311). In fact Medley and Coker (1987) concluded that principals' judgments have little to do with teachers' effectiveness in promoting student achievement. They have discovered a number of common weaknesses in research design and instrumentation that cause the problem. One such weakness is caused by using a sample of teachers drawn from different schools in order to have enough teachers to allow a relationship to be detected. Therefore, judgments made by different principals in different schools could not be treated as interchangeable. Also, statistical procedures used to estimate the effectiveness of teachers violated important assumptions. Medley and Coker proposed a promising alternative called "measurement evaluation, which would base teacher evaluation on records of classroom performance made by observers trained to record behavior without evaluating it" (p. 140). They agreed that this alternative should be given further study and development. Until educational researchers can find clearer links between teacher-evaluation systems using the highly acclaimed instructional models of Hunter (1986) and others and student-achievement gains, principals are going to balk at using narrowly defined criteria to evaluate teachers. Any evaluation system too narrowly defined and artificially implemented will be viewed by teachers as threatening and coercive and is against the professional administrator's better nature and training. They also know that a restrictive system will destroy teacher efficacy which Berman and McLaughlin (1977) called the single most powerful explanatory variable related to student performance.

The challenge facing policy makers and administrators is to make teacher-evaluation systems actually improve teaching performance and produce positive student outcomes. Until that happens, teachers and administrators will continue to complain that most systems do not distinguish between clearly outstanding and mediocre teaching. Moreover, the incompetent teacher remains. These complaints and other concerns about the motives behind the aforementioned evaluation systems have not turned administrators away from learning new skills to improve their supervisory roles. They realize the potential value of solid broad-based teacher evaluation. Lewis (1982) found that the overwhelming concern among administrators was how to convey that evaluations are for improvement, how to relate evaluation to learning improvement of students and how to develop a personal improvement plan for each teacher. Graduate programs in educational administration, state departments of education, and administrator in-service conducted by professional education associations are providing training to strengthen principals' supervisory, diagnostic, and prescriptive skills. This new emphasis on teacher evaluation trains principals and other staff to observe classroom practices, assess teacher solutions to classroom problems, and analyze the quality of the instructional processes. This training confirms the generally held belief about the conditional nature of teacher effectiveness and stresses individual teacher judgments within widely held categories for effective teaching (Hoyle, et al., 1985).

This phenomenon of the 1980s to retool school administrators to become instructional leaders has produced some predicted results in terms of new training and teacher evaluation procedures. Both the training methods and the evaluation procedures are strikingly similar across the United States. For instance almost all of the state and university training academies secure the services of the same consultants who bring in the same song with perhaps a little different verse. They each stress the following features of a One Best Model successful evaluation system: (a) involvement of the teachers in the entire developmental evaluation process, (b) performance criteria based on sound research and on local needs and concerns, (c) collaborative goal setting, (d) multidimensional methods for assessing teacher's skills, (e) careful analysis of data gathered in the assessment stage, (f) development of specific job targets, and (g) inclusion of a preobservation conference to acquire background data and a postobservation conference to mutually analyze classroom data and set goals for improvement (Manatt, 1982). This "Mutual Benefit Evaluation" is an adaptation of the management-by-objective (MBO) model from business and is similar to models established by Redfern, Bolton, Manatt, and Hoyle (Hoyle, English, & Steff, 1985). Consultants to the academies and professors in graduate classes not only stress this Mutual Benefit Model but they employ many of the same teaching methods to help administrators improve skills in teacher evaluation and in the teaching process. Through simulations, role modeling, videotapes, and other devices, administrators are given extensive training in clinical observation, note taking, reporting, and conferencing skills. The participants then become mentors and coaches for other appraisers (McLaughlin, 1986).

This remarkable similarity in teacher evaluation training is seen by many as the One Best Model and has many advantages and some disadvantages. The advantages are as follows:

1. The terminology is similar, which improves communication about the process.

2. Involvement of the entire professional staff supports the time-honored notion of team work and organizational culture which, "embraces the norms that inform people what is acceptable and what is not, the dominant values that the organization cherishes above others and the basic assumption beliefs, rule and philosophy that guide the organization in dealing with its employees and its clients" (Owens 1987, pp. 29, 30).

3. The emphasis is placed on improving teachers rather than proving their incompetence.

The disadvantages of the One Best Model are as follows:

1. Excessive time is needed to conduct a thorough evaluation for each teacher if the staff is over 20 in number.

2. The process appears overwhelming to many teachers and they doubt if the system will make any difference in the way they teach.

3. Even after extensive training, appraisers remain inconsistent in assigning scores to teachers' classroom performance. This has been a troubling problem with the Texas Teacher Appraisal System when appraisers tried to determine the highest level or "exceptional quality" of a teacher's performance on each of the five domains. What is exceptional to one appraiser may be satisfactory to another.

According to Stiggins and Bridgeford (1984), who conducted case studies of teachers evaluation systems in four Pacific Northwest school districts, administrators had mixed feelings about the systems. In two districts, administrators were generally satisfied with the evaluation process, but concerned about the amount of time necessary to conduct observations. In the other two districts administrators were less satisfied. Reasons for the dissatisfaction included teachers' lack of trust in the evaluation process, the lack of clarity in the criteria, and the fact that the evaluation seemed more oriented to meeting state standards than promoting improvements. There was also disagreement about the impact of the evaluation system on teacher improvement and its link to staff development and in setting instructional priorities. Evaluation was, however, used by some administrators to help teachers identify individual goals and to specify a plan of action for the year. The completion of these plans and their effect on instruction was seldom monitored.

When asked how evaluation could be more directly related to the improvement of teaching, Stiggins and Bridgeford (1984) reported that the administrators recommended

> changes in system management, including increased staff involvement in goal setting and emphasis in improvement as a district priority, improved methods of conducting observations, more time allowed for evaluation and observations, development of evaluators' skill, a stronger link between evaluation and staff development, and accountability for all principals conducting evaluations. (p. 21)

These suggestions for change parallel those concerns identified in most other national studies in teacher evaluation. Most administrators agree that evaluation could be much more effective in diagnosing teachers' needs, improving their skills and improving student learning if changes are made in the process.

THE TEXAS TEACHER APPRAISAL SYSTEM (TTAS)

In interviews with principals and superintendents in Texas, the author has found both positive support for and calls for change in the Texas Teacher Appraisal System (TTAS, 1987).

Among the positive comments are the following

1. "(The System) standardized teacher evaluation in Texas."
2. "Many of the smaller resource-poor districts would have never instituted a system otherwise."
3. "Made the public more aware of the teacher's role."
4. "It reinforced the good teachers who were already doing these things."
5. "It has helped weak teachers to be aware of better techniques because most teachers really want to be good."
6. "Helped promote a common language about instruction and improving student learning."
7. "Increases the principals confidence to make suggestions about improving teaching effectiveness to bright professional teachers."
8. "The process helps you give more concrete suggestions to each teacher."

Some of the calls for change or negative comments were as follows:

1. "The career ladder was put in place before the teacher appraisal system was in working order."
2. "The State Board of Education and the Texas Education Agency keeps changing the rules in mid stream."
3. "There is not enough state money to pay teachers who have earned level three on the career ladder. If the state wants a merit system they should fund it."
4. "There is too much inconsistency in the appraisals from district to district in terms of the number of teachers who deserve to achieve level three of the career ladder."

9. TEACHING ASSESSMENT 319

   5. "Other appraisers from the central office can cause problems because they frequently have no vested interest in the school and its culture, also no basis for building trust between the faculty and principal."
   6. "We have only hearsay that the TTAS is improving our schools in Texas. The same districts have the same successes or failures."
   7. "So far the system has had no effect on the number of students who drop out."
   8. "Teachers put on a good show when they are being observed because the criteria are so specific and fairly easy to follow."
   9. "It is unrealistic to pretend that I have the time to do each evaluation as the TTAS calls for."
   10. "We really resent the career ladder because of the competition and divisions it causes."

The only research data available to measure the impact of the TTAS and the career ladder was gathered in 1986 after the first year of its implementation. The study gathered attitudes from teachers, principals, and superintendents about Texas School Reform and included several questions about the TTAS and career ladder (Ryon, et al., 1986). The results were not positive. "Eighty percent of the teachers, 78% of the principals and 78% of the superintendents said that the existence of the career ladder had negatively affected teachers morale" (p. 15). When asked, "All things considered, is the career ladder more of a plus or a minus?" 79% of the principals and 77% of the superintendents regarded it as a minus" (p. 18).

The researchers concluded that:

> It would be difficult to arrive at any conclusion other than that most teachers, principals, and superintendents hold views of the career ladder that are largely negative, but they seem favorably disposed toward the increased emphasis on teacher evaluation. It is important to note that the respondents evaluated the career ladder and appraisal system as they knew them in April, 1986. It is difficult to say what their responses would be if the career ladder were somehow restructured or if it were better funded. Similarly, the disposition of teachers toward evaluation procedures could become either more positive or more negative with the introduction of the new statewide teacher appraisal criteria and procedures. (p. 17)

Individual "voices" from the field over 1 year later bring more encouraging news about the TTAS and career ladder. According to Bill Kirby (1987), the Texas Commissioner of Education, the TTAS has been modified and refined in 1987 to respond to the needs and recommendations from teachers and administrators. Some of the changes include a reduction in the number of teaching indicators within certain criteria, clarifications of the use of the "exceptional quality" rating and modifying the overall scoring procedures.

The TTAS is based on the clinical model discussed earlier and is similar to systems in several other states. The system was implemented on a statewide basis in the fall of 1986 after 13,000 appraisers were trained the previous summer. Also, standards were set for the rating of teacher performance for career-ladder decisions. This rather rapid implementation of a massive evaluation activity was fraught with glitches in the system. Teachers were upset because they were all treated alike in the process. Master teachers with 20 years of experience were placed at the starting line along with 1st-year teachers. They were all classified as Level 1 teachers and all were to be observed four times for 50 minutes whether they needed or wanted it. The majority of the master teachers were subsequently promoted to Level 2 within the year, but the morale damage had been done. The appraisers needed more and better training because most of them felt that they had been handed an ill-conceived tool by a politically inspired state-education bureaucracy. Several laws suits were brought by disgruntled teachers who were not promoted because they were not convinced that the most capable teachers were being rewarded. The Legislature, the Commissioner of Education, and the State Board of Education were pressed by teacher and administrator associations to fine tune the system in some areas and "overhaul" it in other areas. Based on these suggestions and advice from educator groups, refinements are being made to the system, and training updates and proficiency checks were conducted for all appraisers during the summer of 1987.

The assumption undergirding the TTAS (1987) includes the caveat that "The state of the art of teacher evaluation is not advanced to an operational level in some areas. Instead the system has been based upon existing classroom-based research on teaching, craft knowledge and experience" (p. 4). Because the appraisal process has been designed to include principles of sound evaluation to reflect the best current practice, and efforts are underway to correct problems the system is slowly being accepted by more Texas educators.

ADMINISTRATORS MAKING TEACHER EVALUATION WORK

In spite of the general knowledge that teacher-evaluation systems to measure teacher effectiveness are based on conflicting classroom-based research on teaching, craft knowledge, and experience and that there exists little agreement between principals' judgments of teachers' effectiveness and the amount that students learn, optimism prevails among educators. University professors and others engaged in improving the state-of-the-art in the assessment of teaching are finding examples of exemplary programs throughout the United States. Many administrators are learning and using the best techniques and processes to improve teaching performance and school districts. Roueche and Baker (1987), authors of a research report on 154 "excellent" secondary schools in the nation, said that "quality in these schools is the function of the school principal backed by the superintendent and school board." Also, they reported that "of 500 teachers in the excellent schools the word most-often used to describe the motivational techniques of the principal was 'inspirational,'" and that "good school leaders spent hours in the classroom, inspecting what they expected" (p. 1).

Pigford (1987), a former principal, made teacher evaluation work for her to improve teacher performance by working with faculty to develop seven clear, specific, and measurable objectives for the school year. By creating a strong collaborative support system using the classical clinical supervision model, major victories were won. For example Pigford reported that "one of our school wide goals was to increase by 5% the number of students who passed the statewide basic skills test in reading. Since the pass rate had risen from 38% the previous year to 48% at the end of the current year, we knew that our students had far exceeded our goal" (p. 142). This report of successful evaluation to improve teaching and student growth is similar to many others with principals who create a climate for success and "inspect what they expect." Where administrators stand firm in their belief that clear instructional goals must be taught by inspired skilled teachers, learning can take place. Not only does learning take place, but teacher evaluation is viewed as a valuable activity by teachers.

LEADERSHIP BY OBJECTIVE AND RESULTS LBO/R MODEL

Based on previous discussion about the unstable history of teacher-evaluation systems and the frayed thread holding principal observation and teacher effectiveness together this writer believes that administrators can use the following system to make teacher evaluation the key to teacher effectiveness and student learning. The system is a version of the One Best Model and is described elsewhere (Hoyle, et al., 1985). The system is called "The Leadership by Objectives and Results Model (LBO/R)" (see Figure 9.1).

The following four points should be considered in applying the LBO/R Model.

1. Each person to be evaluated meets with the evaluator in August. Together, a few specific areas of the job that relate to the goals of the system are selected. Teacher and evaluator agree on specific objectives for the teacher and on dates for classroom visits.

2. Evaluators concentrate on observable skills during classroom visitation. All new teachers and others viewed as needing assistance should have at least two different observers visit *at least three times for a 50-minute period.* Master teachers may need a formal evaluation every other year.

3. The teacher is given a copy of evaluator's comments at the performance follow-up conference following each visit. Both help write new objectives and growth plans. Both sign the evaluation form and indicate agreement or disagreement with the assessment.

4. The final evaluation conference informs the teacher of recommendations concerning employment, and new growth targets are mutually identified. The LBO/R Model should be used for instructional improvement and as a basis for dismissal of ineffective and marginal teachers. The model should be used to determine merit-pay or career-ladder status with much caution.

9. TEACHING ASSESSMENT 323

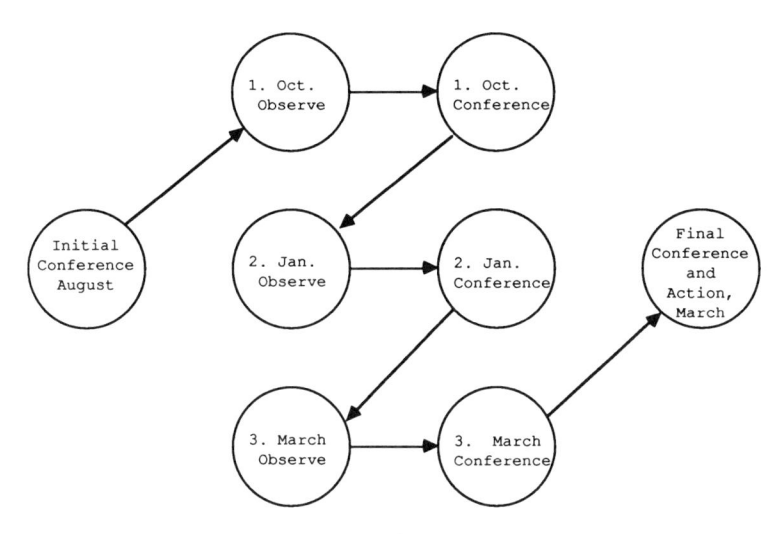

FIG. 9.1. LBO/R Teacher Evaluation Model

The LBO/R model contains the flexibility and the processes to help improve performance through improved supervision, helps plan for individual growth and development, provides information to identify marginal, average and outstanding performance, and identifies special teaching talents, creativity and skills. Note that the LBO/R model should primarily be used for instructional improvement and as a basis for dismissal of marginal teachers. It is not recommended that the LBO/R be used as the sole means to determine merit-pay or career-ladder status.

INDICATORS OF TEACHING EFFECTIVENESS

The LBO/R teacher-evaluation model can be very valuable for beginning teachers and teachers who need assistance. They should have at least two different observers who visit at least three times for a 50-minute period. The primary observer is the principal and the second could be an instructional supervisor, associate superintendent, assistant principal, or a retired teacher. Each observer must be trained to do the following things:

- Identify strengths and weaknesses of the teacher and provide assistance.

- Recognize "best practice" teaching performance.
- Use the vocabulary of staff evaluation and instructional management.
- Use motivation skills to inspire teachers to do their best.

Current research show that students are more attentive in classrooms that are businesslike and task oriented. A key to this businesslike classroom is not time-on-task alone but "academic learning time" (ALT). ALT is the amount of time students actually spend on an appropriate learning activity in which they are achieving at a high rate of success (90% or better). Researchers have found that in more effective schools teachers waste less time in starting and ending instructional activities and they select appropriate curricular materials that match the students abilities. Also, these teachers build high expectations for each learner and for themselves. Therefore, any teacher-evaluation form should include the following indicators:

- motivates students to achieve
- uses academic learning time effectively
- demonstrates proficiency in subject areas
- demonstrates command of the language
- promotes student academic growth
- learning objectives are clear
- learning strategies are based on objectives
- testing is based on objectives

Obviously, there are other important observable and nonobservable behaviors that contribute to the overall assessment of a teacher's performance. However, if the aforementioned indicators are not measured or present then the other factors hold little value in determining a teacher's ability.

The LBO/R or any other approach to teacher evaluation is only as effective as the administrators and teachers involved. If the administrator is protecting an image of total authority over his or her teachers, then the best evaluation model and instrument will be useless. Likewise, if the teacher feels that he or she needs no supervision, chooses to ignore school policy, and views the principal or any supervisor as the enemy, then any system regardless of its claims of a "mutual approach" is of little help. If the "mutual approach" is taken seriously and becomes embedded into the cultural fabric of the school, then there is little doubt that administrators can make teacher evaluation work much more effectively.

CONCLUSIONS

Administrators in Texas and other states with comparable programs are trying to make the teacher-evaluation systems work to improve schools. Although there appears to be a sense of accomplishment about standardizing the process, reinforcing good teaching, improving weak teachers, promoting a common language about teaching, and improving the instructional leadership image of administrators, gnawing problems remain. The major problems appear to be the weak research base linking teacher-evaluation systems to improved student achievement and the inconsistencies in state-by-state and district-by-district applications of evaluation systems. Another problem appears to be the two-edged use of teacher evaluation. Many observers believe that removing the poorly conceived career ladders and merit pay from the appraisal process is the only answer to making the system operational to improve schools and schooling. Others have doubts about the validity of the One Best Model because it is heavily influenced by popular instructional models with specific inflexible steps that teachers and principals must follow to drive up student test scores. Although time constraints and expertise to help all teachers will remain as obstacles for principals, they want to increase their skills to help teachers teach and students to learn. Workable teacher-evaluation models are available if, and only if, the teachers and the evaluators view them as a positive process to achieve intrinsic rewards of professional growth. It should seem obvious to education policy makers that true professional educators need open, threat-free workplaces that nurture self expression and respect. Any teacher-evaluation process that restricts these rights will fail. Perhaps, time and the kind of disciplined inquiry engendered in this Buros-Nebraska Symposium will raise new questions and lead to better answers for administrators charged with insuring high levels of teacher performance. We must have the courage to try and try again—so much depends on our struggle.

In closing perhaps this story illustrates the kind of persistence we need to improve teacher evaluation. A little 9-year-old boy not endowed with much athletic ability was cut from a Little League team for the second year in a row. In deep despair he went home and told his Dad about the great failure in his life. After a big hug and a popsicle the young lad decided to try again. He headed to the back yard with a ball and bat. He threw the ball in the air and swung—he missed the ball by at least a foot; he tried again and said "strike two" and again, "strike three." Then without missing a breath he yelled, "Man, I'm a great pitcher." So, man, we are great teacher evaluators. If we think we can, we will be.

REFERENCES

Acheson, K. A. (1986). *It is time to share the responsibility for instructional leadership with others.* (ERIC Document Reproductive Service No. ED 267 510), 1–30.

Berman, P., & McLaughlin, M. W. (1977). *Federal programs supporting educational change: Vol. VII Factors affecting implementation and continuation.* Santa Monica, CA.: The RAND Corporation.

Burke, B. T. (1982). Merit pay for teachers: Round Valley may have the answer. *Phi Delta Kappan, 64,* 265–266.

Carey, N. B. (1986, April). *Conceptions of excellence and incompetence in teaching: Implications for teacher evaluation.* Paper presented at the Annual Meeting of the American Educational Research Association, San Francisco.

Cogan, M. L. (1973). *Clinical supervision.* Boston: Houghton Mifflin.

English, F. W. (1985). Still searching for excellence: A preliminary report from the ASCD task force on merit pay and career ladders. *Educational Leadership. 42,* 34–35.

Epstein, J. L. (1985). A question of merit: Principal's and parents' evaluations of teachers. *Educational Researcher, 14,* 3–10.

Frymier, J. (1987). Bureaucracy and the neutering of teachers. *Phi Delta Kappan, 69,* 9–14.

Hoyle, J. R. (1985). Programs in Educational Administration and the AASA preparation guidelines, *Educational Administration Quarterly, 21,* 71–93.

Hoyle, J. R., English, F. W., & Steffy, B. E. (1985). *Skills for successful school teachers.* Arlington, VA: American Association of School Administrators.

Hunter, M. (1986). Knowing teaching and supervising. *Using what we know about teaching.* Alexandria, VA: Association for Supervision and Curriculum Development, pp. 175–176.

Johnson, S. M. (1984). *Merit pay plans: Effects on teachers and their work.* Paper presented at the 1984 National Conference on merit pay for teachers. American Center for Management Development, Sarasota.

Kirby, B. (1987). Comments in the foreword of the 1987–1988 *Teacher orientation manual for the teacher appraisal system.* Austin, TX: Texas Education Agency.

Lewis, A. C. (1982). *Evaluating educational performance.* Arlington, VA: American Association of School Administrators.

Manatt, R. (1982, January). Teacher performance evaluation: Practiced application of research. Ames, IA: Iowa State University, 82–81.

Manatt, R. (1986). How well can we truly evaluate teachers? An interview in *The School Administrator, 43,* 10–12.

McLaughlin, M. W. (1986). Teacher evaluation and school improvement. In a

Lieberman (Ed.), *Rethinking School Improvement* (pp. 162–175). New York: Columbia University Press.

Medley, D., & Coker, H. (1987). How valid are principals' judgments of teacher effectiveness. *Phi Delta Kappan, 69,* 138–140.

North Carolina State Department of Public Instruction. (1986). *Teacher performance appraisal system training: A report of outcomes.* Raleigh, North Carolina.

Owens, R. (1987). *Organizational behavior in education* (3rd ed.). Englewood Cliffs, NJ: Prentice Hall.

Pigford, A. B. (1987). Teacher evaluation: More than a game that principals play. *Phi Delta Kappan. 69,* 141–142.

Peterson, K. D. (1987). Teacher evaluation with multiple and variable lines of evidence. *American Educational Research Journal, 24,* 311–317.

Peterson, K. D., & Finn, C. E. (1985). Principals, superintendents, and the administrator's art. *The Public Interest. 79,* 42–62.

Peterson, K. D., Murphy, J., & Hallinger, P. (1987). Superintendents' perception of the control and coordination of the technical core in effective school districts. *Educational Administration Quarterly, 23,* 79–95.

Roueche, J., & Baker, G. (1987, September). *Profiling excellence in America's schools.* Distinguished lecture presented at the Annual meeting of the Texas Association of School Administrators and the Texas Association of School Boards, San Antonio, TX.

Ryon, J. H., Cross, R., Gonzales, M. A., Guerrero, T., & Pearson, D. (1986). *Voices from the schools: Texas view on public school reform.* Report sponsored by The Texas Coastal Bend Chapter of Phi Delta Kappa and Corpus Christi State University. Corpus Christi, Texas.

Shanker, A. (1986, November 14). No way to grade teachers. *St. Louis Post Dispatch,* p. 36.

Stiggins, R. J., & Bridgeford, N. J. (1984). *Performance assessment for teacher development.* Washington, DC: ERIC clearinghouse on teacher education. (ERIC Document Reproductive Service No. ED 242 717).

Texas Teacher Appraisal System Teacher Orientation Manual. (1987). Austin, TX: Texas Education Agency.

Tirrell, F. J. (1986). Reality lags behind ideal in teacher evaluation. *The School Administrator, 43,* 31–32.

Young, R. (1986). Five reasons why your teacher evaluation form may be faulty. *The School Administrator, 43,* 31.

10

Appraisal: The Teachers' Perspective

Peg Shafer
Prince George's County Educators Association

The Discovery Channel on TV has some terrific programming. Not too long ago I watched a scientist explain why it is that the position of a stranded boat will not change even when it is tossed around by giant storms. The theory is that waves move across the water rather than the water itself moving. The wave moves along in a circular motion, propelled by big or small forces depending on what started it in the first place. As long as nothing interrupts the roll of the wave, it will pass and leave everything as it was before.

At the time, I was in the process of collecting my thoughts for this presentation, reflecting on the rising tide of mediocrity, which you will recall was the alarm raised several years ago by the report *A Nation At Risk*. One of the many outcomes of the increased scrutiny provoked by that and other reports has been the reform of our thinking about appraisal. But long before that, teachers had been bobbing along in a dangerous and stormy sea and the only rising tide they knew about was the criticism that was threatening to swamp them. Anyway, teacher organizations tried to applaud the reports as a welcome SOS. And sure enough, very quickly they were surrounded by would-be heroes and rescuers. Unfortunately, most offers of help have presented new dangers and it has been difficult to distinguish flotsam and jetsam from a life raft. Teachers still aren't at all sure what appraisal reform will turn out to be.

Now for those of you who wish I hadn't started out that way, let me sympathize. You believe that appraisals are an important key to positive change. Your strategy for surviving the onslaught of criticism is to elevate standards and prove accountability. You think I should suspend my cynicism and throw myself wholeheartedly into a project to document success. Resistance, you say, fuels the fires in the critics' eyes—And you're right.

Resistance makes schools look unresponsive, and makes people believe that educators are lazy. And it's true that lazy teachers don't want to change, incompetent teachers can't change, unions want to protect the weak, and stubborn teachers become bad press. And you're right in thinking that I'm going to preach a sermon you have probably heard before. I have a negative message to deliver, and if you take me seriously you're going to experience frustration.

To begin with, here are some additional possibilities that I ask you to consider. There are other reasons educators might resist reforms. For example, good teachers don't want to continually be changed. Good teachers want to be left alone to do what they do well. Good teachers think they improve their performance best with experience, inspiration, sharing, and freedom to plan and dream.

Good teachers don't understand why the public doesn't value what they do and they feel bitter when they think about it. They certainly don't understand why they should interrupt their teaching to process paperwork that will tell the public how well they were teaching before they were so rudely interrupted.

It is also true that a significant majority of teachers belong to organizations that serve as unions as well as professional associations. Those unions work to insure that all teachers, weak or strong, have due process rights. But members of these unions have never enjoyed any unbridled powers. We do not hire and fire teachers, and we do not grant tenure. The vast majority of our members can't understand why school districts would not terminate the employment of teachers who are an embarrassment to the profession. Teachers are very unhappy when they are blamed for that failure. And they are frustrated that those perceived failures stand in the way of fair and reasonable funding for education and deprive them of resources to do the job.

These are the conflicts that rage in the everyday world of teachers. No matter how well meaning and reasonable those responsible, these are conflicts which alternately threaten the teaching profession and the health of public education.

I know that you are often frustrated that teachers won't just "go along" instead of fighting every effort to inspire confidence in our schools. I know that many of you blame unions. I understand how hard it is for school administrators and elected officials to raise money for education, and I know the kind of criticism you take. I will try not to argue, but simply share with you some perceptions of appraisal which have become clear to me over the years that I have served as an advocate for teachers. I do so in the hope that it may help you consider alternative ways to approach changes in evaluation.

I've been around long enough to have swung on the pendulum. I have fought both for and against evaluation plans. Much of what I know about teachers' perceptions of appraisal, I learned over the past 4 years. During that time, Lincoln Public Schools and the Lincoln Education Association have developed their own teacher appraisal instrument and field-tested it in a dozen schools. This experience has given me an unusual opportunity to find out how teachers feel about appraisal.

The Lincoln negotiated agreement establishes a Joint Teacher Appraisal Committee. Although experts generally agree that teachers should help develop their appraisal instrument, teacher input is rarely so formally guaranteed. Prior to this agreement, the District suffered from confrontations on the topic of evaluation, with teachers insisting that they wanted contractual controls and the District insisting that evaluation was not a proper subject for collective bargaining. In negotiations, during the year of the change, it was agreed that a committee, with equal numbers of representatives from the administration and from the teachers' organization, would have the responsibility to develop a new appraisal system. Also provided were contractual guarantees of fair play and the right to grieve in cases of dispute.

The Association did not try to take away the Board's job of setting standards, nor the administrative job of making judgments about quality of work. In return, the administration recognized that the association could help teachers reach an understanding of the District's expectations and help develop an effective process for assessment. The simple but significant gesture of this contractual commitment created a good feeling of partnership.

The Joint Committee studied a number of appraisal systems while creating their own documents. However, they worked hard to develop evaluation criteria really important in Lincoln and the methods Lincoln educators wanted to use to identify success. They created a 3-year cycle of independent formative and summative processes and agreed to an intensive assistance program in an effort to help the administration eliminate deficiencies. When they were done, both teacher and administrator committee members were pleased.

The system was field tested last year and a new draft will be tested in an expanded number of schools this year. Mrs. Marge Willeke of the ESU Evaluation Team studied the procedure, with assistance from members of the Joint Committee. Her evaluation reached every administrator who participated in the field test, and all of the teachers who were appraised. The Joint Teacher Appraisal Committee also had the opportunity to participate in the testing of national standards being developed by the Joint Committee on Standards for Educational Evaluation chaired by Daniel L. Stufflebeam of Western Michigan University. That project is supported by numerous grants and participating organizations, including the Association of School Administrators, the School Personnel Administrators, the American Educational Research Association, the American Evaluation Association, the NEA and AFT, the American Psychological Association, and other equally prestigious groups. Mrs. Willeke's work resulted in an impressively thorough report which told us there is a high degree of satisfaction with the new process and a good match with the proposed national standards.

Our study of the 1rst year of the Lincoln pilot was intended to focus on our committee's efforts to design an appraisal document. We did not ask whether participants thought they ought to be evaluated, and few of them dredged up basic arguments for and against appraisals in general. However, within the union the process brought about many discussions of the basics of appraisal, particularly with regard to its public relations value. Clearly, the public is clamoring for "accountable" schools and teachers with credible stamps of approval. Many educators believe that aggressive appraisal can build greater public confidence and lead to better funding. Others believe that the public has an obligation to increase funding without all this nonsense about evaluation. Whether or not the public has failed to give adequate support, there's no denying that most of the legislation passed in the name of school reform ties new money to measurements alleged to increase accountability and control quality.

Will the efforts have long-term payoffs for teachers and schools? Teachers don't think so. They simply don't believe that evaluation lives up to its promise, and they don't believe the small gains they do make are worth all the extra work.

I believe one teacher in our field test explained that point of view well. This anonymous teacher wrote "I realize that appraisal is necessary, but I doubt if the principals know how to effectively use the appraisal instrument as a tool. There are other ways to grow professionally besides IDM (Instructional Decision Making), and I refuse to be intimidated by some appraisal process—especially when I know nothing will come of it. Why don't you people at the Public Schools Administration Building take a stand on issues that are more meaningful to teachers, like the weak attendance policy or the outrageously poor staff development program. Do something about the quality of our schools in other areas besides the teachers. Make the appraisal process meaningful as well as relevant to teachers, and maybe more teachers would take it seriously."

Although obviously ventilating a lot of frustration, this teacher has raised an important question, silently asked by many—does teacher evaluation help teachers? Does evaluation get at the most critical problems in our schools? How did teacher evaluation rise to such importance in political circles?

There's public relations value in the growing research base which ties teacher behaviors to predictable outcomes in students, and public relations value in making teaching look more scientific and controllable. It has even seemed like a good idea to use impressive sounding jargon. The public wants to believe that *someone* can identify good teachers, tell what a good teacher does, and know why it works. It's comforting to the public to think that a model teacher can be hired, and cannot slip into incompetence if administrators are vigilant. It's easy to sell the public on strenuous in-service training programs to shape up teachers. It's easy to be a critic.

There are, however, nasty side effects. From the belief that a model of good teaching exists, the public can take the short step to the harmful conclusion that anyone can teach if they possess a passable knowledge of a subject and are able to emulate the behaviors in the model. They can erroneously conclude that any deviation from the model must be faulty. They can ignore jargon as pretentious. They can demand inservice after teachers have run out of energy to listen. And they can believe that principals can become overnight experts on teaching—something more believable in shopping malls and barber shops than in America's classrooms.

Good public-relations campaigns are simple and self-perpetuating. Evaluation hype requires too much stirring and damage control because the frustrations are stirred every year in the teaching ranks. Even if their own appraisal is positive, most teachers have some bad feelings about the process. They surely don't go around humming the catchy tune. . . .

The ivory-tower world of the researcher runs into other conflicts with the world of real teachers. Even in training institutions, teachers are taught to strive endlessly for ideal learning conditions. The real world, then, can't help but fall short. Having learned how to reach for the ideal, teachers resist compromise with the practical. They do not learn to quietly accommodate tight budgets, paperwork that leads nowhere in particular, and principals who are only human. In fact, nobody ever tells prospective teachers that they will have "bosses" to contend with. When I was a teacher, I knew my mission and my special calling—to work with the most unlovable teenagers in my school—and I agonized over ways to get through to them. Evaluation never helped me. In fact, I remember nothing of significance which evaluation raised to my attention.

I do particularly remember two of them. I remember an observation conducted by an administrator who had never been a classroom teacher and clearly did not understand what was happening in my class. I also remember an evaluation in the early 1970s when my principal gave me a low mark on an evaluation because I wear wire-rimmed glasses. There are two points to this personal digression. First, it's a mistake for administrators to try to fake knowledge of teaching expertise. Second, righteous indignation prevents one from hearing properly.

Not only would relationships of educators improve, but the image we project to the public might be more positive if we stopped training prospective teachers as though they would one day walk out and hang up a shingle in private practice. We should tell them that they will need to be good employees, and they might not be so publicly appalled when someone drops by to conduct an appraisal. Teachers will continue to resist "management" as long as they are trained for a solo professional mission and then treated like students who must be disciplined and taught. What are the odds? Can a principal ever help idealistic teachers become more effective when he has to assign cafeteria duty, require triplicate paperwork, put too many kids in a classroom, and ask the staff to compromise with misguided parents? The administrator can't provide the resources that teachers need. When the principal can't produce, the principal can't criticize. Teachers think that if they are lucky, the principal will take care of problem students, get them sufficient supplies, and leave teachers alone. They don't need constant coaching to be a good teacher. Having passed the hurdles of college graduation, initial employment, and finally the achievement of "tenure," most teachers expect to fly solo for the remainder of their careers. They have reason to believe that they are good and they most certainly don't expect the administration to pop up on its clay feet one day and suddenly decide that their performance doesn't stack up.

Another interesting problem in organizational psychology is that reformers have begun to believe their own hype. School districts have come to believe that they deserve and can get all super teachers. We talk a lot about our high standards, but the truth is that we can't find enough teachers of that high quality in the first place and we have to "settle" in at least a few cases.

As a result, most systems are usually afraid to specifically articulate their standards, preferring to encourage teachers to psyche themselves up to set their own high standards and to live by their own work ethic. Appraisal is just an annual opportunity to whip them up a little more. The only trouble is that when there's a teacher who really should be fired, the ambiguity testifies dramatically to the absence of any real standards.

Those of you who are practicing administrators no doubt take exception to those remarks. You have probably worked hard to set a tone for your system and you're probably proud of the tough image your schools project. But no matter how proud we are of our own local schools, you still need to be realistic about the fact that most teachers accept teaching assignments based more on location and general demographics rather than on any particular knowledge of the instructional philosophy of the system. I am gratified that a lot of teachers want to work in the Lincoln system, but very few sign on because they think our administrators will come into their classrooms to work with them, or because we have such a strong commitment to Madeline Hunter's Instructional Decision-Making. Nor do new teachers particularly care that principals have learned some new vocabulary and will script tape when they observe. That information will be irrelevant in the new teacher's career unless the principal turns out to be surprisingly helpful or gets in the way.

I can be realistic, too. Teachers know that someone out there has the right to hire, fire, and/or promote them. But most teachers believe those decisions have little to do with appraisal and the ability to teach. Teachers aren't stupid. They see bad teachers untouched by appraisals, bad teachers given tenure, poor teachers promoted, good veteran teachers attacked out of the blue, and they see good student teachers not hired. The end result of all those object lessons from real life is that teachers resist public relations schemes associated with appraisal because they know them to be politically motivated. That is, teachers believe something important will be sacrificed to whatever part of the public has a bone to pick. Few teachers believe that the target will automatically be someone they consider incompetent.

Even the latest trends are scary. Before our very eyes, principals are being transformed from business managers to instructional leaders. Some new young turks are being hired to prove that good coaches can work with teachers to create new excitement about teaching. No one, however, has been able to razzle-dazzle teachers about some of the veterans who can't or won't team up with their teachers to help. Teachers know they won't change and that mass administrative firings would send altogether the wrong message to the public. Teachers try to keep a straight face when they hear that their principal will attend a couple of in-service classes and become instructional leaders.

If we finally do undergo a transition to principals who are instructional leaders, it will mean that teachers have decided to help administrators who show promise. The transition will fail if anyone expects teachers to turn a blind eye to a principal who has a credibility gap in his or her credentials. Teachers feel an almost sacred obligation to reveal the shortcomings of an unrealistic or unhelpful administrator. They think that silence just prolongs the agony. On the other hand, teachers will follow a leader with nothing but good people skills and the ability to rally the team. They will also respect and appreciate someone with expertise in teaching theory and practice. They will probably even try to help an administrator who has limited administrative or management skill. But teachers will never pretend that an administrator is good, or let anyone think they can't tell the difference. That would be as intolerable as a policeman taking a bribe.

You can always tell when teachers have been pushed to the point they feel compelled to "blow the whistle." They begin to talk about teachers having the right to evaluate principals.

The worst news I have for you today is that so far, teachers have not bought into the recent changes in teacher evaluation. Teachers sense danger and they have circled their wagons. The clearest danger is that researchers and testing experts are searching for ways to reduce teaching to paper so that we can convince the public that we can control and improve the way teachers perform. But teachers know that nothing unique and exceptional ever grew from a dry formula. Creativity and flair can't be standardized. Painting by number has never produced any masterpieces. Resistance to "recipes" for improvement is growing every day and there is massive resistance to standardized methods of teaching, both from individuals and organizations. Listen to some of the comments from Lincoln teachers during our field test, keeping in mind that we have *tried* to diffuse any concerns about "standardization," particularly with regard to our IDM in-service program.

> "I need feedback as a teacher, not as a clone of methods which are forced on us. I cannot function as a mechanized teacher, except on evaluation days, and still maintain a relationship with students based on personality."
>
> "The labels he puts to my teaching are often not what I am really doing."
>
> "I feel that I begin worrying too much about IDM model rather than teaching a concept inductively—using the inquiry method—as is my natural style and methodology."
>
> And finally, "While IDM provides a format for evaluation, it also standardizes teaching. In my own school that I attended, I feel that some of my best teachers would not have done well based on IDM. I think individuality makes for more interesting teachers."

In addition to these complaints, standardization will have other unwanted side effects, a few we have already seen. Not long ago the fad was to criticize "textbook-tied teachers." Using teacher-made materials was meant to be more professional than buying commercially developed products. That theory inspired lots of school districts and teachers to abandon professionally produced resources in favor of what those of us who write newsletters call "fast and dirty" materials—volumes of amateur, poorly produced worksheets. Similarly, we have slowly eroded academic freedom in the process of making sure all students study the same skills with the same book on the same page at the same time with the same degree of success.

Behind each of these plans are well-meaning reformers who think that the changes will actually be better or will at least affect public perceptions of education and will work to the ultimate advantage of our schools.

A few years ago when I was working as a lobbyist for the Memphis, Tennessee Education Association, I had the experience of having the governor of Tennessee look me in the eye and tell me that the only way to get money for education was to have a Master Teacher plan. I had fought hard and that made me angry, but he was right. He did raise money for schools that way. But the expense was tremendous: a blizzard of paperwork, elevation of racial tensions, basic skills belabored at the expense of many who should have been able to excel, money used to produce a paper nightmare instead of money put into salary for teachers, and much, much more. When Master Teacher was first implemented in the Tennessee schools, there were 3,000 separate skills supposed to be taught and tested in the first grade. And there was a separate test for each one.

When teachers fought the plan, they were accused of fearing evaluation and accountability. But the truth is simply that teachers knew the price tag of the political campaign. Teachers have heard governors tell them that such plans will pay off. They've heard the same from Madeline Hunter zealots, merit-pay fans, "concerned" taxpayers groups and the two Secretaries of Education of the United States. And not one of them has made it easier for teachers to do what the public has hired them to do.

The growing frustrations among teachers have many origins. One which is rarely discussed is the basic character of people who enter the profession. There can be no questions about teaching being a highly demanding and modestly paid profession. In the cold light of day, one would have to surmise that those who would undertake such a career are dedicated, hard working, thick skinned, and altruistic. Almost all of them give us much more than we deserve.

Consider now what happens when we get "picky" about such people, or want to make them punch a time clock, or want to add unnecessary paper work. The resentment is strong.

Compounding the problem, most middle-aged to older teachers believe they are teachers for life. When the bitterness and anger well up, such people see nowhere to go. They are not competitive, and are generally uncomfortable with the private sector. Younger generations of teachers may have more bravado, and talk often and manipulatively about getting out of teaching. The truth is that a few will, but most will not. Whether our work force suffers from limited or exaggerated options, we have some unhappy people in our classrooms. Managers need to figure out a way to stop rubbing salt into the wounds and begin building pride and self-esteem.

Appraisals, particularly when school boards or administrators deliberately insist on always finding room for improvement, contribute to the depression and stress. Teachers brace themselves for the recitation: I observed you building a positive-feeling tone by reinforcing the student's ideas, but I did not see. . . .

Now you tell me, wouldn't that just warm the cockles of your heart and make you glad you went into teaching?

A new trend in appraisal which might help solve that problem is the separation of formative and summative processes. It's far too early to expect results from the formative field test in Lincoln Public Schools because we concentrated heavily on the summative process this 1rst year. But, I can share with you some of the interesting deliberations within the Joint Committee. The teachers in Lincoln firmly believed that formative appraisal should be voluntary. We argued that most teachers like to enhance their skills and credentials, and that teachers generally grasp every opportunity to share ideas that work. We were able to point, for example, to all of the teachers who attend far more than the required inservice sessions.

On the other hand, the District was uncomfortable saying that teachers weren't required to have any growth plan at all. We compromised by agreeing that teachers would have a plan at least one out of the two formative phase years. That's a start, but the teachers on the committee would like to have a plan that would allow a teacher to attempt their own challenging growth plans with the "no-risk" option of retaining possession of all the results. We believe teachers would soon discover that they really had some time for dreaming and growing. We trust that most would stay true to form and find meaningful ways to keep their teaching in top form. We think they would find exciting ways to share successes, and we are pretty sure that some of them would discover possibilities that the administration hasn't dreamed about.

Debate on some of these points will come in 1990, and we already anticipate that the administration will argue that some teachers will opt for no change and begin to moss over. The administration thinks that it will be better to be able to assure the public that everyone is required to practice. Teachers prefer to show the public that teachers are working voluntarily to upgrade the education we deliver. Once again, public relations considerations control both sides of the argument.

Notwithstanding the decisions that we still face, teachers are natural learners who like formative activities. They like the idea of helping each other. Although individuals like to work together for improvement, it is an idea that unions are approaching cautiously. They have several strong concerns. First, teachers learn group processes from working with students. Few of them have the opportunity to relate regularly with other adults in the work force. Although I am very fond of teachers, I have to tell you that they can be unrelentingly critical of each other. Unless trained and assisted, a teacher with quasi-supervisory authority over another can leave an impressive trail of destruction.

Nothing will scuttle peer assistance programs and/or formative evaluations any faster than confusing teachers with administrators. The two greatest dangers are using teachers to testify against teachers in employment decisions and thinking that teachers can do some of the appraisal work for the principal.

The dangers should be crystal clear: exposing shortcomings and vulnerabilities requires absolute trust. Peer coaching and "informing" cannot coexist.

For years, principals have experienced the tricky interpersonal problems associated with performance evaluation and they have learned the realities of human nature with widely differing degrees of success. How any experienced manager could imagine that time could be saved by delegating some of those management responsibilities to untrained workers is beyond me. Nevertheless, as principals try to spend more time on becoming instructional leaders, they more frequently want to drag department chairpersons, team leaders, lead teachers, and so on into the evaluation process. We could profit from thinking about why, as parents, we discourage tattlers in order to nurture positive strong relationships between our children. Above all else, we need for our teachers to work well together.

Administrators may very well need more help to do the new job that has been defined for them, but there are other ways to solve the problem. They either need additional administrators or they need to stop doing other kinds of work, or they need to trust other schools to deliver the new training. We could save our administrators a lot of work if we trusted our own certification requirements for continuing education, and trusted our local colleges and universities to keep our teachers up to speed. It's an irony that our colleges and universities are searching for students and funding while school districts are taking over expensive teacher training and research functions. Formative evaluations sound good, but our time and money might be better spent getting the results a different way.

As for summative evaluations, the results of Lincoln's field test look good. Teachers generally agreed that the criteria are essential to good teaching. That good start, however, led to some interesting "no win" disagreements. After the experience, participants encouraged the Committee to do everything from throw the whole thing away to expand the form because it needed to include every conceivable contribution any teacher might ever make. That kind of diverse input should tell us there's no way to win, and appraisal won't really help our public-relations campaign. If teachers believe in their hearts that appraisal is a farce, they will scuttle the plan in their churches, the grocery stores, their neighborhoods, and everywhere they feel safe to speak their minds.

Let's consider whether teachers believe that appraisals are a farce. Routine appraisals aren't very telling because they generally just provide an opportunity for the administrator to say something nice about the teacher's work. Once in a while a principal will deliver an unpopular message and ruffle feathers for a while, but usually everything will get back to normal by the start of the next year. But how about when push comes to shove? Do appraisals deal with incompetents? Possibly. Observations provide opportunity, at least. If the administrator has a good grasp of communications, he or she ought to be able to tell whether the teacher and students are connecting. When they are not, the administrator should be insightful enough to understand the reasons and offer help. If efforts to help don't pay off, the teacher should be fired. Have they been? Not in the public's mind, at least.

Well, there are some reasons. The most important in current reform movement thinking is that tenure stands in the way. The public believes that teachers can't be fired. A lot of administrators think that teachers can't be fired. Some facts might help us ascertain the truth of the matter. According to the Nebraska State Education Association, the division of teacher rights opened 321 job security case files last year. Nebraska has about 18,000 teachers, so that makes the percent of teachers in trouble about 1.7%. Sometimes, teachers anticipated trouble and solved the problem, sometimes they overexaggerated an incident which was quickly forgotten. Of those 321 cases, however, 197 teachers were really given notice of dismissal or contract amendment. Of those, 138 were reinstated without a hearing, and 34 were re-signed.

There were Board hearings in 25 of the cases. In 20 of those, the Board upheld the administration, and it reversed the administration in only 5 instances. Clearly, the politicians aren't thwarting their administrators. Moreover, there have only been an average of 9 litigations concerning teacher terminations in each of the past 3 years, and those were generally instances where there were gross procedural errors, such as failure to give timely notice. The myth that a teacher can't be fired is certainly bigger than the reality.

So why would there be incompetents in the classroom? And why would evaluation have such a bad name? For one thing, our evaluations often don't present persuasive documentation, so they invite disagreement. For another, administrators have too long taken the easy way out and "counselled" teachers out of the profession. I say they have taken the easy way, because when a problem teacher goes away, nobody has to say for certain what was wrong. No one has to prove a case. No one has to risk looking bad. Some administrators pride themselves on the kind way they handle the teacher to save them public disgrace.

On the other hand, life is a private nightmare for the person who decides to leave because of such counseling. I can tell you why someone would voluntarily resign under such circumstances. It's because they become convinced that they aren't good. Or, they become afraid not to. They become increasingly unhappy on the job, and frustrated with what they consider unreasonable obstacles. Or, they believe that their co-workers think they are awful. Whatever the particular reason, you can be sure that the devastating effects of such administrative "counseling" ruin lives far more often than termination actions. Take it from the person who talks them into hospitals or out of suicidal thoughts or just helps them through the endless late night hours on the phone chasing the personal feelings of uselessness. It's kinder to let an employee be angry because they were fired.

Without all of the manipulation and effort to reveal to a teacher that he or she has a terrible professional flaw, school boards can and do take quick, unwavering action to dismiss incompetent teachers. Few straight-forward, well-documented cases make it to a hearing. Almost all of the hotly contested, hard-fought termination cases arise from administrative overkill that reeks of unfairness. Don't all those cases where the teachers were reinstated prove that it's hard to fire teachers? That all depends on whether we believe that remediation cured them. It is certainly possible for teachers to be able to change troublesome behavior when it is spelled out for them with sensitivity and a sincere desire to help. In that respect, appraisal processes can clearly work when the administrator is able to state the deficiencies and solutions.

Are there other reasons teachers would think appraisals are a farce? Well, the process of formative appraisal that we would all like to think takes place, generally boils down to the teacher having to think up some good sounding "job targets" or goals, or what have you. Sometime during the year, the principal will come into contact with the teacher, and make a judgment about how they are doing, in general. If the teacher doesn't do anything to cause trouble during that year, life goes on uneventfully.

Many of you are probably out there thinking to yourselves, "That's certainly the way it used to be, and it sounds lousy. Good thing we've moved into the new era of principals as instructional leaders and we make them set job targets, too."

Don't kid yourselves. Look at the way job targets for educators have been improved. On the theory that student improvement can be measured, most job targets these days set goals for effecting student outcomes. How could anyone argue with the fact that good teachers get good results from students? I won't argue this involved question here, but I will tell you that virtually every teacher I have represented in termination has produced valid evidence of student achievement on standardized tests. The link between cause and effect does not stand up under challenge, and may create a new nightmare school districts don't need.

Of course it helps a school to have a leader who sets high expectations. Some new principals attack their employees with an enthusiastic, energetic involvement in instruction. And it works just fine with teachers who are ready for a new burst of inspiration and with relatively new teachers who are still fresh and rested. I predict, however, that these efforts are doomed to failure, too. Why? Simply because most of the new breed of administrators do not focus on how to make the teacher's work easier. Far too often, they want to change the cosmetics: make everyone look energetic, have everyone smiling, keep teachers on task at fast-forward speed. Or worse, they want all teachers to teach just like they do.

Most of us, even educators, never face the truth that we ask elementary teachers to teach 16 or 17 subjects to 29 individual students in 6 1/2 hours every day. They revise curriculum, or at least implement new curriculum in about a fifth of the subjects every year. In addition, we demand that they learn about Madeline Hunter, begin using computers, coordinate their work by meeting with a team of people, help plan for special education students, stay healthy so they don't use much sick leave, attend open houses and PTA meetings, stop smoking at work (if they ever had time to anyway), walk the kids to and from the cafeteria, conference with parents, and stop arguing about having to stay for required meetings. A principal who wants something additional better not expect them to rejoice. We're lucky that we have as few insurrections as we do. Every new, bright idea that we heap on our classrooms diverts energy from teaching.

Still, in spite of those who muddle around with things, our schools are effective. That's a good start to what I have to tell you about how teachers believe appraisals can help them.

First, administrators can use the current trends in appraisal to help teachers become more effective. As the administrator spends less time on office work and more time out in the classrooms, he or she should be able to discover ways to simplify the work load of teachers and provide needed resources. In the course of revising curriculum, we need to clean it up: take away irrelevant and less important material; find ways to reduce clerical demands and stop unnecessary paper work; listen to teachers' ideas about how to solve problems; eliminate unnecessary meetings; give teachers options about materials and supplies; and not create new problems by pitting teachers against each other and dumping administrative duties on them.

Administrators should be able to find ways to encourage creativity and improvement in teaching. They should be able to reward professional development if they have time to find out what the teachers are really working on instead of running around trying to get everyone to look busy with the latest fad. Administrators should be much better able to appreciate what's good about their staffs and be able to defend them from critics and promote them to the general public.

Given everything that we know about what works in the classroom, and what we know to be the truth about education law, administrators must be able to get rid of teachers who can't perform. If administrators ever want to build credibility and inspire loyalty in teachers, they are going to have to produce—by solving the most dramatic problems. Appraisal will no longer be a farce if administrators get rid of bad teachers before they start "fixing" good ones.

I have discussed appraisals as teachers see them: the good, the bad, and the ugly. The good is encouraging. Schools can improve if we are smart about it. Teachers like to grow and feel fulfilled. Teachers will live up to extremely high expectations when they are allowed to dream up ways to flourish. Once some teachers move forward, others will follow, when they are encouraged to do so in a natural, nonthreatening way. Schools can use what psychologists know about developing self-actualized veteran workers to build a highly motivated teaching force.

The bad seems too easy. In our efforts to combat the critics and build good public relations, we can get the definition of success so warped that schools can never succeed. We can all (public, educators, and legislators) be diverted by the irrelevant, and teachers can spend so much energy and time on "reforming" that they have nothing left to give their students. Good teachers can be thrown "off stride" by uninformed advice or directives and stop connecting with student learners. And they can become so suspicious, afraid, or just tired of the boss that good communication with management becomes impossible.

Finally, there are some ugly possibilities lurking below the surface. Our systems can revert to unhappy, paternalistic days where "bosses" didn't have to earn respect. Bigotry can be allowed to feed on "demerit" pay and selection processes for staffing elitist schools. Academic freedom may be lost as teachers are forced to "teach to tests" and standardize all results and achievements. Finally, teachers may continue to live in fear that as the political atmosphere shifts with various public expectations of the schools they may at any time get snarled in the termination trap.

Those of us in positions to understand the high cost of progress have an obligation to cut out the false starts. We can just stop imposing faddish new programs and making irrational demands on teachers. If we want public education to succeed, we have a responsibility to protect schools from unworkable quick fixes by standing up to be counted. Good administrators need more common sense than instructional leadership.

Education can look around at other social problems in order to better understand our dilemmas. As with teaching, a number of professions are experiencing an explosion of potential. Consider what we know about medicine these days. There are new cures and new medicines every day. Local hospitals must all have state of the art equipment and high-quality specialists available for every procedure. And medical costs are astronomical. Just like in education, what we can afford to provide can't possibly live up to what we could provide in theory.

If we let the public demand the ideal, they will have to find a way to pay—by giving up some of the service they value as well as by paying out tax dollars. Good general practitioners would probably not have time to serve as good practitioners if we insisted that they had to try to stay abreast of all the new advances in organ transplants.

The same is true of teachers. The advances in what we know about teaching aren't necessarily affordable. Can we afford low class size? Computerized and highly individualized materials?

How about releasing teachers from classroom responsibility every 4 or 5 years for retraining? How about giving teachers release time and paying them to write curriculum that really works? How about giving teachers time to coordinate their work?

Are you thinking that the public won't every pay for such things? Maybe you're right. That's why teachers think appraisals are presumptuous. With all of the relatively inexpensive ways to lighten the burden and make schooling more successful, it's almost sinful to attack teachers first.

When was the last time you heard a teacher say that it would be helpful if the principal would just come into their room and tell them which students aren't on task? Or tell them how much time they spent trying to organize their materials? When did you last hear a teacher say that if the principal would only get all teachers to make out lesson plans in a uniform way it would make teaching a lot easier? Maybe it's time for the rest of us to use appraisal to find out what is happening in our classrooms and to look for effective ways to help. Maybe if we knew enough to really be proud of our teachers, we could eliminate much of our public relations problem. If you haven't looked lately, you can't possibly understand the amazing work of our teachers. If you do know all the miracles being performed, when was the last time you told anyone about it?

Now, that's the kind of appraisal that teachers would find helpful!

11
The Assessment of Teacher Assessment: Concluding Thoughts and Some Lingering Questions

James V. Mitchell, Jr.
University of Nebraska-Lincoln

In a recent update on teacher testing practices across the United States, Rudner (1988) reported that 44 states have developed teacher-certification-testing programs, with 26 states currently testing prospective teachers as a certification requirement and another 18 states scheduled to implement such programs in the near future. It is obvious that teacher testing has become a very extended endeavor. It has also stimulated extended debate.

It was in acknowledgment of the importance of this extended teacher testing and associated debate that the Advisory Committee of the Buros Institute of Mental Measurements decided to devote its 1987 annual symposium to the topic of teacher assessment. As we developed the plans for this symposium, we tried to keep in mind two principles to guide our thinking and planning: (a) our treatment of teacher assessment was not to be narrowly conceived and focused on a singular aspect of teacher assessment (e.g., assessment for certification), but rather was to address the larger measurement and implementation issues that were generic to many or all teacher assessment settings; and (b) we hoped that we could avoid the mere rehashing of old issues and instead effectively advance thinking about teacher assessment in ways that, in

John Dewey's words, would represent "a level deeper and more inclusive than is represented by the ideas and practices of the contending parties" (Dewey, 1949, p. v). We hope that we have accomplished that, at least to some degree, both in the symposium and now with the book. The purpose of this concluding chapter is to work within this context to highlight and compare some of the salient thoughts of the several contributors, to reflect on their meaning and implications, and to point out some of the issues that remain. Each contributor is considered in turn, with summary comment to follow about their combined contributions. W. James Popham, the keynote speaker, is considered first.

When we first asked Jim Popham to present the keynote address at the symposium, we had in mind both his extended and important contributions to this area and the fact that this experience would qualify him admirably for addressing the questions implied by the topic we had tentatively suggested: "Teacher Assessment: Why and for What Purpose?" When he accepted the invitation, Popham asked whether he could "spice up" the title, and the final result was a "spicing up" of both title and topic by focusing on an issue that he felt had very potent implications for the future of teacher assessment: "Face Validity: Siren Song for Teacher Testers."

Popham's contention that we are being lured away from more important concerns by becoming preoccupied with face validity considerations is an important and timely one for many participants in the teacher-testing enterprise, particularly those who are not as indoctrinated with the holy trinity of validity classifications as most measurement people are. But measurement people are only a small contingent in the teacher-testing arena, and the lure of face-validity considerations over the more important consideration of the validity of score-based inferences is but another example of the miscommunication, differing (and sometimes unknowledgeable) expectations of different groups, and downright wish fulfillment that often seems rampant whenever the issue of teacher testing arises. The "quick fix" mentality often found in the public, legislators, governmental agencies, and even in some educators creates a setting where the siren song of face validity becomes irresistibly appealing. Popham is to be congratulated for warning us of the risk.

I am almost totally in accord with the major points made by Popham, and this should be kept in mind in the following discussion. However, there were some issues that were raised in my mind that did not necessarily lessen the effect of Popham's arguments but were stimulated by the major directions that his arguments took. If these are side issues, they are important side issues, and they are an interesting example of how a focus on one particular issue can raise other issues for which the answers sought are important in their own right as well as for their contribution to the understanding of the original issue.

The first issue relates to Popham's definition of face validity, a definition that I believe most of us would find acceptable: *"Face validity constitutes the perceived legitimacy of a test for the use to which it is being put."* As I read that definition I was struck by the extent to which "perceived legitimacy" plays a role not only in the face-validity setting but also in the content-validity exercises that are so much a part of the local validation effort for teacher tests like the National Teacher Examinations (NTE). It is sometimes hard to determine why "perceived legitimacy" is accorded so much more professional approval in the case of content validity than it is for face validity. For the NTE, for example, a typical content validity exercise would have a college-based panel address the question of the content appropriateness of each test item by asking each panelist whether 90% of the applicants for entry-level certification have had the opportunity to acquire the knowledge or academic skills being tested; another panel, in this case a school-based panel, would address the question of the job relatedness of each test item by asking each panelist how important the knowledge or skill was for the beginning teacher in general. If this isn't a "perceived legitimacy" question, I don't know what is. There are differences, of course, but are the differences critical? In the case of the NTE panels, for example, the panelists are supposed to be either experts or very knowledgeable people who have direct personal experience with the content or job that defines the judgment setting. Face-validity judgments usually refer to judgments by less qualified or knowledgeable people. Another difference is what is judged. The NTE panels judge either content relatedness with teacher-training curricula or relatedness to the job of teaching. Face-validity considerations involve judgments about whether the test or test items look appropriate for the testing of teachers. But they are both "perceived legitimacy" judgments with all the human frailties usually associated with such judgments.

The greater respect and status accorded to content validity exercises of the kind employed for the NTE must reside in the knowledgeability ascribed to the judges and the relatively systematic methods used in arriving at the judgments. This is in contrast to the naivete or lack of knowledgeability presumed to be present in the face validity situation and the unsystematic and impressionistic judgments that are supposed to characterize that situation. The drawing of these contrasts is forced, however, in the light of the indeterminacy and confusion that often accompany these NTE content validity exercises. In contrast to face validity, content validity is supposed to involve a kind of focused rationality, but in practice it can be noticeably short in both focus and rationality. Face validity is certainly the ogre that Jim Popham says it is, but the content-validity measures that are often offered as the antidote have much more in common with the inadequacies of face-validity judgments than we are commonly willing to recognize. "Perceived legitimacy" is a siren song for teacher testers wherever it appears, and its ill effects can be felt in the presumedly more antiseptic environment of the content-validity exercise as well as the nasty context of face-validity perceptions. Both involve perception and judgment, and while we are casting out the one we should recognize that the other, pure and white because of its presence in the holy trinity of measurement, evokes the same kind of cognitive processes and is susceptible, hopefully but not assuredly in lesser degree, to the same kinds of bad habits.

The second issue that was raised in my mind as I read the Popham chapter was again not an issue prompted by disagreement, but rather an issue stimulated by the development of the argument. I took special note of Popham's contention that: "Typically, in the case of teacher tests, we administer tests so that we can make inferences about how a teacher is apt to behave in an instructional setting." This seems to connote a confidence in the predictive efficacy of teacher tests that is not shared by all members of the measurement community. This confidence is shown again in a concluding statement: "If, however, an increase in face validity causes a decrease in the validity of score-based inferences, then efforts to enhance face validity should be foregone." If something can cause a decrease in the validity of score-based inferences, the clear implication is that there was some legitimate validity to begin with. An in-house review of the validity of the earlier National Teacher Examinations revealed a median correlation of .11 for seven studies that involved the correlation of a weighted total score for the Common Examinations and ratings by supervisors and principals during the 1st year of teaching (Quirk, Witten, & Weinberg, 1973). This does not inspire confidence. Yet even within the group of authors contributing to this volume there are substantial differences about the kinds of validity evidence required and whether acceptable validity levels have been achieved. Popham and Mehrens, for example, are optimists on these issues, and Madaus and Mitchell take a much more pessimistic view.

Regardless of one's requirements or interpretation of the data, however, I find it somewhat difficult to conceive of many situations where you would actually be required to trade off the validity of score-based inferences for face validity, especially if in the former case we were referring to the criterion-related validity suggested by Popham's statement that we administer these tests "so that we can make inferences about how a teacher is apt to behave in the instructional setting." I can think of possible situations where we might have to trade off someone's judgment about the curricular validity or job relatedness of test content for someone else's judgment about whether test content seems to have perceived legitimacy for the job of teaching. If I stated it in its most outrageous terms, I would say that the choice is sometimes between face validity and no validity or face validity and pretend validity. In that kind of situation I'm not sure that I would even bother to make the choice; the choice is not worth making and the test is not worth giving.

Popham's major point, however, is well worth making and is cogently argued: Face validity can be a snare and a delusion. Unfortunately, content validity is sometimes susceptible to very similar ills.

Edward Haertel's chapter on "Teacher Performance Assessments: A New kind of Teacher Examination" is a very useful status report on the current work of the Teacher Assessment Project (TAP), sponsored by the Carnegie Corporation and under the direction of Lee S. Shulman, from the point of view of an active participant in the project. In a report entitled *A Nation Prepared: Teachers for the 21st Century* (Carnegie Forum on Education and the Economy, 1986) the Carnegie Foundation Task Force on Teaching as a Profession recommended the creation of "a National Board for Professional Teaching Standards, organized with a regional and state membership structure, to establish high standards for what teachers need to know and be able to do, and to certify teachers who meet that standard" (p. 55). The measurement problems inherent in such an effort are immense, of course, and the Teacher Assessment Project has accepted the heady task of developing the teacher performance assessments that might serve as the basis for board certification.

Haertel's discussion of the TAP project must be in the nature of unfinished business, because the project has been in existence for only a short period of time. The nature of some of the challenges to come, however, may be clearly grasped from descriptions of steps taken to date. One particularly important statement, in my judgment, is the following:

> By design, nearly all of the questions posed in the various exercises have several correct answers. In scoring, it is necessary to recognize the validity of alternative instructional approaches while maintaining distinctions among different degrees of response quality (p. 23).

The immensity and inherent difficulties of the task of developing valid scoring procedures for the TAP structured performance assessments are here cast in bold relief. It is admirable for teacher-assessment procedures to have the flexibility that acknowledges the many alternative patterns that may constitute effective teaching, but the determination of which of many alternative patterns constitute "correct" answers and have the requisite "response quality" will be certain to magnify appreciably the problems of establishing the validity of the assessment. One of the first problems will be a classificatory problem: classification in terms of the essential features of the phenomenon being observed, and classification in terms of the quality of response observed. The TAP program has chosen initially to structure the first classification issue in terms of five "scoring dimensions" described as "content-specific pedagogy," "subject matter knowledge," "professional responsibility," "class organization and management," and "pedagogy, sensitivity, and responsiveness to students." "Professional responsibility" and "pedagogy, sensitivity, and responsiveness to students" are examples of such broad and ambiguous categories that one wonders about the definitiveness of any inclusion criteria that could be developed and the reliability of the assignments to such categories. The reliability of assignments to these categories raises another problem that Haertel also acknowledges in his own discussion: Will these categories have the convergent and discriminant validity that is required of them, or will cross-dimension correlations be so high as to negate their hoped-for utility?

The classification or scoring of response quality is not without its problems, either. The attempt to identify discrete, scorable elements of a teaching performance and then to combine these scorable elements "following a more or less explicit rule" is a procedure having evident heuristic value but also one that cries for reliability and validity evidence that provides some ultimate justification for the ad hoc nature of the approach. Haertel rightly warns us about premature insistence on validity evidence, but validity evidence is critical and cannot be long postponed if the people most immediately involved are to have confidence in the procedures developed. The alternative scoring procedure described, "holistic" scoring, involves a matching of performance elements to descriptions of previously rated prototype performances. This matching process seems to proceed in terms of relatively inexplicit criteria as well, and once again its justification can only come from sound evidence of its reliability and validity.

All of these problems are doubtlessly well known to Haertel, the TAP director, and their collaborators. It is a brave effort and a very necessary one, and it is imperative that the effort be supported and the problems addressed. There are two major dangers that concern me. The first is that the validity and scoring problems will be so time consuming that, eventually, compromises will have to be made and there will be a retreat to face validity justification of the type Jim Popham decried. Because face validity could certainly be ascribed to these exercises, the temptation would always be there. The second danger is that the procedures themselves will be found to be so time consuming that those who inherit them will have neither the time, patience, nor professional expertise to apply them as well as their developers. Such conditions would again have immense consequences for validity.

Donald Medley's chapter on "Improving Teaching Through the Assessment Process" is a tribute to systematic thinking and the scientific method. His model of the teaching-learning process helps to avoid much of the conceptual confusion that can occur in the teacher-assessment area long before any of the measurement issues are addressed. His choice of measurement techniques then follows naturally from the model chosen, and the reader can appreciate the final result in the context of its conceptual underpinnings. His model also acknowledges the complexity of the teacher-assessment problem and provides a manageable structuring of that complexity to facilitate understanding about where one might most effectively enter the system and how one might most effectively take advantage of its measurement implications. Scholars can also be realists, and it is this happy combination that makes Medley's contribution so worthy of careful thought. He more than proves the case for his contention that "there is a better way to assess competencies than the conventional tests presently used."

The last section of Medley's chapter is devoted to assessment procedures that meet the requirements of his model and focus on the "skills . . . a teacher needs to do well during interactive teaching," which he perceives as having little in common with the skills a student needs to do well on a conventional multiple-choice test of professional knowledge. The following comments are directed to the two assessment procedures discussed in this part of the chapter: the simulation exercises and the instrumentation used to assess teacher competence in the Beginning Teacher Assistance Program (BTAP).

The two simulation exercises illustrated are doubtlessly far more related to the problems a teacher in the classroom would face than the typical item in a typical teacher assessment test. In this sense Medley has done what he set out to do. Both exercises represent a face validity that has inherent appeal; at the same time both conjure up some of Popham's concerns about the issues that may lie beyond initial impressions of face validity. Verisimilitude in relation to actual classroom problems is certainly a strong characteristic of these simulation exercises, but that verisimilitude does not necessarily guarantee that the responses will better predict what that same person would do in the actual classroom situation with the same problem. There are at least four concerns that arise in relation to simulation exercises of the type described: (a) demand characteristics of the setting; (b) fakability, (c) the affective components of most problem situations in teaching, and (d) the determination of an acceptable definition of what constitutes "professional knowledge."

Demand characteristics are different for different exercises, and the demand characteristics of the first exercise (the cheating episode) are probably the strongest of the two simulation exercises. In view of the fact that the two participants in the cheating episode are described as normally well behaved and even docile, is there much doubt that the more severe punishments for cheating would be regarded as unacceptable by the powers that be? Because the cues for what is wanted are likely to be stronger and more evident than the cues for what the respondent would *actually* do in the situation (which may be unpredictable even to the respondent), and because the motivation would also be correspondingly stronger for these demand cues, the "wrong" responses can be rather easily eliminated for the wrong reasons. The influence can be unconscious in nature, but in most cases it will probably be conscious and will then demonstrate what we usually refer to as the "fakability" of the item. One can always take the position that the exercise represents professional knowledge, not actual professional performance in the classroom, but in that event the exercise is not better than an item similarly unpredictive of actual performance that is totally without verisimilitude. Neither way can we predict accurately what the person is going to do in the classroom.

Another concern is that exercise verisimilitude is incomplete at best if it only reflects the cognitive components of a problem situation. Many problem-solving situations in the classroom have strong affective overtones caused both by the teacher's own affective needs and self-concept and by the nature of the teacher's previous and present interactions with pupils in the classroom. It is probably impossible to reflect these affective variables in any teacher-assessment procedure except an actual classroom observation, but their existence does make prediction difficult even from the most realistic of problem depictions. One can again retreat to the position that it is professional knowledge that is being assessed, not actual professional performance, but again one can question what gains have really been made over conventional methods by the effort to create verisimilitude—not predictive gains, certainly.

Still another concern is the problem of defining what constitutes professional knowledge, the very gist of what is being assessed. Many of those who are cognizant of the literature on the prediction of teaching effectiveness would probably conclude that well-verified empirical results in this area are few and far between and the evidence uncertain and inconclusive. It is interesting to note that the first simulation exercise was taken from a self-instructional package developed for in-service teacher education and that the keyed answers were those consistent with the "recommendations" given by those who developed the packets. One can wonder whether this kind of "knowledge" is deserving of the term *professional knowledge* or whether it is a combination of common sense, good judgment about the probable consequences of actions, and personal and professional values. Even if it did not meet the criteria of empirically verified knowledge, perhaps it could be excused for that if it adequately predicted performance in the classroom. But there is no evidence that it does that, either; if we are realistic we have to challenge both its legitimacy as "knowledge" and its predictive efficacy for actual classroom performance.

Medley acknowledges that "interactive performance skills," unlike professional knowledge, cannot be assessed adequately by simulation. The very different kinds of interactional settings that exist between students and teacher cannot be accurately reflected in the typical simulation, and other methods must be sought. For this he advocates the measurement-based teacher evaluation that was implemented in the Virginia Beginning Teacher Assistance Program (BTAP). There is little doubt that the Virginia program constitutes one of the most credible and creditable programs around, and it is much advanced over most of its competitors. It is not the simulation of setting and the simulation of performance choice; it is the actual setting and the actual choice and execution of performance options. What has been done to develop and implement the program is impressive. The fact that certain questions can still be raised about the program is not so much a reflection of program shortcomings as it is a reflection of the complexity of the problems that can bedevil any effort to assess teacher performance.

Although the BTAP program reduces some of the problem of generalizability that occurs with simulation, some of the problems remain, even if in somewhat different form. Demand characteristics are still very much in evidence. With the simulation exercises it is the problem of showing that you know and can choose the correct professional knowledge. With the BTAP program someone else has chosen the professional knowledge, in this case the 70 research-based categories of teacher behavior labeled *indicators of competence*, and you have to demonstrate the behavior required. But whether you choose on demand or act on demand, there is still the very real problem of what you are really going to do when the demands are removed. If the problem setting is not effective in predicting that future behavior, and if fakability is still a serious issue, both the predictive efficacy of the program is in question, and the potential of the program to improve future teaching behavior can be seriously doubted.

Because teachers are required to demonstrate "indicators of competence" (e.g., ending a unit with a summary or review) in an actual classroom setting, the BTAP program does much more than the simulation to include both the affective and cognitive elements that together produce the climate of a real teaching situation. This is a decided plus. The setting is no doubt influenced, however, by the likelihood that the teacher is showing off his or her very best behavior, and the affective requirements and responses for this setting may be quite different from what occurs when the observer leaves the classroom.

The knowledge base for the "indicators of competence" is also at issue. The 70 categories of teacher behavior that served as the knowledge base were identified from the research literature on teacher effectiveness. The strength and relevance of these research findings are a matter of professional judgment, and that judgment is likely to be varied. The weights to be assigned these indicators in anyone's implicit set of judgments about what constitutes effective teaching is also open to question; it certainly seems that in any implicit *or* empirical set of weightings for defining effective teaching, "making interrelationships among parts of the lesson clear to learners" should be assigned greater importance than "beginning the lesson or unit with a statement of purpose." What is one person's knowledge base seems to be another person's morass of inconclusiveness. In such a setting professional value judgments seem to play a large role.

The issues of scoring procedures and passing scores also loom large in an assessment undertaking of this nature. According to Medley, "A temporary scoring key was constructed for each of the 14 competencies by first identifying a set of events that reflected the indicators that defined that competency, and summing the standard scores ... in each record" (p. 69). Subsequent revisions of the keys were undertaken to maximize coefficient alpha. To be included an indicator had to be perceived as supported by research on teaching, and once included its weight appeared to be equal to weights of all other indicators included. The pass score was based on an estimate by principals of what percentage of teachers in the state possessed that competency. This is another judgment game that does not have very precise rules. What is important to recognize here is that the actual observing and recording procedures in this system are low-inference procedures; where the high inference occurs is in selection of indicators, the scoring procedures, and the setting of the passing scores. High-inference procedures, wherever they occur, need constant study and verification.

Because the complexities are so great, any teacher-assessment program will have its stronger points and its weaker points. It is far easier to critique than to create. Donald Medley has created a conceptual scaffolding and a teacher-assessment program that demonstrate remarkable improvements over earlier state-of-the-art efforts, and his work has resulted in major contributions that have advanced and will advance teacher assessment for some time to come.

William Mehrens' "Assessing the Quality of Teacher-Assessment Tests" is an extremely comprehensive and useful compilation of facts and insights about the development of teacher-assessment tests and methods of assessing and assuring their quality. Of particular interest is the extensive treatment of validity considerations in the development of teacher-assessment tests. Readers of this volume encounter very different judgments about the adequacy of most current efforts to establish validity for teacher-assessment instruments; Mehrens probably represents the most optimistic end of the continuum and George Madaus represents the most pessimistic end. Perhaps this author ought to indicate his predilections before commenting further about the Mehrens' chapter, for I must admit to a more pessimistic view of present methods of establishing validity evidence for teacher-assessment tests and also the quality of validity evidence so produced. With this as context I offer the following as a basis for discussion.

Mehrens spends a great deal of time and effort in the discussion of methods of establishing *content* validity for teacher-licensure tests, and his faith in the procedures and results of these content-validation efforts is admittedly much greater than mine. His discussion of the development of a list of competencies, the analysis of job requirements, the development of test specifications, and the development and validation of items is thorough, thoughtful, and stimulating. But as I read this discussion I could not help being impressed by two statements that summarized the basic weakness of the foundation of the entire structure. In speaking of the test development procedure just described, it is stated that "It [the test] will be assessing those competencies that experts in the field *thought necessary* [italics added] for beginning professionals to have in order to protect the public" (p. 99). Then later, in a discussion of criterion-related validity, it is indicated that "there is no clear definition of what it means to be an effective teacher" (p. 102), with a reference to a paper by Webb (1983).

The appeal to authority, to "experts in the field," whether they be practicing elementary or secondary teachers or university professors of education, is not one to inspire confidence, especially in view of the fact that there is so little agreement among experts or anybody else on "what it means to be an effective teacher." The latter has just as many implications for content validity as for criterion-related validity. Whether one is looking for the ideal empirical criterion or the ideal of teaching effectiveness as fashioned by several disagreeing "experts," the goal is just as unattainable. The "thought necessary" criterion, stripped of its verbal superstructure, is nothing more than simple opinion, expert or not, and it is simple opinion based on nonexistent or at least unimposing scientific findings. Sometimes it can be little more than ideology or value judgment. Furthermore, there is little doubt that often the "experts" who are asked to apply the "thought necessary" or similar criteria are uncertain and frustrated about their task. Whether they actually feel "expert" in either their final judgment or the certainty with which that judgment is held is open to serious question.

The "thought necessary" criterion applied by "experts in the field" seems particularly worrisome in the context of Webb's (1983) painfully evident contention that there is no clear definition of what it means to be an effective teacher. The paragraph in which she expresses that contention is a thought-provoking one that deserves to be quoted in its entirety:

> Although no one would question the importance of good teaching to the provision of good education, the appraisal of teacher performance has presented numerous and nettlesome problems. One major problem inherent in teacher evaluation is that there is no clear definition of what characterizes an effective teacher or constitutes effective teaching and, consequently, no definitive measures to be used for teacher evaluation. Any evaluation process is essentially a comparison of desired outcomes with actual outcomes. If the situation exists where not only the results but in many cases the desired outcomes are in question, then the task of evaluation becomes extremely difficult. (Webb, 1983, p. 69)

Although Webb seems to be talking about teacher assessment in general, she is also talking about evaluation involving minimum competency testing, and her comments apply with equal force to assessment for licensure. If there is no clear and agreed-upon definition of what it means to be an effective teacher, the specific competencies of an effective teacher will be difficult to define or agree upon, and the further difficult task of defining what *minimum* levels of competencies should be for licensure or other purposes becomes an unstructured and confusing enterprise. And it has often been just that. Through compromise and adjustment, teacher-assessment instruments do get constructed, but the gap between the ideal of content validity and the actuality of practice typically makes the final product very vulnerable to challenge.

Mehrens' discussion of the establishment of validity evidence leaves no doubt that it is content validity evidence that should shoulder all the burden. He cites several authorities who have argued that it is both "unfeasible and inappropriate to expect criterion related validity of a licensure examination." He quotes the *Standards for Educational and Psychological Testing* (1985) to the same effect. He cautions that when a rating is used as a criterion, and a test as a predictor, it is difficult to determine whether a failure of the test to predict the rating is the fault of the test or of the rating.

In view of Mehrens' conviction of the unfeasibility of collecting criterion-related validity evidence for licensure tests, I am a little surprised that at the end of his discussion he indicates that:

> It does not follow from all of the preceding statements that it is inappropriate to attempt to find out what, if any, correlates of teacher-licensure tests exist. Although correlational data are somewhat sparse, they are consonant with the logical inference that knowledge about teaching and the subject matter being taught (competence) should be related to both performance and effectiveness in teaching. (p. 104)

Mehrens then reports data he apparently feels is consistent with this statement. Two of the studies he cites involved the correlation of NTE scores with aptitude tests. In what way does teaching performance or effectiveness play a role in either one of these? Is NTE now the criterion instead of the predictor? High correlations between general ability and achievement tests have been recognized for a long time, but the relationship says nothing about how knowledge about teaching might be related to actual teaching performance or effectiveness. Mehrens cites another study (Piper & O'Sullivan, 1981) as reporting a correlation of .43 between the NTE Common Examinations scores and a supervisor's rating on a Performance Evaluation Instrument. Actually, the correlation of .43 was between the NTE Elementary Area examination and the Performance Evaluation Instrument. The study was a half-page brief research report with only 32 subjects, and there were aspects of the study that were puzzling and required additional explanation. Overall, it may be better not to depart at all from one's contention that criterion-related validity evidence is unfeasible than to place much reliance on data of this type.

The Mehrens' chapter stimulated a great deal of thought on my part, and that is a tribute to its author. There are times when I think we should change our direction completely. Predicting teacher performance or effectiveness (even for licensure purposes) may be a pretty hopeless task. There may be a problem of what, for want of better terminology, I refer to as a "shifting criterion": There may be 1001 ways of being an effective teacher, and 1001 ways of being an ineffective teacher. This only acknowledges the complexity of what goes on in teaching. There are other ways to satisfy the public's concern about teachers. Why not start with the basic proposition that it simply isn't good to have an ignoramus in front of an elementary or secondary classroom? Don't suggest or imply that this has anything to do with effective teaching, because we really don't know the point at which it does; it is simply desirable, for modeling and social learning purposes alone, to have a well-educated person in front of either elementary or secondary students. Forget your list of competencies or your job analyses; they sometimes seem to contribute more to problem confusion than problem solution. Require instead that prospective teachers pass a general education examination that attests to their achievement in reading, writing, speaking, mathematics, reasoning, and knowledge of the culture. Require that this examination be passed before the person can be admitted to a teacher-education program. Do not pretend that this will ensure effective teachers, and strongly disabuse the public of any such thoughts. Don't do that which we may not be able to do; do that which should be done for its own sake, and avoid the tortuous route of collecting content-validity evidence that may have very limited or no meaning and even less predictive efficacy. And let the higher-education subject areas, in cooperation with teacher-education specialists, determine whether a prospective teacher has sufficient knowledge to teach a given subject at the secondary level. If all this seems a little iconoclastic, it should be attributed to this author's continuing frustration with the validity problems of teacher-assessment tests and the conviction that a better direction must be sought.

For those who feel that content-validity exercises, as they are now or as they will presumably be improved, are the royal road to better teacher assessment (or licensure) tests, William Mehrens points the way with his usual thoroughness and illuminating insights. For those like me who are experiencing doubts and frustrations, Mehrens' contributions serve masterfully to stimulate careful thought about where we are, where we are going, and what the alternatives might be.

Linda Darling-Hammond's chapter on "Teacher Evaluation in the Organizational Context" serves an extremely useful function for this volume on assessment of teaching. When the symposium and book were being planned, it was felt that the influence of organizational context on the nature, processes, and results of teacher assessment was so profound that we had to include one chapter that would emphasize the importance of context and shed some useful light on the specific processes by which these contextual influences affect the nature and implementation of teacher assessment. Darling-Hammond's chapter does that extremely well. Her focus is not at the state level and on licensure examinations but rather on evaluation activity as it occurs at the teacher, school, and system level. She forces us into some healthy reality testing by delineating convincingly the several influences of the organizational context and demonstrating the consequences if these are poorly understood or ignored. The chapter stands by itself, and thus my comments will be restricted.

When all the organizational context variables are brought to bear, as they are in this chapter, one can develop a much more profound grasp of why teaching presents so many difficult problems for evaluation. The descriptions of the various "Conceptions of Teaching Work," with teaching conceived alternatively as labor, craft, profession, or art, underscore the very different purposes and procedures that would govern the evaluation of teaching so differently conceived. The cited experience of the Beginning Teacher Evaluation Study conducted for California's Commission for Teacher Preparation and Licensing is interesting in relation to the earlier discussion of Mehrens' chapter; they concluded that their findings suggested "that the legal requirement for a license probably cannot be well stated in precise behavioral terms" (Bush, 1979, p. 15). Interesting also is the evidence given that the effort to specify specific teaching behaviors related to increased student achievement can often result in two- or three-way interactions that are difficult to translate into rules of practice. The generalizability of such interactions for classroom practice is thus severely constrained. Furthermore, any relationships found with achievement are often curvilinear, which provides additional limits on generalizability. She reports that "Research on nonteaching variables in the educational environment indicates that many factors other than teaching behaviors have profound effects on student learning" (p. 146), and later quotes approvingly from Doyle's (1979) statement that such an ecological approach, which acknowledges the influence of important nonteaching variables on achievement, "would seem to call into question the very possibility of achieving a substantial number of highly generalizable statements about teaching effectiveness" (Doyle, 1979, pp. 203–204). Thus performance-based teacher-evaluation models, based on the presumption that there are generalizable rules for teaching behavior that will lead to increased student achievement, are procrustean models that too often fail to acknowledge the contextual complexity of teaching and fall short as a result. Predetermined approaches to teaching, and their associated predetermined approaches to the evaluation of teaching, fail to acknowledge the many student, classroom, and school variables that the effective teacher must react to in the decision making that will ultimately shape his or her teaching behavior. For once one senses in this discussion a forthright recognition of the true complexity of what we are up against. It is refreshing.

It is equally refreshing to benefit from Darling-Hammond's discussion of the logistic, financial, and political realities that have so much impact on the usefulness of an evaluation program. She reports Knapp's (1982) contention that in actual practice schools follow the lines of least resistance and evaluate "aspects of teachers and teaching in more vague terms so as to simultaneously satisfy diverse constituencies." This is a humbling statement, but the satisfaction of these diverse constituencies is doubtlessly a very potent political reality and an accurate portrayal of the typical setting. She quotes a very interesting statement from Knapp (1982) that includes a sentence to the effect that "Value choices are nowhere more clearly at issue than in decisions about the aspects of the teacher and teaching to be evaluated" (p. 4). This acknowledgement of the importance of *values* in teacher evaluation is a very critical consideration. If research on teacher effects does not provide as strong a foundation for teacher evaluation as we should like, and if logistic, financial, and political influences are prepotent in the typical setting anyway, it is likely to be *values* that will have as much or more influence than anything else on what is finally developed for teacher-evaluation purposes. The process of "satisfying diverse constituencies" will eventually result in an averaging process that represents the "lines of least resistance," and the value directions emerging will somehow get embedded in the final teacher-assessment program. The final program may not reflect that imperfectly emerging value system as well as it should or as well as most people might have hoped, but that may be a function of the vagueness already referred to and the difficult leap from value perspective to instrumentation. It is realistically useful, in my judgment, to recognize the important role of value choice in the development of teacher-evaluation programs; if you don't know what an effective teacher is, construct an effective teacher from your value repertoire and try to embed it in your evaluation system. This may sound cynical, but it is only meant to prevent us from kidding ourselves about what most teacher-evaluation systems actually are. Any item in any teacher-evaluation instrument I have seen reflects a value about a characteristic a good teacher is supposed to have. We may hope that such items are based on what little research evidence we have, but they are most likely influenced greatly by the political realities Darling-Hammond discusses so trenchantly. Those political realities are ignored only at great peril. Thank you, Darling-Hammond, for forcing us to jump into the muddy waters of reality testing.

Richard Stiggins' chapter 6 "Measuring Performance in Teacher Assessment" is a helpful analysis of the role that performance assessment can play in the assessment of teachers and the steps that must be taken to insure the quality of those performance assessments. Performance assessment as he describes it has a philosophical and procedural kinship to Medley's chapter; perhaps equally true is that many of the concerns and cautions expressed in the Popham chapter might well be applied to what Stiggins is advocating. In a sense Stiggins is teaching us the ethics of performance assessment—the "thou shalls" and the "thou shall nots"—and in the process the criteria, decision points, and procedures are all systematically described.

It appears to this reader that more performance assessment, a higher quality of performance assessment, and more adequate training for performance assessors should all be instituted in the various settings for which Stiggins advocates performance assessment—particularly in teacher-education programs. His points are well taken and his advocacy is enlightened, especially if Popham's cautions are carefully considered and applied. My greatest concern is that in the process of applying the "shalls" and "shall nots" of performance assessment we may lose sight of the provisos that must be attached to those "shalls" and "shall nots" by the inevitable interactions and complexities of teaching. From Darling-Hammond's chapter we learn about the fearful lack of generalizability that seems to occur with teacher-effects research, and the consequences this has for teacher assessment. In Stiggins' chapter there seems to be a tendency to believe that performance assessment effectively applied will somehow overcome this complexity and lack of generalizability. In concentrating on the "shalls" and "shall nots" the interactions between the conceptual structure and the terms of the teaching milieu are not salient considerations, and this leads to some rather sweeping statements that may sometimes oversimplify the task at hand.

Two examples of this tendency appear in the discussion of the application of performance-assessment procedures to summative assessment. In discussing various decision contexts Stiggins indicates that "In each of these cases, the first requirement is that the performance criteria be based on a thorough task analysis of the teaching process" (p. 205). Then in the next paragraph he reports that "The sample of exercises—whether naturally occurring or structured exercises—must reflect in a representative manner the full range of situations in which the student or teacher will be expected to demonstrate proficiency when teaching" (p. 205). A "thorough task analysis of the teaching process" and exercises that reflect the "full range of [teaching] situations" may be admirable ideals, but they may also be ideals that are contrary to the research evidence and not realizable in practice. Performance assessment is not a panacea that will solve all of the problems of teacher assessment or allow them to be ignored; it is a useful assessment procedure, with rules of application very well described by Stiggins, that is intended to add an additional measure of realism and validity to the assessment process. That realism and validity may be compromised if the complexity and interactions of the teaching situation are oversimplified or are not given the full attention required in both principle and practice.

Stiggins has provided an important service by warning us that in the hiring of teachers it is not always a "defensible assumption" that all preceding performance assessments were sound. The lack of training in performance assessment that may characterize many instructors, supervisors, and principals may be cause for justifiable skepticism. The effective use of performance assessment requires careful study of its concepts, principles, and rules of application. Stiggins' chapter provides a useful first resource for guiding that study.

Before commenting on the George Madaus chapter "Legal and Professional Issues in Teacher-Certification Testing: A Psychometric Snark Hunt," I should probably make a confessional statement about my predilections with respect to teacher-assessment tests. Madaus quotes a statement I made about one such teacher-assessment test, and that statement then reflected and doubtlessly continues to reflect my professional evaluations of most or all such teacher-assessment tests. My position on such matters is extremely similar to that of Madaus, and it is my considered judgment that Madaus is one of the most perceptive debunkers on the measurement scene since Oscar Buros passed away. If Madaus were not here, someone would have to invent him so that his clearheaded and realistic insights into what is really going on in teacher assessment would be available for all to ponder. Fortunately, he *is* here, and we can all profit immensely from his analysis and cautions.

From this preliminary statement I can then state without remorse the many Madaus contentions that I agree with, and also take up one issue that continues to perplex me in spite of my very extensive agreement. I agree with Madaus that "extant, generic multiple-choice teacher-certification tests make little sense, and are simply not valid" (p. 246). I agree that most or all validation studies generated by the commercial test publishers are "minimalist exercises designed to obtain a positive result" (p. 210), or at least usually achieve that result whether by conscious intent or not, and that current practices of content validation for these tests "redound to confirmation rather than disconfirmation" (p. 211). I agree with his statement that:

> the precondition of "legal defensibility" drives applied validation efforts to the detriment of a careful consideration of the evidence needed to sustain the inferences and decisions made from the test scores. The form and technique to construct a "legally defensible" test has almost completely overshadowed the essential question of the meaning behind the test score. (p. 226)

I also agree that teacher-assessment tests have been reified to such an extent that in the minds of some, particularly the public, they are perceived to measure that which even their designers did not design them to measure; I also wonder, however, whether those representing measurement have always done what they could to disabuse them of that notion. I particularly agree that content-validity evidence, based as it usually is on opinion alone, is not sufficient for teacher-certification tests generally and certainly not for the inferences typically drawn from them. I believe, along with Madaus, that the validation of teacher-certification tests must include evidence from all three traditional validity categories: content, criterion-related, and construct.

It is precisely at this point, however, that I begin to have qualms. It is not at all difficult to be consistently realistic in one's assessment of a very difficult problem and yet not be equally realistic in charting directions for its solution. In chapter 4 Mehrens tends to derogate the role that construct validity might have for licensure tests, and his thoughts about this exhibit a realistic tenor that should be considered as carefully as the realistic concerns brought up by Madaus with respect to the present status of teacher assessment as a whole. Yet Madaus advocates a "functional analysis of what minimally competent teachers actually do in their classrooms" (p. 246), for each and every area of certification, and the generation of convincing criterion-related and construct-validity evidence appropriate thereto. That's a large order in view of the generally accepted conclusion that reliable and valid criteria are extremely difficult to identify in this area, and the generation of a nomological network of relationships is extremely hazardous because of the ill-defined nature of the construct of "teaching effectiveness" and the earlier described "shifting" criterion that can result both in teaching effectiveness attributable to entirely different causes and teaching effectiveness that interacts with student and situation. The comparison of correlations between what a given teacher-assessment test is supposed to measure and what it isn't supposed to measure may result in such small or nonexistent differences between the two (due to unreliable criteria and inherent construct definitional inadequacies) that defensible conclusions are difficult or impossible to draw. The construct of "teaching effectiveness" simply does not lend itself to construct-validity evidence as well as other constructs in psychology and education. In addition to the usual well-documented problems with establishing construct-validity evidence in the typical setting, we have in this instance a construct that is unusually difficult to work with in terms of construct-validity requirements.

Despite the tremendous difficulties in establishing criterion-related and construct-validity evidence for teacher-assessment instruments, I agree with George Madaus that it is absolutely essential that we try to do it. If we can do it, we are far ahead in the game; if we can't, perhaps that very fact can demonstrate that the present practice of relying on raw opinion euphemized as content-validity evidence must by comparison be even more hopelessly short of the goal. George Madaus has made an extremely important statement in this chapter; ignore it at extreme risk.

Ronald Berk's chapter "Limitations of Using Student-Achievement Data for Career-Ladder Promotions and Merit-Pay Decisions" is a well researched and very comprehensive account of how the public's most popular panacea for evaluating teachers can lead us into a morass of pitfalls. Although this is a more specialized chapter than most of the other chapters, dealing only with the use of student-achievement test scores to evaluate teachers, this kind of approach has such face validity for the public that it more than deserves this concentrated attention. It tends to evoke thoughts and concerns similar to those Jim Popham was discussing in his chapter warning about "Face Validity" as the "Siren Song for Teacher-Testers." Anything with this much face validity and this many problems demands potent weaponry, and Berk certainly brings such weaponry to bear. First he reviews professional standards and court decisions relevant to his topic and concludes that "There are no professional standards or court decisions to support the use of achievement data for any type of teacher evaluation" (p. 298). Then he conducts a review of the research literature that identifies "several factors that can influence a teacher's measured effectiveness that are beyond his or her control" (p. 277); he identifies 42 such factors. To this he adds 11 factors relating to pretest-posttest gain that can cause confusion or make impossible any inferences regarding the teacher's actual contribution to such gain. He also discusses criteria for defining superior teacher performance and finds them wanting. It is a convincing exercise.

Regardless of the evidence that can be marshalled against the use of student-achievement–test gains as criteria of teaching effectiveness, however, the public is not likely to abandon this appealing gambit. We must return to Darling-Hammond's plea that we deal with the realities of our situation. Faced with the evidence that Berk has presented to us, we can attempt to accomplish at least three things: (a) we can take *every* opportunity to immerse the public in interpretable data and argument that will disabuse them of the notion that student-achievement test score gain is the panacea for evaluating teacher effectiveness; (b) we can make an equally strong effort to encourage the adoption of teacher-evaluation systems that make use of *multiple* indicators of teaching effectiveness in the hope that such systems will tend to counterbalance any constant measurement errors that may inhere in the individual indicators; and (c) we should forthrightly recognize that at this stage in our development any evaluation system (as mentioned earlier by this author) involves a value choice of those indicants that are perceived to define what we mean by teaching effectiveness, and in the absence of weightier logical and scientific evidence we should simply fill the gap with conscious choices consciously and openly defended. And we should always make clear exactly what we are doing, and the status of what we are doing in terms of knowledge base and scientific underpinnings (or lack thereof).

We turn now to a consideration of John Hoyle's chapter "Teaching Assessment: The Administrator's Perspective." When the symposium and this book were first planned, it was always a high priority to make sure that our treatment of teacher assessment

11. THE ASSESSMENT OF TEACHER ASSESSMENT   369

would make a very conscious and strong attempt to bridge the gap between theory and practice that often exists for such topics. With this in mind, we resolved to obtain some first-hand commentaries from representatives of two groups that are most integrally involved in the actual application of the teacher-assessment process: the administrators who administer the evaluation programs and often conduct the evaluations, and the teachers who are the objects of the evaluation and profit or suffer from them. To represent the administrator's perspective we selected John Hoyle of the Department of Educational Administration of Texas A&M University; to represent the teacher's perspective we selected Peg Shafer, who has been a teacher and who now represents teachers in her capacity as a teachers' union official. At the panel discussion I chaired at the conclusion of the symposium, I asked whether the researchers and the practitioners were speaking the same language when they discussed the topic of teacher assessment. There was a difference of opinion in response to that question; my personal opinion is that there is still an appreciable gap in communication and understanding. Readers may have felt that they were entering a different world as they read the Hoyle and Shafer contributions. Earlier we discussed the reality testing that Darling-Hammond required of us. Hoyle and Shafer force us into a reality-testing mode again, and with a vengeance. But the shock of reality testing is good for us, because it forces us to recognize that all the theorizing, researching, and discussion comes to naught unless it leads to practical outcomes that are sound in practice and facilitative of improvement.

In speaking from the administrator's perspective John Hoyle sounds the first jarring note when he asserts that the school principals who are required to do much of the teacher evaluation have only haphazard training at best in teacher evaluation, do not have the time to do an adequate job of teacher evaluation, and often feel there is a conflict between their evaluation and supervision roles. As a result the job typically doesn't get done very well. It seems that principals are not really obtaining a realistic grasp of what is going on in the classroom, either; it is interesting that he reports that one of the criticisms of the Texas Teacher Appraisal System was that "Teachers put on a good show when they are being observed because the criteria are so specific and fairly easy to follow" (p. 319). There is obviously a certain amount of game playing going on here, and it would be foolish not to recognize it as a source of invalidity in teacher evaluations. It also constitutes a good reason for "involvement of the teachers in the entire developmental evaluation process" (p. 316), which is the first recommendation of the "One Best Model" format for a successful evaluation system.

The One Best Model system contains some recommendations that seem quite sound to me and may have some potential for reducing the gap between theory, research, and practice. They are worth quoting in their entirety:

> (a) involvement of the teachers in the entire developmental evaluation process, (b) performance criteria based on sound research and on local needs and concerns, (c) collaborative goal setting, (d) multidimensional methods for assessing teachers' skills, (e) careful analysis of data gathered in the assessment stage, (f) development of specific job targets, and (g) inclusion of a preobservation conference to acquire background data and a postobservation conference to mutually analyze classroom data and set goals for improvement. (p. 316)

There are certain features of these suggestions that recommend themselves because they effectively acknowledge the state of the art and the limits thereto. The involvement of teachers in the entire developmental evaluation process is good because it involves teachers in working with the system instead of against it. Performance criteria based on sound research and on local needs and concerns are good because they require a careful evaluation of available research and its practical utility, and the further recognition that value choice of criteria based on local needs and concerns is a perfectly legitimate practice if it is recognized for what it is—value choice. Collaborative goal setting is good because it again involves the teacher working with instead of against the system, and also emphasizes what may be by far the most important component of any evaluation system: the setting of goals for the future. Multidimensional methods for assessing teachers' skills are good because they implicitly acknowledge that any method or instrument is subject to its own peculiar error and criticism, and that there is greater safety in using multiple methods that can cast light on construct validity and counterbalance error. The development of specific job targets is good because it again focuses not on evaluation for evaluation's sake but rather on the all-important goals for future improvement. Maybe we can't always evaluate very well, but *any* evaluation that produces the outcome of a convinced teacher setting important professional goals has achieved the most important outcome of all.

One of the most interesting statements in the Hoyle chapter for

11. THE ASSESSMENT OF TEACHER ASSESSMENT 371

me is the statement that "any teacher evaluation form should include the following indicators:

- motivates students to achieve
- uses academic learning time effectively
- demonstrates proficiency in subject areas
- demonstrates command of the language
- promotes student academic growth
- learning objectives are clear
- learning strategies are based on objectives
- testing is based on objectives (p. 324)

The reason this statement was of such interest to me was that it seemed to illustrate several things about teacher-evaluation programs that are important to recognize. First, the list includes several items that almost no one would argue are not desirable for a teacher to exhibit. Second, in spite of the foregoing sentence many (perhaps the majority of) people would probably create a list of their own that would differ somewhat in terms of what was included and excluded and what the overall emphasis was. Third, there is nothing in this list that is mandated by research (including research on the prediction of student achievement), with the possible exception of time-on-task research. Fourth, when this list is examined in relation to the foregoing statements, the importance of *value choice* in defining teacher effectiveness emerges more potently than ever before. Many of the values represented are so general and generally accepted that they probably don't even stimulate much thought; the items they represent may be so general and vague that they are equally difficult to evaluate (e.g., "promotes student academic growth"). Other items are based on state-of-the-art ideology; the last three items, for example, all relate to *objectives;* yet I dare say you could identify teachers of excellence that would not rank high on these items and would yet deserve the label of *excellent* teacher. This again relates to the "shifting criterion" of teacher effectiveness mentioned earlier in this chapter; there may be 1,001 ways to be an effective teacher, and 1,001 ways to be an ineffective teacher. Into this mass of teacher behaviors you insert certain vectors that represent value-laden items, and if a given teacher has high loadings on the vectors you have inserted, that teacher is labeled a *superior, average,* or *inferior* teacher, as the case may be. But there is an interaction between the vectors chosen and teacher behavior such that one's standing could vary from system to system, with repercussions of consequence. Notice what happens, for example, if I should enter the notion of "discipline" into the aforementioned list. In today's educational climate many would protest that my ideology was wrong, my values were wretched, my items were atavistic and inappropriate, and my intent was malicious. The maliciousness of my intent, however, is limited only to illustrating the importance of *value choice* in the defining of teacher effectiveness and its measurement. In the absence of definitive research, value choices, pure and simple, step in to fill the gap.

Peg Shafer's chapter "Appraisal: The Teacher's Perspective" may have impressed some readers as being comprehensively negative about most or all forms of teacher appraisal. Peg Shafer's presence in person at the symposium, however, projected a somewhat different image from Peg Shafer's words in writing. Her presentation was characterized by cordiality, spontaneity, vigor, and a deep commitment to realism and honesty. Here is a person who is very deeply identified with teachers and their aspirations, needs, and problems, and she intends to "tell it like it is" and set the record straight. As a well-respected and effective leader of teachers she provides us with a striking opportunity to perceive appraisal issues as those do who are most affected by them. When we planned this symposium and book, we decided it was important to have this point of view, and we got it in full measure. Anyone who ignores teacher reactions as Peg Shafer describes them might as well give up all hope of effecting a valid teacher-evaluation system. As she says in her own inimitable manner, "If teachers believe in their hearts that appraisal is a farce, they will scuttle the plan in their churches, the grocery stores, their neighborhoods, and everywhere they feel safe to speak their minds" (p. 341). That's not advice to be taken lightly.

There is a great deal said in this chapter, and it is impossible for me to comment on it all; instead I shall briefly discuss some issues that particularly piqued my interest as I read the chapter. One point I may have known before but perhaps did not recognize for its widespread implications is that teachers often perceive teacher-evaluation programs as public relations gimmicks. It also appears that the more "farcical" the evaluation program is in their eyes, the more it is perceived as PR. It would be wrong to dismiss this as mere cynicism, because this attitude undoubtedly contains at least some measure of truth. Principals may also have doubts about the validity or utility of some teacher-evaluation programs, but they go through the motions because the motions represent a response, whether adequate or not, to the public's cry for getting rid of the incompetents and identifying superior teachers for reward. Public dissatisfaction with schools and teachers must somehow be responded to, and a teacher-evaluation system may be regarded as a good first line of defense, or at least one of them. What all this underscores is that a teacher-evaluation system must be perceived as having some inherent real benefits for teachers in order to compensate for an apparently ubiquitous and strong tendency for them to perceive such systems as mere PR. If it is not realistic to assume that teacher-evaluation systems can have real benefits for teachers, then passive-aggressive behavior will be the likely result and the "selling" job will be correspondingly difficult. Teacher-evaluation programs perceived by teachers and others as mostly PR mechanisms define a setting ripe for disgruntlement and low morale.

Another issue that had tremendous import for me was well expressed by two excerpts from the Shafer presentation:

> From the belief that a model of good teaching exists, the public can take the short step to the harmful conclusion that anyone can teach if they possess a passable knowledge of a subject and are able to emulate the behaviors in the model. They can erroneously conclude that any deviation from the model must be faulty.... (p. 333).
>
> The worst news I have for you today is that so far, teachers have not bought into the recent changes in teacher evaluation. Teachers sense danger and they have circled their wagons. The clearest danger is that researchers and testing experts are searching for ways to reduce teaching to paper so that we can convince the public that we can control and improve the way teachers perform. But teachers know that nothing unique and exceptional ever grew from a dry formula. Creativity and flair can't be standardized. Painting by number has never produced any masterpieces. Resistance to "recipes" for improvement is growing every day, and there is massive resistance to standardized methods of teaching, both from individuals and organizations. (pp. 336–337)

These two passages are reminiscent of the "shifting criterion" I have occasionally referred to as constituting a problem for teacher evaluation and my conjecture, colloquially expressed, that there may be 1,001 ways to be an effective teacher and 1,001 ways to be an ineffective teacher. You cannot fault teachers for concluding that teaching is an art rather than a science; many of them have concluded that the science we have offered them is conflicting and inconclusive and of little help. To the extent that any teacher-evaluation system presents or implies a rather singular model for effective teaching, they may have a right to rebel. As a university teacher I would rebel myself. Shafer is right to say that "Creativity and flair can't be standardized." But it can be thwarted by evaluation systems that rigidly define by competencies or otherwise what an effective teacher is, and then leave little room or acknowledgment for departures from the standard ideal that may be as effective or more effective than what was originally defined. If teacher-evaluation systems turn out to be procrustean beds fashioned by people who claim to know, on insufficient evidence, what "the" effective teacher is, the rank-and-file teacher has a right to be disbelieving and defensive.

Many people who read Shafer's chapter may conclude that she and the teachers she represents are being *too* defensive. They may be right. But the concerns that Shafer describes must be carefully attended to for purposes of good communication. One of the often-stated standard requirements of an effective teacher-evaluation program is that teachers should be an integral part of the developmental process for such a program. If that is so, teachers should be heard, and heard well. Shafer has helped us to hear them well.

This completes my discussion of the contributions made by chapter authors to this book on teacher assessment. These authors have addressed varied topics and have certainly provided a wide variety of professional judgments and opinions. My own comments have also been wide ranging; as a former dean of a college of education, a vice president for academic affairs, director of the Buros Institute of Mental Measurements, and now a university professor again, I have had the benefit of many different perspectives, and these different perspectives undoubtedly came into play as I reacted to a topic as encompassing and with as many ramifications as this one. Much work still remains to be done in this area, and we have tried to consider some of the questions to be addressed for further progress to occur. The title of this chapter makes reference to concluding thoughts and lingering questions about this topic of teacher assessment. If I were to summarize these concluding thoughts and lingering questions with a few broad statements, those statements would include the following:

1. There is great danger in oversimplifying the task of teacher assessment, or allowing the hazardous oversimplification of the teacher assessment task by the public.

2. The appeal to face validity in teacher-assessment tasks may bring satisfaction in the short term but invalid inferences as a final outcome.

3. Any teacher-evaluation system must allow for multiple "correct" responses that do justice to the complexity of teaching and acknowledge that there are many *patterns* of teaching behavior that can be designated as "effective" teaching.

4. The validation of teacher-assessment instruments and procedures is fraught with many difficulties, and there is a difference of opinion among measurement professionals about what kinds of evidence are acceptable and required.

5. The determination of cut scores and the validity of cut-score decisions continue to be major issues with most teacher-assessment tests.

6. Many factors other than teacher behaviors have profound effects on student learning, and any teacher-assessment system that does not take this into account is closing it eyes to reality and confounding its efforts to predict.

7. The legal, political, social, and organizational context of teacher-assessment efforts has immense impact on what is developed and the nature of its consequences.

8. In the absence of definitive scientific findings, value choice plays a significant role in the selection of variables for the development and implementation of teacher assessment programs.

9. The attitudes of teachers and principals to a teacher-assessment program can make a tremendous difference in its acceptance, validity, and consequences; teachers are truly the "make or break" agents in the implementation of a teacher-assessment program.

10. Clear communication among the many parties interested in teacher assessment is critical; at the present time such communication is in short supply, and both teacher assessment and the democratic process suffer as a result.

I hope the present volume has helped to meet the critical need expressed in this last statement for clarification of issues and facilitation of communication.

REFERENCES

American Educational Research Association, American Psychological Association, & National Council on Measurement in Education. (1985). *Standards for educa-*

tional and psychological testing. Washington, DC: American Psychological Association.

Bush, R. N. (1979). Implications of the BTES. *The Generator, 9*(1), 13–15.

Dewey, J. (1949). *Experience and education.* New York: Macmillan.

Doyle, W. (1979). Classroom tasks and students' abilities. In P. L. Peterson & H. J. Walberg (Eds.), *Research on teaching* (pp. 183–209). Berkeley, CA: McCutchan.

Knapp, M. S. (1982). *Toward the study of teacher evaluation as an organizational process: A review of current research and practice.* Menlo Park, CA: Educational and Human Services Research Center, SRI International.

Piper, M. K., & O'Sullivan, P. S. (1981). The National Teacher Examination: Can it predict classroom performance? *Phi Delta Kappan, 62*(5), 401.

Quirk, T. J., Witten, B. J., & Weinberg, S. F. (1973). Review of studies of the concurrent and predictive validity of the National Teacher Examinations. *Review of Educational Research, 43*(1), 89–113.

Rudner, L. M. (1988). Teacher testing—An update. *Educational Measurement: Issues and Practice, 7*(1), 16–19.

Task Force on Teaching as a Profession. (1986). *A nation prepared: Teachers for the 21st century.* Hyattsville, MD: Carnegie Forum on Education and the Economy.

Webb, L. D. (1983). Teacher evaluation. In S. B. Thomas, N. H. Cambron-McCabe, & M. M. McCarthy (Eds.), *Educators and the Law* (pp. 69–80). Elmont, NY: Institute for School Law and Finance.

Author Index

A

Abeles, S., 18, *35*
Aburto, S., 22, *34*
Acheson, K. A., 311, *326*
Adams, N. E., 173, *176*
Adams, P. T., 47, *75*
Aickin, M., 217, *257*
Airasian, P. W., 283, *303*
Alabama State Board of Education, 81, *129*
American Educational Research Association, 8, *14,* 28, *34,* 83, 85, 86, 88, 97, 98, 102, 105, 106, 107, 109, 119, 125, 126, 127, *129,* 227, 246, 247, *256,* 267, 268, 269, 277, 282, 286, 298, *300,* 359, *375*
American Psychological Association, 8, *14,* 28, *34,* 83, 85, 86, 88, 92, 97, 98, 102, 105, 106, 107, 109, 119, 125, 126, 127, *129,* 227, 246, 247, *256,* 267, 268, 269, 277, 282, 286, 298, *300,* 359, *375*
Anderson, B. D., 146, *176*
Anderson, C. S., 174, *176*
Angoff, W. H., 285, 287, *300*
Applegate, J. M., 49, *75*
Armor, D., 173, *176*
Aylesworth, M. S., 55, *75*
Ayres, Q. W., 105, *129*

B

Bacharach, S. B., 264, *300*
Baker, G., 321, *327*
Baldus, D., 217, *256*
Bales, J., 252, *256*
Baltes, P. B., 290, *304*
Bandura, A., 173, 174, *176*
Baron, J. B., 18, *35*
Beady, C., 281, *301*
Beaton, A. E., 279, *303*
Beatty, R. W., 275, *300*
Beckham, J. C., 148, 149, *176*
Benson, C. S., 281, *300*
Bereiter, C., 288, *300*
Berk, R. A., 32, *34,* 84, 98, 118, *129,* 251, *256,* 277, 278, 282, 283, 285, 286, *300*
Berliner, D. C., 43, 51, *74,* 102, *129,* 142, 151, *177, 178*
Berman, P., 150, 168, 173, *177,* 315, *326*
Bernardin, H. J., 275, *300*
Bernstein, H., 154, 161, 162, *181*
Berry, B., 148, 162, *177, 181*
Betz, N. E., 173, *177*
Bickel, W., 247, *257*
Biddle, B. J., 145, *178*
Biniaminov, I., 277, 278, 279, 280, 281, *301*
Bird, T., 23, *35*
Bloom, B. S., 95, *129*
Boardman, A. E., 279, *300*
Bodine, R., 174, *177*
Bond, L., 88, *129*
Bower, R., 283, *301*
Boyd, D. R., 121, 127, *129*
Brandt, D., 290, 291, *304*

377

AUTHOR INDEX

Brennan, R. L., 84, 129, *130*
Bridge, R. G., 277, 281, *301*
Bridgeford, N. J., 317, *327*
Bridges, E. M., 17, *34*
Brinkerhof, R. O., 63, *75*
Brookover, W., 173, *177*, 281, *301*
Brophy, J. E., 66, *75*, 145, *177*, 289, *301*
Broudy, H. S., 141, 142, *177*
Brown, I., Jr., 173, *177*
Bryk, A. S., 291, *301*
Bull, B., 149, *180*, 276, *305*
Burke, B. T., 310, *326*
Burns, R. L., 91, *130*
Buros, O. K., 248, *256*
Burry, J. A., *258*
Busch, 123
Bush, R. N., 145, *177*, 362, *376*
Bushman, J. H., 174, *177*

C

Caldwell, M. S., 64, *75*
Calhoun, F. S., 264, *301*
Cameron, D., 79, *130*
Campbell, D.T., 291, 292, *301*
Capie, W., 47, *75*, 154, *178*
Carey, N. B., 308, *326*
Carlson, H. S., 113, *130*
Carlson, R. E., 79, *130*
Carnegie Task Force, 79, 80, 121, *130*
Carroll, L., 209, *256*
Cascio, W. F., 275, *301*
Celotti, L. D., 175, *178*
Centra, J. A., 146, *177*, 277, *301*
Cogan, M. L., 311, *326*
Cohen, D. K., 261, 266, *301, 304*
Cohen, E., 171, *177*
Cohen, J., 296, *301*
Cohen, M., 175, *177*
Cohn, E., 277, 281, *301*
Coker, H., 55, *75*, 145, *177*, 266, 276, 277, 278, 285, *303*, 314, *327*
Cole, J., 217, *256*
Coleman, J. S., 105, *130*
Collins, J., 173, *177*, 243, *259*
Collins, J. L., 91, 92, *136*
Colton, D., 92, 93, 95, *130, 132*
Colton, T., 252, *256*
Commerce Clearing House, Inc., *256*
Conry-Oseguera, P., 173, *176*

Consalvo, R. W., 283, *303*
Coody, C. S., 121, 127, *129*
Cook, T. D., 291, 292, *301*
Cooley, W., 247, *257*
Cooley, W. W., 284, *302*
Copelin, L., 238, *257*
Corder-Bolz, C. R., 290, *301*
Cork, B., 238, *257*
Corrigan, D. C., 48, *75*
Cox, M., 173, *176*
Cronbach, L. & Associates, 247, *257*
Cronbach, L. J., 86, 90, 94, 102, 112, *130*, 145, 278, 288, *301*
Cross, L. H., 122, *130*
Cross, R., 319, *327*
Cruickshank, D. R., 49, *75*
Cureton, E. E., 283, *301*

D

Damarin, F., 290, *305*
Darling-Hammond, L., 80, 108, *130*, 140, 148, 152, 154, 156, 161, 162, 248, *257*
Davis, O. A., 279, *300*
D'Costa, A. G., 109, *130*
Deal, T., 170, 171, *177*
Deal, T. E., 175, *178*
Deci, E. L., 174, *178*
Dembo, T., 173, *179*
Dempsey-Atwood, N., 142, 145, 147, 147n, 158, *180*
Denemark, G. W., 48, *75*
Denham, C., 43, *75*
Dewey, J., 348, *376*
DiClemente, C. C., 173, *178*
Dornbusch, S. M., 171, 174, *178, 179*
Downs, S. L., 126, *130*
Doyle, R. W., 178, *376*
Doyle, W., 145, 146, *362*
Duke, D. L., 199, 199n
Dunbar, S. B., 291, *303*
Dunkin, M. J., 145, *178*
Durham, R. L., 275, *302*

E

Ebel, R. L., 85, 96, 102, 103, 104, 105, *130, 131*
Echternacht, G., 93, *131*

Educational Testing Service, 109, 124, *131*, *257*
Eignor, D. R., 283, *302*
Eisdorfer, S., 88, *131*
Eisner, E. W., 142, 143, *178*
Ekstrom, R. B., 112, *131*
Elias, P., 145, *179*
Ellett, C., 47, *75*
Ellett, C. D., 154, *178*
Elliot, S. M., 93, 94, *131*
Elman, A., 294, *301*
Elmore, R. T., 150, *178*
Englert, R. M., 168, *178*
English, F. W., 312, 315, 316, 322, *326*
Epstein, J. L., 307, *326*
Equal Employment Opportunity Commission, Civil Service Commission, Department of Labor and Department of Justice, 92, *131*
Estes, C., 92, 93, 95, *132*
ETS Visiting Committee, 245, *257*
Evendon, E. S., 261, *301*
Evertson, C., 145, *177*

F

Feiman, S., 152, *178*
Feldt, L. S., 85, *131*
Feldvebel, A. M., 152, *178*
Fenstermacher, G. D., 151, 172, *178*
Festinger, L., 173, *179*
Finley, C. J., 294, *301*
Finn, C. E., 307, 309, *327*
Flanagan, J. C., 285, *301*
Floden, R. E., 152, *178,* 283, 284, 285, *305*
Flood, P., 281, *301*
Forgione, P. D., Jr., 18, *35,* 92, *133*
Fredericksen, N., 19, *34*
Freeman, D. J., 283, 284, 285, *305*
Freeman, H. E., 168, *180*
Freeman, L. D., 80, *131*
Frymier, J., 313, 314, *326*
Fuller, B., 171, 174, *178*
Furby, L., 288, *301*
Furst, N., 144, *180*

G

Gabrys, R. E., 79, 126, *131*
Gage, N. L., 143, 144, 145, *178*

Galambos, E. C., 89, *131*
Gallup, G. H., 79, 122, *131,* 148, *178*
Gifford, B. R., 121, 126, *131*
Glasman, N. S., 277, 278, 279, 280, 281, *301*
Glasnapp, D. R., *258*
Glass, G. V., 32, *34,* 89, *131*
Goertz, M. E., 112, *131,* 251, *257*
Gonzales, M. A., 319, *327*
Good, 172
Good, T. L., 66, *75*
Gorth, W. P., 124, *135*
Gramenz, G. W., 283, *302*
Green, D. R., 282, *302*
Gronlund, N. E., 96, *131*
Grossman, P., 218, 226, 230, 231, *258*
Guerrero, T., 319, *327*
Guion, R. M., 86, *132*
Gupta, N. C., 85, *131*

H

Hackett, G., 173, *177*
Haefele, D. L., 154, *178*
Haertel, E., 105, *132,* 267, 277, 280, 281, 287, *302*
Haertel, E. H., 22, 23, *34*
Hall, B. W., 127, *132*
Hallinger, P., 313, *327*
Hambleton, R. K., 84, 97, *132,* 283, *302*
Haney, W., 231, 241, 248, 250, 251, 252, 253, *257*
Hanushek, E. A., 279, *302*
Hardy, A. B., 173, *176*
Hardy, R., 284, *302*
Harnisch, D. L., 291, *303*
Harnischfeger, A., 281, *305*
Hastings, C. N., 291, *303*
Hastings, J. T., 95, *129*
Hayes, L. J., 59, *75*
Hecht, K. A., 101, *132*
Hersey, P. W., 22, *34*
Hildrup, R. P., 79, *132*
Hills, J. R., 96, *132*
Hoffman, P. E., 140, *180*
Holmes Group, The, 79, 80, *132*
Hopkins, K. D., 96, *132,* 283, *302*
Horst, D. P., 286, 291, 294, *302*
Howells, G. N., 173, *176*
Howsam, R. B., 48, *75*

Hoyle, J. R., 309, 315, 316, 322, *326*
Huff, D., 219, *257*
Hunter, J. E., 119, *134*
Hunter, M., 315, *326*

IJ

Innes, A. H., 55, *75*
Inouye, D. K., 173, *177*
IOX Assessment Associates, 32, *35*
Jackson, P. W., 49, *75*
Jaeger, 123
Jaeger, R. M., 118, 120, *132*
Jenkins, J. R., 283, *302*
Jensen, A., 241, *257*
Johnson, C. E., 47, *75,* 154, *178*
Johnson, R. C., 283, *302*
Johnson, S. M., 310, *326*
Johnson, S. T., 101, *132*
Joint Committee on Standards for Educational Evaluation, 267, 270, 271, 273, 277, *302*
Jones, B. G., 283, *302*
Joyce, B. R., 146, *178*
Judd, C. M., 277, 281, *301*

K

Kane, M., 93, *130*
Kane, M. T., 84, 88, 91, 92, 93, 94, 95, 102, 107, 108, *132*
Kauchak, D., 145, 149, 152, 154, *179*
Kaye, D. H., 217, *257*
Kazdin, A. E., 173, *178*
Kean, M. H., 168, *178*
Kerchner, C. T., 142, 149, *179*
Kerr, M. E., 105, *133*
Kiesling, H. J., 281, *302*
King, N., 173, *176*
Kingsbury, C., 92, 93, 95, *132*
Kirby, B., 320, *326*
Kleiman, L. S., 275, *302*
Kleine, P. F., 148, *178*
Knapp, M. S., 145, 150, 152, 168, 174, 175, *178*, 363, *376*
Koenigsberg, R. G., 108, 121, *134*
Koerner, J. D., 248, *257*
Kounin, J. S., 51, 61, *75*
Kreitzer, A., 231, 241, 248, 250, 251, 252, 253
Kreitzer, A. E., 100, *134*

L

Landholm, L. J., 22, *35*
Lareau, A., 19, *35*
Leblebici, H., 174, *179*
Lehmann, I. J,. 87, 96, 106, *133*
Leinhardt, G., 284, 285, *302*
Levin, H. M., 279, *302*
Levin, J. R., 296, *305*
Lewin, K., 173, *179*
Lewis, A., 149, 154, *179*
Lewis, A. C., 315, *326*
Lieberman, A., 43, *75*
Light, R., 253, *257*
Linn, R. L., 88, 102, 106, 118, *132,* 286, 287, 288, 289, 291, 294, *303*
Lipsky, D. B., 264, *300*
Lipsky, M, 168, *180*
Livingston, S. A., 84, 118, *132*
Lord, F. M., 288, 290, *303*
Lortie, D., 141, *179*
Lowther, M. A., 102, *105*

M

Madaus, G., 231, 241, 248, 250, 251, 252, 253, *257*
Madaus, G. F., 95, *129,* 215, 241, 248, 251, *257,* 283, *303*
Madaus, G. M., 241, 242, 246, 248, *257*
Manatt, R., 309, 316, *326*
Manatt, R. P., 78, *135*
Mann, D., 168, *179*
March, J., 175, *177*
March, J. G. 170, *179*
Maughan, B., 173, *180*
Mayeske, G. W., 279, *303*
Mazmanian, D., 168, *180*
McCarthy, M. M., 226, *257*
McCloseky, M., 20, *35*
McClung, M. S., 283, 284, *303*
McDonald, F. J., 145, *179*
McDonnell, L., 149, 173, 176, *179*
McFague, S., 240, *257*
McKenna, B. H., 146, *179*
McLaughlin, M., 154, 161, 162, *181*
McLaughlin, M. W., 150, 168, 173, *177,* 307, 315, *326*
McNergney, R. F., 55, 64, *75*
McPhee, S. A., 105, *133*
Medley, D., 145, *177,* 314, *327*

Medley, D. M., 55, 63, 64, *75,* 80, 106, *133,* 144, 155, *179,* 266, 276, 277, 278, 285, *303*
Mehrens, W. A., 79, 80, 87, 96, 106, 124, *133,* 282, *303*
Melnick, S. L., 248, *257, 258*
Messick, S., 290, *305*
Messick, S. A., 86, *133*
Meyer, J., 170, 171, *177*
Meyer, M. H., 174, *179*
Michelson, S., 279, *303*
Miller, M. D., 88, *132, 258*
Millman, J., 83, 95, 96, 99, 125, 126, *133,* 154
Millman, S. D., 277, 281, *301*
Mitchell, D. E., 142, 149, *179*
Mitchell, J. V., Jr., 231n, *258*
Mook, P. R., 277, 281, *301*
Moore, B. C., 265, *303*
Mortimore, P., 173, *180*
Mosier, C. I., 11, *14*
Munnelly, R. J., 152, *179*
Murnane, R. J., 261, 266, 280, *304*
Murphy, J., 313, *327*
Murray, S. L., 3n, *14*

N

Nash, R. J., 48, *75*
Nassif, P. M., 97, *133*
Nathan, B. R., 275, *304*
National Council on Measurement in Education, 8, *14,* 28, *34,* 83, 85, 86, 88, 97, 98, 102, 105, 106, 107, 109, 119, 125, 126, 127, *129,* 227, 246, 247, *256,* 267, 268, 269, 277, 282, 286, 298, *300,* 359, *375*
National Evaluation Systems, 100, *133*
Natriello, G., 171, *179*
Nelson, J., 94, *131*
Nesselroade, J. R., 290, *304*
Nitko, A. J., 96, *133*
North Carolina State Department of Public Instruction, 310, 311, *327*
Novick, M., 26, *258*
Novick, M. R., 84, *132*
NTE Policy Council, 210n, 226, 230, *258*

O

O'Connor, E. F., 288, 289, *304*
Okey, J. R., 47, *75*

Orlandi, L. R., 283, *303*
O'Sullivan, P. S., 104, *133,* 360, *376*
Ouchi, W.G., 174, *179*
Ouston, J., 173, *180*
Overall, J. E., 190, *304*
Owens, R., 316, *327*

PQ

Pany, D., 283, *302*
Pascal, A., 149, 173, *176, 179*
Pauly, E., 173, *176*
Pearson, D., 319, *327*
Pease, S. R., 80, 108, *130*
Pecheone, R. L., 18, *35,* 92, *133*
Pencavel, J. H., 266, *304*
Peterson, K. D., 102, *133,* 307, 309, 313, 314, *327*
Peterson, P., 145, 149, 152, 154, *179*
Peterson, P. L., 145, *179*
Pfeffer, J., 174, *179*
Pigford, A. B., 321, *327*
Piper, M. K., 104, *133,* 360, *376*
Pitcher, B., 251, *257*
Poggio, J. P., 218, 219n, 221, 222, 223n, *258*
Popham, W. J., 87, 96, 97, *133, 136,* 243, *259,* 284, *304*
Porter, A. C., 283, 284, 285, *304*
Porwoll, P. J., 261, *304*
Potter, D. A., 146, *177,* 277, *301*
Pottinger, P. S., 63, *75,* 96, 119, *133*
Power, 172
Poynor, L., 284, *304*
Pratt, D., 78, *134*
Prom-Jackson, S., 101, *132*
Protheroe, N. J., 264, *301*
Pullin, D., 241, 242, 246, 248, *257, 258*
Quirk, T. J., 57, *75,* 350, *376*

R

Rapoport, T., 171, 174, *178*
Raudenbush, S. W., 291, *301*
Rebell, M. A., 108, 121, *134*
Rein, M., 168, *179*
Rentz, R., 218, 219, 219n, 220, 221, 222, 223, 223n, 224, 226, *258*
Richards, J. M., Jr., 290, *304*
Riley, R. D., 174, *179*

AUTHOR INDEX

Roberts, A. O. H., 294, *304*
Robinson, G. E., 264, *304*
Rogosa, D. R., 290, 291, *304*
Roid, G. H., 97, 134
Rosen, G. A., 102, *134*
Rosenblum, E. P., 64, *75*
Rosenfeld, M., 91, 114, *134*
Rosenholtz, S. J., 174, *180*
Rosenshine, B., 144, *180*, 289, *305*
Rossi, P. H., 168, *180*
Roth, R., 110, *134*
Roueche, J., 321, *327*
Rovinelli, R. J., 97, *134*
Rudner, L. M., 347, 350, *376*
Rulon, P. J., 87, *134*
Russell, J. T., 253, *258*
Rutter, M., 173, *180*
Ryon, J. H., 319, *327*

S

Sabatier, P., 168, *180*
Salancik, G., 174, *179*
Sanday, P. R., 279, *300*
Sandufer, J. T., 17, *35*
Sax, G., 96, *134*
Schaffer, E. C., 174, *179*
Schlei, B. L., 218, 226, 230, 231, *258*
Schmeiser, C. B., 95, *134*
Schmidt, F. L., 119, *134*
Schmidt, W. H., 283, 284, 285, *305*
Schunk, D. H., 173, *176*
Schweitzer, J., 281, *301*
Schwille, J. R., 283, 284, 285, *305*
Scott, R., 170, 171, *177*
Scott, W. R., 174, *178*
Scribner, J. D., 168, *178*
Scriven, M., 80, *134*
Sears, P. 173, *179*
Sechrest, L., 140, *180*
Seewald, A. M., 284, *302*
Seiler, E., 266, *305*
Shanker, A., 79, 82, *134*, 309
Shannon, G. A., 124, 125, 126, *134*
Shavelson, R., 141, 142, 145, 147, 147*n*, 158, *180*
Shearron, G. F., 63, *75*
Shedd, J. B., 264, *300*
Shepard, L. A., 32, *35*, 100, *134*
Shimberg, B., 3*n*, *14*, 88, 95, 101, 102, 113, 114, 118, 119, *134*, *135*

Shulman, L. S., 3, 6, *14*, 18, 19, 23, 25, *35*, 80, 82, 91, *135*
Silvestro, J. R., 126, *130*
Skurnik, L. S., 91, *134*
Slinde, J. A., 288, 289, *303*
Smith, A., 173, *180*
Smith, B. O., 51, 61, 62, *75*, *76*
Snow, R. E., 145, 177, 278, *301*
Soar, R., 145, *177*
Soar, R. M., 278, 285, *305*
Soar, R. S., 55, *75*, 145, *180*, 266, 276, 277, 278, 285, *305*
Southern Regional Education Board, 261, 263, 264, 295, *305*
Sproull, L. S., 168, 171, *180*
Sroufe, 168
Stallings, J. A., 144, *180*
Stanley, J. C., 96, *132*, 283, 291, *301*, *302*
Stark, J. S., 102, *135*
Steffen, M., 85, *131*
Steffy, B. E., 315, 316, 322, *326*
Stern, P., 142, *180*
Stiggins, R. J., 187, 187*n*, 199, 199*n*, 317, *327*
Stigler, S. M., 290, *304*
Stodolsky, S., 158, *180*
Stone, C. N., 168, *180*
Strike, K., 149, *180*, 276, *305*
Subkoviak, M. J., 84, *135*, 296, *305*
Summers, A. A., 279, 280, *305*
Sweeney, J., 78, *135*
Sykes, G., 3, 14, 121, *135*

T

Talbert, J., 174, *180*
Tallmadge, G. K., 286, 291, 294, 297, *305*
Task Force on Teaching as a Profession, 18, *35*, 351, *376*
Taylor, H. C., 253, *258*
Tenopyr, M. L., 86, *135*
Texas Teacher Appraisal System Teacher Orientation Manual, 318, 320, *327*
Thompson, J. E., 174, *180*
Thornton, R. F., 91, 114, *134*
Tirrell, F. J., 308, *327*
Tittle, C. K., 98, *135*
Tollefson, N., *258*
Tomala, G., 92, *133*
Tractenberg, P., 88, *131*
Traub, R. E., 84, 85, *135*

AUTHOR INDEX

Trotter, G., 238, *258*
Tucker, L. R., 290, *305*
Turbayne, C. M., 240, *258*

U

U. S. Civil Service Commission, 92, *135,* 217, *258,* 268, 273, 274, *305*
U. S. Department of Health, Education and Welfare, 82, *135*
U. S. Department of Justice, 217, *258,* 268, 273, 274, *305*
U. S. Department of Labor, 268, 273, 274, *305*
U. S. Equal Employment Opportunity Commission, 217, *258,* 268, 273, 274, *305*

V

Vance, N. C., 64, *75*
Vertiz, V. C., 88, *135*
Vlaanderen, R., 147, *180*
Vold, D. J., 79, 100, *135*
Vorwerk, K. E., 124, *135*
Vroom, V., 173, *180*

W

Watts, G. D., 121, *135*
Weatherley, R., 168, *180*
Weaver, J. R., 126, *135*
Webb, L. D., 102, *136,* 358, 359, *376*
Webster, H., 288, *305*
Webster, W. J., 104, *136*
Weick, K. E., 170, 171, 176, *180, 181*
Weil, M., 146, *178*

Weinberg, S. F., 57, *75,* 350, *376*
Werner, E., 113, *136*
Wigdor, Alexandra, 226, *258*
Wildavsky, A., 168, *181*
Wiley, D. E., 279, 280, 281, *305*
Willett, J. B., 290, 291, *305*
Williams, R. H., 289, 290, *306*
Williams, T. B., 286, *306*
Williamson, J. W., 93, *136*
Wilson, Ann Jarvela, 229n, *259*
Wilson, B., 174, *180*
Wilson, S. M., 22, *35*
Winkler, D. R., 279, *306*
Wise, A., 141, 148, 152, 154, 156, 161, 162, *181*
Wise, A. E., 80, 108, *130*
Wisenbaker, J., 281, *301*
Wisniewski, R., 148, *178*
Witten, B. J., 57, 75, 350, *376*
Wolfe, B. L., 279, *280*
Wolfe, B. W., *305*
Wood, B. D., 87, *136*
Wood, C. T., 286, 291, *302*
Wood, K., 171, 174, *178*
Woodward, J. A., 290, *304*
Wright, S. R., 168, *180*

YZ

Yalow, E., 243, *259*
Yalow, E. S., 87, 91, 92, *136,* 284, *306*
Young, R., 308, *327*
Zellman, G., 173, *176*
Zieky, M. J., 118, *132*
Zigmond, N., 284, *302*
Zimmerman, D. W., 289, 290, *306*
Zimowski, M., 290, 291, *304*

Subject Index

A

AASPB, 114
Academic Learning Time (ALT), 324
Administrators, 316-317, 321, 324
  See also Principals
Admissions Research, 45-46
Adverse Impact, 217-225, 227
Affective Variables, 355-356
Albemarle Paper Co. v. Moody, 217, 232
Allen v. The Alabama State Board of Education, 129, 214-215, 227, 232, 234-236, 238, 241n, 242, 248
Applied Testing, 242-245, 255
Appraisal Reform, 330, 341
Arkansas Educational Skills Assessment (AESA), 11

B

Beginning Educator Support and Training (BEST), 18
Beginning Teacher Assistance Program (BTAP), 59-60, 63-64, 69, 71-73, 356
Beginning Teacher Competence, 65-66
Beginning Teacher Evaluation Study, 145
Beginning Teacher Programs, 148
Best Practice of the Profession, 65-66
Bias, 29-30

Biographical Information, 10-11
Board Certification, 31, 33
Bureaucratic Mentality, 313
Buros Institute of Mental Measurements, 347

C

Career Advancement, 185-187, 203-205
Career Ladder, 5, 9, 261-265, 312-313, 319-320
Carnegie Corporation of New York, 15, 18
Castaneda v. Partida, 220-224
Certification, 3, 17-18, 82-83, 96
Certification of Teachers, 15, 18, 28, 33, 63
Certification Tests, Teacher, 3, 6, 18-19, 27-33, 227, 237-243, 246-253
Classroom Management, 21, 51
Classroom Process Record (CPR), 65
Clinical Professional Knowledge, 62
Clinical Supervision Model, 311, 321
Collaboration, 165
Collective Bargaining Agreements, 149
Collegial Interaction, 21
Communication, 171, 192, 375
Competency Matrix, 53-54, 60
Conceptions of Teaching, 141-145
Confirmatory Teacher Licensure Tests, 5, 10
Consensus, 308
Construct-Related Validity, 8, 28-30, 86, 93, 105-108, 240-241, 246-247, 249, 252, 274, 367

386 SUBJECT INDEX

Content-Related Validity, 8, 28–30, 86, 88, 90, 92, 99, 106–107, 227, 229, 231–236, 240, 241, 246–247, 248–250, 269–270, 274, 349–350, 358–359, 361, 366
Context-Specific Variables, 44, 144–146
Contrasting-Groups Method, 252
Contreras v. City of Los Angeles, 232
Course Achievement, 184, 186, 193–194, 205–206
Criterion-Related Validity, 8, 28–30, 34, 86, 101–102, 106–107, 116, 232, 240, 241n, 246, 249–250, 252, 274, 351, 358, 360, 367
Curricular Evaluation, 112
Curricular Validity, 108–111, 215, 227–229, 282–284
Curriculum Knowledge, 21
Cut Score, 83–85, 89, 96, 118–124, 219–220, 248–249, 251–252, 254, 375
See also Pass Score

D

Debra P. v. Turlington, 108–109, 214–215
Decision Contexts, 184–187
Demand Characteristics, 354, 356
Dichotomous Judgement Model, 97–98
Disparate Impact. See Adverse Impact
Documentation, 127–128, 275
Document Review, 92
Due Process Clause, 214–215, 217

E

Effective Teachers, 359–361, 367–368
Efficacy, 171–174, 315
Efficiency, 30
Eighty Percent Rule, 217–220, 222, 225
Employee Selection Procedures, 273–274
Employment Testing, 221–222, 225–227, 231
Employment Tests, 82–83, 88, 92–93, 119–120
See also Hiring
Equal Protection Clause, 213–215, 217
Estimating Gain, 290
Evaluator Expertise, 157–158, 163–165
Events, 67–69
Examination for the Certification of Educators in Texas (ExCET), 100

Expert Panels, 28, 31–33, 91–92, 95, 97–99, 128, 247–248, 251, 349, 358–359
Expert Teachers, 163–164

F

Face Validity, 2, 8–14, 349–351, 354–355, 367, 375
Factory Worker-Teacher Productivity Analogy, 266
Failure Charts, 249
Fakability, 354, 356
False Acceptances/False Rejects, 118–120, 122–123
False Positives/False Negatives, 252–254
See also 239
Financial Costs, 166–167
Formative Assessment, 206–207, 339–340
Four Fifths Rule. See Eighty Percent Rule
Fourteenth Amendment to the Constitution, 213–215, 217, 228n
Functional Professional Knowledge, 56, 58–59, 65–66, 70, 72
See also Professional Knowledge

G

Gain Score, 288–294, 296
Generalizability, 146–147, 364
Generic Teaching Function, 48
Grade Equivalents, 285–287
Griggs v. Duke Power Co., 231–232
Guardians Association of the New York City Police Department v. Civil Service Commission, 232–233, 234n

H

Hiring, 185–186, 198–199, 205
See also Employment Testing; Employment Tests
Holistic Scoring, 24, 31
Hypothesis Testing, 93

I

Improving Teacher Performance through Evaluation, 321
Improving Teacher Quality, 148
Improving Teaching (through Evaluation), 37–39, 41, 45–46, 52–53, 60, 71

SUBJECT INDEX

Indicators of Competence, 66
Individual Pupil Characteristics, 44-45
Initial Certification, 185-186, 197-198, 205
Instructional Evaluation, 112
Instructional Leadership, 311, 315
Instructional Validity, 282, 284
 See also Curricular Validity
Interactive Teaching Problems, 48-49, 51, 53, 56-60
Interstate Teacher Assessment and Support Consortium, 18
Item Bias, 241-242
Items, 67-69, 93-99, 235-236, 248-249

J

Job Analysis, 92-96, 107, 233-235, 250, 269-271, 275-276
Job Competencies, 246
Job Dimensions, 275-276
Job Elements, 92-93
Job Relatedness, 92-94, 217, 227-228, 231-232, 234-236, 241, 349
Joint Committee on Standards for Educational Evaluation, 332
Joint Teacher Appraisal Committee, 331-332, 339
Judgment, 30-32

K

Knowledge Base of Teaching, 28
Knowledge of Curriculum, 26

L

Leadership by Objective and Results Model (LBO/R), 322-324
Legally Defensible Tests, 210, 226, 231, 233, 237, 254
Licensure, 2-3, 82-83, 93, 113, 118, 148, 359
Licensure Tests, 17, 83-95, 99-104, 106-115, 118-121, 124-126
Lincoln Appraisal Pilot Project, 331-332, 339, 341
Literature Review, 91, 93
Logical Analysis, 92
Logistic Costs, 166
Loose Coupling, 170

M

Manuals, 127-128
Marker Items, 97
Measurement-Based Teacher Evaluation, 55-56, 60, 63
Measurement Evaluation, 314-315
Measurement Methods, 186-187
Mentor Teacher, 262-263
Merit Pay, 261, 263-264, 312-313
Method Dependence, 249, 251
Minimum Level of Competency, 359
Minimum Teaching Competence, 185-186, 200-201, 205
Motivating Change, 172-174
Multiple-Choice Item, 95-98
Multiple-Choice Test, 96
Mutual Benefit Evaluation, 314-316

N

National Board for Professional Teaching Standards, 16, 18, 29, 31, 33-34
National Teacher Examination (NTE), 103-105, 108-111, 210n, 227-230, 238n, 245, 349-350
National Teacher Examinations, 2

O

Objective Measurement of Human Performance, 55-56, 59, 62, 70-71
Objectives, 96-97, 234-235
Objectivity, 30-31, 68, 267
Observation, 92
Observation Instruments, 308
One Best Model, 314, 316-317, 370
Organizational Commitment, 162-163
Organizational Context, 165, 168-170, 174
Organizational Factors, 138-140, 150, 161
Oversimplification, 374

PQ

Pass Score, 69-70, 219-220, 357
 See also Cut Score
Pedagogical Content Knowledge, 19-21, 23, 25-27, 28
Percentile Ranks, 286
Perceptual Skills, 49-51, 53, 60-61

Perceived Legitimacy, 349-350
Performance Assessment, 26-27, 41-43, 188-193
Performance Assessment Design Process (or Development), 188-192
Performance Dimensions, 275-276
Performance Skills, 49-50, 52-53
Permanent Certification, 185-186, 197-198, 205
Personnel Evaluation, 137, 270-271
Policy Context, 147-150, 165, 168-169
Political Context, 8, 138-139, 147-150, 165, 168-169, 338
Political Costs, 167
Preactive Teaching Problems, 49, 51-53
Predictive Efficacy, 350, 355-356
Predictive Validity, 101, 119-120
Preexisting Teacher Characteristics, 39, 45
Pretest-Posttest Design, 265
Pretest-Posttest Gain, 288-293, 298-299
Principals, 164, 307-315, 336, 340, 343-344
Problem Solving, 355
Process-Product Research, 144-146
Professional Development, 185-186, 201-203, 206
Professional Judgment, 49, 51-53, 60-61
Professional Knowledge, 49, 52-53, 60-62, 67, 354-355
    See also Functional Professional Knowledge
Professional Training Variables, 44, 46
Professions, 140-141
Public Relations Value of Appraisal, 255, 332-334, 338-339, 345, 372-373
Publishers, 127-128
Pupil Learning Experience, 42-45
Purpose of Evaluation, 157, 159-160, 163, 165-166
Quality of Assessment, 193-207
Questionable Items, 248-249

R

Rating, 189, 191-192, 275-276
Reality Testing, 362, 368-369, 375
Real-World Teaching, 334
Research in Teaching, 45, 72
Reflective Teaching Problems, 49, 53
Reliability, 30-31, 83-85, 125-126, 273, 289-291
Research in Classroom Learning, 45

Research in Teacher Competence, 45
Research Suggestions (validity), 115-117
Role Conflict, 164, 311-312
Rule of Reason, 127-128

S

Sample Size, 221
Sampling, 93
School Characteristics Variables, 280-281, 292-293
School Improvement, 140, 147-148
School Incentive, 262-264
School Variables, 146
Schware v. Board of Bar Examiners, 213
Score-Based Inferences, 8-11, 13, 86-88, 237-239, 248, 254-255, 350-351
Scores, 23-32, 68-69, 124-127, 189, 191, 210, 247, 249, 287, 357
    See also 242
Scoring Dimensions, 23-24
Setting Variables, 44-45, 68-70
Shifting Criterion, 360, 371, 373
Situational Items, 67
Snark Hunting, 209-210, 255
Stability, 146-147
Standard Achievement Tests, 308-309
Standard Error of Measurement, 83-85
Standardization of Teaching, 337
Standards, 31-33, 149-150, 271, 275
Standard Score, 68-69
Standards for Evaluating Teacher Performance, 267-271
Statements of Competencies, 96-97
Structured Performance Assessment, 18-21, 25
Structured Performance Exercises, 28-29, 34
Student Achievement, 264-283, 285, 288-289, 293, 308-309, 314-315, 368
Student Learning Factors, 375
Student Outcomes, 144-146
Student-Teaching Performance, 184, 186, 195-197, 205-206
Student Variables, 44-45, 146, 266-267, 278-280, 292
Subject Matter Knowledge, 26, 89-90
Subscores, 85, 125-126
Summative Assessment, 205-206, 339, 341
Superior Teacher Performance Criteria, 295-298
Supply and Demand, 118-122
Symbol Management, 170-171

T

Task Inventory, 92
Teacher Assessment Points, 39, 41-45
Teacher Assessment Project (TAP), 15-16, 18, 20-23, 25-30, 33, 353
Teacher Behavior Items, 67
Teacher-Certification Tests. See Certification Tests, Teacher
Teacher Certification Test (TCT), Georgia, 218-221
Teacher Competence, 39-42, 44-47, 49, 52-54, 63-66, 70, 72, 81, 106, 108, 155, 157, 237-240
Teacher Competency, 40, 45-46, 49-55, 59-60, 64-67, 69-73, 80, 91-93, 96-97, 108, 111, 115, 155
Teacher-Competency Tests, 79, 81, 90-91, 101, 105-107, 112-114, 120-121, 123, 126, 148
Teacher Education Programs, 19, 28, 72-73, 111-112, 148
Teacher Education Screening Tests, 4
Teacher Effectiveness, 44-45, 81, 116, 145-146, 155-157, 359-361, 367-368
Teacher Evaluation, 41, 44-45, 103, 108, 137-140, 142-143, 146-154, 156-162, 175-176, 276, 307-324, 359, 368, 375
Teacher Incentive Programs, 261-265, 277
Teacher Judgment, 248
Teacher Judgments, 241-242
Teacher Licensure, 114-115, 122-123, 184-186, 197-198
Teacher Licensure Tests, 4-5, 18-19, 31-32
Teacher Performance, 41, 44-45, 52-53, 63-65, 69, 81, 108, 146-148, 155-157, 261, 264-265, 267-269, 272
Teacher Performance Exercises, 31-34
Teacher Performance Record (TPR), 63-65, 67, 69, 71
Teacher Performance Skills, 21
Teacher Preparation Programs, 2, 39-41
  See also Teacher Education Program; Teacher-Training Programs
Teacher Relicensure Tests, 6-7, 11
Teachers' Perspectives on Appraisal, 334-337, 341-344
Teacher Tests, 4-9
Teacher-Training Programs, 228-231
  See also Teacher Education Programs; Teacher Preparation Programs

Teaching as Art, 143
Teaching as Craft, 142-143
Teaching as Labor, 142
Teaching as Profession, 141-142
Teaching Behaviors, 145-147
Teaching Context, 159-160
Teaching Environment, 144, 146
Teaching Problems, 48-50, 52-54, 66
Teaching Research, 144-146
Technical Factors, 138
Tenure, 341-342
Test Auditing, 244-245, 255
Test Characteristics, 282-287, 294
Test Contractors, 210-211, 228, 233, 241-244, 247, 248, 250, 255
Test Development, 22, 86-88, 90, 96-97, 99, 106-107, 114, 127-128, 233-236, 241, 244, 247
Test Quality, 126-127
Texas Examination of Current Administrators and Teachers (TECAT), 100
Texas Teacher Appraisal System (TTAS), 317-320
The Georgia Association of Educators v. State of Georgia, 216-226
Threshold-Loss Function, 84
Title VII of the Civil Rights Act of 1964, 216-227, 231-232
Turner v. Fouche, 224
Two or Three Standard Deviation Rule, 220-223

U

Unions, 11, 330-331, 340
United States and North Carolina Association of Educators v. North Carolina, 216
United States v. South Carolina, 109-110, 227-231, 239
Utility, 166-167

V

Validity, 8-9, 13-14, 28-31, 44, 85-87, 112-115, 210, 227-229, 231, 237, 240-245, 248, 251, 254-255, 268-269, 272, 274, 350, 353, 358, 361, 375
Value Choices, 168-169, 363, 368, 371-372, 375
Verisimilitude. See Face Validity

W Y

Washington v. Davis, 228–231
Wesman Personnel Classification Test (WPCT), 104

Wisdom, 41, 48
Wisdom of Practice, 23
Withitness, 51, 61
Work Environment Variables, 272
York v. Mobile, 238n